Cambridge Studies in Early Modern British History

CRITICISM AND COMPLIMENT

Cambridge Studies in Early Modern British History

Series editors

ANTHONY FLETCHER
Reader in History, University of Sheffield

JOHN GUY
Reader in History, University of Bristol

and JOHN MORRILL
*Lecturer in History, University of Cambridge, and
Fellow and Tutor of Selwyn College*

This is a new series of monographs and studies covering many aspects of the history of the British Isles between the late fifteenth century and the early eighteenth century. It will include the work of established scholars and pioneering work by a new generation of scholars. It will include both reviews and revisions of major topics and books which open up new historical terrain or which reveal startling new perspectives on familiar subjects. It is envisaged that all the volumes will set detailed research into broader perspectives and the books are intended for the use of students as well as of their teachers.

Titles in the series

CRITICISM AND COMPLIMENT

The politics of literature in the England of Charles I

KEVIN SHARPE

Lecturer in History, University of Southampton

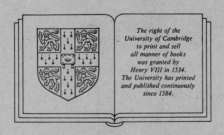

The right of the
University of Cambridge
to print and sell
all manner of books
was granted by
Henry VIII in 1534.
The University has printed
and published continuously
since 1584.

CAMBRIDGE UNIVERSITY PRESS

Cambridge

London   New York   New Rochelle

Melbourne   Sydney

Published by the Press Syndicate of the University of Cambridge
The Pitt Building, Trumpington Street, Cambridge CB2 1RP
32 East 57th Street, New York, NY 10022, USA
10 Stamford Road, Oakleigh, Melbourne 3166, Australia

First published 1987

Printed in Great Britain at the University Press, Cambridge

British Library cataloguing in publication data

Sharpe, Kevin
Criticism and compliment: the politics of
literature in the England of Charles I.
– (Cambridge studies in early modern
British history).
1. English literature – Early modern,
1500–1700 – History and criticism
I. Title
820.9′004   PR431

Library of Congress cataloguing in publication data

Sharpe, Kevin
Criticism and compliment.
(Cambridge studies in early modern British history)
Includes index.
1. English literature – Early modern, 1500–1700 –
History and criticism.   2. Politics and literature –
Great Britain – History – 17th century.   3. Politics in
literature.   4. Great Britain – Politics and
government – 1625–1649.   5. Great Britain – Intellectual
life – 17th century.   I. Title.   II. Series.
PR438.P65S48   1987   820′.9′358   87–5204

ISBN 0 521 34239 2

*For Hugh Trevor-Roper and
Anne Whiteman*

CONTENTS

ILLUSTRATIONS

PREFACE AND
ACKNOWLEDGEMENTS

This is a book about literature by a historian. I hope that by making such an announcement I do not deter either side of its intended audience: literary scholars on account of a suspicion that a historian may wish to 'reduce' the plays and poems to 'mere' historical artefacts; historians because they tend not to accept literature as 'real' historical evidence. For it is my purpose both to argue for the importance of this material as primary evidence for the history of ideas and politics, and to re-read literary texts as documents of the culture and values of Caroline England.

Recently, the new historicist literary critics have valuably questioned the premise upon which for too long criticism has rested: the premise of an autonomous aesthetic, a realm of 'art' which may be differentiated from, and studied apart from, society, ideology and culture. The historicists have called for a new methodology, even a new discipline of 'cultural criticism' that would dispense with the conventional boundaries of literature and history, boundaries which are themselves constructs of our own culture and which may have obstructed our perception of others. Such recent work offers the exciting prospect of a reinterpretation of Renaissance society.[1]

This book, however, did not originate in any such theoretical reflection. It began life, more modestly, as a chapter of a book on *The Personal Rule of*

[1] See, for example, S. Greenblatt, *Renaissance Self-fashioning* (Chicago, 1980); Greenblatt, ed., *The Forms of Power and the Power of Forms in the Renaissance*, *Genre*, 15 (1) (1982); L. A. Montrose, 'The purpose of playing: reflections on Shakespearian anthropology', *Helios*, n.s. 7 (1979–80), 57–74; Montrose, 'A poetics of Renaissance culture', *Criticism*, 23 (1981), pp. 349–59.

Since this book was completed, Lauro Martines has become the first historian to add his voice to the call for a new cultural criticism. See L. Martines, *Society and History in English Renaissance Verse* (Oxford, 1985), a manual for the historical reading of literary evidence. In the introduction to his *Collected Essays* (Brighton, 1985), Christopher Hill also argues powerfully for the value of literary evidence, but undermines the claim by reading that literature from *a priori* assumptions.

Charles I on which I have been engaged for some years. I went to the masques, plays and poems of the Caroline court initially as another source for an elucidation of the values of Charles I and his court. But what I discovered on further reading was not material that nicely illustrated accepted views (I fear the usual use made of literature by historians), but evidence that challenged those views. Evidence, that is, of debates and tensions, anxieties, doubts and criticisms articulated within the culture of the court, indeed opinions akin to those often identified only with the ideology of the 'country'. Clearly this was material that questioned established historical and critical interpretations and merited close examination.

Recent works, several published since this book was drafted, have begun to identify currents of dissent in the drama and poetry of Renaissance England, drama and poetry which for too long has been read as literary homilies to the religion of order and obedience preached from the Tudor parish pulpits and promulgated by royal proclamations. But Caroline courtly modes are still characterized *a priori* as a culture of absolutism, the expression and justification by hired hands of the absolutist aims of an authoritarian monarch. It is the argument of the pages that follow that such a characterization rests upon often anachronistic assumptions – about the nature of the court, about puritanism, about a supposed polarity between court and country – and upon preconceptions – about genre, patronage, the position of the poet or playwright and about the possibilities for dissent.

My study neither rests on nor offers any new methodology. It does attempt to question the assumptions – both historical and critical – from which the literature has hitherto been read. Whilst it is not my primary purpose to offer an aesthetic reappraisal of Caroline court literature, I would suggest that traditional critical description and evaluation have been in part politically determined. When we speak of 'cavalier' drama or poetry, we may have predetermined our reading and confined to a (defeated) party a literature that articulated the concerns of an age. For it is my contention that, far from being simply monotonous or partisan, the literature of the Caroline court reveals debate, ambiguity and anxiety, and so offers a rich case study of political discourse, of social and political ideas in early Stuart England.

In the traditional accounts of Caroline court culture, the masque has been taken as the ultimate courtly mode, that literary form which had its raison d'être in celebration and whose authors were the most sycophantic of the hired admirers of the king. I therefore decided to take as the core of my study of court literature the drama, poetry and masques of the three authors who succeeded Ben Jonson as devisers of court entertainments in the reign of Charles I: William Davenant, Thomas Carew and Aurelian Townshend. It might be said that such men exemplify the court, its concerns and values. However, after a discussion of the contentions that have consciously or unconsciously obstructed our historical and critical understanding, and a re-examination of their literature, I wish to argue that these men belong in a broader context of humanism and should not be confined to the narrow constraints of a party or decade. And I hope too to have shown that, working within the conventions and modes of court drama, masque and love poetry, they engaged in a searching examination of the ethical and political issues of their age, and proffered counsel to the ruler both through criticism and through compliment. If I have established a case, then the culture and politics of Caroline England await a full reconsideration.

Research in the humanities requires primarily three things: financial support to travel to archives and libraries, time for research reflection and writing, and stimulation and support from colleagues – by means both of criticism and of compliment. I have many to thank under each head. I am most grateful to the Wolfson Foundation, the British Academy, the National Endowment for the Humanities and Southampton University for funds that made this research possible, as indeed that of my wider study of the 1630s. And I should like to thank the staff of those libraries and record offices who kindly facilitated my researches and enquiries. The illustrations from the Devonshire Collection, Chatsworth, are reproduced by permission of the Chatsworth Settlement Trustees. I should like to thank Mr Peter Day and the Courtauld Institute of Fine Art for permission to use photographs of the Jones drawings. Two places, both in the United States of America, provided the invaluable opportunity of time away from the usual chores of a university lecturer. Both the Institute for Advanced Study, Princeton and the Hunting-ton Library, San Marino, California provide the most stimulating environments a scholar could wish for, and I should like to thank them both for their kindness in electing me to visiting fellowships and especially Professors John Elliott and Martin Ridge respectively for all they did to make my time there productive, stimulating and enjoyable. To those institutions too I owe introductions to literary scholars and to friendships which proved a major stimulus for this work. I would like to thank Leah Marcus and David Riggs, with whom I enjoyed many helpful lunchtime conversations, and, most of all, Steven Zwicker, from whose own work, conversation and encouragement I gleaned so much, and with whom I have recently edited a volume on literature and politics which has proved an unparalleled stimulation.

As a historian embarking on a study of literature I owe more debts to many scholars than conventional acknowledgement can convey. First, my historian friends and colleagues have been remarkably tolerant of long conversations about literature and invaluably helpful in their questions, suggestions and criticisms. I would especially like to thank my friends George Bernard, John Morrill, Gerald Aylmer, Penry Williams and Brian Lyndon. Second, working in the field of literary studies I have been extremely grateful to long-

standing and new acquaintances and friends who have offered encouragement, advice and necessarily searching criticism to an amateur working in
their midst: Michael Brennan, Cedric Brown, Katherine Duncan-Jones, John
Kerrigan, Jeremy Maule, David Norbrook, Sara Pearl and especially my
colleagues John Peacock and Jim (A. J.) Smith. Most of all I would like to
thank those without whose stimulation and support I should never have
embarked upon this book. For this study originated from conversations with
Anne Barton, Jonathan Goldberg and Stephen Orgel, and has continued to
benefit from their own work and suggestions and their hospitality and
support.

After the book was first drafted, Anne Barton, Cedric Brown, Jonathan
Goldberg, Stephen Orgel, Conrad Russell, Jim Smith and especially David
Riggs passed on detailed comments which proved of great value, as did the
editors of Cambridge Studies in Early Modern British History. I am very
grateful to the above for all they have done. Finally, I would like to thank
Alison Hamlin and Dee Marquez, who valiantly deciphered and translated
into typescript the scrawl that I delivered to them, Russ Foster, who checked
it and made helpful suggestions on style, and Mary Montegna, who provided
encouragement and succour when they were most needed.

The dedication expresses not only my greatest scholarly debts, but friendships which have inspired my historical studies.

Stanford Humanities Center 1986   KEVIN SHARPE

ABBREVIATIONS

The following abbreviations have been used:

Bodleian Quart. Rec.	*Bodleian Quarterly Record*
Cal. Stat. Pap. Dom.	*Calendar of State Papers Domestic*
Cal. Stat. Pap. Venet.	*Calendar of State Papers Venetian*
E.H.R.	*English Historical Review*
E.L.H.	*English Literary History*
Eng. Lit. Renaiss.	*English Literary Renaissance*
Hist. Journ.	*Historical Journal*
H.M.C.	Historical Manuscripts Commission
Hunt. Lib. Quart.	Huntington Library Quarterly
Journ. Warburg & *Courtauld, Inst.*	*Journal of the Warburg and Courtauld Institutes*
Trans. Roy. Hist. Soc.	*Transactions of the Royal Historical Society*

Culture and politics, court and country: assumptions and problems, questions and suggestions

CULTURE AND POLITICS

Historians and literary scholars seldom meet on the same ground (almost never at the same conference or seminar). When they do encounter each other, it is even more unusual for them to agree. But to both generalizations, early seventeenth-century England stands out as a conspicuous exception. It should not surprise us that students of the literature and history of the early Stuart period often find each other toiling in adjacent fields – or even the same patch. The age of Shakespeare, Jonson and Donne has been as exhaustively tilled by critics as the half century before the English civil war has been raked over by historians. But what is noteworthy, all the more so given the vast numbers of scholars, is the consensus that has emerged concerning the nature of the relationship between culture and politics, and more particularly between the literature and history of the reigns of James I and Charles I.

An agreement that there was *a* relationship should not surprise us. Culture cannot be divorced from politics in any age, and in Renaissance England their interdependence and interpenetration were consciously acknowledged and even deliberately pursued.[1] The humanists ascribed to the literary and visual arts an ethical and a didactic function. And because the public life and the private were viewed as one world, because, that is, the function of the state was held, following Aristotle, to be the provision of the good life, what we delineate as 'the arts' was interrelated with the world of politics too. Renaissance theory, and even practice, integrated aesthetics, ethics and

[1] For an incisive analysis of this interpenetration, see D. Javitch, *Poetry and Courtliness in Renaissance England* (Princeton, 1978). Louis Montrose points out that in *The Arte of English Poesie* Puttenham shows a sophisticated awareness that 'poetry is more than an analogue of courtliness: it is a medium of courtliness'. L. A. Montrose, 'Of gentlemen and shepherds: the politics of Elizabethan pastoral form', *E.L.H.*, 50 (1983), p. 451.

politics. And the product of that integration is manifest in the literature of politics, that is in mirrors for magistrates and handbooks for courtiers, as it is in the politics of the literature.[2] Both are evidence of an age which was concerned simultaneously with the capacity of literary and artistic symbols to affect reality, to have authority, and with the presentation and representation of authority – with the power of image and the image of power.[3] Such an interrelationship, perhaps even the consciousness of the interrelationship, is as old as government itself. Coins and seals have borne the images of kings which have given authority to their value since the earliest times. But the centuries of the Renaissance may claim a special place in the history of culture and politics for two reasons. For the period we term the Renaissance saw renewed study of the classics and a self-conscious return to attitudes to poetics, ethics and politics voiced by classical authorities. At the same time it witnessed the consolidation of princely and monarchical courts, centres of magnificent display as well as of authority, sources of cultural as well as political patronage.

In both these senses, the Renaissance came to England in the sixteenth century. The sixteenth century in England saw the emergence of the royal court as the centre of authority and government, as the crown consolidated its power and established the rule of law.[4] By the end of the century, the court, the principal centre of patronage, was seen as the centre of the realm as well as the household of the monarch. The Tudor monarchs, in consolidating their strength, were quick to appreciate the importance of the court as the image of their rule, and the value of artists and scholars in the representation of their authority. The printing press offered the opportunity to disseminate an ideology to the literate political nation, and, in an oral culture, beyond. The monarch became one of the greatest patrons of learning and the arts; and the court emerged as a cultural as well as a political focus. Painter, poet and courtier became embraced within one world. It was a world in which reality and the representation of reality were not distinct.[5] The paintings of Holbein and Hilliard, the treatises of Starkey, Morrison and Sir Thomas Smith, the poetry of Spenser and Sidney were as real expressions of the monarchy as were the orders and proclamations issued in the king's or queen's name: they were alike documents of courtly rhetoric. Nor in an age when politics was the art of 'winning compliance' can their significance be exaggerated. For the

[2] L. B. Campbell, ed., *The Mirror for Magistrates* (Cambridge, 1938); B. Castiglione, *The Courtyer*, translated by T. Hoby, 1561; W. H. D. Rouse and D. Henderson, ed., *The Book of the Courtier* (London, 1928).

[3] C. Geertz, 'Centers, kings and charisma: reflections on the symbolics of power', in J. Ben-David and T. N. Clark, eds., *Culture and its Creators* (Chicago, 1977), pp. 150–71. And Greenblatt, *The Forms of Power and the Power of Forms*.

[4] G. R. Elton, 'Tudor government: the points of contact. III. The court', *Trans. Royal Hist. Soc.*, 26 (1976), pp. 211–28.

[5] See R. Strong, *Splendour at Court: Renaissance Spectacle and Illusion* (London, 1973).

Tudors, as we cannot be too often reminded, had no independent paid bureaucracy, nor a standing army to enforce their will. Government rested upon co-operation and consent; authority depended upon attitudes to royal authority. The perception of power was central to the exercise of power itself; and the perception of power could be influenced, even moulded, by the images of authority represented by the artists of the court.[6]

This is to say nothing new. Historians and literary scholars have for long appreciated, even if they have not yet fully investigated, the 'use' made by Henry VIII, and more particularly by Elizabeth I, of the power of images and symbols in inculcating or influencing attitudes to authority.[7] But we have only recently, perhaps, come to appreciate better just how effective such images were, the more we understand that they established and preserved illusions that were often distant from reality. The solid, wilful, mighty Henry VIII of Holbein's canvases is a very different figure from the king of some recent historical scholarship, a king who has been described as malleable, capricious and even weak.[8] No less, the instability, crises and chaos of Elizabethan government now stressed by some historians are far removed from the omniscient and omnicompetent realm of the goddess, virgin Queen Astraea.[9] But our sense of the distance between what was and what was idealized should sharpen, not blunt, our interest in the symbols of authority in sixteenth-century England. Indeed it may be that the success of Tudor government in a period of religious change, economic and social dislocation and threats from abroad lay in its effectiveness in presenting an image of order and authority which was convincing.[10] This cannot be separated from 'real' power: when power depends upon perception, what men perceive and believe to have authority possesses that authority. If the Tudors on the shaky foundations of a crown snatched at Bosworth field founded a dynasty where others had scarce survived a lifetime, it was not least because they appreciated that the representation of authority, the politics of art, was a principal art of politics. Today, we are tempted to describe this as propaganda, with all its pejorative undertones of wilful separation of truth from presentation. But

[6] The phrase comes from P. Williams, *The Tudor Regime* (Oxford, 1979), ch. 11; S. Greenblatt, 'Invisible bullets: Renaissance authority and its subversion', *Glyph*, 8 (1981), pp. 20–61.

[7] S. Anglo, *Spectacle, Pageantry and Early Tudor Policy* (Oxford, 1969); R. Strong, *Splendour at Court*; Strong, *The English Icon* (London, 1969); Strong, *The Cult of Elizabeth: Elizabethan Portraiture and Pageantry* (London, 1977); E. C. Wilson, *England's Eliza* (Cambridge, Mass., 1939); D. Bergeron, *English Civic Pageantry 1558–1642* (London, 1971).

[8] D. Starkey, 'From feud to faction: English politics c. 1450–1550', *History Today*, 32 (1982), pp. 16–22; Starkey, 'Representation through intimacy', in Joan Lewis, ed., *Symbols and Sentiments* (London, 1977).

[9] See, for example, C. Haigh, ed., *The Reign of Elizabeth I* (London, 1985), especially the editor's introduction.

[10] On ideas of order see E. Tillyard, *The Elizabethan World Picture* (London, 1943); A. Lovejoy, *The Great Chain of Being* (Cambridge, Mass., 1961); W. H. Greenleaf, *Order, Empiricism and Politics* (London, 1964); R. Eccleshall, *Order and Reason in Politics* (Oxford, 1978).

this would be to attribute to the sixteenth century a cynicism, even a clear sense of a distance and difference between object and image, which may be anachronistic. And significantly it would be to employ a term (propaganda), as well as a concept, which had then no such modern or sinister meaning beyond the Latin sense of the dissemination of a doctrine or faith.[11] The ceremonies and symbols of courtly and monarchical life were – to the monarch no less than for his subjects – the rituals of divine kingship. The artists and poets were priests and apostles of this faith.

The power or effectiveness of image rests upon two fundamentals. It requires a language or symbolism that may be understood through reason or grasped by faith: an image of authority needs to be communicated if it is to influence, and communication requires some common language. Secondly, the political success of representations of authority depended upon the projection of images of power which carried conviction with both common subjects and the gentry who ruled in the localities. For from that conviction the court drew its authority to govern. The achievement of the Tudors, it has been argued, lay in both: in their capacity to communicate and in the image of a monarchical order which they projected and promoted. Elizabeth I skilfully transformed the real danger of heirless virginity into a cult of the virgin queen and so appropriated the iconography of the Catholic virgin Mary to Protestant rule.[12] The symbolism surrounding the worship of Elizabeth has been shown to be complex, multi-layered and mystical.[13] But if only the learned few could unravel the tangled layers of image in Spenser's *Fairy Queen*, or comprehend the cult of Astraea, most men were evidently prepared to take the step of faith, celebrating the queen's deliverance from death, and her birthday and accession day long after her death, with bonfires and bell-ringing.[14] This unlikely success, it has been suggested, owed much to the queen's preparedness to speak to men in their own language – through the public procession and familiar speech as well as the formal address.[15] By such means Elizabeth I helped to create the political ideology that sustained her rule.

[11] *O.E.D.*

[12] Strong, *Cult of Elizabeth*, p. 125.

[13] *Ibid.*; Wilson, *England's Eliza*; F. Yates, 'Queen Elizabeth as Astraea', *Journ. Warburg & Courtauld Inst.*, 10 (1947), pp. 27–87; Yates, *Astraea: The Imperial Theme in the Sixteenth Century* (Harmondsworth, 1977); L. Montrose, '"Eliza, Queene of Shepheards" and the Pastoral of Power', *Eng. Lit. Renaiss.*, 10 (1980), pp. 153–82.

[14] R. Strong, 'The popular celebration of the Accession Day of Queen Elizabeth', *Journ. Warburg & Courtauld Inst.*, 21 (1958), pp. 86–103; cf. Strong, *The Cult of Elizabeth*, pp. 117–27.

[15] See J. Nichols, *The Progresses and Public Processions of Queen Elizabeth* (3 vols., London, 1923); I. Dunlop, *Palaces and Progresses of Elizabeth I* (London, 1962); Bergeron, *English Civic Pageantry*; R. Strong, 'Queen Elizabeth and the Order of the Garter', *The Archaeological Journal*, 119 (1962), pp. 245–70; G. Parry, *The Golden Age Restor'd: The Culture of the Stuart Court* (Manchester, 1981).

It has become conventional, and not unreasonable, to suggest that the Stuarts failed to sustain that mystique, and to argue that the respect accorded to monarchy declined as the image of kingship became tarnished. The Stuarts are arraigned by historical and literary judges on two charges: that they presented an image that was unattractive; and that even when well intentioned they failed to communicate or represent themselves favourably. As a consequence they opened a rift between the reality and the representation of monarchy, between authority and the perception of authority, and so divided ruler and ruled, the king from the people.[16] The problem was not the same under both kings. James I, we are told, was unpopular as a foreign, Scottish king whose familiar, often over-familiar, style, coarse behaviour and crude language were viewed as affronts to the dignity of monarchy. The mystique of divine monarchy was not fostered by a king who defecated in his trousers.[17] Charles I, by contrast, was dignified, chaste and refined; his court was ceremonious, splendid and cultivated. But, so the traditional argument goes, Charles I's political intentions were autocratic: he wished to rule untrammelled by custom, law or parliaments. Because his political ambitions were not in tune with the customs or constitution of the realm or the attitudes of his subjects, the expression of those political values in court culture was not, as Elizabethan court culture had been, a national culture, but the culture of a political minority to whose tenets the bulk of the country was opposed. Moreover, it has been argued, Charles's refined artistic and architectural tastes served only to compound the problem and to widen the gulf between the court and the country into a cultural and political chasm. For the classicism of Inigo Jones, the flamboyant romanticism of Van Dyck and the baroque extravagance of Rubens were perceived as innovative, foreign, imperialist and, worst of all, Catholic. And the king and the court which embraced them were accordingly suspected of a design to establish a continental monarchical absolutism and to reintroduce popery. The Stuarts' failure to communicate or represent themselves favourably, we are told, left the court unpopular and isolated from the nation.[18]

In early seventeenth-century England, the prevailing orthodoxy now has it, there emerged two cultures: that of the court and that of the country. The two cultures embodied different values and spoke different languages, and they symbolized and reflected two different political worlds: that of Whitehall and that of the rest of the nation. The Stuarts' fragmentation of a national culture

---

[16] The view of Stone, Ashton, Thomas and Parry, for example, as cited in notes below.

[17] R. Ashton, *James I by his Contemporaries* (London, 1969); D. H. Willson, *King James VI and I* (London, 1965); J. P. Kenyon, *The Stuarts* (London, 1958, 2nd edn, 1977). For a splendid critique of the caricatures of James I, see J. Wormald, 'James VI and I: two kings or one?' *History*, 68 (1983), pp. 187–209.

[18] R. Ashton, *The English Civil War 1603–49* (London, 1978), ch. 4; R. Ollard, *The Image of the King* (London, 1979), ch. 2.

was soon to see the division, and ultimately disintegration, of a once united polity. For between 1603 and 1640, the king began to be perceived no longer as the focus of the realm, but, especially after 1628, as a threat to the commonweal – to the institutions, the church, the customs, that is to the culture of England. The interrelationship of culture and politics which the Tudors' skill had exploited for the stability of the realm and strength of the crown was now manifested in the divisions between 'cavalier' and 'puritan', in civil war and the abolition of monarchy.

It is now some twenty years since this interpretative framework for the early Stuart period was promulgated by Professor Perez Zagorin in an article which subsequently spawned an influential book of the same title, *The Court and The Country*.[19] Zagorin argued that by the 1620s the term 'country' came to be applied not only to describe long-held arcadian ideals or an inclination to retreat, but a set of values distinct from and consciously opposed to those of the 'court'. Moreover the labels were used to denominate if not actual parties then clear political groupings: 'The appearance of *Court* and *Country* as political descriptions signalized the enlarging conflict.' The divide they represented 'was the polarity in which the English revolution had its beginning'.[20]

Though somewhat crudely mechanistic, Zagorin's thesis won general acceptance among historians. It was stamped with authority and enshrined as orthodoxy in one of the most widely read and influential texts on early Stuart history. In *The Causes of the English Revolution*, Lawrence Stone took up Zagorin's work with his customary vigour and eloquence. 'By the early seventeenth century', Stone asserted, now stressing the ideas and values which separated court and country, 'England was experiencing all the tensions created by the development within a single society of two distinct cultures, cultures that were reflected in ideals, religion, art, literature, the theatre, dress, deportment and way of life.'[21] Indeed the terms derived their meaning from contending values, representing what they opposed as much as what they stood for. The country emerged as a synonym for virtues, the court for vice: 'the Country was virtuous, the Court wicked; the Country was thrifty, the Court extravagant; the Country was honest, the Court corrupt; the Country was chaste and heterosexual, the Court promiscuous and homosexual; the Country was sober, the Court drunken; . . . the Country was outspoken, the Court sycophantic',[22] and so on. Indeed, Stone went on to explain, the country stood for custom – for the residence of gentry in their

---

[19] P. Zagorin, 'The Court and the Country: a note on political terminology in the earlier seventeenth century', *E.H.R.*, 77 (1962), pp. 306–11; Zagorin, *The Court and the Country* (London, 1969).

[20] Zagorin, *The Court and the Country*, pp. 39, 331.

[21] L. Stone, *The Causes of the English Revolution* (London, 1972), p. 106.

[22] *Ibid.*, p. 105.

country houses, for charity and hospitality, for things English and traditional – in contrast to the cultural and political innovations of the court.[23] The tension between court and country, as he has recently reasserted, was one tremor leading to the seismic rift which shook the English commonweal.[24]

Many historians who did not subscribe to Stone's essentially Whig thesis of an inevitable escalation of crisis into conflict evidently concurred with him on the cultural rift between court and country. In 1973, Conrad Russell, the prophet as well as protagonist of the anti-Whig 'revisionists' of early Stuart studies, included in *The Origins of the English Civil War* an essay on 'Two cultures? Court and country under Charles I' from the conclusions of which he expressed no dissent.[25] More clearly, in the first major textbook to challenge Stone's account, this aspect of his argument not only remained unassailed, it was endorsed. In *The English Civil War* Robert Ashton took issue with both the Whig and Marxist approaches, with their emphases upon the long-term and structural problems that led to civil war, and focused attention upon the political errors, the follies and misguided actions of James I and Charles I which led first to the alienation of their subjects and ultimately to resistance. Chief among these miscalculations, in Ashton's view, was Charles I's isolation within the confines of a court which the political nation as well as the people perceived as innovative, foreign and popish. Concurring with Zagorin and Stone that 'it is reasonable to speak of the emergence of a distinct court culture', Ashton characterized the culture of the Caroline court as 'exclusive, aristocratic and authoritarian'. And in response to the sycophantic and frivolous masques and plays which were to him its expression, he identified a literary genre 'which expresses in a similarly idealized way the contrasting ideals of the country'.[26]

Since historians of the seventeenth century have agreed about little else, this consensus concerning a cultural rift is noteworthy. But it is even more remarkable that students of literature have tended to concur. Peter Thomas writes, 'There were it seems two warring cultures' emerging in the 1630s, as an Elizabethan national culture expressed in 'a literature that had been the authentic voice of patriotic high seriousness and Protestant nationalism' fragmented, leaving a Caroline court which 'seemed to speak for narrow snobbery and effete indulgence'.[27] The distance between the two cultures, Thomas argued, was the gap that separated Milton from the court. It was the

[23] *Ibid.*, p. 106; see also Ashton, *The English Civil War*, ch. 3.
[24] L. Stone; 'The results of the English revolutions of the seventeenth century', in J. G. A. Pocock, ed., *Three British Revolutions: 1641, 1688, 1776* (Princeton, 1980), pp. 24–5.
[25] P. Thomas, 'Two cultures? Court and country under Charles I', in C. Russell, ed., *The Origins of the English Civil War* (London, 1973), pp. 168–96. Cf. P. Thomas, 'Charles I: the tragedy of absolutism', in A. G. Dickens, ed., *The Courts of Europe* (London, 1977), pp. 191–212.
[26] Ashton, *The English Civil War*, pp. 22, 29, 30 and *passim*.
[27] Thomas, 'Two cultures?' pp. 175, 184. See also Parry, *passim*. Christopher Hill has recently subscribed to the same thesis in his introduction to *Collected Essays I* (Brighton, 1985).

puritans who were the heirs of the Elizabethan humanist tradition. By the 1630s, ideals of domesticity and hospitality, once part of a common culture, prevailed little at the centre. 'In Puritan literature they were reasserted.'[28] And in the 1640s a court which no longer expressed the values of a nation 'went for ever'.[29]

Such agreement itself repays some reflection. Perhaps for the literary scholars the thesis of two cultures held out an attractive explanation for one of their own most taxing problems: the passing, as they have seen it, at least since Eliot and Leavis, of the golden age of drama and poetry, of the age of Shakespeare, Donne and the best of Jonson, by the beginning of the reign of Charles I. It is tempting to look to politics for an explanation. Culture, some would argue, requires certain conditions for its healthy growth; the best literature, that which engages major questions and issues, depends upon the capacity for free expression and perhaps even upon some fundamental values held in common within the context of which disagreements may be articulated without danger. Such conditions, it is said, did not exist in Caroline England, where the court demanded conformity. So as Charles I led the commonweal towards autocracy, literature and the arts were debased to the menial rôle of slavish servants to his absolutism. Such circumstances, it has recently been argued, produced in the seventeenth century, as they have in more modern totalitarian regimes, a culture that was derivative, imitative, sycophantic and, in a word, second-rate. In *The Golden Age Restor'd*, Graham Parry has depicted Charles I's cultural interests as the handmaidens of his political ambitions. Thus the king's plans for building a new palace at Whitehall were evidence of his 'burgeoning megalomania'.[30] Even more sinisterly, Parry suggests, when criticism of or obstacles to his policies arose, Charles I regarded it as the function of culture to dispel them, to present an ideal image which might mould a more tractable reality. Or when the arts could not change reality, in the guise of spectacular entertainments or romantic pastoral, they might at least divert men from it. So in the cult of Neo-Platonism, Parry maintains, Charles I saw 'an admirable means of projecting the royal image in a way that *distracted attention* from the political aspects of his kingship'.[31] Such attitudes fostered in culture no less than in politics 'the grateful, uncritical mind favoured by the atmosphere of Charles's court'.[32] The men of free spirit, independent judgement and creative genius found no home there. 'Almost predictably', Parry concludes,

---

[28] Thomas, 'Two cultures?' pp. 185–90, quotation from p. 189.
[29] *Ibid.*, p. 192. A reminder that much of the criticism of Caroline literature has rested upon assumptions about Caroline politics.
[30] Parry, *The Golden Age Restor'd*, quotation from p. 162.
[31] *Ibid.*, p. 189 (my italics). Cf. p. x: 'The court isolated itself from the threatening trends in politics and religion that developed during the 1630s.'
[32] *Ibid.*, p. 190.

the genius who might claim succession to Shakespeare and Jonson was found outside the court. And John Milton was to become the exponent of the cause that brought down the court along with the king.[33]

There are a multitude of problems presented by this established interpretation; to many of them we shall return time and again throughout this book. Some difficulties, however, present themselves immediately. The attributes for example which Professor Stone identifies with the ideology of the 'country' – hospitality, chastity and the rural residence of the gentry – not only clearly concerned the king and the court, they were commanded by royal order and proclamation. It was Charles I who gave teeth to the proclamations ordering the nobility and gentry to remain in the country, so as to provide hospitality and good governance.[34] And it was the king himself who insisted upon the moral reformation of the court, upon sobriety, chastity and marital fidelity.[35] In general it must be clear to anyone who has read the literature of the 'cavalier' poets and playwrights that the *ideal* of the 'country' was celebrated at court as elsewhere, that pastoral, especially in the Caroline period, was a courtly mode.[36] Similarly, Professor Ashton's thesis runs into trouble when he marshals as evidence for 'the contrasting ideals of the country' the poems of Ben Jonson and Thomas Carew, who were not only both of the court – Carew as sewer in ordinary to the king, a courtier by the most narrow definition of the term – but authors of that allegedly most effete, exclusive and sycophantic of genres, the court masque.[37] The careers of Jonson and, it will be argued, his Caroline sons make nonsense of the labels of 'court' and 'country' as terms explanatory of cultural and political divisions.

Upon examination many courtiers fail to subscribe to form, as indeed alleged members of the country display no antagonism to courtly modes. The wives of the Earls of Warwick and Bedford, two prominent country peers, commissioned portraits from Van Dyck. And any idea that the civil war was a conflict of two cultures dissolves when we examine the evidence. One of the best collections of Van Dycks in England, for instance, was assembled at

---

[33] *Ibid.*, p. 265; see also Thomas, 'Two cultures?' pp. 185–90.

[34] See 'A Proclamation commanding the repaire of Noblemen, Knights and Gentlemen of qualitie, unto their Mansion Houses in the Countrey, there to attend their services, and keepe Hospitality', 23 November 1626, in J. F. Larkin, ed., *Stuart Royal Proclamations Vol. II: Royal Proclamations of King Charles I, 1625–46* (Oxford, 1983), pp. 112–13. The proclamation was reissued in 1627 (*ibid.*, pp. 170–2); and in 1632 (pp. 350–3). Charles ordered a census of all gentry residing in London in contravention of the proclamation and prosecuted offenders in Star Chamber. Cf. K. Sharpe, 'The personal rule of Charles I', in H. Tomlinson, ed., *Before the English Civil War* (London, 1983), pp. 61, 193.

[35] Lucy Hutchinson, *Memoirs of the Life of Colonel Hutchinson*, ed. C. H. Firth (2 vols., New York, 1885), I, p. 119; Sir Philip Warwick, *Memoires of the Reigne of Charles I* (London, 1701) pp. 64–6; Ashton, *Civil War*, pp. 29–30.

[36] See below, pp. 14–15.

[37] Ashton, *Civil War*, pp. 30, 35. Ashton modifies his own statement by acknowledging that 'the worlds of Court and Country were inextricably intertwined', *ibid.*, p. 41.

Wilton House, a favourite retreat of Charles I and the home of Philip, Earl of Pembroke, who, though he held the position of Lord Chamberlain, was noted as a puritan sympathizer and fought for Parliament in 1642.[38] Graham Parry reveals his discomfort that another puritan parliamentarian failed to react against the romanticism and absolutism of Van Dyck: 'Even the steel clad Northumberland Admiral of the Fleet rests his hand on an anchor as if it were a Cellini bronze.'[39] Yet such an observation merits further reflection. For such cases point to differences both within the politics and the culture of the court and to complexities concerning the relationship between them to which historians and literary scholars have often proved blind. I shall argue that the court/country thesis, rather than illuminating our understanding, has proved to be a blinding glare which has led us along a false trail, while the rich complexities of Caroline court culture have remained, unexplored, in darkness.

A sense of the uncomfortable exceptions and problems lies behind one of the best studies of early Stuart culture and politics, which unfortunately remains unpublished – Professor Malcolm Smuts's doctoral dissertation, 'The culture of absolutism at the court of Charles I'.[40] For Smuts, unlike Parry, begins from an understanding of the complexities of the early Stuart court, or, as he has argued elsewhere, *courts*, of the prince and queen as well as the king; from a knowledge of the factional rivalries, jockeyings for place and favour, the differing political and religious views, the attempted palace coups and heated Council debates which lay behind the illusory uniformity of Whitehall.[41] Smuts perceived that the Caroline court was not a political bloc speaking with one voice. As a consequence he saw too that there could be no simple clash of morality or values between the court and the country when both were engaged in debate within themselves. But, for all his breadth of reading and sensitive analysis of political groupings, of individual poets and texts, Smuts's thesis stops short of the logic of his own research. Though time and again his evidence mutinies against the cause of court *v.* country, in the end he feels obliged to marshal it beneath that banner. And though conspicuous rebels are presented – Carew is enlisted as a spokesman for the country party – the authority of the court/country thesis is upheld. Smuts concludes by an identification of 'two antithetical modes of life'.[42] He sees the

---

[38] Oliver Millar, *Van Dyck in England* (London, 1982); C. Brown, *Van Dyck* (Oxford, 1982), ch. 4; Ashton, *Civil War*, p. 39; below, pp. 21–2.

[39] Parry, *Golden Age Restor'd*, p. 219; Brown, *Van Dyck*, plate 204.

[40] R. M. Smuts, 'The culture of absolutism at the court of Charles I', Princeton University unpublished Ph.D. thesis, 1976. I am grateful to Malcolm Smuts for permission to cite this thesis and for several stimulating discussions of Caroline court culture and politics.

[41] R. M. Smuts, 'The puritan followers of Henrietta Maria in the 1630s', *E.H.R.*, 93 (1978), pp. 26–45; cf. K. Sharpe, 'Faction at the early Stuart court', *History Today*, 33 (Oct. 1983), pp. 39–46.

[42] Smuts, 'Culture of absolutism', p. 468.

civil war as a struggle between two cultures and describes the culture of the Caroline court as no longer in tune with the values of the nation, but as 'The culture of absolutism'.

Absolutism in politics, decadence in culture; it is an enticing equation with the seemingly irrefutable truth of mathematical logic. Perhaps this is why neither side of the equation has been examined more closely. Historians still await a full study of the years of Charles I's rule without parliaments from 1629 to 1640. And literary scholars have paid little attention to the poems and politics of the plays of that decade. Preconceptions about non-parliamentary government and about 'cavalier' poetry and drama have substituted for, even fended off, scholarly investigation.[43] A history of the personal rule, however, is in progress.[44] And meanwhile it is the purpose of this book to examine the poems, plays and masques of those authors closely associated with and at times specifically writing for the court. But before we turn to the texts, we must pause to consider some preconceptions; preconceptions which though flawed in themselves have laid the shaky foundations for that superficially commanding but inherently unstable edifice on the early Stuart landscape: the thesis of a court/country polarity.

COURT AND COUNTRY

When we employ the term 'country' to represent a set of values or to describe an ideology, we think of puritanism as one of its central components. Indeed the argument that there was a widening gulf between the country and the court rests upon assumptions about the nature of puritanism. The puritans of popular image and even of some historical writing were not merely the zealous readers of Scripture, the regular attenders of sermons, the men and women of sober deportment and conversation; they were too the enemies of the arts. Puritans, it is still believed, perceived poets and playwrights as the apostles of Antichrist, inciting men to frivolity and lewdness. Ribald plays, sensuous music and mixed dancing they spurned as ungodly and pagan pastimes. From such a caricature the word 'puritan' in its cultural and moral rather than its religious sense entered the language – though not perhaps until the nineteenth century.[45] It is surprising that after all that has been written to question such a view, we still have to refute the myth of a universal puritan sobriety which damned plays and pleasures. For evidence to the contrary abounds. The puritans were not antagonistic to the arts: among their ranks we find not only poets and musicians, but patrons of theatrical companies

---

[43] Below, pp. 27ff.

[44] The author is currently preparing such a study for Oxford University Press. See Sharpe, 'The personal rule of Charles I'.

[45] See M. G. Finlayson, *Historians, Puritanism and the English Revolution* (Toronto, 1984), ch. 3.

and regular attenders at the playhouse. The Countess of Warwick, daughter-in-law of the leading patron of puritan divines, recorded in her autobiography her regular visits to the theatre.[46] Sir Thomas Barrington, leader of a family also known for its zeal in that citadel of godliness, the county of Essex, went up to London to see plays and held performances in his own household.[47] Bulstrode Whitelocke, the 'improbable puritan' who was to serve as Keeper of the Great Seal to the Republic, not only wrote music for theatrical companies, and for a court masque, but was evidently so well known at the Blackfriars that when he entered the theatre the orchestra played the music which he had composed, as a signature tune to mark the presence of a well-known personality.[48] The Blackfriars was located in one of the most puritan parishes of London, yet amidst its hundreds of seats there were doubtless local men as well as an audience from the West End.[49] And whilst the occasional tensions between the theatre and the local community cannot be denied, they should be attributed more to the noise and disorder to which the theatre at times gave rise, and which concerned magistrates of all religious persuasions, than to the strength of local puritan antagonism to the drama itself.[50] It is noteworthy that Sir Thomas Herbert, Master of the Revels, believed that when the French company of actors led by Floridor was licensed to play for some weeks at the Phoenix in Drury Lane, 'They had the benefit of playing on the sermon days.'[51] Evidently the crowds attracted to the one provided a paying audience for the other.

This is an important reminder that godliness and entertainment were not necessarily exclusive. Indeed they could be, and were often expected to be, complementary. The arts were deemed to have a morally didactic function and even as entertainment, as the concept and term *re-creation* make clear, their purpose was a rejuvenation – of the spirit as well as the body. During the 1630s, as we shall see, John Milton clearly believed in the power of literature as a force for reformation. Even Prynne, whose principal objection to the theatre was the acting, particularly by women, praised the reading of plays, especially those of godly intentions.[52] Not all plays or poems, of course, lived up to this ideal. But it was not puritans alone who discriminated between

[46] *Autobiography of Mary, Countess of Warwick*, T. C. Croker, ed. (London, 1848), p. 4.
[47] W. A. Mepham, 'Essex drama under puritanism and the commonwealth', *Essex Review*, 58 (1949), pp. 155–61, 181–5.
[48] G. E. Bentley, *The Jacobean and Caroline Stage* (7 vols., Oxford, 1941–68), I, p. 40; C. Burney, *A General History of Music* (4 vols., London, 1776–89), III, pp. 377–9; S. Orgel and R. Strong, *Inigo Jones: The Theatre of the Stuart Court* (2 vols., Berkeley and London, 1973), II, p. 540; R. Spalding, *The Improbable Puritan: A Life of Bulstrode Whitelocke 1605–75* (London, 1975).
[49] Bentley, *Jacobean and Caroline Stage*, VI, pp. 11, 17.
[50] *Ibid.*, VI, pp. 26–31.
[51] *Ibid.*, VI, p. 65; J. Q. Adams, ed., *The Dramatic Records of Sir Henry Herbert* (New Haven, 1917), p. 61.
[52] W. Prynne, *Histrio–Mastix. The Players Scourge* (London, 1633), pp. 831–6, 928–36.

substantial and light or foolish productions: courtier and king did so too.[53] Sir Thomas Herbert censored lewd language no less zealously than the puritan preachers condemned it.[54]

The puritans, then, were not necessarily opposed to the theatre. Moreover, there was little to antagonize them in the culture and style of the Caroline court. For in matters of personal morality and in his attitudes to the purpose and tone of court culture, Charles I, unlike his father, was not far from the position of his puritan subjects. As Lucy Hutchinson (whose standards were high) was to acknowledge, the face of the court was much changed in the new king.[55] The licentiousness, ribaldry and drunkenness of James I's court were rapidly out of season. Charles's personal style was strict and serious: he ate modestly, was punctilious in his personal devotions, refined in his speech and decorous in his behaviour. He was chaste and even prudish.[56] Moreover the king insisted that his personal example be emulated and that his court become a worthy model for the reformation of manners. Any 'prophane person' or 'ribald', 'notorious drunkard' or 'swearer' was to be banished.[57] One of the queen's favoured attendants, Harry Jermyn, was dismissed the court when his clandestine affair with one of the maids became obvious by her pregnancy.[58] The king expected the highest personal standards of his ministers and servants, and with some conspicuous and ironically some 'puritan' exceptions,[59] his expectations were realized. Indeed William Laud, for all his disagreements with the puritans over matters of church doctrine and ceremony, in attitudes to morality and discipline was at one with them. Laud's own life was ascetic, even monastic; he had little time for plays.[60] Laud's friend and correspondent, Thomas Wentworth, a figure of intense

---

[53] Below, pp. 36–7; P. Simpson, 'King Charles the First as dramatic critic', *Bodleian Quart. Rec.*, 8 (92) (1936/7), pp. 257–62.

[54] Adams, *Dramatic Records of Herbert*, pp. 21, 22, 23.

[55] 'The face of the court was much changed in the king, for King Charles was temperate chaste and serious, so that the fools and bawds, mimics and catamites of the former Court grew out of fashion.' Hutchinson, *Memoires of the Life of Colonel Hutchinson*, I, pp. 119–20. The testimony is all the more powerful from a puritan opponent of the king.

[56] See Warwick, *Memoires*. Warwick, as gentleman of the bedchamber, knew Charles I intimately.

[57] P.R.O., Lord Chamberlain's department, L.C.5/180, Orders for the royal household, 1630. See K. Sharpe, 'The court and household of Charles I', in D. Starkey, ed., *The English Court from the Wars of the Roses to the English Civil War* (forthcoming).

[58] J. Flower to Sir J. Scudamore, 11 May 1633, P.R.O., Chancery Masters Exhibits (Duchess of Norfolk deeds), C.115/M.30/8151.

[59] E. Hyde, Earl of Clarendon, *The History of the Rebellion and Civil Wars in England*, ed. W. D. Macray, (6 vols., Oxford, 1888), I, pp. 75–80; B. Donogan, 'A courtier's progress: greed and consistency in the life of the Earl of Holland', *Hist. Journ.*, 19 (1976), pp. 317–53.

[60] H. R. Trevor-Roper, *Archbishop Laud, 1573–1645* (2nd edn, London, 1962), p. 34; cf. 'The Diary of . . . William Laud', in W. Scott and J. Bliss, eds., *The Works of William Laud* (7 vols. in 9, Oxford, 1847–60), III, pp. 131–255.

self-discipline, was a self-confessed convert to the doctrine of Stoicism.[61] There was little in a court of such men to antagonize a puritan sense of sobriety. The Sunday performances at court may have played upon some puritan consciences, but they evidently did not disturb the Bridgewaters, who, for all their sympathies with the godly, held their own.[62] Puritanism, as a description of a personal and social morality, was not necessarily at odds with the court any more than with the theatre. Rather the champions as well as critics of a puritan morality were found both in the court *and* the country.

Nor should the term, idea and ideology of the 'country' be assumed *a priori* to be antagonistic to the court. For the ideals associated with the term were part of the common heritage of a classical culture, the legacy of an education which embraced Virgil's *Georgics* and *Eclogues* in grammar schools and universities.[63] The association of 'the country' with the inclination to retreat from public life was one of the *topoi* of classical political rhetoric. This itself should remind us that the idea of the country was not a concept divorced from or opposed to government, but part of the common language of political debate concerning the nature of the polis. In Elizabethan England, the starting point for reflection concerning the nature of government was the works of Aristotle.[64] Central to Aristotle's *Ethics* and *Politics* is the idea that virtue must be active – and active on the public stage. Because man is a political animal, he fulfils his nature only by participation in the polis. Retreat was at times the necessary response by the good man to a society of vice and corruption which threatened to compromise his virtue. But it was never the ideal. For the state existed to make the good life possible, to make the good man and the good citizen one.[65] It is in this context that we should understand the idea of the country. Like the use of the word 'nature', the term 'country' described not so much a place as an ideal. As a model of purity and virtue, of honesty and nature, the 'country' was an ideal *for* the conduct of political life; it was not a rejection of political life.

As such the ideology of the country was expressed at the centre of politics – at the court – no less than outside it. This is one reason why it was at court

[61] *The Earl of Strafforde's Letters and Despatches*, W. Knowler, ed., (2 vols., London, 1739), II, p. 40.

[62] See Bentley, *Jacobean and Caroline Stage*, VII, appendix B; J. Creaser, 'The present aid of this occasion: the setting of Milton's comus', in D. Lindley, ed., *The Court Masque* (Manchester, 1984), p. 117.

[63] H. F. Kearney, *Scholars and Gentlemen: Universities and Society in Pre-industrial England, 1500–1700* (London, 1970), pp. 43, 124; P. Alpers, *The Singer of the Eclogues: A Study of Virgilian Pastoral* (Berkeley, 1979), pp. 86, 94, 105; M. Curtis, *Oxford and Cambridge in Transition 1558–1642* (Oxford, 1959); J. Simon, *Education and Society in Tudor England* (Cambridge, 1967), pp. 83–4, 86n, 112, 144n.

[64] Kearney, *Scholars and Gentlemen*, p. 82.

[65] J. A. K. Thomson, ed., *The Ethics of Aristotle* (Harmondsworth, 1955), pp. 37, 41–2, 126–7, 251, 301, 302–5; T. A. Sinclair, ed., *Aristotle: The Politics* (Harmondsworth, 1962), pp. 28, 52, 107, 120–1, 152. See below, ch. 6.

that the pastoral flourished as a genre, and at court that Arcadian ideals were a recurrent motif throughout the English Renaissance. The reconciliation of virtue and politics was perhaps the central concern of a society which could react only with horror to Machiavelli's attempt to justify a separate morality for the state.[66] If 'the good life', that is the virtuous as well as happy life, is indeed a chief end of the state, there could be no conflict between ethics and politics. Renaissance England still believed that the aristocracy, those who governed, should also be the best men (by merit as well as birth), as the Greek etymology affirmed. They maintained that the king could do no wrong because his authority lay in his virtue.[67] That the realities often fell short of the ideal escaped few men. Courtiers could, and did, indulge in peculation and corruption; the world of politics, a world of intrigue, dishonesty, sleights of hand, often seemed far from the state of virtue. But the perception of this reality reinforced rather than eroded the ideals. Within the court as well as outside it, poets and politicians presented visions of innocent nature and virtuous government in order to rearticulate ideals to a society which, during the later years of Elizabeth's reign, they began to see as in decline.

Such ideals, and idealizations, of 'the country' were not only expressed in the literature of early seventeenth-century England. They underlay the rhetoric and the action of the government no less than they influenced its critics. In Charles I's and William Laud's programme to re-establish the parish church as the centre of worship and as the focus of the parish, we may detect a perception, an idealized perception, of the community of the parish threatened by wandering preachers and puritan hostility to church-ales.[68] More obviously, royal proclamations (issued from the 1590s) ordering the gentry to reside on their local estates and to provide hospitality and good governance embody the language and image of a paternalist aristocracy and rural good order.[69] It is easier to mock even the more sophisticated expressions of belief in a rural 'Merrie England' than it is to appreciate their enduring hold on men's minds. Perhaps if no motif more insistently pervades the court poetry of early Stuart England than 'an idyllic image of English rural life', it was because such an image was still central to political thought and to political action.[70]

The court then did not occlude country ideology nor did country ideology

---

[66] F. Raab, *The English Face of Machiavelli* (London, 1964); J. G. A. Pocock, *The Machiavellian Moment* (Princeton, 1975), ch. 10.
[67] Cf. Aristotle, *Politics*, Bk. IV, ch. 2.
[68] Trevor-Roper, *Archbishop Laud*, e.g. pp. 77–100, 155–8; T. G. Barnes, 'County politics and a puritan cause célèbre: Somerset churchales, 1633', *Trans. Roy. Hist. Soc.*, 9 (1959), pp. 103–22. I shall be developing this point in *The Personal Rule of Charles I*.
[69] Above, p. 9.
[70] Smuts, 'Culture of absolutism', p. 409.

exclude the court. It embraced the court.[71] The labels 'court' and 'country' were juxtaposed as contrasts by critics of the court of James I and Charles I. But they were not opposed as contending sets of *values*. It was the short-comings of the court, its *failure to fulfil an ideal*, which was contrasted to the country *as an ideal*. Criticisms of what was perceived as a degeneration from courtly ideals were articulated within the court itself, even from the throne, and not surprisingly those criticisms were articulated through represen-tations of the country as a model for reform. In other words, as expressions of ideas and ideals, the 'court' and the 'country' were part of a common language and of common values which were shared by the political nation, and even beyond. The commonweal was one ethical community. It was also one political community from the highest, as Richard Hooker had asserted, to the lowest. In early modern England there was no retreat from political life. The personal and the public, like the country and the court, interpenetrated and were interdependent.[72] And no more in ideas than in action could they be conceived as distinct. A good illustration for our purposes is provided by the country house poem – a genre which Professor Ashton views as the exemplifi-cation of country values.[73] Not only are the poems written by artists connected with the court; the houses – Penshurst, Saxham and Wrest – are the rural residences of courtiers. At times they entertain the court. Moreover they are themselves courts, public and political worlds, worlds of harmony and order which are political models, not rejections of or retreats from politics.[74] Like the royal entertainments offered at Buckden, Bolsover or Welbeck, the country house poems are the expressions of a realm in which court and country could not be opposed to each other but were of one world.[75] The values embodied in the 'country' were the common values of that world.

One constituent of the country ideology to which both historians and literary scholars have recently drawn attention was an expression of nostalgia – especially for the days of Good Queen Elizabeth. In the literature and in the political rhetoric of the early Stuart period we encounter the frequent association of Queen Elizabeth's reign with the virtues of literary talent, true nobility, martial valour, model government and the unity of the com-monweal. Such nostalgia focused particularly on the renowned figures of the

---

[71] Historians of politics have argued powerfully for their interpenetration and interdependence. See D. Hirst, 'Court, country, and politics before 1629', in K. Sharpe, ed., *Faction and Parliament* (Oxford, 1978), pp. 105–38.

[72] See J. Goldberg, *James I and the Politics of Literature* (Baltimore, 1983).

[73] Ashton, *English Civil War*, pp. 35–6.

[74] See below, ch. 3, for my discussion of 'To Saxham' and 'To my Friend G.N. from Wrest'. The high moment of Penshurst is when the house becomes a court.

[75] Below, pp. 52–3.

reign – on Sidney and Drake, or on Ralegh.[76] Certainly a central purpose of the celebration of the age and rule of the Virgin Queen was to point up a contrast which was intended to be unflattering to and critical of her successor. This was true in particular and in general. Those who invoked the names of Drake and Hawkins did so in order to discredit what they regarded as the pusillanimous pacificism of Jacobean foreign policy in a Europe divided by the Thirty Years War and threatened by the spectre of popery. William Camden's purpose in the *Annales* of Elizabeth's reign was broader: to present the *'aevum Elizabethanum'* as an entity, as a historical condition which revealed the failings, decadence and decline of values in the institutions as well as in the individuals of the reign of her successor. Camden's study, of course, was not a mere antiquarian description. It was, and was probably intended as, a model – the presentation of ideals through the portrait of a golden age.[77]

It is important to appreciate, however, that in early Stuart England this nostalgia for Elizabeth's reign, like other forms of criticism, found expression at court as well as outside the court. In Jacobean and Caroline England those who voiced nostalgia for Elizabethan values can often be found within the court. Camden himself was Clarenceux King-of-Arms; Prince Henry evidently consciously portrayed himself as the heir to Elizabeth, appropriating to himself as Oberon the Fairy Prince, the iconography that had become associated with the Fairy Queen.[78] Ben Jonson's late plays, *The New Inn*, *The Magnetic Lady* and *A Tale of A Tub* were, as Anne Barton has argued, conscious revivals of Elizabethan dramatic modes and deliberate expressions of nostalgia for Elizabethan values;[79] and these were written and performed while Jonson was still within the employ of the court.[80] There is something of the same tone in plays of William Davenant, an admirer and conscious imitator of Sidney and Shakespeare, who was employed as the queen's

[76] C. V. Wedgwood, *Oliver Cromwell and the Elizabethan Inheritance* (London, 1970); K. Sharpe, *Sir Robert Cotton, 1586–1631* (Oxford, 1979), pp. 233–4, 244–5; see Fulke Greville, 'Poems of Monarchy', in A. B. Grosart, ed., *The Works of Fulke Greville* (4 vols., London, 1870), I.

[77] W. Camden, *Annales, The True and Royall History of the Famous Empresse Elizabeth*, translated A. Darcie (London, 1625); H. R. Trevor-Roper, *Queen Elizabeth's First Historian: William Camden and the Beginnings of English Civil History* (London, 1971); Sharpe, *Sir Robert Cotton*, pp. 89–94; Sharpe, 'The foundation of the chairs of history at Oxford and Cambridge: an episode in Jacobean politics', *History of Universities*, 2 (1982), pp. 127–52.

[78] J. W. Williamson, *The Myth of the Conqueror* (New York, 1978), pp. 95–102; J. Briggs, *This Stage-Play World* (Oxford, 1983), p. 152. I am grateful to John Peacock for helpful discussions of *Oberon*. See also N. Council, 'Ben Jonson, Inigo Jones, and the transformation of Tudor Chivalry', *E.L.H.*, 47 (1980), pp. 259–95.

[79] Anne Barton, 'Harking back to Elizabeth: Ben Jonson and Caroline nostalgia', *E.L.H.*, 48 (1981), pp. 701–31; see also Barton, *Ben Jonson, Dramatist* (Cambridge, England, 1984), ch. 14. I am grateful to Professor Barton for sending me a typescript of this article and for stimulating discussions of this subject.

[80] Bentley, *Jacobean and Caroline Stage*, IV, pp. 619–20, 623–4, 633.

servant throughout the 1630s.[81] William Cavendish, Duke of Newcastle, Governor to the Prince of Wales, wrote plays which were appeals for the restoration of Elizabethan modes and in one, *The Variety*, presents a character, Manly, in antique Elizabethan ruff and trunk hose.[82] For much of the 1630s, Newcastle kept a distance from the court.[83] But the same could not be said for Thomas Howard, Earl of Arundel, who was on close terms with the king and entrusted with sensitive diplomatic missions and the command of the army against the Scots.[84] In the van of the *avant-garde*, in the fashions for collecting paintings and marbles, Arundel was yet known for his sombre and simple attire, an appearance which his biographer and the Earl of Clarendon clearly interpreted as a commitment to antique values whose demise he lamented.[85] If an Elizabethan plain style represented, as it often does in the drama of the early Stuart period, a rejection of continental foppishness – in dress and in manners – it would be over-simple to identify the first with the country, the second with the court.[86] Just as there were many in the country whose newsletters reveal an obsession with the pursuit of the latest fashion, be it in ribbons, coifs or plays, so there were those at court who decried such ridiculous vanities.[87]

In certain respects, we may see in the policies of Charles I himself a conscious revival of Henrician and Elizabethan styles, in matters of politics and conduct, if not in architecture and art. In reorganizing the royal court and household, for instance, Charles's commissioners, as a contemporary perceived, 'looked back to Henry the Seventh, Henry the Eighth and Queen Elizabeth's time'.[88] The king's personal style had little in common with the posturings and modishness that allegedly characterized the courtier. Charles's own dress was simple and plain; he spoke little and then without rhetorical embellishment.[89] The king dismissed the queen's French attendants and seemed anxious to keep her and his own contacts with the French court, for all its emergence as the arbiter of fashion, to a minimum.[90] He addressed the French ambassadors in English, despite his perfect com-

---

[81] Below, ch. 2.
[82] Barton, 'Harking back to Elizabeth', pp. 707–8.
[83] Margaret, Duchess of Newcastle, *The Life of William Cavendish, Duke of Newcastle*, ed. C. H. Firth (London, 1886), p. 5.
[84] M. F. S. Hervey, *Thomas Howard, Earl of Arundel* (Cambridge, 1921).
[85] B.L., Harleian MS 6272, a biography of Arundel by Sir Edward Walker; Clarendon, *History of the Rebellion*, I, pp. 68–70.
[86] See, for example, Davenant's criticisms, below, pp. 62–3.
[87] Madam Ann Merrick to Mrs Lydall, 21 Jan. 1639, *Cal. Stat. Pap. Dom. 1638–9*, p. 342.
[88] P.R.O., P.C.2/48/403; Knowler, *Strafford Letters*, II, p. 140; Hawkins to Leicester, 21/31 Dec. 1637, H.M.C., *De Lisle MSS*, VI, p. 84.
[89] Warwick, *Memoires of the Reigne of Charles I*, pp. 64–6; *Cal. Stat. Pap. Dom. 1611–18*, p. 273.
[90] *Cal. Stat. Pap. Dom. 1625–6*, pp. 198, 417, 607.

mand of French.[91] For all the emphasis that has been laid on the continental influences in Caroline culture, on the classicism or the baroque extravagance of royal iconography, we should not lose sight of the Englishness or Britishness of Charles as he was and as he was represented. The Albanactus and Britanocles of the masques were idealized as the embodiment of British virtues, as the heir of Brutus.[92] There is more work to be done here. The plays of the reign which poked fun at the ridiculous lengths to which courtiers (among others) might go in order to appear *à la mode*, far from offending the king, may have reflected his own values. And the nostalgia for lost days of harmony, unity and order informed the policies of the king no less than the rhetoric of the country.

It has been our purpose then to argue that as moral, social and even political idea, the ideology of the 'country' was not the preserve of a distinct political group, let alone a political party; it was a component of the common language and currency of values in the context of which political questions were discussed in Renaissance England. We must now come to appreciate that this is equally true of the term 'court'. For the idea of the court was a common ideal too – not an opposed ideology, nor one held uniformly or only by those who held office at court. With the court, with 'courtliness', were associated manners of behaviour and personal qualities to which all men were to aspire. Just as the ideology of the country was an ideal for public life as opposed to a retreat from it, so from the court came the values and language which established models for the conduct of private life: in making requests or petitions (*to court*), in modes of love (*courtship*), and in civilized manners in society (*courteous*). A courtesy was, of course, a generous action of the sort befitting the conduct of the court. The language of the court in everyday use is the legacy of those centuries for which the business of government was still believed to be the rule of virtue.[93] As the abode of the most virtuous man (the king) and the best men (the aristocracy), the court was the natural arbiter of human behaviour.

That not all kings or courtiers lived up to it did little to tarnish the ideal of the court. Castiglione's *The Courtier*, itself the product of a world at Urbino where the lapses from ideal standards were all too apparent, remained the most popular handbook of manners throughout the early seventeenth century.[94] Indeed the hostile and bitter invectives against court corruption in late Elizabethan and Jacobean England only make sense if we acknowledge that there were still powerfully influential expectations that were not being

[91] P.R.O., C.115/N3/8544, Sir Henry Herbert to Scudamore, 3 July 1629.
[92] Orgel and Strong, *Inigo Jones*, II, pp. 454–8, 662–7; see *Coelum Britannicum, ibid.*, II, pp. 576–80, especially lines 870–1048; T. D. Kendrick, *British Antiquity* (London, 1950).
[93] See Javitch, *Poetry and Courtliness*.
[94] *Ibid.*, pp. 118–24.

fulfilled. Like the modern sport or pop celebrity, the king and court dictated what was thought to be good; and early modern Englishmen reacted with the same outrage as modern moralists when such influence was exercised without responsibility.[95] The disgust we can discern in newsletter comments concerning the behaviour and court of James I expresses a concern for the consequences of such bad example. This should not surprise us if we appreciate that the court was not just a distant irrelevance, but the centre of culture and power to which most of the important men of the realm had at least occasional resort and of which many literate (and some illiterate) were by the 1620s receiving regular news. John Owen, the epigrammatist, versed succinctly the belief of his age:

> All subjects in their manners follow Kings
> What they do, bids; forbearing forbids things
> A King's behaviour sways his subjects livès
> As the first mover all the fixt stars drives.[96]

Owen's epigrams, after widely circulating in manuscript, were published in 1628. After more than twenty years of Jacobean slovenliness and debauchery, a reminder that monarchs did, and should, set personal and ethical examples may not have been untimely. Charles I seems to have been especially aware of the importance of his own example and that of the court. His orders of 1630 for the regulation of the royal household announced their purpose as 'to establish government and order in our court which from thence may spread . . . through all parts of our kingdoms'.[97] That is to say, of course, that Charles I realized that the image of the court was powerful in the country – indeed he intended that it should be.[98] In Caroline England, then, neither the king's subjects nor the king himself saw the court or its culture as an insulated, exclusive or separate world of values. Like the ideology of the country, the values of the court penetrated and permeated society, the private world as well as the public.

If then the ideals associated with the court were held in common, did the image and culture of the Caroline court debase that common currency and so fragment a world of shared values? It has become customary to argue that this is so, that court culture in the reign of Charles I pandered to the 'narrow snobbery and effete indulgence', as Peter Thomas put it, of a few, and so became the exclusive preserve of a coterie at Whitehall insulated from the rest of the nation.[99] Before we concur, we should pause for several reflections.

[95] J. S. Morrill, 'William Davenport and the "silent majority" of early Stuart England', *Journal of the Chester Archaeological Society*, 58 (1975), pp. 115–30.

[96] J. Owen, *Certaine Epigrams* (London, 1628), p. 31.

[97] P.R.O., L.C.5/180.

[98] See below, ch. 5, pp. 236–7, for Carew's treatment of Charles I's intentions in *Coelum Britannicum*.

[99] Thomas, 'Two Cultures?' p. 175.

First, as recent researches in political history have made clear, we should recognize the diversity of attitudes, personalities and personal styles within the Caroline court.[100] Charles I was served almost equally by English and Scots. Among his leading ministers was a Lord Treasurer, Weston, who was believed to be pro-Spanish and Catholic; a Master of the Horse, the Marquis of Hamilton, and a Groom of the Stole, Holland, who were deemed of strongly Protestant sympathies and pro-French. Alongside the austere self-disciplined style of Wentworth and Laud worked Weston, whom Laud regarded as a slouch, and Cottington, whom he thought a wag. Holland had a reputation as a womanizer for all his puritan connections; Van Dyck evidently kept a mistress.[101] The king, as we have seen, was prudish. A culture that could express the style of such a heterogeneous court can hardly be regarded as exclusive. Nor when so many factions were represented there is it easy to describe the court as isolated. For through the connections of powerful courtiers as diverse in attitudes as Weston and Holland, Cottington and Northumberland, most of the views aired in the country could find an advocate at court.

Secondly, we should consider the nature of and responses to the Caroline courtly style. The classicism of Jones's architecture, it is argued, was seen as foreign, popish and alien. By the reign of Charles I, however, Jones's most productive period as an architect was all but over, curtailed by royal insolvency. And though in the 1630s Jones designed the spectacular west portal of St Paul's Cathedral, we should recall that his other major commissions, for the church in Covent Garden and for Wilton House, came respectively from the Earl of Bedford, who remained distant from the court for most of the decade and who was to emerge as a champion of the country in 1641, and from the Earl of Pembroke, who fought for parliament.[102] There are to my knowledge no horrified reactions to Jones's architecture during the reign of Charles I; it may be that his buildings were disliked as incongruous to English style and helped to foster fears of popish innovation, but the contemporary record of the thirties is silent. In 1641 Sir Simonds D'Ewes had to ask who Jones was. Van Dyck, as we have seen, was not the painter of only the cavaliers. As well as Northumberland and Pembroke, the Countess of Bedford, Anne Cavendish, wife of the Earl of Warwick, and Elizabeth Howard, Countess of Peterborough ('a lady of ... strong republican

---

[100] See Smuts, 'The puritan followers of Henrietta Maria', and Sharpe, 'Faction at the early Stuart court'.

[101] B.L., Egerton MS 1636, f. 102.

[102] J. Harris, 'Inigo Jones and the courtier style', *Architectural Review*, 154 (July 1973), pp. 17–24; H. Colvin, *A Biographical Dictionary of British Architects, 1600–1840* (London, 1978), pp. 467–74.

sympathies') sat to his brush.[103] So too did Arthur Goodwin who, a year after his portrait, was returned with John Hampden for the county of Buckinghamshire, whose cavalry he commanded for parliament during the civil war.[104] Even the masque, as *Comus* and many other entertainments illustrate, was not a purely courtly mode. Indeed printed texts of the court masques themselves were disseminated to the country.[105]

Finally, we should take note of an important observation by Professor Smuts: that the very idea of a systematic, or what we might term 'official' court culture is something of a misleading fiction. For in early modern England there were no institutions at court through which an official culture could be organized, nor did Charles I appear to have had any desire to establish them. Inigo Jones held only the medieval office of Surveyor of the Works, whilst Van Dyck enjoyed a pension but no official position. Moreover, at court and in London, the king's was only the largest of several sources of patronage.[106] And, as the career of Thomas Howard, Earl of Arundel, underlines, the civilization of the court 'grew from the initiative and investment of many individuals, including some who arguably had a greater impact than the king',[107] and some who did not share his values.

The term 'court culture', then, is a convenient and simple shorthand, but it must not substitute for the more complex fuller story. The court was not one body, but a diversity of men and attitudes; the painters, poets and playwrights we find at court were never the exclusive preserve of the court; there was no official court culture marshalled for political ends. Only a sense of the common world of values, of the interpenetration of court and country, of the factions and differences of court politics, and of the difficulties involved in talking of an official 'court culture' will enable us to examine the literature of the court free from assumptions that it was by necessity frivolous and exclusive, authoritarian and sycophantic. Only an understanding of the complexities of the court will open our ears to the differing and discordant voices of courtly literature, and to refrains of dissent that we have ignored from an assumption that all at court perforce sang in harmony.

THE PREMISES OF CAROLINE CULTURE

In the masques, plays and poems of the reign of Charles I scholars have identified a unifying philosophy – the philosophy of Neo-Platonism, and

---

[103] C. Russell, *The Crisis of Parliaments* (Oxford, 1971), p. 179. I owe this reference to James Robertson; Millar, *Van Dyck in England*, p. 76.
[104] Millar, *Van Dyck in England*, p. 95.
[105] Below, ch. 5.
[106] R. M. Smuts, 'The political failure of Stuart cultural patronage', in G. F. Lytle and S. Orgel, eds., *Patronage in the Renaissance* (Princeton, 1981), pp. 165–90.
[107] *Ibid.*, p. 177.

especially the cult of Platonic love. The Neo-Platonists of the Italian Renaissance expounded their mentor's philosophy of forms, or ideals which were the reality beside which particular material objects were but shadows.[108] Though man lives in the world of time and corporeal substance, he has a soul which, at its height, may enable him to comprehend the world of forms. In the Neo-Platonic system, it is the purpose of life to come to a knowledge of the form, or essence, by an ascending process of cognition – through an elevation from the world of sense to that of intellect. It is the rôle of education, philosophy and the aesthetic to make possible that cognition. In the *Symposium*, Plato depicted the attainment of love in this way: as an ascent from a sensual appreciation of earthly beauty to a knowledge of the true form of beauty – virtue. Such a love brings man to the realization of his highest self – to virtue and self-regulation. This is the ethical doctrine for which Ficino coined the shorthand 'Platonic love' in his *Commentary on Plato's Symposium* of 1469.

From the beginning there were sceptics and critics of Platonic love – and it is important that we find them among the ranks of those who wrote theoretical treatises expounding the doctrine. In the works of Torquato Tasso, for example, scholars have detected tensions between the theoretical expositions of Platonic love and the unabashed sensuality of the poetry.[109] The Aristotelians who came to dominate the academies of the sixteenth century placed a far greater emphasis upon the integration of body and soul, of substance and form, and expressed reservations about the implications for ethics and politics of Platonic metaphysics. Though the debate continued, it was a Christian Aristotelianism rather than Ficino's rigid Neo-Platonism that gained the ascendancy in the universities of early modern Europe.

Platonic love, however, had gained a following beyond the circles of scholarship. It became the fashion of polite society and especially of the princely courts where the need to regulate sexual appetite was felt most. Among the leading contributors to the fashionable literature of Platonic love were Pietro Bembo and Castiglione, noted public figures as well as scholars and the latter the author of *The Courtier*, the best-selling guide to conduct in the world of affairs. Bembo's *Gli Assolani*, five books of dialogues on the nature of love, became a favourite text for the Italian gallants of the sixteenth century. Reprinted many times and translated into French, Bembo's treatise was the inspiration for Honoré D'Urfé's *Astrée*, a pastoral romance consisting of discourses on the nature of love which became popular throughout

[108] The following summary is based upon A. H. Armstrong, ed., *The Cambridge History of Later Greek and Early Medieval Philosophy* (Cambridge, 1970); P. Kristeller, *The Philosophy of Marsilio Ficino* (Gloucester, Mass., 1964); J. C. Nelson, *Renaissance Theory of Love* (New York, 1958); P. Kristeller, *Renaissance Thought and its Sources* (New York, 1979).
[109] Kristeller, *Renaissance Thought*, p. 62.

Europe.[110] It was probably through *Astraea*, translated into English in 1620, that the idea of Platonic love became more widely known in England.[111] As a fashionable cult, however, Platonic love came to England through Henrietta Maria, who had grown up during the years when the Marquise de Rambouillet had established her salon to refine manners and sexual mores at the French court. Its influence at court was first noted in 1634, by the newswriter James Howell:

The Court affords little News at present, but that there is a love call'd Platonick Love, which much sways there of late; it is a Love abstracted from all corporeal gross impressions and sensual Appetite, but consists in Contemplations and Ideas of the Mind, not in any carnal fruition. This love sets the Wits of the Town on work; and they say there will be a Mask shortly of it, whereof her Majesty and her Maids of Honour will be part.[112]

Howell's tone suggests scepticism about the seriousness of Platonic love. The sophistication of the queen's or king's understanding of Neo-Platonic philosophy is, unfortunately, something which we cannot document. When, at the end of a chapter on love in his own copy of Bacon's *Advancement of Learning*, Charles wrote, 'Love is the Mother of all Noble action', we cannot be sure whether the sentence represented a philosophical belief or a proverbial commonplace.[113] But the king and queen appear to have taken the idea seriously. Platonic love became a central motif of the masques and some of the court plays.

Most, however, appear to have found the idea unattractive and ridiculous, and such criticisms of Platonic love were heard from within the court as well as outside it. Anyone who has read the drama of the 1630s will know that many Caroline playwrights treated Platonic love as the subject of bawdy humour and derision. Good examples are Constant and Sadd in Killigrew's *The Parson's Wedding*, characters who adopt Platonic love only for fashion's sake, or lady Love-All who in the same play excuses her flagrant sexual promiscuity by arguments about transcending the merely physical. At the other end of the sexual spectrum is Sir Ralph Winterplum of Brome's *Court Beggar*, a self-announced Platonic lover who is in fact a castrated bachelor horrified by every allusion to sex.[114] Such examples lampoon Platonic love as a trivial and empty deceit. Not only were these plays performed at court, playwrights intimately connected with the court voiced the same criticisms.

[110] *Biographie Universelle*, 42, pp. 371–2.
[111] Honoré d'Urfé, *The History of Astraea* (London, 1620); Sears Jayne, 'Ficino and the Platonism of the English Renaissance', *Comparative Literature*, 4 (1952), pp. 214–38.
[112] J. Jacobs, ed., *Epistolae Ho-Elianae* (London, 1890), p. 317.
[113] Francis Bacon, *Of the Advancement of Learning* (London, 1640). A copy in the British Library (6.46 v 1) bound in plum velvet with the royal crest is Charles I's own and bears extensive annotation in his own hand. Quotation from p. 318.
[114] J. L. Davis, *The Sons of Ben: Jonsonian Comedy in Caroline England* (Detroit, 1967), pp. 185–206.

Sir John Suckling's name, for example, is inseparable from our concept of cavalier culture – in poetry, drama and public affairs.[115] Yet the character of Orsamnes in his play *Aglaura* (performed at court and printed in 1638) parodied Platonic love as 'a mere trick to enhance the price of kisses'.[116] Sir William Davenant, the queen's servant and masque writer, wrote a mordant satire, *The Platonic Lovers*, which was printed and probably performed at court as well as the Blackfriars.[117] Such comedies exposed the pretence and dissimulation of a fashion. But, as I shall suggest, Davenant's concern went deeper, for if the court was engaged with a trivial fashion, it was abnegating its responsibility to proffer moral examples. And if, as he came to suspect, there was a more serious commitment to Neo-Platonism on the part of the king, then its ethical and political implications were both novel and unattractive. In either case, Davenant was sufficiently concerned to make it the subject of critical examination. Platonic love by no means inspired the artists of the Caroline court.

Those who argue that Caroline court culture was frivolous, exclusive and authoritarian usually point to the masque.[118] The masque was the quintessential courtly mode. In its very structure it embodied a Neo-Platonic philosophy; the masque was concerned with forms, idealizations. Whereas drama took as its subject matter the ambivalence and debates of human life, the purpose of masque was to transcend them.[119] The conclusion of the masque was triumph over uncertainty; the revels symbolized the harmony which transcended the dialogue, the ambivalence of the spoken word. At the centre of the action was the king himself – whether or not he participated. For the masque was a political expression and idealization of the king and the court – an observation which once led scholars (and still leads some) to discuss it as narcissistic and sycophantic.

In *The Jonsonian Masque*, however, Stephen Orgel demonstrated that the Jacobean masque did not preclude criticism. From 1609 onwards, Ben Jonson introduced progressively longer antimasques which became vehicles for satirical discussion and topical allusion. In the end the form of masque required the transcendence of antimasque burlesque by revels and the arts of illusion effected through the machinery developed by Inigo Jones. But in many Jonson masques the antimasque leaves a powerful impression. In some texts they predominate and even in performance some suggest that the

[115] T. Clayton, ed., *The Works of Sir John Suckling. The Non-Dramatic Works* (Oxford, 1971), p. xlvii.
[116] A. Harbage, *Cavalier Drama* (New York, 1936, 2nd edn, 1964), pp. 110–12; Knowler, *Strafford Letters*, II, p. 150; Bentley, *Jacobean and Caroline Stage*, V, pp. 1201–6; L. A. Beaurline, ed., *The Works of Sir John Suckling. The Plays* (Oxford, 1971), pp. 33–114, quotation from Act II, Scene II, lines 28–9, p. 56.
[117] Below, ch. 2.
[118] Ashton, *English Civil War*, pp. 30–1.
[119] S. Orgel, *The Jonsonian Masque* (Cambridge, Mass., 1965), p. 17.

conflicts and criticisms of antimasque were never dispelled. The tensions could be radical: *Pleasure Reconciled to Virtue*, as Orgel argues, concluded with a celebration of the mean between antimasque misrule and masque order, not in the triumph of the latter.

But in the Caroline masque, it has been argued, the tensions and criticisms disappear. Unlike his father, Charles was not attracted by the burlesque and repartee of antimasque. In accordance with royal tastes, critics suggest, Caroline masques placed greater emphasis upon the visual spectacular of masque and all but banish the antimasque.[120] The dismissal of Jonson and elevation of Inigo Jones saw the complete triumph of spectacle over poetry, idealization over a sense of reality and of sycophantic flattery over any counsel or criticism.[121] The first to make such a charge was Jonson himself, and literary scholars and historians have never quite resisted the power of his denunciations of Jones and his invective. Where Jacobean masques are understood to be ambivalent and critical in tone, the Caroline masques are seen as transient spectacle and trite flattery. To Professor Ashton they are 'distinctly narcissistic and inward looking'; to Graham Parry they are the sycophantic gestures to authority of the 'hired admirer'.[122] Even Stephen Orgel, whilst appreciating their serious purpose, has described the 1630s masques as expressions of 'the developing movement toward autocracy . . . if we can really see the king as the tamer of nature, the queen as the goddess of flowers, there will be no problems about Puritans or Ireland or Ship Money'.[123] The Caroline masques, in other words, were an escape from important questions and problems into the self-supporting world of illusion.

It is precisely this characterization that I wish to challenge in a later chapter from a close re-examination of the texts. But some preliminary and obvious objections present themselves. What strikes the reader immediately is the nature and length of the Caroline masque texts. The length alone of masques such as *Coelum Britannicum* seems sufficient to question Harbage's assertion that poetry became subordinated by spectacle. What discredits the view completely is the attention paid by the Caroline authors to the masques as texts. Printed editions, carefully corrected and revised, bearing descriptions of scenes and costumes and explanation, notes and prologues indicate that the Caroline authors, no less than Jonson, conceived of the masque as a genre with an audience outside the court and with a life more enduring than the night's performance. Those in the country who avidly sought copies of

---

[120] Orgel, *The Jonsonian Masque*; Orgel, *The Illusion of Power* (Berkeley, 1975); Orgel and Strong, *Inigo Jones: The Theatre of the Stuart Court*; D. J. Gordon, *The Renaissance Imagination*, ed. S. Orgel (Berkeley, 1976). For a greater emphasis upon the ambivalence and irony of masque, see below, ch. 5.

[121] Parry, *Golden Age Restor'd*, ch. 9.

[122] Ashton, *English Civil War*, pp. 30–1; Parry, *Golden Age Restor'd*, pp. 185, 191.

[123] Orgel, *The Illusion of Power*, pp. 51–2.

masques, as well as those at court who bought, as it were, 'the book of the show' confirm the continuing importance of the texts and of the masques as discourse and poetry, as well as spectacle. Indeed it is not only the survival of the masque as literature which strikes us; it is the continued vitality and importance of the antimasques.[124] It has become fashionable (inexplicably fashionable) to dismiss the Caroline antimasques as trivial episodes transcended by the dazzling displays of the illusionist's art. So according to Graham Parry the lengthy dialogue between Publius and Platonicus served only as 'an engaging interlude' to the real subject of *Albion's Triumph*; the twenty entries of the antimasque to *Salmacida Spolia* he dismisses as suggestive of recreations allowed by the king. Even the throng of hundreds who processed before the king as the antimasque introduction to the *Triumph of Peace* is discounted: 'Even if the points were seriously intended, it is difficult to imagine that Charles would have sensed them in that setting of splendour and gaiety.'[125] This is of course superficially to prejudge the issue, and we shall need to examine the antimasque more closely than that. For not only do the antimasques loom large in the texts of the 1630s masques, they were evidently the subject of considerable attention – to costume, display and iconography as well as to prose and verse – in the performance. I shall suggest too that not only do they introduce and explain the masque itself, but that an understanding of these antimasques and their function within the formal structure of masque lends support to the view that the Caroline masques were as literary, as serious, as ambivalent, at times even implicitly as critical, as the Jonsonian productions.

To make any such suggestion or to raise the word 'criticism' is to launch a fundamental challenge to the idea of 'cavalier culture' and so to jeopardize the utility of descriptive labels, such as 'cavalier poetry' or 'cavalier drama', which historians and literary scholars have employed in order to make sense of an age. We must not shrink from this challenge, nor rue the demise of such terms, for like 'puritan' and 'country' they often incorporate assumptions and become explanations rather than, as descriptive terms ought, facilitate deeper understanding. Quite simply there were no cavaliers in the 1630s – if the term is intended to delineate a coherent political group. And as description of a style, gallant and swaggering, it was by no means confined to the court.[126] Indeed many of those known as 'cavalier poets' – Carew and Suckling for example – died before the first blood had been spilled in the English civil war.

[124] Below, ch. 5.

[125] Parry, *Golden Age Restor'd*, pp. 190, 193, 201.

[126] For example, Thomas Howard, Earl of Arundel, used the term to describe the gentlemen of the Inns of Court, Arundel to Wentworth, 22 Feb. 1634, Sheffield Central Library, Wentworth Woodhouse MS WW13/201. I am grateful to Sheffield Central Library and the Wentworth Woodhouse Trust for permission to cite this manuscript. Conrad Russell has reminded me that the first Royalists were not courtiers.

This is not merely the pedantic complaint of a historian. For there is more than a suspicion that assumptions about the political sympathies of poets have infected the critical discussion of their verse by literary scholars and historians alike. Where Jonson and Donne speak with the voices of a courtly world resonating with internal tensions yet still united with the realm in common values, the cavalier poets, it is alleged, sang the swansong of an exclusive and authoritarian caste doomed to be defeated.[127] So to George Parfitt 'Cavalier poetry shows a narrowing of range of reference and interest, becoming courtly in a sense which suggests a decisive split between "court" and "country" and a consequent concentration upon few areas of emotional experience.'[128] And so, C. V. Wedgwood argued, cavalier poets 'stimulated . . . an attitude of mind which weakened the judgement and made king and courtiers alike unable to read the harsher signs of the times'.[129]

Perhaps as a consequence of this dismissive disdain, the Caroline poets have gone long unedited, unstudied and, except in anthologies, unread. When they were subjected to close critical investigation by Earl Miner in 1971 the assumptions began to fall away. The poets were found to be concerned with the life of virtue, to be seeking their values in the country as well as the court, to be concerned with disorder as well as order and to reveal 'doubts about the actual court'.[130] If such observations were not sufficient to discredit the usefulness of the term 'cavalier', one might have thought that a mode that took in a century from Ben Jonson to Cotton was too broad in range and chronology to suit the specific associations of the label. In what he called *The Cavalier Mode*, Miner offered in fact an implicit rebuttal of the term and a re-evaluation of a poetic which, in the 1620s and 1630s as in other decades, engaged with the ethical and political questions of the age from a variety of viewpoints and perspectives. Prejudices, however, die hard and Miner's suggestions have not prompted further investigations. In *The Golden Age Restor'd* Parry critically condemns 'a poetry that was more refined and more uncritically flattering than the earlier mode . . . more artificial, more superficial'.[131] And even the most recent anthology introduces the selection in a slightly apologetic tone.[132] There is no need for apology. Herrick and Suckling, Carew and Lovelace belong within the traditions of Donne and Jonson, but deserve fully to be read for themselves, separately and independently. Later chapters on Aurelian Townshend and Carew will

---

[127] Parry, *Golden Age Restor'd*, ch. 9; Thomas, 'Two Cultures?'
[128] G. Parfitt, 'The poetry of Thomas Carew', *Renaissance and Modern Studies*, 12 (1968), pp. 55–68; p. 56.
[129] C. V. Wedgwood, *Poetry and Politics under the Stuarts* (Cambridge, 1960), p. 30.
[130] E. Miner, *The Cavalier Mode from Jonson to Cotton* (Princeton, 1971), *passim*; quotation p. 200.
[131] Parry, *Golden Age Restor'd*, p. 264.
[132] T. Clayton, ed., *Cavalier Poets* (Oxford, 1978).

suggest that they spoke ambivalently, and sometimes critically, of the court society in which they lived.[133] We should not prejudge them from a position that assumes *a priori* that they could not.

If much Caroline poetry has been confined to occasional perusal in the anthology, most 'cavalier drama' now remains unstaged and unread. Indeed one might be led to believe, if literary criticism were to be our guiding light, that from the days of Jonson's successes, *Volpone* or *Bartholomew Fair*, to the world of Restoration comedy, the theatre was plunged into darkness. The names and plays that literally packed the Caroline theatres – Killigrew and Davenant, Nabbes and Brome, and Shirley – mean little to the student of drama. The reason for their neglect stems once again from preconceptions. After Jonson's years of greatness, it is argued, the theatre became dominated by the court.[134] Controlled, it is said, by court censorship and dictated by courtly preoccupations, tainted by the frivolities and vanities of masque, Caroline drama descended to uncritical, sycophantic spectacle, depicting the foolish concerns (Platonic love, honour) of an exclusive and snobbish coterie. Alfred Harbage indeed described the theatre of Caroline England as *Cavalier Drama*. For, he argued, the plays for the private and public theatres too were dictated by courtly patterns.[135] Their model was *The Shepherd's Paradise*, a tedious pastoral penned by one of the queen's minions, Walter Montagu, and performed by her ladies at court. It was an inauspicious mould which formed the pattern for a drama that revolved around the subjects of courtly romanticism: plays of lustful villains, friends who were rivals in love, long lost siblings, heroes resurrected from (apparent) death, in short trivial plots. Lacking the developments of real characterization, 'the people in Cavalier plays are precieux'.[136] The comic underplot which provided the vigour and satire of so much Jacobean drama was surrendered to a uniformity of form which was 'prevailingly serious, sentimental, romantic' – a reflection of the queen's influence and taste.[137] Feminine sensibilities, Harbage argued, dictated too the suppression of lascivious jests and sexual innuendo and favoured a treatment and language 'of almost uniform freedom from ribaldry and coarseness'.[138] Expressions of criticism fell victim to the political

---

[133] Below, chs. 3, 4.

[134] For some remarks on the political determination of literary canons, see K. Sharpe and S. Zwicker, eds., *Politics of Discourse: The Literature and History of Seventeenth Century England* (forthcoming), introduction.

[135] Harbage, *Cavalier Drama, passim*. For a recent corrective, see P. Edwards, ed., *The Revels History of English Drama, Vol. IV, 1613–1660* (London, 1981), especially section III. But note that in his recent *Collected Essays* (I, p. 5) Hill writes, 'The tone of the drama favoured by the court and the coterie theatres became increasingly "Cavalier".'

[136] Harbage, *Cavalier Drama*, p. 38. See below, pp. 39–44, for a different interpretation of *The Shepherd's Paradise*.

[137] Harbage, *Cavalier Drama*, p. 73.

[138] *Ibid.*, p. 40.

ambitions of the court. When they cannot be denied, as in the case of
Orsamnes' speeches in Sir John Suckling's *Aglaura*, Harbage plays down
their impact: 'this element is subsidiary and affects the major characters not
at all'.[139] Almost all the plays fit the mould. The court dictated the subjects
and style of Caroline drama which adopted too the values and ideals of the
court uncritically.

Not only do assumptions about politics underlie this thesis; political
attitudes and sympathies appear more strongly than evidence in its exposition. For Harbage was clear that we should not condemn the playwrights, but
rather 'blame the *zeitgeist* than the authors themselves'.[140] After all, 'Talent
was not lacking; conditions in the reign of Charles I were simply adverse to its
development.'[141] A developing autocracy was not the field in which the finest
literature could be expected to grow. Those closest to the court were most
choked by the weeds of absolutism: a writer like Suckling was 'spoiled by his
times'.[142] A few honest men distanced themselves from the court and so
preserved their integrity: among them Heywood, Brome and Nabbes and, as
a shining example to all, the Duke of Newcastle who, for all his wealth,
position and status, 'refused to write like a courtier'.[143] For the rest we are left
with the 'petty creations of a petty circle'. No wonder then that few have been
drawn to read them.[144]

Remarkably, there has been little dissent from Harbage's characterization
since its first publication in 1936. If the critical consensus has endorsed
Harbage for nearly fifty years it is not least because the assumptions on which
it is based have themselves remained unquestioned, and hence the problems
and questions to which they give rise have rested unexplored. Let us start with
the term 'cavalier drama'. In Harbage's usage this was evidently not simply
drama performed at court – for Marmion, Nabbes, Heywood and Brome,
who were all staged there, are specifically exempt from his castigations of the
mode; and Shirley, another independent, was commissioned to write a court
masque.[145] Nor were 'cavalier plays' those penned by courtiers – for
Newcastle, whose work escapes the label, was governor to the Prince of
Wales. What then was 'cavalier drama'? We are left with the conclusion that
it was a dramatic mode which reflected a fashion at court, but which was
neither the only courtly mode nor one to the taste of all those at court. To
recognize this is important, for it is to acknowledge that there was more than
one courtly style and a more complex theatrical world than the phrase

---

[139] *Ibid.*, p. 110.
[140] *Ibid.*, p. 124.
[141] *Ibid.*, p. 132.
[142] *Ibid.*, p. 115.
[143] *Ibid.*, p. 117.
[144] *Ibid.*, pp. 3, 258.
[145] All evidence for the staging of plays is taken from Bentley, *Jacobean and Caroline Stage*.

'cavalier drama' conveys. And it is further to acknowledge the potential for debates and differences – between playwrights and courtiers, and even within the individual play.[146] Like his title and organizing concept, Harbage's other generalizations are disturbingly unsatisfactory. For anyone sampling Caroline plays without his preconceptions will soon encounter bawdiness and ribaldry, comic underplot and satire; nor can one fail to suspect a questioning and critical undercurrent which cannot be dismissed as 'purely incidental'.[147] One might begin to wonder, as Harbage seldom does, how a scene might have been adapted in performance, how a tone of voice or gesture might have underlined the satirical topicality of a speech. And when one begins to read further and reflect, one becomes unhappier still about generalizations which fewer and fewer of the plays seem to fit. For Harbage imposed a thesis upon the plays and so left himself with the task of explaining away 'exceptions'.[148] This even results in unconvincing suggestions concerning the redating of plays in order that they conform to the patterns allegedly set by *The Shepherd's Paradise* in 1633.[149] Because Harbage began from a belief that the court was an autocratic monolith, his ears detected only monotone. Suckling's discontented Colonel could have no place in the work of a gentleman of the Privy Chamber to Charles I and so his voice, audible in the drama, is subconsciously silenced.[150] Starting from similar assumptions, other commentators have proved no less deaf. For Parry, the decadence of drama, as of masque and poetry after Jonson, reflected a fundamental change in politics at court. Whereas Jonson was a tireless intermediary between Bankside, Whitehall and the City, and his drama rang with echoes of those worlds, his successors were confined to the more rigid and exclusive domain of Whitehall and their plays 'lost touch with the broad spread of experience that animated ... Jacobean drama'. Cavalier drama, it was recently concluded, 'reflected back an idealized version of its audience's aspirations'.[151] Court *v.* country has cast a shadow across our study of the Caroline stage.

There is just now a glimmer of illumination. In a thesis and, at the time of writing, a book entitled *Theatre and Crisis*, Dr Martin Butler has issued a challenge to the critical consensus that followed Harbage.[152] Butler explodes

---

[146] We may note that Harbage sees the puritan Earl of Pembroke as a courtier holding identical views by that position with Charles I or his queen. *Cavalier Drama*, p. 141.

[147] As was recognized, for example, by Earl Miner, *The Cavalier Mode*, p. 53 and Davis, *The Sons of Ben, passim*.

[148] E.g. Harbage, *Cavalier Drama*, pp. 77, 107–8, 110, 164, 165.

[149] *Ibid.*, p. 128.

[150] *Ibid.*, pp. 112–13.

[151] Parry, *Golden Age Restor'd*, p. 203; *Revels History of English Drama IV*, p. 257.

[152] M. H Butler, 'The English drama and its political setting', University of Cambridge unpublished Ph.D. thesis, 1982. I am most grateful to Dr Butler for lending me a copy of this thesis. M. Butler, *Theatre and Crisis 1632–1642* (Cambridge, 1984). Dr Butler's book appeared after this chapter had been drafted. I have changed references to pages from the thesis to the book.

the myth of 'Cavalier drama'.[153] Following G. E. Bentley, he testifies to the
vitality of the Caroline playhouses. The emergence of London society assured
performances to full houses. In private as well as public playhouses, at the
Blackfriars as well as the Globe, the audience was far broader than the
exclusive circles of Whitehall. The dramatists of Caroline England were not
dependent upon the court and seldom wrote only or specifically for the court.
Even within courtier plays Butler has identified outspoken and critical voices
dismissed or denied by others. He has appreciated that within the conventions of courtly romance playwrights could pose serious ethical and political
questions: 'In particular plays about princes in love provided useful devices to
enable discussion of the problems of a king whose resources and popularity
were, in the late 1630s, coming to look increasingly limited.'[154] Butler's
literary re-evaluation stems significantly from a rejection of Harbage's
historical assumptions. From the perspective of the recent demonstration by
historians of divisions and differences within the court, Butler is able to see
the plays as 'an important focus and voice for anxieties and dissent existing in
tension' there.[155]

   This is an important step forward. But Butler's new framework also
presents problems and rests on some questionable assumptions. For he
wishes to argue for a 'fundamental distinction between the theatres, between
drama written principally for the court and drama intended for other wider,
audiences'.[156] The first, the more purely courtly tradition, commands little of
the author's respect: it is 'both the least interesting and least significant aspect
of the period'.[157] It is in the private and public playhouses that Butler
identifies the most vital expressions of Caroline drama. Here variety
flourished away from the restricted medium of the courtly mode. The
contrast between courtly and other drama rests squarely on a sense of distinct
political worlds. The public theatres' 'relatively free treatment of political
subjects corresponds with their detachment from the court'.[158] According to
Butler, Charles I acknowledged and feared the threat of that independence to
his autocratic ambitions. His proclamations ordering the gentry to leave
London 'may be seen as an attempt to disperse a potentially critical opposition'.[159] The attempt, however, failed. The playhouses of the 1630s did
something to substitute for the absence of parliaments: they brought the
politically active together and staged radical debates of political issues.
Theatrical circles overlapped with the membership of the Long Parliament.

---

[153] Butler, *Theatre and Crisis*, p. 3.
[154] *Ibid.*, p. 56.
[155] *Ibid.*, p. 82; Smuts, 'Puritan followers of Henrietta Maria'.
[156] Butler, *Theatre and Crisis*, p. 4.
[157] *Ibid.*, p. 4.
[158] *Ibid.*
[159] *Ibid.*, p. 118.

Meanwhile the popular dramatists of the thirties, Massinger and Shirley, Brome and Nabbes, carried the torch of freedom during the years of darkness. The opposition plays deserve the most attention, Butler concludes, because they were in touch with the 'most lively and challenging currents of opinion in the decade'.[160]

Obvious difficulties present themselves. First, Butler's use of terms such as 'country' or 'opposition' is, if the phrase may be pardoned in these circumstances, often cavalier.[161] How helpful are such constructs when some of Suckling's works are listed as country plays and when the Earl of Newcastle's work is associated with the popular playwrights, both men being as office holders definitely part of the court? Butler's own confusions with his explanatory labels are evident here as they are in his doubts about whether to 'count' William Davenant as a courtier playwright.[162] Secondly, in insisting upon the contrast between courtly and non-courtly plays, Butler drives an artificial wedge between the worlds of the Blackfriars and Whitehall. He rightly stresses the relative breadth of audience at the Blackfriars but largely ignores the communication and exchange between court and city stages and court and playhouse companies, an exchange which undermines any thesis of opposed dramatic styles.[163] Thirdly, by its concentration on the professional stage, *Theatre and Crisis* gives shorter shrift to plays written for the court and so fails to discern within them the expressions of attitudes often similar to those lauded in Nabbes and Brome – and incidentally fails to mention Brome's visible jealousy of Suckling and Killigrew.[164] Later we shall suggest that in the drama of Sir William Davenant Butler might have found much of the ambivalence and criticism that he sees in the 'opposition' plays. Finally, it is evident that Butler's account still rests upon unsupported historical assumptions. Though he is sensitive to the contending factions within the court and to the different religious and political attitudes they represented, Butler always assumes that the king's ambitions were towards an absolutism untrammelled by law. It was the parliamentary leaders, he maintains, who alone appealed to moderation and balance; the king's own claims to be ruling in accordance with law are ignored.[165] In fine, Butler's own politics colour his history and his criticism. When he concludes that the country plays expressed 'the most central and passionate current of feeling' or that Brome wrote 'the

---

[160] *Ibid.*, p. 281.
[161] Butler acknowledges here the influence on his work of the naive and crude study by M. C. Heinemann, *Puritanism and Theatre: Thomas Middleton and Opposition Drama under the Early Stuarts* (Cambridge, 1980). See K. Sharpe, 'Court and commonwealth', *Hist. Journ.*, 3 (25) (1982), pp. 735–49.
[162] Butler, 'The English drama', pp. 195, 253–8; Butler, *Theatre and Crisis*, p. 101.
[163] A. J. Cook, *The Privileged Playgoers of Shakespeare's London 1576–1642* (Princeton, 1981); Butler, *Theatre and Crisis*, appendix II.
[164] Bentley, *Jacobean and Caroline Stage*, VI, p. 38.
[165] *Theatre and Crisis*, pp. 34, 82, 100, 118, 134 and *passim*.

most committed play of the decade', Butler perhaps tells us more of what is central to his own political passions and commitments than to those of the 1630s.[166] For all the importance of his commentary, Butler's central tenet of division and distinctions in style and politics between the courtly and professional drama must remain, what he himself confesses, a contention – a suggestion requiring substantiation rather than a position already proven.[167] It deserves further exploration.

Thanks to the monumental researches of Professor Bentley we probably know as much about the early Stuart theatres and their repertoire as we are ever likely to know.[168] Bentley categorizes them as private playhouses – the Blackfriars and Phoenix or Cockpit in Drury Lane, the favourite resorts of the gentry; the public theatres – the second Fortune, the Globe and the Red Bull, known for a more popular audience and the last often disdained for slapstick and burlesque; and the court stages – the Cockpit-in-Court completely remodelled specifically for plays and opened in November 1630, the Banqueting House, the special masquing house built in 1637, and the Great Halls of royal palaces at Whitehall, Somerset House, Hampton Court and others. As broad categories these are helpful: the theatres evidently presented different images to contemporaries, the Blackfriars and Phoenix being held in higher esteem not least by the playwrights themselves. But it is important to keep in mind that the distinctions were not rigid. Works of nearly all the major dramatists were performed in public and private theatres and at times, as in the case of Shirley's *The Doubtful Heir*, a play intended for the Blackfriars had its preview at the Globe.[169] Nor, as Butler rightly emphasizes, were the audiences distinct or separated. Whilst the Globe evidently attracted a more common clientele than the private theatres, when in the summer season the King's Company moved there, many of their Blackfriars audience moved with them.[170] Though there were different styles associated with the London theatres, there was also interaction and movement between them – of playwrights, plays and spectators.

There was even greater interaction between the private theatres and the court. And this was very much an inter-communication in both directions: plays transferred from the Blackfriars to the court and court plays were acted in the private playhouses; the king and especially the queen visited the private theatres.[171] A list of the plays from the professional stage which we know to

---

[166] Butler, *Theatre and Crisis*, pp. 276, 281.
[167] *Ibid.*, ch. 1, 'Some contentions'.
[168] Bentley, *Jacobean and Caroline Stage*.
[169] James Shirley, 'A Prologue at the Globe to his Comedy call'd The doubtfull Heire, which should have been presented at the Black-Friers', *Poems by James Shirley* (London, 1646), pp. 154–5.
[170] Bentley, *Jacobean and Caroline Stage*, VII, pp. 15, 194, I, p. 4; Butler, *Theatre and Crisis*, p. 133.
[171] Below, pp. 35 n. 174.

have been performed at court is already long and if we knew more details about the hundreds of performances of works not named it would doubtless be much longer.[172] The works transferred to court include those of almost all the dramatists praised by Butler for their noble independence from the sycophancy of the cavalier mode. During the decade of personal rule we find performances at court or before the king and queen of plays by Brome, Fletcher, Heywood, Jonson, Randolph, Rowley, Shirley and Wilde, and an intended entertainment for the prince by Nabbes. The court appears to have staged a broad spectrum of plays from the professional theatre. It would seem too that most court plays subsequently enjoyed a life on the public stage. Plays by Carlell and Davenant, Mayne, Denham and Suckling originally presented at court transferred to the Blackfriars. Moreover this appears to have been expected of all court premiers: the actors of *The Royal Slave* at Hampton Court were given an extra £20 as compensation because Laud had requested that 'neither the play, nor clothes, nor stage might come into the hands and use of the common players abroad, which was graciously granted'.[173] Royal visits to the theatres were not infrequent. We have evidence that the king and queen attended performances at the Blackfriars and the Phoenix – Henrietta Maria is known to have attended the Blackfriars alone three times between 1634 and 1638 and there may have been other visits of which no record has survived.[174] On some occasions royal attendance indicates a special performance staged at the public theatre for the court – Davenant's *The Unfortunate Lovers* for example was acted at the Blackfriars on 23 April 1638 'for the Queene' – but there is no evidence to suggest that this was usual.[175] The queen, who attended the Christmas Revels of the Inns of Court, in peasant garb, and sat with her ladies on the benches, evidently joined the audience at Blackfriars for ordinary as well as special performances.[176]

The royal visitors did not shun the playwrights renowned for an independent streak, and dramatists were quite prepared to mock courtly vanities in performances before the king. On 13 May 1634, for example, the queen went to the Blackfriars to see a play by Massinger, probably not in ignorance of the occasional scandals surrounding his career, nor of the recent refusal of a licence to print his *Believe As You List*.[177] On the royal visit to Cambridge University in 1632 the king and queen were presented with a performance of Peter Hausted's *The Rival Friends*, which, in a parody of the

[172] See Bentley, *Jacobean and Caroline Stage*, VII, appendix C.
[173] G. Blakemore Evans, ed., *The Plays and Poems of William Cartwright* (Madison, Wis., 1951), pp. 182–3.
[174] Bentley, *Jacobean and Caroline Stage*, VI, pp. 740, 774; III, pp. 220–1; VI, pp. 34, 63.
[175] Adams, *Dramatic Records of Herbert*, p. 75.
[176] *Ibid.*, p. 56.
[177] *Ibid.*, pp. 19, 65.

Platonic love celebrated in a court masque only days earlier, ridiculed the
Platonic rivals as homosexual fools.[178] Such instances suggest that neither the
royal presence nor royal taste dictated the exclusive mode, narrow effeteness
or uncritical flattery generally associated with plays favoured by the court.
There is little in the drama of the 1630s indeed to suggest that authors felt
themselves constrained by (supposed) canons of royal taste or barred from
questioning, comic satire or criticism. In so far as the playwrights felt the need
to defend themselves against hostile reaction, they justified themselves and
directed their satirical venom not against the disapproval of the court, but the
strictures of certain puritans. A repeated claim that the drama was an ethical
and didactic medium by which men might be 'laughed into wit and virtue' can
only have been intended to convince those who dismissed plays as frivolous
and wanton.[179] The court did not need to be persuaded. Whilst playwrights
despaired at times of the ignorance and philistinism of their audiences – at
court as in the theatres – there is little to suggest that they regarded the king or
the court as obstacles to expression or as the determinants of their art.

There was really no need for them to do so. For the evidence we have
suggests that official censorship of the drama was neither common, nor
severe, nor, in the forms it often took, effective. This is not to say that
censorship did not affect what was performed nor to argue that no plays fell
foul of the censor. Sir Thomas Herbert, the Master of the Revels, had his own
clear ideas about what it was fit and not fit to license, and applied strict
standards of decency and propriety which might have allied him with many of
the puritan critics of the stage.[180] But it is not clear that courtiers or the king
himself always shared these standards. Herbert, for example, prohibited
Fletcher's *The Woman's Prize*, which was performed at court and well
liked.[181] Davenant's *The Wits*, initially refused a licence by Herbert, was
rescued by the king, at the instigation of a courtier, and published with
evidently only minor emendations.[182] Even when plays dealing with politically sensitive subjects were refused a licence, censorship was seldom perma-
nent or complete. Massinger's *Believe As You List*, for example, was refused
a licence in January 1631, on account of its critical references to the Spanish
occupation of Portugal, references which might have compromised delicate
Anglo-Spanish negotiations. The play was licensed and acted in May after
Massinger revised it to relocate the action in Carthage. England and Spain
were removed from the story, but Massinger 'did nothing', in Annabel

[178] Davis, *The Sons of Ben*, p. 176.
[179] I shall suggest that there was an ideological objection to puritanism in the didactic humanist
   drama of the period, as well as a defence of profession. Below, ch. 6. Thomas Randolph, *The
   Muses' Looking Glass*, Act I, Scene IV, cited in Davis, *Sons of Ben*, p. 76.
[180] Adams, *Dramatic Records of Herbert, passim*.
[181] *Ibid.*, p. 20.
[182] *Ibid.*, p. 22.

Patterson's words, 'to remove the . . . allusion to the situation of Frederick, King of Bohemia'. Moreover the empire of Carthage of the revised play was 'easily identified with that of early modern Spain'.[183] Massinger made his point. In 1638 the king personally requested the excision from Massinger's *The King and The Subject* of a speech in which the monarch claimed the right to unparliamentary taxation – a delicate subject in the year of the ship money trial.[184] In 1640, the manager of the Cockpit, William Beeston, was committed for a play which 'had relation to the passages of the king's journey into the North'.[185] These are clear instances of political censorship, but we should be careful of the conclusions we draw from them. For as remarkable as the censorship is the licence given to the plays after the offensive passage had been removed. As we shall argue, it was the directly obvious, the immediately topical criticism that was censored and this by no means obstructed the articulation of doubt or dissent. It is noteworthy, too, that even authors in trouble with the censor on several occasions continued to be staged throughout the decade, and sometimes at court. Jonson remained popular despite the king's annoyance at his bitter attacks on Inigo Jones; Massinger's plays were performed despite his frequent brushes with the censor.[186] We know of no voice that was silenced.

Indeed there were no real institutions or mechanisms of organized censorship. The Master of the Revels was responsible for approving performance and licensing publication. But influential courtiers could and did bypass his authority by special representations on behalf of friends or clients. *The Woman's Prize*, for example, was sent back to Herbert for his reconsideration 'at my Lord of Holland's request'.[187] Requests from powerful courtiers were hard to refuse and, as Endymion Porter's support for *The Wits* suggests, could even be influential with the king.[188] When courtiers could exercise such independent authority and sway, and when the court contained men of such different attitudes and lifestyles, there could be no absolute official censorship of the drama.

Many plays, moreover, required no licence at all: courtier plays and, at least until 1633, revivals.[189] In the first case only blindness would prevent us

[183] Annabel Patterson, *Censorship and Interpretation* (Madison, Wis., 1984), pp. 86–8, 248.
[184] The offending passsage reads:
> Monys? Wee'le rayse suppliés what way we please,
> And force you to subscribe to blanks, in which
> Wee'le mulct you as we shall think fit. The Caesars
> In Rome were wise, acknowledginge no lawes
> But what their swords did ratifye . . . (Adams, *Dramatic Records of Herbert*, p. 23)
[185] *Ibid.*, p. 66.
[186] Bentley, *Jacobean and Caroline Stage*, VII, appendix C.
[187] Adams, *Dramatic Records of Herbert*, p. 20.
[188] *Ibid.*, p. 22.
[189] Harbage, *Cavalier Drama*, p. 99.

from seeing that courtiers such as Suckling, Killigrew and Davenant used this freedom in order to air specific political positions and criticisms. In the second case, of course, the potential freedom was unlimited. Under the guise of a revival of a play, there was wide scope for adaptation and interpretation, especially in performance. We have one conspicuous case of a play presented at the Fortune in 1639 in which an altar and candlesticks were set up on the stage and the gesture of genuflection prescribed by Laud was mocked in clownish manner. There was evidently no doubt that 'although they allege it was an old play revived and an altar to the heathen gods, it was apparent that this play was revived on purpose in contempt of the ceremonies of the church'.[190] Such cases on many other occasions might well have escaped the censor's notice. The liberties that were taken in performing old plays can be imagined by any of us familiar with modern practice.

Even when offensive passages or interpretations were brought to his attention, Herbert did not automatically act to ban a play. Often he seems to have been content with no more than assurances from the playhouse managers that what was amiss would be amended. Shirley's *The Ball* was permitted on no better security than the manager Beeston's word that the players would cease to impersonate courtiers in future performances.[191] Whether or not they always kept their promise cannot have been easy for Herbert to have known. In other words, there were limits to the censor's effective power, even when he wished to exercise it. And overall the evidence would suggest that it was not much exercised. Over five hundred editions of plays and masques were published during the reign of Charles I – over half of them during the decade of personal rule.[192] Theatrical performances ran into thousands, and (with the Globe's capacity of 3,000 and the Blackfriars 500–600) played before hundreds of thousands.[193] Against this background of dramatic proliferation and diversity and given the paucity of examples of censorship, it would be foolish to believe in any orchestrated or official campaign to impose either artistic uniformity or political orthodoxy. When, from the experience of our own, more monitored age, we read through many Caroline plays, it is the open-mindedness of the court that appears striking. As Anne Barton comments of Massinger's *The Emperor of The East*, 'The only really surprising thing . . . is that Massinger, who was often in trouble

---

[190] Edmund Rossingham to Edward Viscount Conway, 8 May 1639, *Cal. Stat. Pap. Dom.*, 1639, pp. 140–1. The episode suggests that Herbert's attempts in 1633 to secure greater control over revivals had failed. See Adams, *Dramatic Records of Herbert*, p. 21.

[191] Adams, *Dramatic Records of Herbert*, p. 19.

[192] Bentley, *Jacobean and Caroline Stage*, VI, p. 225; Butler, *Theatre and Crisis*, p. 104, points out that 263 plays were published between 1631 and 1642 compared with 162 between 1606 and 1615.

[193] Bentley, *Jacobean and Caroline Stage*, VI, pp. 11, 184.

with the censor, should have managed to write such a play during the period of Charles's personal rule and get away with it.'[194]

The expression of surprise, of course, reflects assumptions about Charles I's autocratic inclinations and about his attitude to court culture. We must leave the first question for the moment and return to it later.[195] What has now become clear is that there is little substance to the spectre of censorship that stalks Butler's (and others') pages, and in general studies of the relationships between culture and politics during the reign of Charles I. Moreover there seems to be no evidence of any political preferences or criteria in Charles I's list of favourite plays, a list that ranged over Fletcher and Shakespeare, Davenant and Massinger.[196] Indeed Habington's *Cleadora, Queen of Aragon*, a play convincingly interpreted by Butler as counselling moderation on the eve of the Short Parliament, was 'commended . . . as very well acted by the king and queen'.[197]

Charles's love of the theatre requires no documentation: of all the buildings projected for a grandiose new palace of Whitehall, only the Cockpit-in-Court was completed.[198] But contrary to traditional generalizations about 'cavalier drama', the evidence suggests that the king's taste ranged widely and did not occlude political debate and discussion. A list of performances at court dispels any myth of a uniform courtly mode characterized by effete style, trivial subjects and fawning flattery. From such an interpretation it might be thought that we will have to exclude those plays that obviously pandered to courtly taste: *The Royal Slave*, for example, performed before the king at his visit to Oxford; *The Gamester*, the plot of which was dictated by Charles I himself; or *The Shepherd's Paradise*, that tedious pastoral indulging the queen's obsession with Platonic love. But in fact they bear out our case. These plays not only support our conclusion that Caroline drama was characterized by variety rather than uniformity; they reveal an engagement with political questions and a tone of political criticism. And they introduce us to what will be our central argument: that love was the metaphor, the medium, through which political comment and criticism were articulated in Caroline England.

THE NATURE OF CAVALIER DRAMA: THREE CASE STUDIES

The Shepherd's Paradise, the pastoral which, Harbage maintained, set the pattern for courtly drama of the 1630s is more often cited than read. There

[194] Barton, 'Harking back to Elizabeth', p. 18.
[195] Below, ch. 6, pp. 290ff. On censorship, contrast Hill, 'Censorship and English literature', *Collected Essays I*, pp. 32–71, with the more sophisticated analysis of Annabel Patterson, *Censorship and Interpretation*.
[196] Adams, *Dramatic Records of Herbert*, pp. 53–4. There is a folio of Shakespeare annotated by Charles I in the royal library at Windsor.
[197] Adams, *Dramatic Records of Herbert*, p. 58; cf. Bentley, *Jacobean and Caroline Stage*, IV, p. 523; Butler, *Theatre and Crisis*, pp. 62–76. [198] Parry, *Golden Age Restor'd*, p. 203.

has been no edition since 1659 and little critical analysis.[199] To Harbage the play presented few problems other than the tedium of reading it: it was a stylized, foppish and pretentious statement of an equally modish and trivial subject – Platonic love. It was penned by a lightweight, Walter Montagu, an intimate of the queen who converted to Catholicism.[200] More recent comments have not been kinder: to Philip Edwards it is 'a tedious pastoral'. Stephen Orgel is more graphic: 'Beside Montagu's pastoral, *Parsifal* is a romp.'[201]

The play is extremely long – it lasted seven or eight hours – and the plot is immensely complicated: Suckling for one claimed not to understand it.[202] Superficially the play revolves around the favourite themes of cross loves and passions, the reappearance of characters believed dead, the resolution of conflicts and marriages. But the meaning, as Suckling's failure of comprehension acknowledges, is not so easily discerned or superficial. An understanding and appreciation of the play must await a full critical edition, which will have to attempt, as a beginning to comprehension, an elucidation of the ideas, the essences, represented by the names. For in the names may lie the more serious intentions of the play. Saphira, for example (also Bellesa, the Queen of the Shepherdesses), suggests Sappho, who in Mytilene led a circle of young maidens who worshipped Aphrodite, but evokes too the sapphire, a name then applied to all precious transparent varieties of crystal, with the concomitant associations of beauty, purity, light and honesty. The name Genorio assumed by Agenor (counsellor to Prince Basilino) indicates one who begets or brings forth, an appropriate adopted name for Agenor, one who acts. Prince Basilino takes the name Moramente, perhaps that of one who obstructs or delays. Fidamira, whom he courts, represents in the play the extraordinary faith enshrined in her name; she is too the lost princess Miranda, a revelation like her original name (and her faith), indeed to be wondered at. Martiro, who advocates a love elevated beyond the senses, bears witness to his faith and so realizes his name. Pantamora, who endeavours to persuade him to more natural, physical passions, doubtless owed something to Pan, who wooed his mistress with the present of a ram, a symbol of sexuality and fertility. Camena, one of the shepherdesses, is clearly, as the Roman Goddess of that name, Poetry herself. Significantly only the king has no name. The relationship of names and adopted names to ideas and

[199] W. Montagu, *The Shepheard's Paradise: A Comedy Privately Acted Before the Late King Charles by the Queen's Majesty and Ladies of Honor* (London, 1659).
[200] Harbage, *Cavalier Drama*, pp. 2, 22–3, 94–5.
[201] Edwards, *Revels History of English Drama IV*, p. 13; Orgel and Strong, *Inigo Jones*, I, p. 63.
[202] Beaulieu to Puckering, 10 Jan. 1632/3, in T. Birch, ed., *The Court and Times of Charles I* (2 vols., London, 1848), II, p. 216; '(The Wits) (A Sessions of the Poets)', lines 81–8, *Non-Dramatic Works of Sir John Suckling*, pp. 74–5.

to actions requires more careful exposition than is possible here.[203] For it becomes apparent that *The Shepherd's Paradise* is an allegory concerning the nature of beauty, sense, virtue and love, both physical and spiritual, and a discourse on the relationship of each to government – of the self, of the world of nature and of the polity. It is both Neo-Platonic and Aristotelian in its treatment of forms, names and ethical and political questions. Whatever its success as entertainment, it was evidently not intended to be trivial.

Nor is *The Shepherd's Paradise* an unambiguous apologia for Platonic love. For it is less a statement than a debate, a debate between corporeal and spiritual love which is not resolved simply by the triumph of the latter over the former. The heroine, Fidamira, played by the Queen, despite her extraordinary faith, her conquest of sense and her eventual devotion to chastity, expects for much of the play to *consummate* her love for Agenor. Martiro, whose love is not 'that material flame' but 'lightning in my soul', stands in the play for spiritual love,[204] but his beliefs are powerfully contested. Melidoro and Moramente argue against him that *all* love begins with the senses. And though Martiro converts Genorio to his creed, as Melidoro informs us, 'there is no danger of Genorio making a sect'.[205] Martiro even begins to question his own position as a consequence of the debates. He sees that the essence of love lies in the senses as well as the spirit, in the union of sense and spirit in marriage (recommended by Melidoro to Camena the goddess of poetry) and in propagation and procreation. Martiro ends up denouncing the falseness of what had been a purely spiritual love for Bellesa (beauty): 'I have been guilty all this while of treason to her, of parting her body and her soul which heaven united for no less a miracle than the propagation of them on earth.'[206]

Moreover, the play concludes in marriages, that is in the reconciliation of sense and soul, and in the actual marriages of characters revealed in their true identities. Bellesa, whom Agenor has courted in the shepherdesses' paradise, emerges as that same Sapphira whom it had been arranged for him to marry: beauty and action are conjoined and will be fertile as Agenor's assumed name, Genorio. Fidamira, his first love, emerges as his sister. These are not Platonic conceits but real human relations, relations in some cases of blood, the ultimate corporeal connection. As the couples go off to wed, Melidoro points out to Martiro how 'your impossibility that is fallen to earth hath ingendered here this day, and is delivered of so many miracles'.[207] The ideal has become real and, as the metaphoric language of fecundity indicates, will propagate the virtues of their union. Fidamira alone, now vowed to chastity, remains as Queen of the Shepherdesses. But in his valedictory speech to her,

[203] See Barton, 'Names: the chapter interloping', ch. 8 in *Ben Jonson, Dramatist*.
[204] Montagu, *Shepherd's Paradise*, p. 94.
[205] *Ibid.*, p. 148.   [206] *Ibid.*, p. 146.   [207] *Ibid.*, p. 166.

Martiro, formerly the spokesman for the abnegation of the sense, wishes she too be fulfilled through sense as well as spirit:

> May you have all the joyes of innocence,
> Injoying too all the delights of sense.[208]

The Shepherd's Paradise concludes with the moral that the pattern for love, as for life, is neither surrender to passion, nor subscription to the abstract sterility of spiritual love as described by Howell, but marriage, that union of sense and spirit which fulfils man's nature and orders nature.

The subject and language of the play have clear political implications. Love stands as an analogy for, indeed represents, the nature of government. True government, like true love, is virtuous. But wherein do virtue and virtuous government lie? It is not always to be found in palaces and courts. Innocence resides, as Fidamira, its personification, well knows, 'but in Courts sometimes' – 'and passeth on'. For innocence 'wants that pliable complacency that is required in the Society of Courts'.[209] The citadel of virtue, the shepherds' paradise, may, however, provide the model for good government, a version of that arcadian idyll which, we have argued, dominates thinking about rather than retreat from politics. In the shepherds' paradise things are what they seem and what they are called. The Queen *is* Bellesa: she owes her title to her beauty, which expresses her virtue. But she is a princess by birth too and the crystal of her name Sapphira reflects the purity of her nature. The newly elected Queen of the Shepherdesses is also a princess by birth and the emblem of faith which her name Fidamira implies. Here then there is no dissimulation, as in courts, no divorce of truth from representation, nor of virtue from government. Such characters need no schooling in the arts of politics: being virtuous by nature they know the nature of virtuous government. Taking her oath as elected Queen, Bellesa promises

> To keep the honour and the regal due,
> Without exacting anything that's new
> And to assume no more to me than must
> Give me the means and power to be just
> And but for charity and mercies cause
> Reserve no power to suspend the laws.[210]

The virtuous person, who knows how to govern himself, knows too that the business of government is to bring men to self-government; it is the exercise of example and persuasion, not of power. Fidamira tells the king that 'Liberty is the greatest blessing kings are entrusted with'.[211] And the king knows it too.

---

[208] *Ibid.*, p. 175.
[209] *Ibid.*, p. 38.
[210] *Ibid.*, p. 22. The phrase 'Without exacting anything that's new' may be significant given the recent levy of knighthood fines.
[211] *Ibid.*, p. 18.

Dominated by his uncontrollable passion for Fidamira, he resigns his throne because 'sensual appetite would not suit with the divine image' of kingship.[212] Unable to govern his nature, the king knows that he is unfit to rule; in the shepherds' paradise he recovers his self-control and his kingship, and so he presides over the election of the new Queen as a true monarch, the arbiter of virtue.

Virtuous government, however, like love, does not deny the world of sense, of the self or the will. It too lies in the union of sense and spirit in the commonweal as in man. Marriage, Melidoro informs Camena in a significantly legalistic phrase, is not the surrender of 'the propriety' (the property) of the self; the nuptial bonds 'rather do enlarge the owning of your self'.[213] So the union of sense and soul, of will and reason enlarges man, fulfils his nature as a being who may order his passions. And, as Bellesa knows, the true nature of monarchy lies in the marriage of will and law in the polity and in the person of the king. To separate these is to abuse the nature of man and of monarchy. Let us recall Martiro's confession about his false love delivered in the language of politics and law: 'I have been guilty all this while of *treason* to her, of parting her body and her soul.' And so it was treason to divide the king's will from the law, indeed the king from the people to whom he, as monarchs were fond of saying, was wedded. In a few years the trial of the Earl of Strafford for treason was to focus on this offence.[214] Monarchy is here presented as the union of soul and sense, of the will and the law, of the king and his people. The commonweal is that marriage in which each gives in order to enlarge himself. It is a pattern for government given in the country.

The Shepherd's Paradise is a treatise on love and the politics of love. Once we read it as a complex debate about ethical and political questions, we can no longer dismiss it as slight or foppish and we may come to find it more interesting. We cannot know how the king and queen perceived the play, or whether their comprehension exceeded Suckling's. We do know that Walter Montagu was close to Henrietta Maria and might have been expected to know her taste. Many at court evidently found his play tiresome, though one of the foremost poets of the decade, Thomas Carew, greatly admired Montagu.[215] Montagu was a serious figure who risked his political future for his faith in converting to Catholicism; he penned devout essays during an

[212] *Ibid.*, p. 39.
[213] *Ibid.*, pp. 50–2.
[214] See article VII of Strafford's impeachment; F. Hargrave, *A Complete Collection of State Trials* (11 vols., London, 1776–81), I, p. 723.
[215] Bentley, *Jacobean and Caroline Stage*, IV, pp. 920–1; R. Dunlap, ed., *The Poems of Thomas Carew* (Oxford, 1949), pp. 76, 252. For the playwright William Davenant's praise of Montagu, see 'To Mr. W. M. Against Absence', in *Sir William Davenant. The Shorter Poems*, ed., A. M. Gibbs (Oxford, 1972), pp. 133–4.

active political career. It would be tempting to speculate on the relationship of his personal and political experience to his drama. But we must leave *The Shepherd's Paradise* in the knowledge that the pastoral which allegedly established the Caroline mode did not retreat from social and political engagement, but staged a serious examination of contemporary issues and questions.

Indeed serious treatment of its subject characterizes Montagu's pastoral throughout: positions are articulated through rational argument, and speeches border on rhetoric and oratory. Characters are subordinated to discourse; the play lacks significant variety of tone, or any humorous or satirical voice. It may be such reflections that deter readers and that led Harbage to argue that the drama of the whole decade was 'prevailingly serious', decorous, and eliminated comic underplot.[216] But it would be wrong to conclude that royal taste precluded the satiric or comic mode. *The Shepherd's Paradise* was performed by the queen and, like the queen's masques, suggests Henrietta Maria's preference for the more serious mode. Our second example of the type of play favoured at court, James Shirley's *The Gamester*, was, in the words of the Master of the Revels, 'made by Shirley out of a plot of the king's given him by me . . . The king said it was the best play that he had seen for seven years.'[217] *The Gamester* was presented at court on 6 February 1634 and acted at the private house in Drury Lane in 1637, when it was also published.[218] Like *The Shepherd's Paradise* it had serious things to say. But compared with Montagu's pastoral it illustrates a very different tone and style of court drama, and may suggest differences of taste between Charles I and his wife.

The Gamester is quite out of character with Harbage's portrait of a dramatic mode that was refined and decorous. Lust and infidelity are its subjects. Mr Wilding, married to a widow who has brought him a fortune, finds his fancy turn to a young maid, Penelope, who is the distant kinswoman of his wife. Mistress Wilding invites him freely to pursue his sexual pleasures and even offers her assistance with the seduction of the girl. Penelope, however, refuses any liaison that compromises her honour. So assured, Mistress Wilding proposes a plot to her in order to deceive her husband into thinking that his lustful desires are to be satisfied. The two women arrange a midnight rendezvous, at which Mrs Wilding contrives to be in Penelope's stead. Wilding, however, is distracted from the (what he believes to be) illicit appointment by a gambling session at a tavern, his greed having got the mastery over his libido. He sends in his place one Hazard as his proxy to an

[216] Harbage, *Cavalier Drama*, pp. 40, 68, 73.
[217] Adams, *Dramatic Records of Herbert*, p. 54.
[218] *Ibid.*, pp. 54–5; J. Shirley, *The Gamester. As It was Presented by her Majestie's Servants At the private House in Drury-lane* (London, 1637).

adulterous union. Hazard encounters not the maiden he had been promised, but Mrs Wilding, with whom he too joins in the ruse to teach her husband a lesson. The lesson is painfully learned. Hearing Hazard boast of the joys of a (fictitious) night of sexual passion with Mrs Wilding, Wilding comes to appreciate his wife and lament his horns of shame. In the end the truth comes out. Reconciled with her, Wilding promises reform: 'Thy virtue shall instruct me.'[219] All ends happily: illicit passion is exposed and ridiculed, constancy is lauded, virtue has its reward. The ethical framework is conventional enough. But within that framework *The Gamester* presents what are thought to be illicit liaisons described in bawdy language and a comic subplot which offers the opportunity for social satire as well as clowning.

The satire is sharp. Shirley's play and tavern are populated with those who dissipate their lives and livelihoods and men whose names signify their condition: Acre-less, Little Stock and Sell-Away. Even the nobility join in the frivolous squander of their patrimony: 'They are well coupled a lord and a sell-away.'[220] In this topsy turvy world of social dislocation the wrong men rise and fall as social status no longer reflects the claims of nature or merit. Barnacle (a social leech if ever there was one) admits he is one of those citizens 'Ambitious to make all our children gentlemen's apprentices'.[221] Society here is organized around such rapid gains and losses: Hurry seeks a quick and profitable marriage for his daughter; Hazard chances all on the game. Morality is dissolved as all centres on money.

> Two thousand pound will make a maiden-head
> That's crooked straight agen.[222]

The court sets the bad example. Pages, we are told, service their ladies elsewhere than at table. Modesty is out of fashion.

Platonic love is spoken of and influences some in the play, but it is seldom practised:

> how ever some men do want heat
> Their is no generall winter.[223]

Platonic love is in any case shown to be a front for promiscuity. Wilding believes Plato's doctrines on love will permit him to marry Penelope to another and retain her as his mistress.[224] The world of the country is no purer. The pretentious country gentleman who dispenses justice only when in his cups is in town to borrow, or to raise money from a project to sell his jests.

[219] Shirley, *The Gamester*, Act V.
[220] *Ibid.*, Act III; sig. [E 4ᵛ].
[221] *Ibid.*, Act I; sig.B 3–3ᵛ.
[222] *Ibid.*, Act V; sig.[H 3ᵛ].
[223] *Ibid.*, Act III; sig.E 2.
[224] *Ibid.*, Act III; sig.D 4ᵛ.

Like his judgements and philosophizing, they have little worth or substance.[225] Parish constables are portrayed as company fit for whores and as
lacking in virtue.[226] And the language which they all speak befits their world
of bawdy bravado in which all moral standards have been breached. The tone
could hardly be described as 'decorous'.[227] Wilding in anticipation of the
pleasures of his sexual rendezvous boasts:

> I swell with my imaginations
> Like a tall ship, bound for the fortunate Islands;
> Top, and Top-gallant my flags.

Hazard pricks the bubble of his fantasy:

> Pray heaven rather
> You do not spring a leake, and forfit your
> Ballast . . .[228]

Wilding, like the rest, has forfeited his virtue to lust, greed and chance. Only
Mistress Wilding and Penelope emerge well, as champions of constancy and
fidelity. But their virtues are not quiescent. It is a combination of the maid's
honour and the wife's ingenuity that brings Wilding to his senses – or more
appropriately perhaps lifts him above them. His recognition of the value of
his marriage and his wife's qualities may restore him to dignity and virtue, as
Penelope's marriage at the end to Hazard qualifies chance and daring by
constancy. In these marriages and the harmonies which they signify may lie
Shirley's whole point: virtue lies in the reconciliation of extremes or
opposites. For Platonic lovers who renounce all physical pleasure, even when
in earnest, are mocked along with puritans by Penelope, for all her commitment to chastity and honour.[229] Fulfilment of the self is found neither in lust
nor abstinence but in a marriage which orders and legitimizes passion.

Shirley's play also seems to have intended a political comment. In the
tavern talk the revellers discuss two kingdoms. One is *terra incognita* in
which dwell a

> cursed kinde of people that have
> Neither law, nor Religion but for their own purposes.[230]

The second is Perwiggana, a country where the moon shines all day and the
sun at night, and where the name implies a dedication to fashion and
foppery.[231] The first, though *incognita*, is clearly the Dutch Republic, for

---

225 *Ibid.*, Act III; sig.F 1ᵛ.
226 *Ibid.*, Act V; sig.H 4ᵛ.
227 Harbage's term in *Cavalier Drama*, p. 28.
228 *The Gamester*, Act III; sig.E 4ᵛ.
229 *Ibid.*, Act III; sig.E 1ᵛ.
230 *Ibid.*, Act III; sig.F 2.
231 *Ibid.*, Act III; sig.F 2.

Barnacle's nephew reports that the country 'is somewhat low and open to the sea'.[232] Republicanism, religious licence and the exploitation of everything for commerce are its characteristics. Perwiggana, Sell-Away knows, is an analogy for England where the gentry, living *à la mode*, debauch the night in drink and go to bed at dawn. And in England, 'In this province the king never comes out of his palace.'[233] Here the world was upside down. For nature dictates that the sun not the moon should shine all day. Only the sun could bring light to this world of darkness. In the commonweal the monarch, as metaphor often depicted him, was the sun. But the king, the sun of the commonweal, also remained in seclusion when his light was needed to restore the natural order. It was the fate of *terra incognita*, a country that was (because a republic?) no country at all, to live without religion or laws. But religion and laws were the growths of monarchies, as indeed kings lived by them. In order for them to flourish and for virtue to seed and flower, monarchy needed to be active, not withdrawn; the king must stand as the light of example. Wilding and Hazard discovered their higher selves in marriage. And monarchy too might realize its true form by union with the body politic, which might lift the commonweal from immorality to virtue.

If my reading is persuasive, we must see Shirley's comic farce as an acute ethical and political comment. Indeed it not only argues a position, it presents a plea, even ventures a criticism of a style of kingship that has become cut off from the realm. That Charles helped devise the play and that it was 'well likt' by the king may cause us to reflect on Charles I's response to criticism, or indeed upon his own attitudes to kingship. We shall return to take up these questions only after we have examined many other cases and felt more and more the need so to stop and reconsider. For the present, we must note that whatever the purpose of Shirley's play, it was certainly comic, satirical and irreverent. In treatment, subject and style, *The Gamester* not only contrasts with the lofty prose and noble sentiments of *The Shepherd's Paradise*; it bears no resemblance to Harbage's identikit of the face of cavalier drama. A royal taste which embraced two such plays left the Caroline dramatists considerable room for manoeuvre.

It was a space of which they took full advantage even when plays were commissioned for royal entertainments, as the last of our case studies makes clear. William Cartwright's *The Royal Slave* was written and performed for the visit of King Charles I to Oxford University in the summer of 1636. Charles presented to the university as its official code the new body of statutes

---

[232] *Ibid.*, Act III; sig.F 2.
[233] *Ibid.*, Act III, sig.F 2^v.

drawn up under the direction of William Laud.[234] The king visited, that is to say, as ruler in an immediate and particular as well as a general sense, as the governor of the university as well as of the realm. The king's own appreciation of the value of learning for the commonweal was lucidly articulated by the Secretary of State, Sir John Coke.[235] And the central importance of education for the business of government was the subject also of the university's entertainment for the king. To argue that *The Royal Slave* was not only a serious work but a didactic political statement is to ascribe to the play an importance denied by its editor. For to Blakemore Evans it is true to the type of cavalier drama: 'an exotic, usually serious plot dealing with exalted and unreal characters, moving in an atmosphere falsely moral and saturated with the doctrines of a sentimentalized and sophisticated Neo-Platonism, the whole tricked out in a multi-coloured rhetorical coat'.[236] To dismiss *The Royal Slave* so is to give it only the most superficial reading.

The central subject of the play is the nature of monarchy and government. Whilst Neo-Platonic philosophy and Platonic love pervade the plot, the play by no means echoes the court's fashionable cult, nor its political values. Cratander, along with other Ephesian soldiers, is captured by the victorious King of Persia. In accordance with Persian custom, one of the captives is to be selected and elevated as a king for three days, then led, at the end of his brief rule, to execution. The gaoler chooses Cratander, who seems inappropriate for the title as a man 'wondrous heavy and bookish'.[237] Indeed Cratander fulfils no expectations. The vanquished Ephesians, anticipating at least the pleasures of three days in which their countryman may command all delights, are soon disappointed. Cratander emerges as a man of true virtue who sets out immediately to rule for the good. Though a slave in his own country as well as a captive in Persia, Cratander is perceived by all as a natural ruler, as one that

> beares
> A Kingdome in his looke; a kingdom that
> Consists of Beauty, seasoned with Discretion[238]

Far from giving vent to licence, Cratander uses his authority to bridle the licentiousness of his compatriots. He rescues the court ladies from the rape

[234] William Cartwright, *The Royal Slave . . . Presented to the King and Queene by the Students of Christ Church in Oxford August 30, 1636. Presented since to both their Majesties at Hampton Court by the Kings Servants* (London, 1639). A modern edition is in Blakemore Evans, *Plays and Poems of Cartwright*. For a discussion of the play and the king's visit to Oxford, see K. Sharpe, 'Archbishop Laud and the University of Oxford', in H. Lloyd Jones, V. Pearl and B. Worden, eds., *History and Imagination* (London, 1981), pp. 146–64.
[235] W. Scott and J. Bliss, eds., *The Works of the Most Reverend Father in God William Laud* (7 vols., Oxford, 1847–60), V, pt. I, pp. 126–32.
[236] Blakemore Evans, *Plays and Poems of Cartwright*, p. 172.
[237] *Royal Slave*, Act I, Scene II, *ibid.*, p. 203.
[238] *Ibid.*, Act I, Scene IV, p. 208.

threatened by his fellow captives; he crushes a plot to betray Persia to the Ephesians and so wins the love of the queen and the respect of the king. His natural claim to royalty is recognized and he is saved from death to be created monarch of his own country.

Cratander stands as an ideal of kingship. His claim to monarchy stems from his control of his own passions, his self-governance. He resists the temptations of the senses and virtue is externally manifested in his beauty. His virtue moreover is seen to be effective, that is capable of changing and reforming, or as one courtier puts it in words reminiscent of masque, 'why then hee'le turne the Scene'.[239] And turn the scene is what Cratander does, changing anticipated anarchy into order and death into life. Cratander, the exemplar of Plato's philosopher-king, exposes the corruptions of Plato's teaching which have become a disguise for licentious practices. Those plotting rape, for example, defend their designs as

> A little Love-sport only; we were arguing
> *Pro* and *Con* out of *Plato*, and are now
> Going to practise his Philosophy.[240]

As a philosopher himself who has written 'a discourse o' th' Nature of the Soule' Cratander decries the abuse of Plato's name:[241]

> the giddy People
> Are ready to transpose all crimes upon
> Him that should moderate them.[242]

Cratander's philosophy, unlike the Ephesians' falsehoods, teaches self-discipline and self-governance. And it is these qualities that he seeks to teach by example. His fellow captives are dismayed and uncomprehending: 'We live not under / A King but a pedagogue.'[243] They fail, that is, to perceive that Cratander's natural claim to rule lies in his capacity to teach virtue. Indeed Cratander has much to teach the real king, Arsamnes, crowned King of Persia.[244] During his three days of rule, the royal slave demonstrates by personal example his dictate that a throne 'May stand without those tumults of delight / That wayte on big and pompous luxury'.[245] More important, he instructs that power is exercised for the good and through example rather than by means of constraint; that the business of monarchy is to bring men to self-government through example and instruction. Queen Atossa is won by

[239] *Ibid.*, p. 208.
[240] *Ibid.*, Act II, Scene V, p. 217. Cf. G. F. Sensabaugh, 'Love ethics in Platonic court drama 1625–42'. *Hunt. Lib. Quart.*, 1 (1937–8), pp. 277–304.
[241] *Ibid.*, Act I, Scene II, p. 203.
[242] *Ibid.*, Act II, Scene V, p. 217.
[243] *Ibid.*, Act V, Scene II, p. 224.
[244] In Act I, Scene II (p. 203), Arsamnes had himself observed that Cratander had 'a serious and Majestique looke, / As if hee'd read Philosophy to a King'.
[245] *Ibid.*, Act II, Scene I, p. 211.

Cratander's virtue and comes to understand his teaching. 'Honest Pow'r', she appreciates, is 'To command only what the free are wont / To undergoe with gladnesse'.[246] Arsamnes, at first jealous of Cratander, through the mediation of Atossa, also comes to perceive his qualities and emulate his example. In the end, he appoints Cratander King of the Ephesians: 'thy Vertues there / May shine as in their proper Sphere . . .'[247] He whose learning and self-governance have equipped him to rule is appointed as the best ruler over others. The philosopher, the 'pedagogue' who has taught the court, the queen and the king, becomes what he is fitted by nature to be, the ideal of monarchy itself.

There was much here for the courtly audience to take in along with the spectacular Persian costumes and the scenic innovations of Inigo Jones. The play does not only point to particular courtly abuses and extravagances, but offers a searching examination of the nature and qualities of kingship. Within the context of the king's visit to present the statutes, we might also see the play as the university's statement concerning the claims of learning to rule: as, one might say, the other side of the relationship between the university and the crown to that expressed by the statutes, namely the king's authority to rule learning. Scholars have debated whether the figure of Cratander or Arsamnes was meant for Charles I himself.[248] But it is more important, perhaps, to observe that the two depend upon each other: without Cratander, Arsamnes would not have learned the virtues of true monarchy, but without Arsamnes (and Atossa) Cratander would never have become king. And this, I suggest, is Cartwright's point about the relationship between learning and government. The university might teach the rulers of the commonweal the virtues of self-regulation which equipped them for government, but it was the king who gave authority to the university and places of power to its students. Even Cartwright's play, presented to the king, owed its very existence to the king – to the royal visit for which it was written. Charles I was, as the prologue to the Oxford production reminded him, both guest and entertainer.[249] As guest he might learn from the university as Arsamnes had from Cratander: the value of learning, the nature of government and the rôle of the king as example and teacher. And as entertainer, the king could give life to the university and its entertainment and so make virtue and self-discipline the pattern for rule. The epilogue instructed the royal visitor on his part in this process as much as it sought his approbation for the play:

[246] *Ibid.*, Act V, Scene III, p. 244.
[247] *Ibid.*, Act V, Scene VII, p. 250.
[248] Barton, 'He that plays the King' in M. Axton and R. Williams, eds., *English Drama: Forms and Development* (Cambridge, 1977), pp. 69–93, 190–2; M. Butler, 'Royal slaves. The Stuart court and the theatre', *Renaissance Drama Newsletter*, Supplement 2 (1984), pp. 1–23; Butler, *Theatre and Crisis*, pp. 44–9.
[249] 'The Prologue to the King and Queene', p. 195.

> The Slave though freed by th' King, and his Priest too,
> Thinkes not his pardon good, till seal'd by you.[250]

Virtue in order to be effective required the stamp of royal action and authority, just as the play, in order to be successful, required royal approval. Like Cratander, the university and its play could only offer an example or ideal

> for 'tis our forward duty that hath showne
> These loyall Faults in honour to your Throne.[251]

In the ambiguity of the last line we may detect a defensiveness, a hint that Cartwright feared that he may have spoken with too much forthrightness. The apologetic tone seems louder in the revised epilogue written when the play was presented again at Hampton Court. For a royal palace was the centre of monarchy where Oxford was the seat of learning. Cartwright expressed his apprehension of 'favour altring with the time and place'.[252] Charles, who had bestowed his favour on the play (as Arsamnes on Cratander) at Oxford, might now revoke it. Alternatively he might express, as the epilogue exhorts him, the virtue of constancy and so endorse in the centre of government what he had approved at the centre of learning:

> Tis then your Countenance that is the price
> Must redeeme this, and free the Captive twice.[253]

At Hampton Court as at Oxford, Charles alone could validate Cratander, *The Royal Slave*, the philosophy which the play advanced, and the university which produced it.

The play met with royal approval; it was also commended by 'all the nobles' and by the Lord Chamberlain in particular.[254] William Cartwright secured the post of overseer of the university press and was close to the king when the royal court moved to Oxford in 1642.[255] If he had had misgivings about how his play or its implications might be received, they had evidently not been necessary.

CONTINUOUS AND COMMON CONCERNS

Our examination of three texts has led us into different worlds – that of Walter Montagu and the queen's household, that of James Shirley and the public stage, that of William Cartwright and the university. The case studies have also illustrated very different modes: the philosophical, the comic and

[250] 'The Epilogue to the King and Queene', p. 251.
[251] *Ibid.*, lines 7–8. The 'loyall faults', of course, could be those of the players, of the characters that they personated, or of the king's own government.
[252] 'The Epilogue to their Majesties at Hampton-Court', line 16, p. 253.
[253] *Ibid.*, lines 19–20.   [254] Blakemore Evans, *Plays and Poems of Cartwright*, p. 171.
[255] Sharpe, 'Archbishop Laud and the University of Oxford', p. 152.

the allegorical. In subject matter too the plays are different: *The Shepherd's Paradise* a treatise on love, *The Gamester* a drama of infidelity, *The Royal Slave* a study in kingship. The differences dispel any notion of a uniform cavalier drama; they illustrate the spectrum and variety of court taste. But by way of conclusion, it is their common characteristics that must concern us. For the plays engaged questions concerning love, morality, social relationships, the court, kingship, government, and indeed the relations between them – between virtue and social position, between the court and morality, between love and government. These are not the concerns of a narrow coterie, nor are they issues specific to the reign of Charles I. These Caroline plays address questions and concerns common to the country and the court; and they take as their themes subjects common to Renaissance drama from the reign of Elizabeth I. They rearticulate in the circumstances of the 1630s the ideas which informed expectations of the court and monarchical government. To argue for common and continuous concerns in Caroline literature is to depart radically from the notions of a cultural rift, or of retreat from social engagement after the demise of Shakespeare and Jonson. But such a reinterpretation does, I believe, take us closer to the world of the English Renaissance. What has separated us from that world has been a series of assumptions about it: assumptions that values and society were polarizing in early Stuart England, that there was a 'cavalier' culture that looked inward on itself and brooked no criticism, that the king and court escaped from reality into frivolous diversions that reinforced their own self-perception, that 'court' and 'country' described two distinct and opposed cultural and political worlds. Such assumptions do not stand the test of closer examination. They originate perhaps from that most dangerous of historical ailments, anachronism; from, that is, the translation into early Stuart England of the ideas and politics of a later age.

For from the late seventeenth century gradually, though never entirely, the once common values expressed in the terms 'court' and 'country' began to change their meaning. 'The court' began to describe a political group, as much as, if not more than, an idea or ideal of monarchy and political life. And the ideal of the 'country' was appropriated by men who employed it in order to separate themselves from the politics of the court, in some cases from central government and all ambitious political manoeuvring. The shift was never absolute, nor clear cut: the terms remained in use as common ideals at the same time that they were employed in practice to delineate divided groups. Their political usefulness indeed lay in this very ambiguity.[256] But the world had changed: men were prepared to acknowledge and even defend the politics of interests and factions. They could even begin to see the public life,

[256] See the perceptive essay by David Hayton, 'The "country" interest and the party system', in C. Jones, ed., *Party and Management in Parliament 1660–1784* (Leicester, 1984), pp. 37–79.

politics, as a world separate from private behaviour with different codes of conduct.

But this was not the world of the 1630s. We should not read these later values or attitudes, or these shifts of language, back into the reign of Charles I. Nor should we approach the plays, poems and masques of Caroline England from the perspective of civil war or a divided nation of which many of the writers remained in ignorance for all or much of their lives. The culture of the court was part of the common values of Renaissance England. Within those values were questions and tensions – about virtue and government, between order and disorder.[257] And those questions and tensions are reflected in courtly literature no less than on the public stages. If we wish to understand them we must read the plays, poems and masques of the 1620s and 1630s not with a hearing blocked by preconceptions, but with our ears open to the language and metaphors through which they spoke to the concerns of their age.

In the chapters that follow we shall listen carefully to three men: William Davenant, Thomas Carew and Aurelian Townshend. They are men from different backgrounds who came to various fortunes – in the queen's household, in the king's privy chamber, in poverty in the Barbican, on the fringes of the court. Between them they wrote all the verses for the Caroline masques after Ben Jonson's fall from favour. Perhaps that alone has condemned them to oblivion, or branded them as courtly sycophants. We should not dismiss them. For in their plays and poems – and even within their court masques – they addressed ethical and political questions which entitle them to a central place 'of an age' and to some recognition as 'for all time'.

[257] S. Greenblatt, 'Invisible bullets: Renaissance authority and its subversion', *Glyph*, 8 (1981), pp. 40–61.

Sir William Davenant and the drama of love and passion

William Davenant, who rose to become servant to Queen Henrietta Maria and Poet Laureate, was born in 1606, the son of an innkeeper from Oxford.[1] After a less than brilliant educational record under the private tutelage of Edward Sylvester and then at Lincoln College, Oxford, Davenant became a page to the Duchess of Richmond, and so ascended the first rung of the ladder of preferment. This first step proved unsure; for it appears that the young Davenant lost his place as a consequence of economies in the Richmond household. But as his first foothold fell away, Davenant was fortunate enough to be taken into the service of Fulke Greville, Lord Brooke, whose patronage was to prove a firmer foundation for his social, literary and perhaps political ambitions. In Brooke's house, Davenant embarked upon his writing for the stage, doubtless with the encouragement of a patron who was himself, in the mid 1620s, still revising two tragedies of his own.[2] It may be too that Davenant was fired by Brooke's fervour for the Protestant cause, for in 1627 it appears that he volunteered to join the expedition to relieve the besieged Huguenots of the Ile de Rhé.[3] Shortly after his return from the wars, however, Davenant was robbed of his mentor when in February 1628 Lord Brooke was murdered by a disgruntled servant.

After Brooke's death Davenant ardently sought patronage, assisted by his kinsman John Davenant, Bishop of Salisbury.[4] It was probably a search for

[1] My account of Davenant's life is based upon A. Harbage, *Sir William Davenant: Poet Venturer* (Philadelphia, 1938); A. H. Nethercot, *Sir William Davenant* (London, 1938); A. M. Gibbs, ed., *Sir William Davenant. The Shorter Poems* (Oxford, 1972), introduction.

[2] On Greville, see R. Rebholz, *The Life of Fulke Greville* (Oxford, 1971); J. Rees, *Fulke Greville, Lord Brooke, 1554–1628* (London, 1971); G. Bullough, ed., *Poems and Dramas of Fulke Greville* (2 vols., London, 1939). Harbage detects the influence of Greville on Davenant's poetry: *Davenant*, p. 33.

[3] Nethercot, *Davenant*, p. 39; J. L Hotson, 'Sir William Davenant and the commonwealth stage', Harvard University unpublished Ph.D. thesis, 1921, pp. 9–10.

[4] Nethercot, *Davenant*, p. 60.

useful connections rather than a serious intention to pursue a legal career that led Davenant to enter the Middle Temple in 1628. At the Temple, Davenant shared chambers and friendship with two young men who, albeit perhaps more serious about their legal studies, were also to make an important contribution to the literature of their age – Edward Hyde, future Earl of Clarendon and historian of the great rebellion, and Sir John Suckling, the poet, dramatist and courtier.[5] Anxious to seize every opportunity for place in the months after the assassination of the Duke of Buckingham, Davenant began to address himself to members of the Duke's family, sending commendatory verses to the Duchess and to the Countess of Anglesey, Buckingham's sister-in-law.[6] There were other potentially powerful patrons for whose favour Davenant made his bid. In 1629, he dedicated his tragedy *Albovine* to Robert Carr, Earl of Somerset, the former favourite of James I – perhaps with a view to the possibility of Somerset's return to power.[7] The following year *The Cruel Brother* and *The Just Italian* were presented respectively to Richard Weston, Lord Portland and Lord Treasurer of England, and to Richard Sackville, Earl of Dorset, Lord Chamberlain to the queen.[8] The year 1630 also saw Davenant's highest bid for favour: a new year's ode addressed to Henrietta Maria.[9] Davenant in the volatile and uncertain circumstances that followed Buckingham's death, then, shrewdly placed a wide range of bets. His strategy paid dividends. For Davenant attracted the attention of Henry Jermyn, the queen's favourite, and also of Endymion Porter, a former client of the Duke's and gentleman of the bedchamber who was an influential figure in the fiscal, cultural and political history of the court of Charles I.[10] Secure now under their patronage, Davenant might have continued upon a productive career of writing for the stage. But his promising start was halted again in 1630 by a serious illness which brought him close to death and took him off the stage for three years.

Davenant's syphilis was evidently the consequence of a profligate lifestyle (especially for a married man), and in particular the memento of a casual

[5] *Ibid.*, p. 67; *Cal. Stat. Dom. 1628–9*, p. 435.

[6] Nethercot, *Davenant*, pp. 71–2; 'Elizium. To the Duchesse of Buckingham', 'The Countess of Anglesey lead Captive', Gibbs, *Davenant Shorter Poems*, pp. 22–3.

[7] W. Davenant, *The Tragedy of Albovine, King of the Lombards* (London, 1629), 'To the Right Honourable The Earl of Somerset', in *The Dramatic Works of Sir William D'Avenant* (5 vols., 1872–4), I, p. 17. All references to Davenant's plays are to this edition. We await a full critical edition.

[8] Davenant, *The Cruell Brother. A Tragedy* (London, 1630), 'To the Right Honourable The Lord Weston', *Dramatic Works*, I, p. 117; *The Just Italian* (1630), 'To the Right Honourable The Earl of Dorset', *Dramatic Works*, I, p. 207.

[9] Nethercot, *Davenant*, p. 74, 'To the Queene, upon a New-yeares day', Gibbs, *Shorter Poems*, pp. 67–8.

[10] D. Townshend, *Life and Letters of Mr Endymion Porter* (London, 1877); G. Huxley, *Endymion Porter: The Life of a Courtier 1587–1649* (London, 1959).

encounter, if Aubrey is to be trusted, with a 'black handsome wench' who infected him.[11] At a time when little was yet known about the 'French disease', the cure, in this case an excessive concentration of mercury, proved worse than the malady. Davenant lost much of his nose and so bore a visible deformity which became his distinguishing mark, the subject of cruel ridicule by enemies and of affectionately ribald banter by friends.[12] But, despite the condition of his nose, Davenant, thanks to the attention of Porter, recovered his health and his muse.[13] He returned to the stage with *The Wits* in January 1634. Though less than a success at the Blackfriars, the play was well liked at court and launched its author upon a new literary path as it raised him to higher positions of favour.[14] For in 1634 Davenant was commissioned by the queen to write the verses for a court masque to be produced in partnership with Inigo Jones. The success of *The Temple of Love*, performed in January of the following year, established Davenant as the author of a series of entertainments for the queen and the king.[15] In 1637 he succeeded as semi-official Poet Laureate on the death of his predecessor in the devising of those entertainments, Ben Jonson.[16]

Unlike Jonson (after 1617), Davenant did not, as writer of masques for the court, turn away from the professional and public stage. His comic masterpieces, *The Platonic Lovers* and *News from Plymouth*, were performed within months of *The Temple of Love*,[17] and three more plays, *The Unfortunate Lovers*, *The Fair Favourite* and *Love and Honour*, graced the stage after the subsidence of the plague of 1637 allowed the playhouses to

---

[11] John Aubrey, *Brief Lives*, ed. A. Clark (2 vols., Oxford, 1898), I, p. 205.

[12] Nethercot, *Davenant*, pp. 90–1. Nethercot went so far as to suggest that Davenant killed a tapster who joked about his pox-deformed nose (*ibid.*, p. 102). The evidence, however, does not support the suggestion, but indicates that Nethercot may have confused Sir William Davenant with another of the same name, dwelling at Halstead, Essex. See J. P. Feil, 'Davenant exonerated', *Modern Language Review*, 58 (1963), pp. 335–42.

[13] See 'To Endimion Porter', Gibbs, *Shorter Poems*, pp. 26–7.

[14] Davenant, *The Witts: a Comedie [The Wits]* (London, 1636), in *Dramatic Works*, II, pp. 107–244; 'To The Chiefly Belov'd ... Endymion Porter', p. 119; Adams, *Dramatic Records of Herbert*, p. 54. Below, p. 69.

[15] Garrard to Wentworth, 11 Jan. 1635, *Strafford Letters*, I, pp. 360–1; Davenant, *The Temple of Love. A Masque Presented by the Queen's Majesty and her Ladies ... By Inigo Jones ... and William Davenant, her Majesties Servant* (London, 1634), in Orgel and Strong, *Inigo Jones*, II, pp. 600–30. See below, pp. 243–56.

[16] Nethercot, *Davenant*, p. 166; Aubrey, *Brief Lives*, I, p. 205. Davenant was granted a pension of £100, not the official title of Laureate. See E. K. Broadus, *The Laureateship: A Study of the Office of Poet Laureate in England* (Oxford, 1921), pp. 225–6; Royalists attributed Thomas May's adherence to the parliamentarian cause to his own disappointment at not being chosen, B.L., Add. MS 24,487 (Hunter's Lives), p. 318.

[17] *The Platonic Lovers* was probably performed both at court and the Blackfriars in the season of 1635–6, and printed in 1636; *News from Plymouth* was performed at the Globe in the vacation of 1635. Bentley, *Jacobean and Caroline Stage*, III, pp. 209–12.

reopen.[18] Davenant was undoubtedly committed to the theatre and to the drama. Even after the necessity of writing for the stage had passed, he maintained a steady output of a play a year and even experimented with a vacation play for the Globe, consciously directed at a more plebeian audience that filled the seats there out of the aristocratic season.[19] He continued too to write verse compliments and poems, a volume of which was published in 1638.[20] During the 1640s, when the theatres were closed by order of parliament, Davenant turned his hand to a major verse epic of five books – the unfinished (and largely unstudied) *Gondibert*.[21] But Davenant's muse always led him back to the stage. Under the ingenious disguise of entertainments 'by declamations and music', Davenant was able to bypass the objections and obstructions to the drama during the Protectorate regime and so to reopen the theatres in the England of the interregnum.[22] After several, probably furtive private performances, the appropriately entitled *The First Day's Entertainment* in May 1656 brought back a paying audience not seen since the war.[23] With the Restoration and the end of restraint, Davenant fulfilled a dream nurtured since the 1630s, taking charge of his own company of actors and his own playhouse near Portugal Row, which he governed personally until his death in 1668.[24]

Davenant's life is a catalogue of what some have regarded as contradictions – of what might at least appear incongruities. The son of an innkeeper, Davenant rose to favour and, in 1643, a knighthood in that allegedly most snobbish and aristocratic environment, the court of Charles I.[25] And whilst he too often expressed his disdain for the poor understanding and bad taste of the vulgar,[26] Davenant, for all his acceptance by the court, clearly never lost contact with the worlds of city and country, and even of the underworld of poverty and petty crime.[27] More strikingly, Davenant, who was commissioned to write in celebration of the cult of Platonic love, fell victim to the pox

---

[18] *The Unfortunate Lovers* was performed at the Blackfriars in April 1638, at the Cockpit in May, and at Hampton Court in September. *The Fair Favourite* was performed at the Cockpit in November and December of the same year; *Love and Honour*, first played in 1634, was performed at Hampton Court in January 1637.

[19] *News from Plymouth, Dramatic Works*, II, pp. 105–99; cf. 'Epilogue To a vacation Play at the Globe' in Gibbs, *Shorter Poems*, p. 67.

[20] Davenant, *Madagascar with Other Poems* (London, 1638).

[21] Davenant, *Gondibert* (London, 1651).

[22] Hotson, 'Sir William Davenant and the commonwealth stage', pp. 185–90; Hotson, *The Commonwealth and Restoration Stage* (New York, 1962), pp. 149–53.

[23] *The First Dayes Entertainment at Rutland House, by declarations and Musick, 1657; Dramatic Works*, III, pp. 195–230.

[24] Hotson, *Commonwealth and Restoration Stage, passim*.

[25] Nethercot, *Davenant*, p. 207.

[26] Eg. 'To the Right Honourable, The Earl of Dorset', epistle dedicatory to *The Just Italian* (*Dramatic Works*, I, p. 207); the prologue to *The Wits* (*ibid*, II, pp. 117–18); prologue to *The Unfortunate Lovers* (*ibid.*, III, pp. 12–13).

[27] See below, p. 89.

and was known for his debauchery.[28] Such ambiguities not only force us to question generalizations about court style, they take us to the heart of the drama of Davenant's own nature, and are essential too for an understanding of the nature of his drama. For all his loyal devotion to the queen and the king – a loyalty which twice nearly cost him his life[29] – Davenant could write satirically of courtly fashion and critically of royal policies. Neither the man nor his plays reflects the narrow preoccupations of an isolated courtly world, but a rich variety of experience and a wide range of perspectives.

As a playwright, Davenant regarded himself as a son of William Shakespeare. Biographers since Aubrey have taxed themselves over the possibility that Davenant was a natural son of Shakespeare, who visited The Crown at Oxford, John Davenant's inn, on his annual journey to Warwickshire and became a close friend of the family. For all the allusions, the question cannot be finally resolved and need not detain us.[30] What is important is that Davenant declared that he admired Shakespeare before any other dramatist.[31] This was no mere lip service, for scholars have detected the influence of Shakespeare in early works such as *Albovine*, and a case could be made for others.[32] Shakespeare, however, was not his only dramatic mentor. Davenant also perceived himself as one of the sons of Ben and some of his comic characters, as we shall see, would alone qualify him for the title, even if one were not to accept the claim that the purpose and structure of the plays follow Jonson in many respects. Critics have convincingly argued for other influences and picked up the echoes of other writers – of Donne (as well as Jonson) in the verse, of Middleton, Fletcher, Shirley and Ford in the drama.[33] If, in other words, Davenant must be discussed within the context of 'cavalier drama', he cannot be divorced, as that drama so often is, from the traditions of Jonson and Middleton, or from the ambivalences, debates and criticisms that marked the Jacobean stage.

Davenant poses many problems to those who would generalize about Caroline dramatic taste, courtly modes and political values. As a result critics have found him an uncomfortable subject for study and have largely ignored him. His most recent biographer, A. H. Nethercot, clearly thought little of much of Davenant's work, discussing several plays as 'appalling', 'spiritless', 'weak' and 'innocuous', epithets befitting the pen of a man described here as a

---

[28] He was described as 'Davenant . . . a loose lived Gentleman', B.L., Add.MS 24,489 (Hunter's Lives), p. 29.

[29] In 1641 when he was charged with involvement in the Army Plot (see below, pp. 100–1) and in 1649 when he was taken prisoner when en route to Virginia (Nethercot, p. 253). *Gondibert* was penned when Davenant believed himself to be facing death in the Tower.

[30] Aubrey, *Brief Lives*, I, p. 204; Harbage, *Davenant*, pp. 17–18.

[31] Aubrey, *Brief Lives*, II, pp. 226–7.

[32] Nethercot, *Davenant*, p. 53; Harbage, *Davenant*, p. 34.

[33] See Davies, *Sons of Ben*; H. S. Collyns, *The Comedy of Sir William Davenant* (The Hague, 1967).

'docile' servant of royal taste.[34] Nethercot was not deaf to the irony and satire in Davenant, nor to the tone of scepticism in his treatment of the courtly cult of Platonic love, but dismissed these as the echoes of an older tradition from which the playwright was striving to break forth: 'nor did he *ever succeed* in freeing himself from the didactic attitude towards poetry which he met in his first master's [Greville's] *Poems of Monarchy and Religion*'.[35] Davenant's true aspirations as a dramatist, Nethercot maintains, were reflected in the 'toploftical idealism' of *Love and Honour* in which he came nearest to the models of taste prescribed for cavalier drama by the queen.[36] Alfred Harbage, who subjected the plays to closer criticism in his own study of Davenant, acknowledged the ambivalences in the works of 'the dramatist who showed the most skill in keeping one foot in the public theatre and the other in the royal banqueting halls'.[37] But instead of seeing the experience of both worlds permeating all Davenant's works, Harbage divided the plays rigidly into professional works and those penned under the patronage and influence of the court.[38] Then in order to support his thesis concerning the nature of cavalier drama, but in defiance of the chronology of Davenant's own career, he concluded that the nobler Davenant of the professional stage 'in a sense sold out to the court'.[39] The man who wrote *The Wits* and *News from Plymouth* as well as *Love and Honour* and the masques clearly caused difficulties to Harbage, who wished to argue for the corrosive effects on the professional stage of an effete and precious courtly mode. He presents no fewer problems to those who would artificially separate the court and professional stages – accordingly Martin Butler does not know how to 'count' him, and discusses him little.[40]

If a perusal of *The Year's Work in English Studies* is a fair reflection of the current critical opinion, there can be still no dissent from Professor Collyns's evaluation of 1967: 'no one reads Davenant today . . . but all who have heard of him are quick to claim that he is tedious'.[41] Collyns's book, *The Comedy of Sir William Davenant*, was the first and remains the only critical study which attempts to read rather than categorize the plays, and significantly it is the first to question the negative judgements passed on them. Collyns read

[34] Nethercot, *Davenant, passim.*
[35] *Ibid.*, p. 49 (my italics).
[36] *Ibid.*, p. 129.
[37] Harbage, *Cavalier Drama*, p. 165.
[38] *Ibid.*, pp. 165–7.
[39] *Ibid.*, p. 154, cf. Harbage, *Davenant*, preface. Harbage describes two distinct political worlds as early as 1629 ('It was a time for choosing sides'), and argues that Davenant had 'elected to become a Royalist' (*Davenant*, p. 42). It is precisely such erroneous political assumptions that flaw his reading of the drama.
[40] Butler, *Theatre and Crisis*, p. 101.
[41] Collyns, *Comedy of Davenant*, p. 8. Cf. C. Squier, 'The comic spirit of Sir William Davenant: a critical study of his Caroline comedies' (University of Michigan, unpublished Ph.D. thesis, 1963).

Albovine as satire and social commentary; in *The Fair Favourite* he saw explicit criticisms of the court.[42] Davenant's comedy, he maintained, was didactic and serious and his commentary sharp and incisive; Davenant, he concluded, was no mere 'court flunky'.[43] This was a significant re-evaluation. But his analysis of the drama remains superficial and the plays are still read in the context of preconceptions about the cavalier mode. Collyns's final verdict adjudges Davenant's comedies a failure. The plots, he argues, lack Jonson's unity and control. And, lacking Jonson's courage, they retreat from the forcefulness of explicit statement. So, Collyns maintains, in *The Platonic Lovers* Davenant 'equivocates throughout and *thus* [my italics] weakens its dramatic force'.[44] Most seriously, Collyns concurs with Harbage that Davenant was too embroiled in the concerns of his age and social milieu to embrace those universals which rescue great art from the ravages of time.[45] And time has condemned Davenant to near oblivion.

Collyns's judgements must remain questions of interpretation on which we may reflect further when we have examined the plays. But the deductions and assumptions on which the interpretation depends cannot pass without comment. If, for example, Davenant failed to sustain Jonson's control (and that is questionable), it may be that he did not strive for it; and if *The Platonic Lovers* equivocates, it may be that therein lies its dramatic force rather than weakness. Most importantly, if Davenant's themes were those of love and honour, chastity and infidelity, honesty and cozening, hierarchy and social dislocation, it may be because these were the themes through which contemporaries examined those fundamental ethical and political questions for which each age has its preferred metaphors. Collyns has no sense that the plays of love and honour expressed any more than the preoccupations of the precieux; as a consequence he fails to appreciate Davenant's works or the drama of values which were his subject.[46] It is Davenant's engagement with the questions and anxieties of Renaissance England that we must attempt to understand. For the more we place him amidst the preoccupations of early Stuart Englishmen, the more we may come to recognize Davenant's claim to greater and broader recognition.

This chapter can be little more than a plea – it may be hoped an inspiration – to read Davenant's plays more carefully. Between 1626 and 1640 eleven of Davenant's plays were written and performed, as well as the five masques to which we will return in a later chapter. Davenant wrote tragedies, tragicomedies and comedies; while plays like *Love and Honour* and *The Fair*

---

[42] Collyns, *Comedy of Davenant*, pp. 81–6, 118–20.
[43] *Ibid.*, p. 17.
[44] *Ibid.*, p. 109.
[45] *Ibid.*, p. 175; Harbage, *Davenant*, p. 248.
[46] There is no evidence that Collyns pondered Davenant's own discussion of his drama in the preface to *Gondibert*. See below, pp. 101–8.

Favourite end in marriage and reconciliation, the close of *The Cruel Brother*
leaves a stage littered with bodies. The tragedies take us to courts, the scenes
of noble sentiments and cunning plots; the comedies are set in the city and the
provinces in which men and women strive to make their way by honesty or by
cozening. For all the differences of treatment, language and even subject
(which would demand a full critical analysis of each play), we may discern
common concerns and problems which the playwright examines in different
settings and from different perspectives. It is these common concerns and
Davenant's discussion of them that we shall attempt to elucidate. We will
pause to consider one or two texts more closely in order to convey something
of Davenant's verse and tone. We shall attempt some analysis of Davenant's
own attitude to the purpose of his drama. We shall look briefly at his poetic
works in which he often expressed his attitudes and artistic philosophy more
succinctly. And throughout our purpose will be not primarily to assess the
artistic merits of the work, but to understand the ethical, aesthetic and
political values which Davenant expressed in his poems and plays.

SOCIAL DISLOCATION AND NATURAL VIRTUE: THE ETHICS OF LOVE

Davenant's plays all take place in a world of dislocation. Set in the courts of
Italy, the city of London, or Plymouth, the society they represent is one in
which standards, values and morality have been overturned. Men have
become effeminate, martial ardour has gone, nobility is decayed, hierarchy
has collapsed as peers match with haberdashers, prayers have been
abandoned, and charity is so little practised that wounded soldiers are left to
the highways. Characters cheat and cozen; men say the opposite of what they
mean. And in this world of moral anarchy, as Claramante observes in the play
that best depicts it, *The Distresses*:

> Virtue and truth are only names on earth,
> And their realities are fled to heaven.[47]

Virtue and truth, however, are still to Davenant the absolute standards which
prescribe and ought to determine how men behave in society and in politics.
The central concern of his drama is a reassertion of these standards. To a
world of the 1620s and 1630s that had come to suspect that survival and
advancement depended upon cunning and dissimulation, Davenant proclaimed that the good man was still the good citizen and the good ruler.
Virtue, he asserted, could not only be reconciled with, it had to be the pattern
for, society and government. The metaphor through which Davenant
examined the tensions of ideal and reality, of personal inclination and public

[47] *The Distresses*, Act III, Scene I, *Dramatic Works*, IV, p. 313; cf. *Coelum Britannicum*, lines
408–15; below, p. 239.

duty, of sincerity and dissimulation, anarchy and order, was that of love – the cynosure of human relationships. The plays of rival lovers and crossed loves, of debauched profligates and models of feminine chastity and fidelity, the drama, as I have described it, of love and passion, was not a retreat from the moral and political questions central to Renaissance England: it was a searching and incisive examination of them.

The mark of a society that had fallen into decline, in which traditional standards and values had been abrogated was, for Davenant, a preoccupation with fashion. Though he became a member of fashionable society, Davenant never lacked a sharp sense of the ridiculous poses and postures of those who slavishly followed the dictates of fashion. And though he became the queen's servant and a familiar within her household circle, Davenant did not shy from identifying the worst excesses and consequences of such vanity with the influence of the French and of the court. Fashion corroded society in mistaking the outer style for the inner substance or, at least, in attributing more importance to display than to worth. *The Fair Favourite*, performed in 1638, opens with courtiers debating the capacity of travel and acquaintance with fashions to perfect 'Your very ape'.[48] Saladine mocks the prevailing belief that the 'rude and unqualifi'd' may be easily refined by 'having once seen countries' and satirizes a society which judges the refinements of travel only superficially by behaviour 'most Monsieur like'.[49] The 'very ape', of course, remains no more than an animal: the inner qualities of men are not so easily transformed, nor are they to be so superficially evaluated. French customs, Davenant makes clear, are not the patterns from which men should mould their manners. In his earliest play, *Albovine*, probably written shortly after Henrietta Maria's arrival in England (and printed in 1629), the French are associated not only with superficiality, but with cowardice and promiscuity, the very inversions of honour, bravery and self-control, the traditional virtues of men and those expected most of the nobles. Grimold, a rough old captain of the wars who for all his lack of sophistication stands for bravery and plain speaking, comically mocks the absurd postures of those who defy nature in order to emulate a French gait.[50] Fashion leads men into worse sins than folly – into misrepresentation and the subversion of truth by show. The

---

[48] *The Fair Favourite*, Act I, Scene I, *Dramatic Works*, IV, p. 207.
[49] *Ibid*. IV, p. 207; cf. *Albovine*, Act IV, Scene I, *Dramatic Works*, I, p. 77.
[50]   You pinion up
     Your elbows thus, – like pullets trust upon
     A spit; then wreath your hams in thus, and move
     With a discreet leisure, as if you meant
     To number all the pebbles in the street.
     And then you fleer – as if y' had wash'd your gums
     In vinegar. This you admire for gesture
     of the newest fashion . . . (Act V, Scene I, *ibid*., I, p. 94).

courtiers who, infected by French fashions, paint their face with stars, as Gondibert protests, 'abuse Astrology'. They are guilty of 'perfuming your very shadows'[51] – and indeed they are no more than men who, to borrow Plato's metaphor, live in a world of shadows, ignorant of true forms and ideas, unenlightened, with the lowest forms of life ('your very ape'). They inhabit a realm of sense, not understanding, and so debase their humanity. Vollterri advises them:

> If you will take physic for your soul's health,
> Retire into that part of the kingdom
> Which lies farthest from France.[52]

And we know with Gondibert that

> He counsels well; for the French air hath made
> Many of our gentry drunk.[53]

Fashion and superficiality have corrupted language and values. Men mouth French phrases ignorant of their meaning, as ready to use them in warfare as in wooing. 'Randee vous', Jasparo tells Gridonell in *The Platonic Lovers*, is a command to yield to love, a fitting error for those whose words and style are at odds with their meaning and substance.[54] The world Davenant satirizes is one in which all is valued for what it appears to be, not what it is, in which representation and reality have become divorced. And this is at the heart of the dislocation of all order that he identifies and grapples with. Rampino, who in *The Unfortunate Lovers* thinks not of his old debt to his tailor, but only of the latest sartorial detail, exemplifies how fashion and outward appearance have corroded social bonds and personal integrity.[55] Rampino's honour lay more in the fulfilment of a long-standing obligation than in his new suit. And the honour of all men, Davenant implies, lay in a rejection of superficiality and novelty for traditional codes and standards.

   Wherein then did virtue lie in society? How was the good man to conduct himself in a world of change and flux? Ideally, the answer to such questions led one in Renaissance England to the court. The court was expected still, as we have seen, to be the pattern of virtue as well as the seat of government.[56] But the courts of Davenant's tragedies do not live up to this expectation; they are themselves microcosms of a society in which, as well as some honest men, there are scheming Machiavels, corrupt counsellors, flatterers and rogues. Courts which ought to prescribe behaviour had themselves turned traditional

[51] *Ibid.*, I, p. 94.
[52] *Ibid.*, I, p. 95.
[53] *Ibid.*
[54] *Platonic Lovers*, Act III, Scene I, *ibid.*, II, p. 54.
[55] *Unfortunate Lovers*, Act II, Scene I, *ibid.*, III, p. 36.
[56] Above, ch. 1.

values upside down. King Albovine in love with his queen is described by his courtiers as defying nature:

> In love with his own wife! that's held incest
> In Court: variety is more luscious.[57]

Because it prescribes, the court has the power to subvert language – to make marriage 'incest' – and in consequence to invert morality. And this is what it has done. For what the court practises it effectively legitimizes for the country as well as for itself. In *The Just Italian,* for example, a play dominated by the theme of sexual infidelity, Alteza claims that she may take an illicit lover, 'my stallion if I please', because he is 'A courtly implement and much in use / Among ladies of my growth and stile'.[58] In the tavern at Plymouth, Cable and Topsail voice the same belief. They can defend their plan to share the widow Carrack because ''tis fashion' and subscribed to by gentry and courtiers.[59] In Plymouth emulation of courtly manners is the key to status – to Topsail's precedence over Cable, for example – though often the antithesis of desert.[60] When the court no longer prescribed patterns of virtue it subverted all society, language and behaviour, hierarchy and morality – and even nature – for at court some 'There be that sin / with feeble ushers and the wither'd dwarf.'[61]

In the 1630s, however, the court offered a model for the ordering of human sexuality and, as Orgel has argued, a metaphor for patterns of self-government and government: the cult of Platonic love.[62] Davenant was unhappy with the philosophy. Claiming not to understand it himself, he believed it would be incomprehensible to the country – to those to whom the court ought to communicate patterns of behaviour.[63] Even in the masque that he wrote to celebrate it, *The Temple of Love*, his discomfort with the 'strange doctrines' is evident.[64] In the poems and plays his hostility is more pronounced. Davenant rejected Platonic love as a code for human behaviour because he perceived it as an abstraction which denied the sensual side of man and so offered no solution to the reconciliation of human nature with virtue and order. Man's physical desires, Davenant indicates, were not to be denied or necessarily condemned: sexual passion is frankly acknowledged in the songs of *News from Plymouth*, and sexual encounters are described as 'That fight which Jove himself held not a sin'.[65] Sexual passion could be creative as

---

[57] *Albovine*, Act III, Scene I, *Dramatic Works*, I, p. 52.
[58] *The Just Italian*, Act II, Scene I, *Dramatic Works*, I, p. 223.
[59] *News from Plymouth* (1673), Act II, Scene I, *Dramatic Works*, IV, p. 127.
[60] *Dramatic Works*, IV, pp. 126–7.
[61] *The Just Italian*, Act II, Scene I, *Dramatic Works*, I, p. 226.
[62] Orgel and Strong, 'Platonic politics', *Inigo Jones*, I, ch. 4.
[63] Prologue to *The Platonic Lovers*, *Dramatic Works*, II, p. 6.
[64] *The Temple of Love*, line 190, in Orgel and Strong, *Inigo Jones*, II, p. 601. See below, ch. 5.
[65] Gibbs, *The Shorter Poems*, pp. 215–17. Douglas Bush, *English Literature in the Earlier Seventeenth Century* (Oxford, 1962), pp. 127–8.

well as destructive: the blood spilled by virgins ushered in life.[66] Platonic love, then, in that it denied physical passion, in all senses sterilized humanity and human nature. Philosophers might dismiss the eyesight, their physical nature, for the mind

> But Lovers (whose *wise* Sences take delight
> In *warme* contaction, and in *reall* sight)
> Are not with leane imagination fed.[67]

Abstract ideas, Davenant's contrasting epithets make clear, that do not allow for the fulfilment and expression of human nature offer no guide to human behaviour. Platonic love offered no solution to the tensions of order and human passion which form the subject of Davenant's plays.

But Platonic love preoccupied the queen, the king and in various ways the court. And it may well be that it was the hold of what he believed to be a sterile and false philosophy that led Davenant to write a play in which it was examined and discredited. If Davenant found little of value in the philosophy of Platonic love, he was the more repelled by the abuses of that philosophy in the modish forms of its adoption by fashionable society. *The Platonic Lovers*, performed in 1635, is no less than an exposé of the hypocrisy of what some called Platonic love, but what was the pretence of men of little understanding or, worse, the disguise of vicious men who concealed their evil purposes under the name of a morality. The play itself revolves around inversions – that is around things called what they are not in reality. So, that which the Platonics brand as lust, 'peaceful politicks and cold divines / Name matrimony'.[68] And that which the court creature Fredeline describes as Platonic love is in fact unbridled lust and deceit. The comic subplot of the play features Gridonell, a young soldier sent by his father Sciolto for an education apart from the corrupting influences of women and books.[69] He is described, in his state of innocence, as 'one of Plato's lovers' when, of course, he is no such thing.[70] Gridonell has never seen a woman and is so naive that he does not know that brother and sister are sired by the same father. And he is so ignorant of the philosophy he allegedly subscribes to that he has never even heard of Plato's name, thinking him 'belike some clerk of a company'.[71] His ignorance of Plato's teachings is common to nearly all the characters of the

---

[66] 'Unarme, unarme! no more your fights', a song from *The Triumphs of the Prince D'Amour*, in Gibbs, *Shorter Poems*, pp. 219–20.

[67] 'To I.W. Upon the death of his Mistresse', lines 47–9, *ibid.*, p. 49 (my italics).

[68] *The Platonic Lovers*, Act I, Scene I, *Dramatic Works*, II, p. 17.

[69] It may be of significance that Sciolto has the same name as the lusty young Florentine of *The Just Italian*, 'one of the most obviously erotic young men in all drama', Collyns, *Comedy of Sir William Davenant*, p. 99.

[70] *Platonic Lovers*, Act II, Scene I, *Dramatic Works*, II, p. 26.

[71] *Ibid.*, II, p. 27.

plays. Only Buonalte, a learned philosopher himself, corrects the misunderstanding which has led Sciolto to see his son as a Platonic:

> My Lord, I still beseech you not to wrong
> My good old friend Plato, with this Court calumny;
> They father on him a fantastic love
> He never knew, poor gentleman . . .[72]

Fashionable Platonic love in the play owes nothing to Plato. Indeed it is a shallow conceit employed to justify immorality. The Platonic lovers even announce that they may see their mistresses married and still continue their relationship – what is clearly a sexual rather than purely spiritual relationship.[73]

> The balls, the banquets, chariot, canopy,
> And quilted couch . . . are the places where
> This new wise sect do meditate . . .[74]

They are places quite unfit for meditation, but the appropriate scenes of sexual dalliance as well as the fashionable accoutrements of the beau monde. Platonic love, as here depicted, is no more.

The fashion for Platonic love, the courtiers announce, has greatly influenced the court. Duke Theander and Eurithea live in spiritual engagement only: their union is not likely to be consummated; Theander's kingdom will lack an heir.[75] Theander is so committed to the philosophy that he fails to comprehend why his ally and friend Phylomont should desire a physical relationship with his own mistress, Theander's sister Ariola:

> How! marry her! Your souls are wedded, sir,
> I'm sure you would not marry bodies too;
> That were a needless charge
>
> Lye with my sister, Phylomont? how vile
> And horridly that sounds![76]

Phylomont sees this as 'mad docrine', and it is a madness that threatens to subvert all reason and order.[77] For when Theander refuses his consent to Phylomont's marriage, the two former friends declare war. Platonic love separates not only the sexes, but man and man – and kingdoms too. The courtiers take matters into their own hands and supply the remedy. Fredeline, a scheming creature of Theander, calls in Buonateste to administer a potion to his master so as to enflame Theander's parts. Sciolto, despairing of his son's

---

[72] Act II, Scene I, *ibid.*, II, p. 38. The use of 'father' underlines the point.
[73] Act III, Scene I, *ibid.*, II, p. 52.
[74] *Ibid.*, II, p. 52.
[75] Act I, Scene I, *ibid.*, II, pp. 19–20.
[76] Act II, Scene I, *ibid.*, II, pp. 42–3.
[77] *Ibid.*, II, p. 43.

ridiculous innocence, acquires another dose for Gridonell. The consequence is unbridled sexual passion which would lead Gridonell, by his own admission, to unnatural liaisons and which makes Theander, by his own confession, a slave to his baser self.[78] This was not to be preferred to their former chastity. The resolution, as the initial effects of the powder wear off, approaches a middle course — marriage to which all the parties become reconciled. Phylomont has known it all along to be naturally part of 'the order and the course of things'.[79] And he advises Theander, who has been infected by an unnecessary jealousy of his mistress, that

> When you
> Possess your lady's bed yourself, y'are the
> Best sentinel to hinder th'onslaught of the enemy,
> Whining and puling love is fit for eunuchs ...[80]

Theander learns the lesson: 'I shall incline in time.'[81]

The Platonic Lovers, as well as a satire on a courtly fashion,[82] is a rich and complex comedy which provides the setting for several debates — the role of nature and learning in education, for example[83] — as well as the central discussion of love and passion. In the end, however, it is hard to see Davenant equivocating.[84] The abuses of Platonic love are sharply exposed and even Theander (who took it seriously) acknowledges that he has subscribed to an erroneous doctrine: 'I have thought a virtue what more pregnant men may term a dull mistake.'[85] The play acknowledges that there are sincere Platonic lovers, but the implication is that they are similarly mistaken and 'but few'. Davenant cannot see any in his audience, and so closes his play with a dedication to 'soft ladies'.[86] There is more than a hint that he had in mind those fashionable ladies who, we are told in the play, take 'a sad Platonical servant' to help them with their meditations![87] Such ironies are central to Davenant's comment. The dedication to Jermyn who had recently seduced and impregnated one of the queen's maids itself makes the point.[88] The empty language of Platonic love bears little relation to the reality of court promis-

[78] Act III, Scene I, *ibid.*, II, pp. 61–2; Act IV, Scene I, *ibid.*, II, pp. 75–6.
[79] Act IV, Scene I, *ibid.*, II, p. 68.
[80] Act V, Scene I, *ibid.*, II, p. 104.
[81] *Ibid.*, II, p. 104.
[82] Davis argues correctly that *The Platonic Lovers* 'deals more critically with Court Platonism ... than do Jonson, Marmion, Hausted or Shirley', *Sons of Ben*, p. 186. Butler does not mention the play.
[83] In the character of Gridonell, *Dramatic Works*, II, pp. 13, 26–7.
[84] Collyns, *Comedy of Davenant*, p. 109; above, p. 60.
[85] *Platonic Lovers*, Act IV, Scene I, *Dramatic Works*, II, p. 69.
[86] Act V, Scene I, *ibid.*, II, p. 104; 'Since not these two long hours amongst you all / He can find one will prove Platonical.' Epilogue, *ibid.*, II, p. 105.
[87] Act III, Scene I, *ibid.*, II, p. 52.
[88] *Ibid.*, II, pp. 3–4; J. Flower to Scudamore, 11 May 1633, P.R.O., C.115/M.31/8151.

cuity. And virtue is not secured by calling vice by another name. The reconciliation of human appetite and social order, Davenant suggests here, was to be found in marriage – in the mean between Theander's sterile preciseness and the rage of sexual passion. In reality, of course, the marriage of Charles and Henrietta Maria, which was fecund and physical as well as spiritual, exemplified what Davenant advocates. But it was not that reality which was represented as the court's prescriptive pattern for emulation in the cult of Platonic love. Moreover, what could not be understood could not be a guide for conduct. The idea of Platonic love, Davenant warned in the prologue, passed over the heads of the 'city audience', who scarcely knew how to spell it; in the country it was incomprehensible. It divided the court from the realm, which still looked to the court for guides to conduct. *The Platonic Lovers* was a critical text which exposed a pretence and criticized a failing – perhaps this was why Davenant appealed with delightful ambiguity to an 'indulgent Court' in presenting his play.[89] In the cult of Platonic love, the court is shown to have pursued yet another empty fashion, to have divorced language and image from truth and to have failed to lead by example. The courtier no longer stood as he was expected to, as the model of manners for the commonweal.

If virtue was not to be found at court, Davenant's comedies reveal no illusion that standards of honesty or models for behaviour were still secure in the country. The targets of some of Davenant's sharpest satire are characters who stand as provincial stereotypes: Thwack and the elder Palatine of *The Wits*, Sir Solemn Trifle and Sir Furious Inland of *News from Plymouth*, the two plays that Davenant set away from courts or Italian principalities in order to examine more obviously the worlds of city and country in early Stuart England.[90] No less than courts and principalities, these too are dislocated worlds in which all men are shown to be out for themselves. Thwack and Palatine come from the country to town specifically in order to cozen and live by their wits at others' expense. Sir Furious Inland, as his name suggests, epitomizes the rough rudeness and provincial ignorance of the country knight, quick to take offence and ever anxious to draw his sword in a frivolous quarrel – a 'weak compound / Of clownery and rashness'.[91] Sir Solemn Trifle is the self-opinionated country justice, rude and unsophisti-

---

[89] 'Prologue', *ibid.*, II, p. 6. Though the play is set in Sicily the references to the English court are explicit as well as implied:
　　The inner room's new hung, and th' garden gallery
　　Adorn'd with Titian's pictures, and those frames of Tintoret . . .
　　(Act I, Scene I, *ibid.*, II, p. 9).
[90] See Davenant, *Gondibert*, preface, pp. 11–12.
[91] *The Wits*, Act I, Scene II, *Dramatic Works*, II, pp. 132–3; *News from Plymouth* (1673), Act V, Scene I, *ibid.*, IV, p. 196.

cated, who is always talking but never well informed.[92] All the characters emerge as inversions of what they believe they are. Thwack and Palatine, who pride themselves on their wits, are naive fools; Inland, for all his belligerent temper, does not display real courage; Trifle, who declaims impertinence and bubbling, is an impertinent bubbler. What he portentously claims to be axioms and truths are empty words – trifles like his name – of 'a weak foundation'.[93] Each receives his just deserts: Thwack and Palatine are gulled by the city women they had hoped to deceive; Inland befriends the Dutch captain who alone might have been a legitimate target for his patriotic violence; Trifle is ridiculed for his pomposity and punished for perpetrating false news. The country offered few examples in characters such as these.

The city in which they are brought to their senses has no more to commend it. For the London to which Thwack and Palatine journey in order to make their living is itself a place of avarice and deception, of the dislocation of human loyalties, ties of blood and all social order. Sir Tyrant Thrift views his wardship of Lady Ample only as a means to profit; the younger Palatine plots, successfully, in order to trick his elder brother out of his estate. Constables cavort with whores and the city watchmen play cards all night and then breakfast on a stolen pig. London is indeed what Thwack sees – 'a false inhuman town'.[94] *News from Plymouth* makes it clear that the provincial town is no better.[95] Lady Love-Right (who does not) lives there because she may debauch herself with sailors, and the three navy men, Topsail, Cable and Seawit, spend all their time in a dishonourable pursuit of ladies. Captain Warwell, a soldier disembarked in the town, is a drunkard. Scarecrow, Prattle and Zeal spread false and seditious rumours around the ignorant countryside. And the local inhabitants of the town seek every opportunity to exploit the visitors: as Cable complains, 'they would make us pay for daylight'.[96] Country, city and town are shown to be worlds in which, as all men strive for themselves by foul means as well as fair, decency and order have collapsed.

In early modern England there emerged a powerful response to the sense of dislocation and fear of collapse of order that seems to have infected the age: the doctrine and discipline of puritanism. As a social code as well as a theology, puritanism, it has been argued, imposed an order upon the potential anarchy of human will and action. In practice, in Calvin's Geneva, it presented to many a model for society and government. Historians of early

[92] Jonson's *The Staple of News* appears to have influenced Davenant's characterization of Trifle.
[93] *News from Plymouth*, Act IV, Scene I, *Dramatic Works*, IV, p. 168.
[94] *The Wits*, Act IV, Scene II, *ibid.*, II, p. 199.
[95] To Captain Topsail, by contrast with Plymouth, London is 'the sphere of light and harmony', *News from Plymouth*, Act I, Scene I, *ibid.*, IV, p. 112.
[96] *Ibid.*

Stuart England have recently stressed the attractions of godly discipline to magistrates faced with the problems of governing a socially volatile and potentially uncontrollable society.[97] For Davenant, however, puritanism was no answer to the problems of decay and disorder. First he suspected, as with the court Platonics, the sincerity of the puritans. In *The Wits*, for example, the devout weaver of Banbury (a renowned centre of puritanism) 'that hopes to entice Heaven by singing, to make him lord of twenty looms' epitomizes the puritan, for whom a show of godliness masks more wordly and more selfish ambitions.[98] Puritans, Davenant implies, like fashionable courtiers, all too often paid more regard to what men appeared to be than to what they were. Young Palatine certainly believes that, for all his quite unholy designs, he will cut a convincing figure among the godly with a 'Geneva band' and 'no more hair left than will shackle a flea'.[99]

These humorous barbs may reveal no more than the stereotyping of puritans which was common to several dramatists of the period. But even in its more sincere expressions, puritanism did not attract Davenant. For, he believed, it was rooted in ignorance, or more accurately in zeal rather than reason. Davenant indicates that zeal subverts reason and truth: in *News from Plymouth* the character called Zeal is even led to believe in the conversion of the Antichrist and to rush to convey the joyful tidings to the exiled congregation.[100] The puritans were a congregation exiled in more than one sense, and Davenant rejects them too for cutting themselves off from society and so denying their own humanity and man's nature as a social animal. Puritanism, the playwright implies, does not order man and society; it denies human nature and divides society. The point is forcefully and scurrilously made in the farcical scene of *News from Plymouth* in which Cable claims to have reformed and renounced his former life of debauchery. In his efforts to convince widow Carrack, a lucrative catch, of his amendment and suitability for marriage, he claims a conversion to strict puritanism:

> This day I'll cut off my main mast, and for
> No other reason, but because me thinks
> It looks like a may-pole.[101]

One suspects from the knowledge of his earlier conversation and preoccupations that Cable is referring not only to his ship. But mast or phallus, to cut it off would be to incapacitate – the ship for sailing and Cable for the marriage

---

[97] See, for example, K. Wrightson and D. Levine, *Poverty and Piety in an English Village. Terling, 1525–1700* (New York, 1979), especially ch. 6; K. Wrightson, *English Society, 1580–1680* (London, 1982); R. Hunt, *The Puritan Moment. The Coming of Revolution in an English County* (Cambridge, Mass., 1983).
[98] *The Wits*, Act I, Scene I, *Dramatic Works*, II, p. 124.
[99] *Ibid.*, II, p. 127.
[100] *News from Plymouth*, Act IV, Scene I, *Dramatic Works*, IV, p. 171.
[101] Act V, Scene I, *ibid.*, IV, p. 185.

which he seeks. And so, Davenant argues, in rejecting the sensual side of man's nature and the society of other men, the puritans deprive human beings of the essence of their humanity. The may-pole, hated by the puritans as an emblem of pagan pastimes, symbolizes village community. In separating themselves, the puritans, like the Platonic lovers, formed a 'sect' or a 'faction' and so divided the commonweal.[102] To Davenant this was to overturn Christianity itself and the very purpose of religion in society. As he was to reflect some years later in *Gondibert*, Christian religion 'hath the innocence of village neighbourhood'.[103] Where, for Davenant, religion should unite men in love and fellowship, puritanism divided and dehumanized them.

The established church too, he suggests, had failed to live up to the ideal. The priest whose first preoccupation is 'Roasting the pig he receiv'd in his last tythes' exemplifies the rapacity of the ministry.[104] The clergy are shown to be ignorant. More seriously, the church too, like the puritans, has denied an aspect of humanity. The studious theologians had smothered human reason, in 'dark School clouds' and so have divided reason from faith.[105] For Davenant reason was a guide for faith:

> When men have several faiths, to find the true
> Wee onely can the aid of Reason use.[106]

Reason was the essence of the higher nature of man. It may then be because the church began to reject reason, 'nature's legate', that Davenant was led away from the church too as the source of instruction for men and for society.[107] John Aubrey, who often conversed with Davenant in the 1660s, tells us that 'His private opinion was that Religion at last . . . would come to settlement, and that in a kind of ingenious Quakerisme.'[108] This may tell us little of Davenant's views a quarter century earlier. But we do know that during the 1630s he was close to Sir John Suckling and that on a trip the two men took together to Bath in 1637 Suckling, equipped with a cartload of books, wrote a tract entitled *An Account of Religion by Reason*.[109] Aubrey

[102] See also *The Temple of Love*, below, pp. 245–7, and the remark in *Gondibert* about the Jews whose religion 'doth still consist in a sullen separation of themselves from the rest of humane flesh', *Gondibert*, p. 9, Cf. the comment: 'the austerity of some divines may be the cause why religion hath not more prevailed upon the Manner of Men' (*Gondibert*, p. 41).

[103] Davenant, *Gondibert*, p. 10.

[104] *The Unfortunate Lovers* (1643), Act III, Scene I; *Dramatic Works*, III, p. 54. Cf. *The Platonic Lovers*, Act I, Scene I, *ibid.*, II, p. 8.

[105] 'To Henry Jarmin', lines 37–42, Gibbs, *Shorter Poems*, p. 76.

[106] 'Sir William Davenant's Reason', B.L., Sloane Ms 2230, f.1 and *passim*.

[107] 'Madagascar. A Poem written to Prince Rupert', lines 11–12, Gibbs, *Shorter Poems*, p. 10; see below.

[108] Aubrey, *Brief Lives*, I, p. 209.

[109] Nethercot, *Sir William Davenant*, pp. 154–7; Clayton, *Works of Sir John Suckling*, pp. xlii–xliii; *Brief Lives*, II, pp. 242–4; J. Suckling, *An Account of Religion By Reason* (London, 1646).

regarded the work as a treatise in defence of Socinianism.[110] It may be, then, that in the 1630s Davenant had become attracted by the ordered morality and belief in the God-given inner light of reason which characterized the teaching of Socinius and of John Foxe. And it may be that he ascribed a greater importance to the place of human reason than was compatible with the teachings of and mounting divisions within the church. We cannot be sure, but what is apparent is that Davenant's values and theory of ethics were built more obviously on a secular than a spiritual foundation.

In his search for standards of virtue, as we have seen, Davenant rejected the abstract order of Platonism, the sterile divisiveness of puritanism, perhaps the church itself. Wherever he looked, in court, country and city he found that decadence and dislocation which he takes as the subject of his drama. We might then be led to conclude that Davenant held a dim view of human nature and beheld as an even dimmer hope the prospect of the good society. It would be wrong to reach such a conclusion. Davenant clearly believed in the intrinsic goodness, the potential for virtue and the inherent reasonableness of man's nature. In many of the plays, as well as scheming villains, we meet characters who make a noble stand for principle, honour and virtue: Amaranta in *The Unfortunate Lovers*, Corsa in *The Cruel Brother*, Eumena and Amadore in *The Fair Favourite*. Perhaps more revealingly, promiscuous and dishonest characters are reformed, led by experience or example to a sense of their own folly or vice: Androlio in *The Distresses*, for example, or Sciolto in *The Just Italian*. The noble and virtuous characters in the plays are those who best know themselves and are themselves. By contrast the scheming villains are men who dissimulate in their every act and word. Take the rough, old and honest Captain Grimold's acute observations on the court favourite Hermegild in *Albovine*:

> He was her father's counsellor; a man
> Created in the dark: he walks invisibly;
> He dwells in labyrinths; he loves silence;
> But when he talks, his language carries more
> Promiscuous sense than ancient oracles.
> So various in his shapes, that oft he is
> Disguis'd from his own knowledge.[111]

Such, Grimold adds with forceful generalization, is 'An error / Much incident to human politics, / Who strive to know others more than themselves.'[112] Evil and dissimulation are identified. The man who is true to his nature is intrinsically good. When men try to appear what they are not, Davenant

[110] *Brief Lives*, II, p. 243.
[111] *Albovine*, Act I, Scene I, *Dramatic Works*, I, p. 21.
[112] *Ibid.*, pp. 21–2.

makes clear, they usually come to grief themselves. The fools of the comedies – Trifle and Inland, for example, or Thwack and Palatine – are ridiculous because they strive to be what they are not, and pay the price. Their names as well as their actions betray their true nature, and only when they are reconciled to it and gain a knowledge of themselves do they possess any human dignity.

Virtue, Davenant argues, resides in knowledge and fulfilment of the self, of one's nature. And the corollary is also true: that the fulfilment of nature leads men to virtue. We have several examples in the many battle scenes of Davenant's drama of men who are unmanned, incapable of fighting, because they have lost their virtue, that is their humanity. In *The Siege* money has so corrupted Captain Piracco that he loses his courage to fight even with a volunteer and a novice: his 'soul' has 'crept / Into one of's pockets'.[113] Galeotto in *The Unfortunate Lovers* cannot duel despite his reputation as a swordsman. A Machiavellian who plots evil throughout the play, he loses his strength and agility in abandoning virtue and natural goodness. In the fight with Altophil, Galeotto's limbs are frozen. He is 'statue like', and like a statue the mere outward show of a man without the humanity.[114] Only death can return him to humanity, in removing the veils of dissimulation with which he has covered his self. As he himself observes, dying, the holes made by Altophil's sword will 'serve to make / My obscure heart transparent to the world'.[115] Altophil goes on to take his revenge on Heildebrand, King of the Lombards, who has cruelly raped his mistress Arthiopa. Though a mighty king, Heildebrand too has lost all his strength as a consequence of his foul crime and Altophil taunts him:

> try what useful strength is left you, now
> Your virtue's gone.[116]

Heildebrand, who could not conquer his own passions, is conquered by Altophil's sword.

The engagement between Heildebrand and Altophil, indeed the latter's own name, focuses our attention upon the central theme and ethical foundation of Davenant's drama: the relationship of love to humanity and goodness. Love and its corrupt expressions – lust, passion and promiscuity – represent the noble and the base in human nature, good and evil in society.[117] True

---

[113] *The Siege*, Act IV, Scene I, *Dramatic Works*, IV, p. 419. *The Siege* is generally thought to be the same play as *The Colonel*, licensed in 1629; Bentley, *Jacobean and Caroline Stage*, III, p. 215.
[114] *The Unfortunate Lovers*, Act IV, Scene I, *Dramatic Works*, III, p. 68.
[115] *Ibid.*, p. 69.
[116] Act V, Scene I, *ibid.*, III, p. 81.
[117] As Davenant himself was later to explain in *Gondibert*. See below, pp. 102–3.

love, sincere, constant and faithful is almost a synonym for virtue in the drama. As Altamont, the Just Italian, puts it in the play of that name:

> 'Tis sympathy
> And love that gives the world continuance
> And life. Each species Love preserves. 'Tis love
> That makes th'eternal wisdom thus forbear
> The silly crimes of dull humanity.[118]

Love expresses man's better nature, as lust and promiscuity debase him. Love, as we have seen from *The Platonic Lovers*, is not a denial of human sense, a spiritual abstraction divorced from humanity; nor is it the mere indulgence of sexual appetite. Love, as Davenant makes clear, in one of the frankly erotic songs from a masque, is the conjunction of two human beings in sense and spirit, the union of complete persons on every plane:

> Breathe then each others breath, and kisse
> Your soules to union;
> And whilst they enjoy this blisse,
> Your bodies too, are one.[119]

Physical love is natural, and therefore intrinsically good. Copulation and reproduction, as Sciolto observes in *The Just Italian*, '[have] been a vocation ever since / The sun spied man thus crawling on the earth',[120] that is from the times of man's innocence. In society, however, love, like humanity itself, had become corrupted. The pursuit of widows for money, fashionable promiscuity, rape, each the central subject of a play, are evidence of the degeneration of cities and courts from love's natural innocence. In such a world the true lover is inclined to yearn for the innocence of nature which love still expresses. As Altamont laments, believing his own mistress to have been corrupted by wordly lust: 'Oft have I said / Let's leave the false, the busy world, and sleep / Beneath our vines; nature, not cunning, then / Augments our wealth.'[121] But retreat is no solution for men who must live in the world, and indeed be part of a society in order to fulfil their nature. And so Davenant makes clear in all his plays that the love that represented man's goodness was best expressed and preserved in society by marriage.

Marriage is at the heart of Davenant's ethics. First marriage, the physical and spiritual union of two beings, reconciles human sexuality and order and so gives legitimate expression to natural appetites that have the potential to

---

[118] *The Just Italian*, Act I, Scene I, *Dramatic Works*, I, p. 213. Cf. *Gondibert*, pp. 15, 42.
[119] 'Unarme, unarme!' lines 13–16; Gibbs, *Shorter Poems*, p. 220.
[120] *The Just Italian*, Act III, Scene I, *Dramatic Works*, I, p. 233. Cf. *Gondibert*, First Book, Canto II, verse 15 (p. 70), in which sexual love is described as 'The secret, vitall heat by which we live'.
[121] *The Just Italian*, Act III, Scene I, *Dramatic Works*, I, p. 247.

be destructive. Fredeline, in *The Platonic Lovers*, seeks by the potion he will administer to Theander and Eurithea:

> to heat their bloods into desire
> And natural appetite; and these desires
> They both may exercise, being married, sir,
> With leave of custom and our laws . . .[122]

More positively, marriage enables men to fulfil themselves, to realize their higher nature. Those characters in the drama who renounce their past and reform often change their attitudes to women and realize their better selves in marriage: the roguish and profligate Cable is 'suddenly reclaim'd' by marriage;[123] Androlio who in *The Distresses* had once believed marriage 'a trap to catch all mankind in' becomes a 'new man', 'seal'd / To marriage articles of living tame'.[124] Sciolto, the highly sexed young Florentine of *The Just Italian*, renounces his own promiscuous past when he falls in love with Scoperta whom he marries: 'false lust, I take of thee eternal leave'.[125] Love and marriage convert these wayward men, and restore them to the nobility of their nature. And marriage and love engender virtue in society. Physical love in marriage will alone give Theander the heir in whom his kingdom will be perpetuated and restore his friendship, his society, with Phylomont. It is in marriage that men in society embrace love 'that gives the world continuance'.[126] And through marriage it may be a world in which love dominates lust, order chaos and virtue vice. Love and honour are reconciled in the play of that name and as he bestows his blessing on the marriage of Alvaro, the Duke of Savoy anticipates the fruits of the union of love and honour as well as of the marriage of Alvaro and Evandra:

> The chiefest happiness of virtue is
> Th' encrease, which to procure, with Hymen's help
> We'll knit, and intermingle lovers' hearts.[127]

It is a fitting epitaph for the morality of Davenant's drama: the ethics of love and nature.

THE NATURE OF KINGSHIP AND GOVERNMENT: THE POLITICS OF LOVE AND MARRIAGE

Davenant identifies virtue in self-knowledge, in the fulfilment of man's higher nature and in love. The function of government was to endow virtue with

---

[122] *The Platonic Lovers*, Act I, Scene I, *ibid.*, II, p. 21.
[123] *News from Plymouth*, Act V, Scene I, *ibid.*, IV, p. 184.
[124] *The Distresses*, Act I, Scene I, *ibid.*, IV, p. 293; Act V, Scene I, *ibid.*, IV, p. 362.
[125] *The Just Italian*, Act III, Scene I, *ibid.*, I, p. 243.
[126] Above, p. 74 n. 118.
[127] *Love and Honour*, Act V, Scene I, *Dramatic Works*, III, p. 183.

authority, to appoint the best man to govern so that by example and persuasion they might lead others to goodness. Politics was, in theory at any rate, the art of doing good, and the good man could not but be active upon the political stage. As the noble Eumena put it in *The Fair Favourite*, 'to be mighty is a just desire in all / That covet to do good'.[128] The nobleman's claim to govern derived from his moral qualities and virtues. The courtier, as Castiglione depicts him, exemplifies the highest morality of his age. Davenant's plays are set at courts because there, in theory and ideal, virtue and government were reconciled. As we have seen, however, the courts of the plays are by no means the shrines of virtue. They have corrupted love, virtue's own expression, by promiscuity, lust and, it is hinted, homosexuality.[129] Courtiers scheme to live off ladies, to seduce innocent maids and to break matrimonial bonds. No wonder the noble lover Altophil sees courts as the antitheses and enemies of love, 'comparing mighty Courts to greater seas, / Where lovers like small rivulets are vex'd . . .'[130] As those who, in Davenant's plays, abuse love and virtue lose their own humanity, so courts which have corrupted love are depicted as having lost all claim to govern.

The courts represented in Davenant's plays are those in which the most vicious men, rather than the virtuous, manoeuvre for place and power. Machiavellian schemers inhabit many of these texts and whilst they come, conventionally, to grief, they yet dominate the stage for much of the drama and bring others, undeserving of their fate, to the grave. Always the Machiavels are 'courtiers' or 'creatures' – men who have lost their humanity: Hermegild in *Albovine*, Galeotto in *The Unfortunate Lovers*, Castruchio in *The Cruel Brother*, Fredeline in *The Platonic Lovers*, and others. (By contrast the virtuous characters often wistfully rue their embroilment in such a world: Altophil and Alteza yearn to be humble rural folk rather than princes and grandees.) The steps to favour at court are taken no longer by the best men; they 'Are worn a little with the num'rous tread / Of fools that climb to gaze upon the top', by men, that is, who seek power not in order to do good but for its own sake and for gain.[131] At court, place and power are abused. Fredeline, the court creature of *The Platonic Lovers*, secures Castruchio's assistance with the rape of Eurithea by the promise of a provostship.[132] The promise is not kept. Those who have no private virtue, Davenant makes clear, exhibit no public morality either.

Indeed good men, knowing it to be a corrupt world, spurned what the young soldier Rampino calls the 'wicked arts of court'.[133] Courts, Davenant

---

[128] *The Fair Favourite*, Act II, Scene I, *ibid.*, IV, p. 232.
[129] Nethercot, *Sir William Davenant*, p. 54.
[130] *The Unfortunate Lovers*, Act III, Scene I, *Dramatic Works*, III, p. 47.
[131] *The Fair Favourite*, Act II, Scene I, *ibid.*, IV, p. 220.
[132] *The Platonic Lovers*, Act V, Scene I, *ibid.*, II, pp. 91–2.
[133] *The Unfortunate Lovers*, Act I, Scene I, *ibid.*, III, p. 16.

is arguing, corrupt men's nature because the 'art' of the court was dissimulation. Courtiers are the opposite of what they seem; they inhabit a world of deceptions. They 'hasten to the privy gallery' not to offer counsel or conduct business, but only to

> whisper there a while; for so
> We may be *ta'en* for cabinet Statesmen,
> And at least be *held* secret, if not wise.[134]

They are neither statesmen nor secret. Rather than governing they spend their time plotting the downfall of their rivals, 'yet in the presence chamber / The opposites can smile, laugh and embrace / Like neighbours'.[135] The court, in short, turns truth and morality upside down. Because in order to survive there it is necessary to practise 'subtle arts', the court divorces men from their humanity.[136] At court, 'wise favourites', those that would keep their place, as Hermegild observes in *Albovine*, 'walk / I' th' dark, and use false lights'.[137] In consequence their own world is dark and false, the antithesis of the light of reason and truth which are the foundation of wisdom. Vicious, deceitful and unwise, the courtier epitomizes a society in which men have departed from their nature, and government has correspondingly become divorced from the good.

In this milieu in which all seems what it is not, or is not what it seems, the worst and most common dissimulation of all is flattery. Flattery is misrepresentation: of the flatterer, of the flattered and of the truth. It is the purpose of flattery to create or to sustain an illusion divorced from the truth. As such flattery was the cancer that threatened the very life of the commonweal. For flattery deprived the body politic of counsel, and counsel, that is advice given from knowledge of the truth for the most virtuous government, was the lifeblood of personal monarchy.[138] The system of personal monarchy assumed as its first premise the inherent virtue, the will to do good, of the king. But personal monarchy depended upon the king being truthfully advised by good men and on virtuous executors of his goodwill.[139] Significantly it is the King who in *The Fair Favourite* tells Eumena, who wishes to resign his favour, exactly this:

> Could every one, that careless sits
> On his high throne, depute his pow'r
> Where it might mingle with such innocence,
> Monarchal sway would be beloved: for 'tis

---

[134] *The Fair Favourite*, Act I, Scene I, *ibid.*, IV, p. 215 (my italics).
[135] *The Fair Favourite*, Act II, Scene I, *ibid.*, IV, p. 221.
[136] *Albovine*, Act II, Scene I, *Dramatic Works*, I, p. 45.
[137] *Ibid.*, I, p. 45.
[138] See Sharpe, *Faction and Parliament*, pp. 37–42.
[139] See the exchanges between the King and Phylenio on the importance of counsel in *The Fair Favourite*, Act V, Scene I, *Dramatic Works*, IV, pp. 268–9.

> Our worst mistake, to think the arts of government
> So hard; since a perfection in the skill
> To rule is less requir'd than perfect will.[140]

Courtiers for whom the 'arts of government' were, as we have seen, no more than the means to stay in power, who lacked Eumena's innocence, failed in the duty of counsel. They sought to 'engross' the King's ears, not to open them to truth. As Grimold observes in *Albovine*, 'They limit still his conversation.'[141] And in closing the King's ears they lead a ruler who has only good intentions into error through ignorance of the truth and the right.

> It is the chief misery of princes,
> Ne'er to understand their own crimes, – to sin
> In ignorance.[142]

The rôle of the counsellor, as the King of *The Fair Favourite* reminded his courtiers, was to inform a well-intentioned ruler 'when's judgement / Is distressed'.[143] It was a rôle fundamental to kingship itself. When counsel was corrupted, monarchy, the rule of virtue, was itself threatened and subverted.[144]

The Fair Favourite examines the question of counsel within the context of a full discussion of virtue, kingship and government. The King (who significantly has no other name) asserts the traditional premise that the good ruler is no other than the good man. But it is the complexities and problems that such a premise does not engage or answer and the tensions between ethics and politics that Machiavelli had so audaciously identified that form the central subject of the play. For the King has married his Queen, not for love, but in order to cement a political alliance. His heart is committed to Eumena, whom he has elevated to high honour and authority. Love (the foundation as we have seen of Davenant's ethics) and duty are presented as opposed. The King voices dramatically the sense of divorce that he feels between his private and public self, between his 'two bodies', a divorce that the tension between his love and his duty exemplifies.[145] The King believes himself to be a monster, that is to have lost his nature in his title.

> What am I else, that still beneath
> Two bodies groan, the natural and the politic?
> By force compounded of most diff'rent things.
> How wearisome, and how unlucky is
> The essence of a King, gentle, yet by
> Constraint severe; just in our nature, yet

[140] Act II, Scene I, *ibid.*, IV, p. 232.
[141] *Albovine*, Act I, Scene I, *ibid.*, I, p. 28.
[142] *Ibid.*, I, p. 29.
[143] *The Fair Favourite*, Act V, Scene I, *ibid.*, IV, p. 268.
[144] See also *Gondibert*, preface, pp. 28ff and Book II, Canto II, pp. 126–7.
[145] For a study of the theory, see E. Kantorowicz, *The King's Two Bodies* (Princeton, 1957).

> We must dissemble; our very virtues are
> Taken from us, only t'augment our sway![146]

The King is virtuous. But, as his own personal experience brings home to him, virtue and nature are not always in practice easily reconciled with public duty and government. Indeed the ruler often had to compromise his own humanity in order to govern. Politics, he admits, in the name of stability requires at times behaviour that as a private man he would regard as neither just nor honest. The King, for example, cannot exercise the charity of an ordinary man, 'for if / the Lord of Laws should compliment / With crimes the law itself that makes him safe / Would be but ceremony thought'.[147] The prerogative of mercy does not belong to kings. This belief that public rôles compromised private virtues is explicitly stated in different ways by others. Eumena (with whom the King has in fact only a chaste relationship) believes that her position as the fair favourite and the King's constant access to her compromise her reputation for virtue.[148] Her brother Oramont bears out her fears, believing his own sister has prostituted herself before royal favour and regal authority. He, believing the King to be debauched, is thereby forced radically to consider the limits to royal authority when kingship no longer rests upon virtue. Though he submits to power and authority, it is clear that for him it is authority that has lost its ethical base:

> What strange divinity is that which guards
> These Kings – the lawful terrors of mankind –
> Keeps them as safe from punishment, when they
> Oppress the tame and good, as it secures
> Them from the treachery of the fierce and bad.[149]

Submission to such an authority produces tensions for the good subject, as the exercise of authority has posed difficulties for the good ruler. The Queen underlines the tensions in her own insistence to Oramont that for all their believed evil, the King and Eumena have a claim to his obedience and love – 'Two bonds upon your duty and your love, / Which you must never forfeit sir; nor can / They e'er be cancelled, but by nature, when you die'.[150] Such natural bonds seem to Oramont at odds with virtue; and at some point in the play all the male characters confront such a tension. In the Queen's case, by contrast, love as well as duty binds her to her husband – for all that he withholds his love from her. And Eumena enjoys royal favour and public influence without compromising her chastity. The Queen and Eumena represent virtue and

---

[146] A classic statement of the dilemma in the relationship between ethics and politics, *The Fair Favourite*, Act I, Scene I, *Dramatic Works*, IV, p. 211.

[147] Act III, Scene I, *ibid.*, IV, p. 245.

[148] Act II, Scene I, *ibid.*, p. 230.

[149] *Ibid.*, IV, p. 223.

[150] *Ibid.*, IV, p. 227.

authority in harmony, for all their difficulties. And ultimately it is they who
resolve the central tensions of the play. Eumena saves Oramont from the
rigours of the law by restoring to health through love Amadore, with whom
Oramont has fought in a duel. She reconciles the two former friends and
spares the King that conflict between law and mercy which he would have
faced in punishing Oramont's crime. The Queen wins her husband's love at
last by her constancy and virtue. Eumena marries Amadore, who fought to
defend her honour; the Queen and the King go off to renew a marriage of love
as well as political convenience. The private good and the public good are
now reconciled.

Once again they are reconciled by marriage. In Davenant's ethical framework, marriage represents the resolution of the tension between sexual
appetite and the need for order. In the world of politics, marriage represents
the reconciliation of private and public virtues. The virtuous man, after all, is
he who knows how to rule his own passions, to govern himself; and the best
ruler, he who must lead all men to self-government, must be master of
himself. So, in *The Fair Favourite*, the King recovers both his humanity and
his kingship *through* his marriage. When his love for Eumena undermines his
marriage, it unkings him too. As one of his courtiers puts it, in significantly
political language, he is 'depos'd by th' cruel tyranny of / Love . . .'[151] Loving
wrongly, he cannot rule, because he cannot order his own passion.
Reconciled to the Queen, the King himself acknowledges the political import
of their union:

> Thy constant virtue hath so
> Vanquish'd me, that all my rash rebellious
> Flames grow pale and sickly now.[152]

Having vanquished himself, the King is once again the ruler. Like the Queen's
and the King's in marriage, the King's two bodies are become one. His love
reconciles his virtue and his authority, his humanity and the law.

In *The Fair Favourite* Davenant tackles the central question of the
relationship between the good man and the good ruler, the question which
taxed an age when traditional theory and political practice seemed themselves to be diverging. Marriage is the metaphor employed for the ordering of
private virtue and the commonweal. Marriage regulates human passion and
human will, as Claramante puts it in *The Distresses*, 'by force of formal
law'.[153] Will and law, that potential tension within the King's two bodies,
must be married for the King to realize his true kingship, as appetite and order

---

[151] Act V, Scene I, *ibid.*, IV, p. 268.
[152] *Ibid.*, IV, p. 278; cf. the King's earlier speech about Amadore: 'thou shouldst not, think / I'll
vanquish him that overcomes himself', Act III, Scene I, *ibid.*, IV, p. 245; cf. *Unfortunate
Lovers*, *ibid.*, IV, p. 64.
[153] *The Distresses*, Act III, Scene I, *ibid.*, IV, p. 322.

must be reconciled for man to fulfil his humanity. The unruly and promiscuous Androlio of *The Distresses*, opposed to the institution of marriage, rejects it as 'A trick your old law-makers first found out / To keep us tame. And then they fob us off / With stale deceptions of *prerogative*, / That every husband is a *monarch* in his family.'[154] Orgemon, who better understands both love and government, sees marriage otherwise – not as the exercise of power or will, but as the mixed polity of love:

> Though I a sceptre held,
> And my imperial rule
> O'ershadow'd all the earth . . .
> . . . yet I should ne'er permit my pow'r
> To lessen or to spoil my love.[155]

Love orders power, and marriage unites love with power, and this is the model for public as for private life.[156] It is lustful kings in Davenant's plays whose passions obey their will, 'Not justice nor the laws'.[157] Such kings are 'tyrants', that is not kings at all. Love and marriage reconcile will and law in the commonweal as well as unite man and woman.

In nearly all Davenant's plays marriages stand not only as metaphors for reconciliation; they actually cement alliances, mend friendships and unite contending families or rivals. In *The Platonic Lovers*, marriage restores Fredeline and Theander to an amity threatened by false love; in *The Siege* the marriage of Bertolina and Florello leads to peace between Pisa and Florence; in *Love and Honour*, Savoy and Milan are joined in alliance by the marriage of Evandra and Lionell. Marriage, we might say, resolves (whilst never quite negating) the dislocations that we have argued were Davenant's central subject and which, as he saw it, were the central problems of his age. In court, country and city Davenant had found the pursuit of ambition and self-interest; in Platonic love and puritanism he feared the denial of man's humanity and the division of society. Self-interest and divisions eroded political as well as social bonds. At Plymouth, for instance, Seawit fails to understand Inland's willingness to fight from *love* of the king: 'Besides divine, and moral reasons, I / Would know what secret interest thou hast . . .'[158] Love, however, as their debate illustrates, is the antithesis of self-interest. It is love that ties men to each other and holds society and the polity together.

---

[154] Act I, Scene I, *ibid.*, IV, p. 293 (my italics). This whole play debates love in highly political language, for, as Orgemon put it, 'Rivals for hearts are like / Competitors for crowns', *ibid.*, IV, p. 352.

[155] Act III, Scene I, *ibid.*, IV, p. 322.

[156] See below, pp. 103, 289–90.

[157] 'Like an old tyrant he bestows his threats, / As if his Anger did obey his will, / Not justice, nor the laws.' *The Just Italian*, Act II, Scene I, *Dramatic Works*, I, pp. 219–20.

[158] *News from Plymouth*, Act II, Scene II, *ibid.*, IV, p. 139.

Through love and union, men and women, society and government, become virtuous. Love was intrinsic to the commonweal, to the good of all.

The conclusions of Davenant's plays present on the stage what they advocate for society: communication, reconciliation, a regard for common interests, union and mutual love. To some extent the playwright united different worlds in his own person: the son of an innkeeper who became a courtier, he yet remained within the worlds of city and country as well as Whitehall. Davenant's poetry and his drama, like Jonson's, evoke the sounds, sights and smells of city and country in which he was deeply involved. We can, reading Davenant, almost taste

> Those lovely Pompeons, which in Barbican,
> Fencers and Vaulters Widowes please to eat,[159]

as we can easily picture the Worcestershire inn in which Davenant and his friends drank humble vinegary wine and exchanged barbs of sour wit.[160] In 'The Long Vacation in London' we catch a glimpse of the poet himself hopping to dodge the bailiff for staying out of season in the city – a city presented as a teeming vibrant world in a vivid and crowded poem which recalls (and the echo in the verse surely intends us to do so) Jonson's Barthlomew Fair.[161] The Worcestershire inn and the city during vacation, like the London of *The Wits* or Plymouth, were worlds far removed from the courts of Albovine, Florence or Savoy. Davenant, however, knew all these worlds from experience. Moreover, it is the necessary interpenetrations and intercommunications of these worlds which are the very subject of several plays. Kings and courtiers may learn from humble soldiers like Grimold of *Albovine*. It is the philosopher who brings the court of the Platonic lovers to its senses. Most obviously, in *The Wits*, it is in the city that the country wits Thwack and Palatine learn their lesson. Each has something to learn from the other and society is good, like individuals, only when it unites these worlds in mutual knowledge and regard. Court and country, courtiers, soldiers and scholars must exist together, not in isolation. Even Trifle (who learns his lesson) may be right in thinking that for all his country news is false, it may 'give satisfaction to the State, / How the people stand affected'.[162] When Lady Ample weds the Elder Palatine, they unite not only themselves but estate and wit, city and country. Those who come to know themselves and each other can also come to realize their common interests and mutual good.

Dislocation and reconciliation. Once we see these as the subjects and object of Davenant's plays, we may also come to appreciate the structure of his drama.

[159] 'To the Lady Bridget Kingsmill', lines 38–9; Gibbs, *Shorter Poems*, p. 30.
[160] 'A Journey into Worcestershire', *ibid.*, pp. 25–7; Nethercot, *Davenant*, pp. 152–4.
[161] 'The Long Vacation in London', Gibbs, *Shorter Poems*, pp. 125–30, N.B. line 92.
[162] *News from Plymouth*, Act IV, Scene I, *Dramatic Works*, IV, p. 171.

For Davenant's plots, as his critics have complained, themselves teeter on the brink of disorder and dislocation.[163] They appear at times to be outside the artist's control. But, as we know from the preface to *Gondibert*, Davenant was greatly concerned about control and structure.[164] And in the end the plays do conclude in order and reconciliation, albeit in some cases (such as *The Cruel Brother*) after a high price has been paid. The dramatic tension then expresses the tension of the drama's subject and of Davenant's own experience: the tension between dislocation and order, but also between what ought to be and what is. For these plays can in no sense be regarded as romantic or escapist idealization:[165] ugly reality stalks the stage leaving death and rape in its train. The triumph of virtue is never inevitable in a world frankly portrayed as deceitful, corrupt and chaotic. But there is hope too, held out by those characters, often women, who stand steadfastly for values that ultimately some of the deluded come to perceive and share. If Davenant's plays never shrink from the ills of society and human nature, they yet proclaim the possibilities of a loftier understanding and of a higher nature. And they urge the power of circumstances and example to lead men to virtue – not through triumphs of one over another, but through men and women finding themselves through and learning from communication with others.

Communication, of course, involves language, speaking to men in ways that they may understand. And, as we have seen, the drama of the 1630s is often charged with having retreated into a precious language of its own, as the discourse of a circle which wished to communicate only to itself. What strikes me, by contrast, about Davenant's plays is the range of languages and voices that they present on the stage – character to character – and from the stage – to the audiences of the Globe, Blackfriars and Whitehall. If some of the speeches of the tragedies are formal and rhetorical, some introspective or soliloquizing, others, in those same tragedies as well as the comedies, are irreverent and unrestrainedly bawdy. Cable's boasts about his 'pinnace'[166] and widow Carrack's reminiscences about her husband and the many noble visitors who have lain 'in several chambers on mine honour, / I should have said my credit'[167] are obviously appropriate to the world of Plymouth – and to a vacation play performed for a more popular audience at the Globe. But

---

[163] E.g. Collyns, *The Comedy of Davenant*, p. 69; Davis, *Sons of Ben*.

[164] 'The Author's Preface To His Much Honor'd Friend, Mr Hobbes', *Gondibert*, pp. 15–16.

[165] As Harbage noted in *Sir William Davenant*, contradicting his own characterization of courtly drama in *Cavalier Drama*.

[166]   *Ca.* To my pinnace, lady
         Car. Is it well rigg'd?
         Ca. And sails well.
    News from Plymouth, Act IV, Scene I, *Dramatic Works*, IV, p. 174. 'Pinnace' of course is a pun as well as metaphoric. Cf. his references to his 'mainmast', above, p. 70.

[167] Act I, Scene II, IV, p. 120. 'Lay' clearly had in the seventeenth century, as today, a sexual connotation.

Davenant does not shy from bringing such characters to court – in the shape for instance of Grimold in his bawdy remarks even in the Presence before the courtly ladies of Lombardy,[168] or in the boasts of Sciolto to Alteza: 'I have a trick to give an easy fall, / And stand to 't stiffly too when I ha' done.'[169] The language and tone of the plays, in other words – from the Queen's calm patience, through courtiers' trivial banter to soldiers' rude innuendo – present the very worlds which are brought together within the drama and led to communicate. They form a society on the stage; they even intermarry. And so, Davenant suggests, they must communicate too in the world in order to come to that mutual understanding upon which society and the polity depend.

For it was a variety of worlds as well as of voices that Davenant presented to his own society in which, as he saw it, each looked to his own. His characters are often universal figures, types who represent qualities common throughout time: honour, bravery, jealousy and ambition, greed, roguery, love. Sometimes they are clearly Jonsonian humour characters named according to their parts – Trifle and Inland, Prattle and Zeal. But always the plays are addressed to his age. Set, conventionally, in the courts or city states of Italy, the plays are rich in topical allusion, and even in specific references to locate them firmly in the England of Charles I. Davenant knows from experience the scenes of the Presence in which the guards sleep, the gallery in which petitioners wait for the king, the privacy of the Privy Chamber and the rooms 'Adorned with Titian's pictures and those frames / Of Tintoret last brought from Rome'.[170] In the courts of Lombardy and Florence, no less than in Plymouth, Davenant's drama clearly debates the questions of Caroline England.

If in arguing that the plays of William Davenant were a serious and independent examination of contemporary problems we defy the critical consensus, our assessment at least comes nearer to Davenant's own. For it would be difficult to deny that Davenant believed that his drama had a serious didactic purpose. In the prologues and epilogues, and in the dedications of the printed editions of his plays, he makes that purpose clear. What is offered is not mere entertainment, even less a romantic escapism from reality. In *The Distresses* Amiana contrasts the romance of 'mourning histories of love' with 'real being here', as in *Britannia Triumphans* the mock romanza beloved by many is satirized for its emptiness: 'how trivial and lost thy visions are!'.[171]

[168] E.g. 'though / My marrow is frozen in my bones, / Yet I melt before her eyes. When I see her, / I grow proud below the navel . . .' etc. Act I, Scene I, *Dramatic Works*, I, pp. 29–30.

[169] *The Just Italian*, Act II, Scene I, *ibid.*, I, p. 227.

[170] *The Platonic Lovers*, Act I, Scene I, *ibid.*, II, p. 9.

[171] *The Distresses*, Act IV, Scene I, *ibid.*, IV, p. 331; *Britannia Triumphans*, lines 372–462; Orgel and Strong, *Inigo Jones*, II, p. 165; see below, ch. 5; cf. 'In the Person of a spy. At the Queens Entertainment by the Lord Goring', Gibbs, *Shorter Poems*, pp. 171, 423–4.

Davenant stuck to his serious purpose even when, as often, his plays did not appeal to his audience. *The Wits*, for example, failed to please at the Blackfriars in 1634. But Davenant revived it after the Restoration and despite minor additions left the play intact, with a defiant warning to his audience:

> If glist'ring shows, or jingling sounds you pass
> For current plays, we justly pay you brass.[172]

Davenant expected his audience to appreciate and understand the serious commentary that was his drama. He was often disappointed. But the hope of bringing men to understanding (that optimism that we have seen in the plays) breeds persistence. Plays were printed (if the texts are to be believed) as performed, even when reaction had been unfavourable. In some cases justificatory and even defiant prologues bitterly condemn the audience's failure to understand and deride the standards of judgement by which the playgoers conferred their applause or disapproval. For 'two great wits that grac'd our Theatre' – Shakespeare and Jonson – had taught a humble and dull-witted audience to distinguish 'a jig, or target fight, a furious tale of Troy' from more serious plays:

> The poets taught you how t'unweave the plot,
> And tract the winding scenes, taught you to admit
> What was true sense, not what did sound like wit.[173]

Discrimination, however, was seldom exercised. Those who boasted of their critical acumen often judged plays not by such high standards but by the dictates of fashion – that is frivolously. The beau monde of the Blackfriars delighted in their liberty to determine the fortunes of a play, not as serious evaluation, but as

> A happy freedom, which y' esteem no less
> Than money, health, good wine, or mistresses[174]

– in other words as a reaction of the appetite rather than the intellect. Whatever the taste of the audience, the purpose of drama lay not in pandering to fashion, but in moral edification and didactic statement:

> to feed you often with delight
> Will more corrupt than mend your appetite.[175]

Davenant despaired of the judgement of his age, believing that even explanatory prologues, as he put it in *Love and Honour*, added only weak

---

[172] 'Prologue Spoken at the Duke's Theatre', *The Wits, Dramatic Works*, II, pp. 226–7. See *ibid.*, II, pp. 109–19.

[173] *The Unfortunate Lovers*, 'The Prologue spoken at Blackfriars', *Dramatic Works*, III, pp. 12–13.

[174] 'Epilogue' to *The Unfortunate Lovers*, *ibid.*, III, p. 84.

[175] 'Prologue' to *The Unfortunate Lovers*.

words to weaker hope.[176] But he persisted. He took his drama into the public houses as well as the private theatres and the court.[177] And even in writing for the more popular audience of the Globe Davenant eschewed frivolous spectacle or slapstick for a didactic Jonsonian comedy in which cozeners are cozened and pseudo wits are exposed. The prologue to *News from Plymouth* indeed combines an assertion of the playwright's commitment to serious drama with a condemnation of the taste of a polite society that has misunderstood it and with a contrasting flattery, perhaps not entirely disingenuous, of the judgement of a more humble audience:

> A NOBLE company! for we can spy,
> Beside rich gaudy sirs, some that rely
> More on their judgements than their clothes, and may,
> With wit as well as pride, rescue our play.[178]

Optimistic of his audience, Davenant announces that though 'This house and season does more promise shows' (spectacles), his purpose is to walk in more 'narrow ways' – that is in the confined world of Plymouth where the scene remains unchanged, but also in the biblical way that is narrow – in the paths of virtue. Davenant refused to pander to popular or to fashionable taste and retained a clear sense of his own purpose. *News from Plymouth* is his play most obviously and most consciously modelled on Jonson. And in the words of the prologue to the audience we cannot but hear the echo of Davenant's own words in praise of Jonson.

> Judgement's force ... more ruled the sense
> Of what he writ, than 's fancy's vaste expence.[179]

The more discerning of Davenant's contemporaries recognized both the didactic purpose of his drama and the Jonsonian model from which the plays were fashioned. Henry Blount, the editor of John Lily's comedies, and a man whose 'clear judgement, great experience [and] much contemplation' were admired by Aubrey, spoke of the 'lofty strains' and 'high rate' of the play, which he compared to Jonson's *Sejanus* and *Catiline*.[180] One Will Hopkins (about whom we know nothing) contrasted Davenant's *The Just Italian* with

[176] Since we have learn'd in Prologues all the scope
Is with weak words to strengthen weaker hope.
(Prologue to *Love and Honour*, *Dramatic Works*, III, p. 99).

[177] Nethercot describes Davenant's scheme in 1639 to build a large playhouse in order to 'adapt as much as possible of the methods and devices of the court theatre to a popular audience' (*Davenant*, p. 169). Unlike Martin Butler, Davenant clearly did not see a rigid distinction between court and popular drama.

[178] *Dramatic Works*, IV, p. 109.

[179] 'To Doctor Duppa, Deane of Christ Church, ... An Acknowledgement for his collection, in Honour of Ben Johnson's memory', lines 19–20, Gibbs, *Shorter Poems*, p. 78. See *Jonsonius Virbius or The Memorie of Ben Johnson Revived by The Friends of The Muses* (1638).

[180] 'Upon the Tragic Muse of my Honoured Friend, Mr William Davenant', *Dramatic Works*, I, p. 13; Aubrey, *Brief Lives*, I, pp. 108–11.

'the fine puppet plays' beloved by his detractors.[181] Davenant, he believed, appealed not to the 'herd' but the wiser few; his purpose was

> To entertain their souls in that high choir,
> Which, not weak fools, but such as know admire.

Thomas Carew made the same distinction. The people, he feared, preferred the empty burlesque of 'Red-Bull, and Cock-pit fight' to 'thy strong fancies, raptures of the brain', which placed Davenant alongside Beaumont and Jonson.[182] In the audience of the early Stuart theatre, Carew reminded his friend, in a metaphor that Jonson had himself employed, there were those who judged by unrefined appetite and those who evaluated by informed taste. Davenant, he knew, wrote 'for the men of better palate' who 'will by it / Take the just elevation of your wit'.[183] The most eloquent testimony to the didactic seriousness of Davenant's drama is that of William Habington, the poet and playwright, who contributed verse-prologues to two of Davenant's plays.[184] Habington admired Davenant's 'bright fancie' and praised in his commendatory verse to *Madagascar* in 1638 a drama:

> Where each Sceane
> Wrought like a charme, and forc't the Audience leane
> To th' passion of thy Pen: Thence Ladies went
> (whose absence Lovers sigh'd for) to repent
> Their unkind Scorne; And Courtiers, who by art
> Made love before, with a converted hart,
> To wed those Virgins, whom they woo'd t'abuse;
> Both rendered Hymen's pros' lits by thy Muse.[185]

Habington comments not only generally on the power and efficacy of Davenant's drama, on the role of art in inculcating morality. He also draws particular attention to the central motif of Davenant's drama and the crux of his moral system: the need to give expression to human nature (in contrast to courtiers' 'art'), and to legitimize and order human passions by marriage. And Habington recognized too the political dimension to this morality. It is courtiers, rulers, who are led from false lust to honest love. And at the court as well as the Blackfriars those 'rendered Hymen's pros' lits' 'did sit / To learne the subtle Dictats of thy wit'.

Among those who sat were the king and queen. Davenant's plays were not only performed at court, they were evidently appreciated by Charles and Henrietta Maria – sufficiently appreciated for Davenant to be chosen as the

---

[181] 'To my friend, M. D'Avenant, on his Legitimate Poems', *Dramatic Works*, I, p. 205.
[182] *Ibid.*, I, p. 206. For Carew's attitude to drama, see below, p. 151.
[183] 'To the Reader of Mr William D'Avenant's Play' (*The Wits*), *Dramatic Works*, I, p. 116.
[184] To *Albovine*, *ibid.*, I, p. 15, and *The Unfortunate Lovers*, *ibid.*, III, p. 11; Gibbs, *Shorter Poems*, p. 342.
[185] 'To My Friend, Will Davenant', Gibbs, *Shorter Poems*, pp. 8–9.

author of court masques in succession to Jonson. *Love and Honour* was played at Hampton Court during the winter season of 1636–7 when plague closed the London theatres; *The Fair Favourite*, perhaps the most explicitly political of Davenant's works, was performed twice at the Cockpit-in-Court in November and December 1638.[186] Henrietta Maria paid Davenant the special compliment of visiting the Blackfriars in April 1638, perhaps for a command performance, to see *The Unfortunate Lovers*, which was revived twice in the following six months at the Cockpit-in-Court and at Hampton Court.[187] *The Wits*, as we have seen, owed its appearance and publication to the intervention of Charles I himself.[188] When it was performed at court it was 'well likt' and the king himself, though he evidently disliked the plot, at least approved the language.[189] Few dramatists enjoyed greater favour at the court of Charles I.

I have argued that Davenant's plays were often satirical of the fashions, corruptions, deceits and dissimulation of the court. I have suggested that they debate questions of counsel, kingship and law, the good ruler and the nature of government; that they advocate order through union, that is the marriage of the king's will and the law, and of the king and his people. At a time when Charles I was ruling without parliaments and seemed, perhaps, distanced from his subjects, Davenant's drama may have been intended to be directly critical – or at least to offer counsel where courtiers were likely to flatter. Davenant evidently felt free to articulate criticisms of the court, even when his plays were performed before a courtly or royal audience. If – and to this condition we must return – the court of Charles I demanded escapist fantasy, the abolition of unpleasant reality, the suspension of criticism and subservience to monarchical autocracy, then Davenant displayed a remarkable independence of that court and made good his own claim:

I am no piece of Houshold Poetry . . .[190]

POET LAUREATE: POETRY AND THE POLITICS OF THE QUEEN'S HOUSEHOLD

Davenant was, in some respects, what he denied: a household poet. He was in the pay of the court. His poetry too is undoubtedly courtly in that most of the verse consists of addresses to the queen and the king, odes on special occasions and epistles to or funeral elegies for courtiers: Endymion Porter, Richard Weston Earl of Portland, the Marquis of Winchester, the Countess of

---

[186] Adams, *Dramatic Records of Herbert*, pp. 57, 76–8.
[187] 'At the blackfryers the 23 Aprill for the queene the unfortunate lov[ers]', *ibid.*, p. 76; *ibid.*, p. 77.
[188] Above, p. 36.
[189] Adams, *Dramatic Records of Herbert*, p. 54.
[190] 'In the Person of a Spy, at the Queens Entertainment . . .', line 5, Gibbs, *Shorter Poems*, p. 171.

Carlisle, the Earls of Dorset and Rutland, the queen's favourite Henry Jermyn. His first collection of poems and addresses took its title *Madagascar* from a court project to colonize the island. But it would be wrong to regard Davenant's poetry as limited by the social milieu, or the preoccupations and values of the court. Rather in the poetry we find the discussions, debates and frank criticisms that characterized the drama.

Like the plays, the poems illustrate Davenant's intimate acquaintance with a wide spectrum of early Stuart society at court, in London, in the provincial town and in the country. Davenant knew – perhaps personally – those at court 'that keepe / The Presence warme and quiet whilst you sleep'.[191] But he knew too the chubby host and hostess of the Worcestershire inn;[192] he joined the vacation walk in Islington, the Aldermen's game of quoits, the archery contest at Finsbury, St Bartholomew's Fair; and he saw the vault and a dancing lass,[193] the 'Ape led Captive still in chaine / Till he renounce the Pope and Spaine'.[194] The condition of Davenant's nose might even suggest a closer than literary acquaintance with the 'Shrove Prentices', 'Drunk in a Brothel house'.[195] From the rich experience of all these worlds, Davenant could not but view the issues of his age from many different angles, not merely from the perspective of the court.

Nor should we assume that the poems addressed to courtiers were empty compliment. The recipient of most of Davenant's verse epistles, Endymion Porter, was indeed both a courtier and the poet's patron. But it is clear that above all else Porter was a friend, a friend who had nursed Davenant through his syphilitic sickness, who had comforted him when his play, *The Wits*, had met with an unfavourable response, and most of all a friend he respected and admired. Davenant does not praise Porter the courtier, but rather the *man* who has retained his integrity even at court:

> Thy wisdome that hath taught the world an art
> How (not enform'd by Cunning) courtship may
> Subdue the minde, and not the Man betray.[196]

This was no mere conceit, let alone flattery. For to Porter Davenant confided his own ambivalent attitudes towards preferment and favour which he both enjoyed and yet viewed with suspicion and disdain. The poet blames Porter

[191] 'To the Queene, upon a New-yeares day', lines 1–2, *ibid.*, p. 61. Davenant refers to the Yeomen of the Guard who remained on duty in the Presence Chamber while the queen slept in her privy quarters.
[192] 'A Journey into Worcestershire', line 65, *ibid.*, p. 26.
[193] 'The Long Vacation in London', *ibid.*, pp. 125–30.
[194] Lines 155–6, *ibid.*, p. 129. 'Apes were trained to climb up a pole or jump over their chain on the mention of a country or religion', E. H. Sugden, *A Topographical Dictionary to the Works of Shakespeare and his Fellow Dramatists* (Manchester, 1925), cited by Gibbs, *Shorter Poems*, p. 407.
[195] 'A Journey into Worcestershire', lines 41–2, *ibid.*, p. 25.
[196] 'To Endimion Porter', lines 28–30, *ibid.*, p. 27.

for raising him above the desires of his humble station to the arduous pursuits of ambition. With the power to 'doe good' place has also brought envy and insecurity: 'now whilst I strive to please / With tedious Art, I lose the lust of ease.'[197] The poem exhibits that frank prevarication about public life that only close friends could indulge. Davenant recognizes the necessity to please even when praise was not justified. In his poem celebrating Brian Duppa's collection in honour of Ben Jonson's memory, he takes delight that

> I now may erne my Bayes
> Without the taint of flatterie in prayse,
> Since I've the luck to make my prayses true.[198]

Truth and praise were not always so comfortably allied as in the case of Jonson or Duppa. But it was precisely Davenant's awareness of this problem and response to it that free him from the charge of subservience or flattery. For within the forms of address and compliment demanded by his position at court, Davenant was able to examine critically the values of the court, the nature of kingship and even prevailing royal policy.[199]

There is little celebration of the court itself in the poetry. Several of the epitaphs and verse epistles commend those who have distanced themselves from the corruption and cozening and from the dissimulation of the court world. The unidentified I. Walker is eulogized in his epitaph as a poet and wit who

> Look'd on ambitious States-men with such Eyes
> As might discerne them guilty, could not wise.[200]

Walker – the terms recall Davenant's own confessions to Porter – preserved his 'Ease', and 'the Prince of mirth', he laughed at the 'grave bus'nesse' of a court which was grave only in its own self-seriousness and self-importance. Davenant directly satirizes such false gravity in the mock heroic *Jeffereidos*, a poem on the captivity of one of the court dwarfs.[201] The pretentiously lofty style of the poem stands in stark contrast to the trivial and ridiculous subject, much as court rhetoric and ceremony are at odds with the base realities of court life. The fates that befall the midget Jeffrey – a humorous fight with a turkey cock for example – become the cause 'for which our deepe *Platonic*

---

[197] 'To Endimion Porter', a different poem, lines 38, 43–4, *ibid.*, p. 36.
[198] 'To Doctor Duppa', lines 39–41, *ibid.*, p. 79.
[199] There has been too much of a tendency to assume that the verse compliment as a form precludes independence or criticism. Jonson's verse epistles, however, often use the form primarily as a vehicle for the articulation of a personal ethical code against which the court is measured.
[200] 'Epitaph on I. Walker', lines 3–4; Gibbs, *Shorter Poems*, p. 50.
[201] We should not forget the references to dwarfs and to the court ladies that even sin with them in the drama (above, p. 64). They seem to represent, for Davenant, the unnatural deformities of the court.

questions heaven'.[202] Court philosophy is no more serious than a dabbling in such trivia and the court wits and poets preoccupied with Jeffrey are men, like himself, small of stature. Like Jeffrey, Davenant concludes, the court too was a stunted and deformed version of its ideal and natural form.

The artificiality and superficiality of the court are sharply exposed in two elegies on peers who are presented as contrasts to it. Francis Manners, 6th Earl of Rutland, though he held office, is depicted by Davenant as a reluctant courtier in a poem that merits close attention:

> How did'st thou smile, to see the solemne sport
> Which vexes busie greatnesse in the Court;
> T'observe their lawes of faction, place, and Time,
> Their precepts how, and where, and when to climbe;
> Their rules, to know if the sage meaning lies
> In the deepe Breast, i' th shallow Brow, or Eyes.
> Though Titles, and thy blood, made thee appeare
> (Oft 'gainst thy ease) where these state-Rabbins were,
> Yet their philosophie thou knew'st was fit
> For thee to pitty, more than study it.
> Safely thou valu'dst Cunning, as 'thad bin
> Wisdome long since distemper'd into Sin.[203]

The many oxymorons – 'solemne sport', 'busie greatnesse', even 'lawes of faction' – express that inversion of meaning and morality for which Davenant taxed the court in his plays. For laws should rise above faction, as precepts ought to be moral injunctions rather than the tactics for acquiring place. Wisdom lay in the soul and mind of man, not in the 'shallow Brow, or Eyes'. Such errors, inversions and hypocrisies were indeed the doctrine of 'state-Rabbins', of false priests who had denied the true religion and even betrayed the innocence of Christ. And such was court philosophy – fitter to be pitied from the 'ease' (let us note the term again) of retirement than aped within. So Rutland shunned this 'mighty noise' and died as he lived in contrast to it – in 'grave silence', a phrase (and a pun) in which, in contrast to oxymoron, epithet and noun, exist, like Rutland's virtue and public life, in harmony. Where courtiers run after empty sounds and appearances and enshrine their achievements in statues and monuments, Rutland's fame lies in his deeds and virtues: gravity, bounty, liberality are his epitaph. The images through which the poet praises them – images of the sun's 'lib'rall Beames', of 'precious Dewes', of growth – contrast Rutland's natural self-integrity to the artificiality of the court. Apart from that world, Manners could remain 'thy Selfe' and so be 'Nature's selfe'.

[202] 'Jeffereidos, Or the Captivitie of Jeffery' in 2 cantos; Canto II, line 40, Gibbs, *Shorter Poems*, p. 41. The turkey cock may stand for the Habsburgs (usually represented by an eagle), against whom England, to the discontent of the queen's circle, had failed to make a stand.

[203] 'Elegie, on Francis, Earle of Rutland', lines 11–22, Gibbs, *Shorter Poems*, pp. 62–3. Francis Manners, 6th Earl of Rutland, died in December 1632.

Rutland died in 1632. During the 1630s Davenant's disdain for the court grew more pronounced and more explicit. In his appeal 'To the Duke of Richmond in the Year 1639', Davenant employs the conventional image of the ship of state but ingeniously twists it to show how courtiers themselves shipwreck the very virtues and values which it is government's purpose to preserve safe. The opening sentence reiterates the accusation of dissimulation which we have seen throughout the plays:

> The court does *seem* a Ship, where all are still
> Busie by office, or imploy'd for skill.[204]

In reality it is no such thing, but the haven of 'cunning statesman' employing deceitful devices in order to manoeuvre for place:

> Wearing their faces often to the West
> When bownd and sayling to the rising East.[205]

In court the virtues natural to the good man have often to be abandoned for survival, as the treasures of a ship in a storm.

> The very Ballast we were poized by
> (Weighty Discretion and Integrity,
> The helps which Time and Nature best afford)
> We for our safety oft throw over-Board.[206]

As the metaphor twists, we come to see that the court is not the ship of state navigating good men through troubled waters. It is the wind that blows the tempest itself ('Courts breed stormes, and stormes are lasting there'),[207] by which human integrity is cast upon the rocks and smashed. The court assails the very virtues it should secure: it is a ship and now not a ship (a storm), because though a court, it is no court when integrity is abandoned. Davenant's criticisms cannot be divorced from personal interest. His poem vents his own frustration concerning his abortive project to build and manage a new theatre in Fleet Street, and his anger at a court faction that has obstructed him.[208] Richmond evidently supported him. But our knowledge of Davenant's personal pique should not lead us to doubt the sincerity of his general attack upon the court (sustained through the drama and poetry), nor see his desire for reform as pure self-interest. When the poet announces that he will be 'In time a mighty Burgher of the Sea', we know that he means to preserve his ballast safe.

Davenant's personal disappointment and his allusion in the poem to the

---

204 Lines 2–3, Gibbs, *Shorter Poems*, p. 132 (my italics).
205 *Ibid.*, lines 11–12.
206 *Ibid.*, lines 15–18.
207 *Ibid.*, line 5.
208 J. Q. Adams, *Shakespearean Playhouses. A History of English Theatres from the Beginnings to the Restoration* (Boston, 1917), pp. 424–31; Nethercot, Davenant, pp. 169–71.

faction which scotches his plans remind us that though he freely employed and utilized the word, there was no one 'court' to condemn or to praise.[209] After all, the Duke of Richmond to whom Davenant addresses his poem is, like Davenant himself, a courtier, indeed one who, as the poem announces, sits near the helm of government. That is to say, it is no contradiction in terms to suggest that opposition to 'the court', or at least to a prevailing faction or policy, was articulated by a courtier, or that criticisms of 'the court' could be made by a courtier to a courtier. It is important for us to bear this in mind when we consider Davenant's addresses to courtiers, and to the queen and the king. And it is essential never to forget it when we examine his attitudes to issues which divided the court and even Charles I and Henrietta Maria.

Davenant wrote only one poem to Charles I, at the beginning of the decade of personal rule: 'To the King on New Years Day 1630'.[210] The ode reads as conventional compliment and eulogy – and at one level it is. The opening images of 'eager Youth' and 'unphysick'd Health', and, perhaps significantly, 'of Lovers, when their Nuptials nie', suggest that the poet placed optimistic hopes in the king as a model of virtue and of government. Davenant wishes in each verse the benefits of peace and unison.

> To *Charles*; who is th'example and the Law,
> By whom the good are taught, not kept in awe.[211]

The couplet encapsulates the values of Davenant's drama: the belief in the identity of virtue and rule, in the efficacy of example, in government as tutelage. It praises a king who fulfils an ideal. But the form of the poem, wishing for particular policies and courses, suggests that it should be read as counsel rather than as flattery. Davenant wishes for a peace, but one 'not compass'd by / Expensive Treaties but a victorie'.[212] He anticipates and desires another meeting of parliament, for all that the 1629 session ended in chaos, with the king issuing proclamations declaring his intention to rule for a time without them:

> A Session too, of such who can obey,
> As they were gather'd to consult, not sway.[213]

Only with the aid of a parliament, he maintains, can the king hope to fulfil the last of Davenant's wishes: for England to play a victorious rôle for the defence

---

[209] Above, ch. 1, pp. 21–2.
[210] Gibbs, *Shorter Poems*, p. 31.
[211] A summary of the view of good kingship presented by Davenant in his drama.
[212] 'To the King', line 10.
[213] *Ibid.*, lines, 17–18. See *A Proclamation about the dissolving of the Parliament* (2 Mar. 1629), and *A Proclamation for suppressing of false Rumours touching Parliament* (27 Mar. 1629), in J. F. Larkin, ed., *Stuart Royal Proclamations*, II, *Royal Proclamations of King Charles 1625–1646* (Oxford, 1983), pp. 223–4, 226–8.

of Protestantism in Europe and so snatch the glory from the King of Sweden, Gustavus Adolphus.

> To make the Northerne Victors Fame
> No more our envy, nor our shame.[214]

If the poem is a loyal address, it is by no means a sycophantic paean. It certainly did not represent royal policy. For, though some counsellors pressed for it, Charles I in 1630 was neither inclined to active involvement in Europe, nor in favour of recalling parliament.[215] Davenant, who was close to Endymion Porter, must have known this to be the case. The poem is an attempt to influence, rather than to celebrate, existing policy.

It may be significant that Davenant, though he became the principal masque writer, penned no more verses to Charles I. He was to write at least five for Henrietta Maria before 1642, and at least another three during the war years. The ode to Charles I may provide some suggestion that political attitudes as well as the accidents of patronage led Davenant to the queen's (rather than the king's) household. For much of the 1630s, Henrietta Maria led a faction of peers and favourites who, in opposition to the royal policy of diplomatic negotiations with the Emperor and Spain, advocated a French alliance and a war against the Habsburgs for the recovery of the Palatinate, hereditary territory first of Charles's brother-in-law, and subsequently of his nephew.[216] Though his plays suggest at times a cynical attitude to war,[217] Davenant appears to have been committed to this policy. In 1636 he wrote the masque *The Prince d'Amour* for the Middle Temple's entertainment of the visiting prince Elector.[218] The queen attended in (transparent) disguise with her ladies.[219] Davenant has the Master of Ceremonies inform the prince: 'You have a num'rous faction in his court.'[220] The ode to Charles I might suggest that Davenant was one of them. More explicitly, in a poem written in 1637, 'when Colonell Goring was believ'd to be slaine, at the siege of Breda',

[214] 'To the King', lines 27–8. Gustavus Adolphus is not named in contrast to the repetition of the name Charles throughout the poem. But the actions of the 'Northerne victor' had loudly proclaimed him, and Davenant may be unfavourably contrasting here Charles's words with Gustavus's actions, as he also criticises parliament for 'Speeches finely pend', rather than subsidies.

[215] Charles had signed a peace with Spain on 5 November 1630. For the debate on foreign affairs in the Privy Council see L. J. Reeve, 'The secretaryship of state of Viscount Dorchester 1628–1632', Cambridge University unpublished Ph.D. thesis, 1983, ch. 6. I am grateful to John Reeve for allowing me to see and cite this thesis.

[216] Smuts, 'The puritan followers of Henrietta Maria in the 1630s'.

[217] See for example the debates between Pert and Meager, two soldiers in *The Wits*, Act I, Scene I: 'Pert: faith! we have been to kill, we know not whom, / Nor why: led on to break a commandment / With the consent of custom and the laws', *Dramatic Works*, II, p. 121.

[218] *The Triumphs of the Prince D'Amour. A Masque presented by his Highness at his palace in the Middle Temple, the 24th February, 1635, Dramatic Works*, I, pp. 328–40.

[219] Garrard to Wentworth, 15 Mar. 1636, Knowler, *Strafford Letters*, I, p. 525.

[220] *Dramatic Works*, I, p. 329.

Davenant praises a hero who was heir to Sidney, and defender of the people's cause.[221] The name of Sidney, who lost his own life at Zutphen, almost represented the Protestant cause to those who yearned for another champion.[222] He was the idol of Davenant's patron, Fulke Greville, Lord Brooke.[223] In 1637, the queen's circle was pressing for active intervention in the war at a time when negotiations with the Emperor had resulted in the collapse of diplomacy with the Habsburgs.[224] By lamenting the honourable death of Goring and by invoking Sidney's name, Davenant stated his own views as well as those of the queen whose servant, as he conspicuously announced, he was.[225]

It is in this context, I believe, that the poem that gave Davenant's collection its title, *Madagascar*, should be read. Charles Louis, Elector Palatine, and his younger brother Prince Rupert arrived in England in February 1636. After many months of being entertained at court, Rupert became interested and interested Charles I in a project to send out the young prince, with a force under his command, to conquer the island of Madagascar.[226] The project was fiercely opposed by Rupert's mother, Elizabeth of Bohemia. She had hoped that the presence in England of her sons would spur their uncle to a greater sense of responsibility concerning their plight and from March 1636 she was manoeuvring to persuade Charles I to allow Charles Louis to put to sea with vessels from the king's substantial ship money fleet.[227] In January 1637 the king had resolved to make 15 ships available.[228] Elizabeth and her English adviser, Sir Thomas Roe, appear to have regarded the Madagascar venture as a 'romance', a fruitless enterprise and, more seriously, a distraction from their plans and delicate preparations to enlist Charles I's support for the recovery of the Palatinate.[229] During the winter of 1636–7, the queen and the

[221] Gibbs, *Shorter Poems*, line 69, p. 71.
[222] See on this theme S. L. Adams, 'The Protestant cause: religious alliance with the West European Calvinist communities as a political issue in England, 1585–1630', University of Oxford unpublished D.Phil thesis 1973.
[223] See Fulke Greville, *Life of Sir Philip Sidney*, ed. N. Smith (Oxford 1907); R. Rebholz, *The Life of Fulke Greville* (Oxford, 1971), pp. 26–32, 205–16.
[224] Smuts, 'Puritan followers of Henrietta Maria'; E. R. to Sir Thomas Puckering, 7 Feb. 1637, T. Birch, *Court and Times of Charles I*, II, pp. 275–6; Correr to Doge and Senate, 17 Apr. 1637, *Cal. Stat. Pap. Venet. 1636–9*, p. 186.
[225] See Huxley, *Endymion Porter*, pp. 176–7. Goring was involved in proposals to equip the Prince Elector with a fleet: see George Goring to his father, 4/14 Feb. 1637, *Cal. Stat. Pap. Dom. 1636–7*, p. 421, and *ibid.*, p. 422.
[226] Elizabeth, Queen of Bohemia, to Sir Thomas Roe, 25 Mar. / 4 April 1636, *Cal. Stat. Pap. Dom. 1635–6*, pp. 320–1.
[227] Sir Thomas Roe to Elizabeth, Queen of Bohemia, 22 Mar. 1636, *Cal. Stat. Pap. Dom. 1635–6*, pp. 313–14.
[228] Sir Thomas Roe to John Dury, 28 Jan. 1637; *Cal. Stat. Pap. Dom. 1636–7*, p. 400; Correr to Doge and Senate, 30 Jan. 1637; *Cal. Stat. Pap. Venet. 1636–9*, pp. 133–4.
[229] Elizabeth, Queen of Bohemia, to Sir Thomas Roe, 25 Mar. / 4 Apr. 1637, *Cal. Stat. Pap. Dom. 1635–6*, p. 321. The queen compared the venture to one of the fanciful exploits of 'Don Quixote'.

leading members of her faction – the Earls of Holland and Northumberland – had been advocating a French alliance.[230] Charles, distrustful of the outcome of negotiations for the restoration of the Palatinate with the Emperor, had despatched the Earl of Leicester to Paris, in order to investigate a treaty of war.[231] Davenant's poem then was written during delicate months when attempts were being made to commit the king to that intervention in Europe which the queen's faction had long advocated. The poem treats the Madagascar venture seriously – as was necessary given the king's own involvement. But skilfully it brings the reader back from that isle to the very different concerns of two queens – Elizabeth and Henrietta Maria. The praise, once again, of 'God-like Sidney', thrice repeated, recalls the reader to the cause of Protestantism and its association with England's model of honour;[232] the reference to Rupert's 'Mother' recalls a lineage and an obligation to relieve the king's sister;[233] hopes for an 'empire of the winds, new kept in awe', for the defeat of Rupert's 'proud foes' who 'conquer'd yesterday' evoke the dreams of Habsburgs defeated;[234] the 'northerne Monarch' who wields a sceptre on land and knows the value of a trident on the seas points to the achievements of Gustavus which could be emulated at sea by England;[235] mention of princes whose 'reason on their courage must rely' echoes perhaps the rhetoric of those who in the winter of 1636–7 were urging Charles I to take to arms.[236] Madagascar becomes in the poem a 'vision' of a very different conquest. And when Davenant discerns 'thy uncle's anger in thy brow' it is, in the poet's 'vision', not the anger of Charles I against Madagascar (anger would be an inappropriate term for a project of conquest), but 'anger' against Habsburg duplicity.[237] And if in his vision the poet saw too 'Thy mighty uncle's Trident in thy hand', it was perhaps the vision of Elizabeth of Bohemia – of her sons at the head of a fleet against the Habsburgs.[238] In *Madagascar* Davenant's vision expressed the hopes and

[230] Smuts, 'Puritan followers of Henrietta Maria', pp. 38–9; H.M.C., *De Lisle MSS*, VI, p. 100.
[231] Leicester went to France in June 1636. See his instructions in A. Collins, ed., *Letters and Memorials of State Written and Collected by Sir Henry Sidney* (2 vols., London, 1746), II, pp. 374–7. The queen urged Charles I in 1639 to appoint him Secretary of State, H.M.C., *De Lisle MSS*, VI, p. 182.
[232] 'Madagascar. A Poem written to Prince Rupert', lines 161, 168, 169, Gibbs, *Shorter Poems*, pp. 10–21.
[233] *Ibid.*, line 54.
[234] *Ibid.*, lines 28, 257, 262.
[235] *Ibid.*, lines 41–4. The reference to Charles Louis as 'universall Admirall' may be a deliberate reference to the subject of Davenant's masque, *Britannia Triumphans*, performed in 1637. See below, ch. 5.
[236] 'Madagascar', line 135.
[237] *Ibid.*, line 244.
[238] *Ibid.*, line 38.

real concerns of a court faction attached not to 'one of Don Quixote's conquests' but to war in Europe.[239]

Active intervention in the Thirty Years War required money (the marriage of Ample and Palatine?). And money on such a scale necessitated the recalling of parliament. Within the queen's household, the Earls of Holland and Northumberland (who were both to fight for parliament in 1642) campaigned for another session of parliament to which the king appeared, for much of the decade, averse.[240] Davenant evidently recognized both the need for and value of parliaments. In his ode to Charles I, as we have seen, he wished for another session. In the same year, almost certainly 1629,[241] Davenant addressed a lengthy rebuke 'To him who Prophecy'd a Successles End of the Parliament'. The object of the attack is almost certainly Alexander Leighton, who was prosecuted in 1630 for his *An Appeal to the Parliament*, printed in Holland in 1628.[242] Davenant saw Leighton as one of those 'fiery spirits' identified by D'Ewes who had wrecked the session of 1629 by 'false fear' and so had led the king to suspect parliament's value.[243] Davenant takes it on himself to be the 'prophet' of that 'Great Senate', but reminds them too of their duties and of the threats to the realm:

> And not the fulness of your Loves express
> By mourning for your Purses emptiness.
> When Thrones are rich, the People richer grow;
>
> . . .
>
> See o're your Heads the Western Eagle fly;
> First towring up, then compassing the Sky.
> Unless our Royal Falcon strait prepare
> To struggle with him in his Native Ayre,
> He will inlarge his growth, new imp his Wings,
> And make the *Hague* an hospital for Kings.[244]

---

[239] *Cal. Stat. Pap. Dom. 1635–6*, p. 321. Above, note 229.

[240] Smuts, 'Puritan followers of Henrietta Maria', pp. 38–9; *Cal. Stat. Pap. Venet. 1636–9*, pp. 124–5, 136. Laud had anticipated a parliament as early as March 1635, *The Works of William Laud*, VII, p. 118.

[241] There is a problem over the date of both 'To the King on New Yeares day 1630' and 'To him who Prophecy'd a Successles End of the Parliament, in the Year 1630'. Charles dissolved parliament in March 1629 and did not recall one until 1640. Gibbs suggests that 'Davenant was expecting, or expressing the hope, that a more pliant Parliament would be recalled in 1630'. But the other possibility he advances that the titles to the poems may have not been given until the 1673 folio of Davenant's works seems much more convincing, for the poem 'To him who Prophecy'd a Successles End' seems clearly addressed to Leighton and to concern the session of 1629. (*Shorter Poems*, pp. 123–4.)

[242] A. Leighton, *An Appeal to the Parliament; or Sions Plea against the Prelacie* (London, 1628); see *Cal. Stat. Pap. Dom. 1629–31*, p. 379.

[243] J. O. Halliwell, ed., *The Autobiography and Correspondence of Sir Simonds D'Ewes* (2 vols., London, 1845), I, p. 402; 'To him who Prophecy'd', line 14, *Shorter Poems*, p. 123.

[244] 'To him who Prophecy'd', lines 53–72. The eagle was the symbol of the Habsburgs whose power had reached its height in 1629 with the Edict of Restitution. The Hague was where the King and Queen of Bohemia, Frederick the Elector Palatine and Elizabeth (sister to Charles I) were living in exile.

Parliaments which alone could finance the crusade against the Habsburgs are urged to look beyond 'their own shores' and purses.[245] Davenant wished for Charles I in 1629 a session of '*Praetors*, who will the publique cause defend, / With timely gifts, not Speeches finely pend'.[246] The session of 1629 failed and parliament was not recalled.[247] But, like others within the queen's household, Davenant continued to place hopes in the 'Great Senate' for the proper ordering of affairs abroad – and, as the 1630s moved on, at home.[248]

By 1640 personal rule was at an end. The war that in the end necessitated the recall of parliament was not the crusade against the Habsburgs but a campaign against the king's own Scottish subjects who had risen in rebellion against the Prayer Book. The Short Parliament of 1640 proved no more successful nor enduring than its predecessor of 1629. But this time personal rule was not an alternative. The Scots invaded England and the king had not the means to resist them; parliament was recalled for November. The signs were not auspicious. The king seemed set to stand firm on his prerogatives and there were privy councillors, most notably the Earl of Strafford, likely to reinforce his inclination.[249]

Other courtiers, however, pursued a different course. During the winter of 1640 to 1641 newsletters report plans to appoint the Earls of Bedford and Leicester, Lord Saye and John Pym, to high office in order to 'make us now hope for a happy success of this Parliament and . . . to make up an entire union between the King and his people'. Important among the movers and supporters of this scheme were Henry Jermyn (to whom Davenant addressed verse) and Sir John Suckling who, sure that 'the great interest of the King is union with his people', prayed that Charles may not be 'too resolved of what is within him'. At some point late in 1640 or early in 1641 Davenant contributed to the debate and attempted to resolve the political impasse by his own appeal to the queen to mediate.[250] This is the purpose of an important poem.[251] Davenant begins from that sympathetic appreciation of the loneli-

---

[245] 'To him who Prophecy'd', line 64.

[246] 'To the King', lines 25–6, Gibbs, *Shorter Poems*, p. 32.

[247] See Christopher Thompson, 'The divided leadership of the House of Commons in 1629', in Sharpe, *Faction and Parliament*, pp. 245–84; Conrad Russell, *Parliaments and English Politics 1621–29* (Oxford, 1979), ch. 7.

[248] 'To him who Prophecy'd', line 46; cf. the reference to the 'city-senate' in *The Unfortunate Lovers*, Act III, Scene I, *Dramatic Works*, III, p. 46.

[249] Strafford had advised Charles I in 1640 that if the Short Parliament failed in its duty to supply the king, 'then he was justified before God and man if he sought means to help himself, though it were against their wills', quoted in S. R. Gardiner, *History of England from the Accession of James I to the Outbreak of the Civil War 1603–1642* (10 vols., London, 1883–4), IX, p. 120; cf. IX, pp. 74–5.

[250] H.M.C., *De Lisle and Dudley*, VI, pp. 365–9; *Cal. Stat. Pap. Dom. 1640–1*, pp. 521–2, Suckling's memorandum (I owe this reference to Conrad Russell). Suckling argued that any who advised the king against union with his people 'was a seducer from the first'. Cf. Davenant's defence of his role in the Army Plot, below, p. 100.

[251] 'To the Queen', Gibbs, *Shorter Poems*, pp. 139–40; see also p. 412.

ness of monarchs and the problems of counsel which he had explored in his drama:

> Madam; so much peculiar and alone
> Are Kings, so uncompanion'd in a Throne,
> That through the want of some equality
> (Familiar Guides, who lead them to comply)
> They may offend by being so sublime,
> As if to be a King might be a crime.[252]

Because 'All less then Kings no more with Kings prevaile', Davenant appeals to the queen 'To cure this high obnoxious singleness' for which he criticized Charles I.[253] The queen, an equal in marriage as well as regality, could be the natural counsellor of moderation free of any suspicion of a desire to erode the prerogative.[254] Davenant urges her to persuade the king '(in the Peoples cause) / Not to esteeme his Judges more than laws', to advise him 'to new forme his Crown' by an alloy of law and prerogative that may make it all the stronger.[255] The queen's intervention was needed because others close to the king counselled a ruinous obduracy – '*Court-Sophisters* who say / When Princes yield, Subjects no more obey'. Davenant appears to allude to Strafford, who was held responsible (not entirely fairly) for the king's rigidity, and whom the Commons tried for treason. Like Northumberland perhaps Davenant believed that such 'acurst' counsellors must pay the price. Nor could the queen shrink from it:

> Madame, you that studied Heaven and Times
> Know there is Punishment, and there are Crimes.
> You are become (which doth augment your state)
> The Judges Judge, and Peoples Advocate.[256]

By her counsel and mediation the queen might secure a settlement which would be her own 'triumph'. The alternative, Davenant prognosticated all too well, might 'cost others Blood'.[257]

In his criticisms of the king's reluctance to compromise, and his attack on advisers who counselled rigidity, Davenant no doubt voiced the grievances of the puritan peers within the queen's household who had become progress-

---

[252] *Ibid.*, lines 1–6.

[253] *Ibid.*, lines 7, 11. Cf. Suckling's sense of the difficulty of counselling kings ('it is not always proper to tell how ill they are') and his concern about Charles's excess resolution, *Cal. Stat. Pap. Dom. 1640–1*, pp. 521–2.

[254] The equality of the love relationship should never be forgotten when reading the love poetry or the drama of love and marriage. Below, ch. 6.

[255] 'To the Queen', lines 17–18, 27. Compare this poem with Carew's 'Upon my Lord Chiefe Justice', discussed below, pp. 142–3.

[256] 'To the Queen', lines 43–6. It may be of significance here that on 14 January 1641 Lord Keeper Finch was impeached (Gardiner, *History of England*, IX, p. 263). For Thomas Carew's attitude to Finch, see below, pp. 142–3.

[257] *Ibid.*, line 50.

ively alienated from Charles I since the Scots war and who were bitter enemies of Strafford.[258] He echoed the counsel to moderation of Jermyn and others. But Davenant articulated his own fears, and his own values too. In 1640–1 that dislocation that had always haunted him loomed as an immediate prospect. The 'obnoxious singleness' of the ruler and the disreputable counsel of courtiers brought it nearer. In his own plays, Davenant would have recalled those queens and models of feminine fortitude who had by their own example led dukes and kings to 'new-forme' their rule. Marriage, as we have seen, raised men to their higher nature; queens, Davenant reminded Henrietta Maria in 1640, 'prevaile by Nature'.[259] Marriage too expressed that union between virtue and rule, between royal prerogative and law that now the poet so urgently advocated. Who better than the royal spouse then to effect in 1640 the reconciliation and union so clearly represented in the royal marriage itself? In the masques of the 1630s, the love of king and queen had dispelled the disorder of antimasque. Now Davenant urged that the visions of Whitehall become reality, that art become life and, as he had so often advocated, representation become reality.

The reconciliation which he sought did not materialize. The royal marriage, the subject of many masques, did not prevent divorce within the body politic. Indeed the queen herself rejected Davenant's counsel of moderation and her own former clients, the 'puritan' peers. Ironically for Davenant, at a time when the king and his parliaments were drifting further apart, the king and the queen were becoming politically closer. Henrietta Maria, far from emerging as the people's advocate, became the staunchest maintainer of a prerogative which she was prepared to defend by violence. Rashly she plotted to appoint the Earl of Newcastle as commander of the northern army, with instructions to lead the troops south to secure London and save Strafford.[260] Startlingly Davenant was implicated in the Army Plot and charged by the Commons with treason.[261] Davenant's part remains unclear. But in his 'Humble Remonstrance' 'To the Honourable Knights, Citizens, and Burgesses of the House of Commons' Davenant disclaimed not only any treasonable rôle in the plot, but any words or actions 'irreverently or maliciously against Parliamentary government'. The poet claimed that his alleged co-conspirators, Henry Jermyn and Sir John Suckling, 'have so often extol'd the naturall necessity of Parliaments here, with extreame scorne upon the incapacity of any that should perswade the King he could be fortunate without them'. He reminded the House of his own position and his own recent poems 'wrot to the Queenes Majesty in praise of her inclination to become the People's

[258] Gardiner, *History of England*, IX, ch. 42.
[259] 'To the Queen', line 15.
[260] See Gardiner, *History of England*, IX, pp. 312–17.
[261] Nethercot, *Sir William Davenant*, pp. 189–98; Harbage, *Sir William Davenant*, pp. 79–85.

advocate'.[262] Though some were sceptical, Davenant's 'Remonstrance' secured his release. It has been described by his biographer as the work of a 'smooth tongue and silver pen' – as, that is, a supreme example of that very dissimulation attacked by the playwright for more than a decade.[263] Before we endorse that judgement or reject Davenant's defence as the insincere apologia of a 'court flunky' engaged in treasonable conspiracy against the people's liberty, we might do well to reconsider Davenant's life work: his attitudes to the court, to government, to the king and queen and the issues of the 1630s. For then we must conclude that if loyalty and principle led Davenant to the king's and queen's side, it was never blind love, nor uncritical loyalty, nor a slavish support for prerogative unqualified by law.

GONDIBERT: ETHICS AND POLITICS AS EPIC

After 1642 Davenant's private and public worlds were both turned upside down, thrown into the disorder he had fought to dispel by his art, his counsel and his intervention. Exiled, captured, imprisoned and under threat of execution, Davenant's fortunes followed those of his king all but to the scaffold. A few months after the execution of his monarch, Davenant lost to death, by natural causes, his Maecenas, his long-standing patron and friend, Endymion Porter.[264] The dislocation of his life drove Davenant back to the order of the Muses. In 1648 or 1649, in exile in Paris, he began to embark upon the most ambitious enterprise of his literary career: *Gondibert: An Heroick Poem*, an epic of (a projected) five books.[265]

Gondibert was an attempt, as the preface boldly announces,[266] to combine the highest forms of literature in one poem: lofty style, an interwoven stanza of four lines, and the five-act form of the drama translated into five books, each divided by cantos as the acts of a play are by scenes.[267] Davenant did not want for ambition. He invokes, as his models, the names of Homer, Virgil and Lucan, of Statius, Tasso and Spenser.[268] He draws upon the work of men of science and philosophers: there are echoes and reflections in his poem of

[262] 'To the Honourable Knights, Citizens, and Burgesses of the House of Commons Assembled in Parliament. The Humble Remonstrance of William Davenant, Anno 1641', printed in full in Hotson, 'Sir William Davenant and the commonwealth stage', pp. 33–4.

[263] Nethercot, *Sir William Davenant*, p. 193. It is indicative of the rapidly altered political circumstances that Jermyn, Suckling and Davenant, who all counselled conciliation during the winter of 1640–1, were involved in the Army Plot revealed in May.

[264] Porter died in August 1649.

[265] Sir W. Davenant, *Gondibert: An Heroick Poem* (1651), ed. D. F. Gladish (Oxford, 1971). All quotations are from this edition. I hope to write further on Gondibert as a case study, together with Milton's *Paradise Lost*, of the poetics and politics of exile.

[266] 'The Author's Preface To His Much Honor'd friend, M. Hobbes', Gladish, *Gondibert*, pp. 3–44. The preface was printed in 1650, before the poem.

[267] *Gondibert*, preface, lines 496–505, 549, pp. 16–17.

[268] *Ibid.*, pp. 4–7.

Pliny, Gabriel Harvey and Thomas Browne, Francis Bacon and Thomas Hobbes.[269] Hobbes read and criticized the entire text as a co-exile with Davenant in Paris.[270] The end product of these ambitious aims and learned influences all but defies description. David Gladish, the editor of *Gondibert*, comments that 'under the mask of historicity, the poem is a prodigious collection of literary, philosophical, and historical bits and pieces'.[271] If this is unsatisfying, it is impossible in brief to say more. The poem expresses an ethical, political and aesthetic philosophy through a love story involving the conflict of love and honour in the life of Gondibert, King of the Lombards. Like Davenant's plays, from which the names of characters are here borrowed, Gondibert offers didactic counsel in a seemingly conventional story of duty and honour, love and passion. Like his earlier plays and poems it reflects immediate political circumstances as well as, or perhaps more accurately in the context of, the universal questions of morality in private and public life. It has been suggested that the entire poem may be a political allegory, a plea to Charles II to rescue England from the horrors and anarchy of the commonwealth.[272] The fictitious characters, it is said, may be exact representations of those who played the drama in life: Gondibert of Charles II, Princess Rhodalind of Henrietta Maria. Certain passages seem clearly to allegorize specific historical events: the hunting of the stag in the second canto of Book I strongly suggests the pursuit of Charles I. Suggestions of this sort are undoubtedly convincing in general, even if they do not seem to work out so well in particular.[273] They would repay further investigation; but they need not detain us now. What must concern us, if only by way of a postscript to our essay, are the values and attitudes expressed in *Gondibert* but more particularly, because there more lucidly and more consciously articulated, in the preface to the poem addressed by Davenant to Thomas Hobbes. In the preface to his epic, Davenant took pains to explain his purpose and his plan – or in his own metaphor the 'provisions' and the 'form' of his 'building'.[274] And in this preface, for all the evidence of attitudes altered or hardened by personal experience and recent historical circumstance, we may read the clearest statement of ethical, political and aesthetic values that had informed Davenant's work from his first venture upon the stage.

The poet, Hobbes told Davenant, if he is to preach a doctrine of moral virtue,

[269] *Gondibert*, p. xi.
[270] Davenant acknowledges that 'you have done me the Honour to allow This Poem a daylie examination as it was writing . . .'
[271] *Gondibert*, p. xiii.
[272] *Ibid.*, p. xv.
[273] *Ibid.*
[274] *Ibid.*, preface, pp. 18, 20.

'must take the Philosopher's part'.[275] *Gondibert*, conceived and produced
under Hobbes's influence, obeys this dictate. It is a philosophical treatise,
albeit one which systematized rather than fundamentally altered Davenant's
long-held beliefs. It crystallizes attitudes that we have seen sprinkled over a
dozen plays and poems across more than a decade. In *Gondibert* and the
preface to Hobbes, Davenant associates the good with the natural. Men are
inclined by nature to virtue. Beauty, that is the beauty of the soul as well as the
body, is nature's expression; it leads men to virtue.[276] Virtue, as here defined,
consists not in retreat or contemplation: it must be active, indeed efficacious.[277] In the sphere of personal ethics, virtue is synonymous with love.
Love is active; it engenders; it unites the soul and the body. Love is that 'by
which Life's name does valew finde'.[278] Love expresses man's higher nature:
'love is the most acceptable imposition of nature, the cause and preservation
of Life, and the very healthfulnesse, of the minde, as well as of the body'.[279]
And so love is the perfect expression of the active virtue of man. Love must
not be confused with the undisciplined licence of the passions, of man's lower
nature. Passions, though part of man's nature, subvert man himself when
they are ungoverned. In the drama Davenant had employed lust and love as
his metaphors for government and self-government. Now, as he states
explicitly, the characters of men who did not know how to regulate themselves, 'I have derived from the distempers of love, or Ambition'.[280] Love,
then, as we saw in the plays, is the governance of the passions, but not the
denial of the senses; it is the expression of man's nature regulated by his
reason. It is the reconciliation of nature and order. Love and government are
therefore closely related, indeed are one. Love's mode of government is
marriage, as lust's preferred polity is anarchic liberty.[281] Marriage is willing
restraint because, as Androlio put it in *The Distresses*, it tames the beast in
man.[282] Obedience, 'like the marriage yoke is a restraint more needful and
advantageous than liberty; and hath the same reward of pleasant quietness,
which it anciently had, when Adam till his disobedience, injoyed Paradise'.[283]
Before the Fall, nature and order, liberty and government were one. By

---

[275] 'The Answer of Mr. Hobbes to Sir Will. D'avenant's Preface Before Gondibert', lines 182–3,
   ibid., p. 50.
[276] *Ibid.*, pp. 7–8, 13, 42.
[277] 'The world is only ill govern'd because the wicked take more paines to get authority, then the
   vertuous; for the vertuous are often preach'd into retirement; which is to the publique as
   unprofitable as their sleep', *ibid.*, p. 14.
[278] *Gondibert*, First Book, Canto IV, p. 91.
[279] *Ibid.*, p. 15.
[280] *Ibid.*, p. 13.
[281] *Ibid.*, p. 15.
[282] *The Distresses*, Act V, Scene I; *Dramatic Works*, IV, p. 362.
[283] *Gondibert*, p. 30.

returning to their innocent nature through love men might come closer to that ideal state.

The good man, as the courtiers in Davenant's plays had graphically illustrated, often had too little appetite for greatness and left the governance of the commonweal to the ambitious and wicked.[284] But virtue active in the world could, as the noble figures in the tragedies epitomize, lead others to an understanding of their wrong. Men may be reformed, as they are in the drama, by love; and love may teach men, even dukes and kings, patterns of government. The poet's rôle is to instil and promote active virtue in men, in society and in the polity. And so, Davenant tells us, poets write of love and of beauty which express men's higher nature and lead them to self-regulation. Beauty and nature have influence and poets may elevate men because poesy 'like contracted essences seemes the utmost strength and activity of Nature'.[285] Poetry, in other words, can itself lead men to the active virtue of their higher nature through images of beauty and love. Hobbes, in his answer to Davenant's preface, caught the purpose of the poem and encapsulated Davenant's philosophy of ethics: 'to adorne vertue, and procure her Lovers'.[286]

If virtue had the best claim to rule, where in the polity was virtue to be found? If the good men, rulers of their own passions, required neither law nor religion, how were those who were not virtuous to be governed? To the first of these questions Davenant had a clear answer, and one which helps us to understand his drama. Courts were the models for political life, he now maintains, because in its best form, the court is the political expression of the ideal of virtue. Courts set the patterns of virtue for others, especially those who were to govern the realm.[287] Courts were 'fit to be imitated by the most necessary Men; and the most necessary men are those who become principall by prerogative of blood (which is seldom unassisted with education) or by greatnes of minde, which in exact definition is Vertue'.[288] In so far as courts were the stages of ambition, this ought to reflect not the vicious machinations of corrupt schemers, but the virtuous strivings of great minds who laboured in 'the rough ways of honour over the impediments of fortune'. Courts, Davenant knew all too well, did not always live up to the ideal. Courts could 'by weak Counc'lers err';[289] favourites could close the king's ears to suits and grievances.[290] But courts were not in themselves corrupt and even the abuses

[284] *Ibid.*, p. 13.
[285] *Ibid.*, p. 40. Since love too is the expression of nature, poetry is concerned with love. Cf. Hobbes's 'Answer', p. 50.
[286] *Gondibert*, p. 48.
[287] Davenant calls them 'the most effectuall Schooles of Morality' (*ibid.*, p. 12).
[288] *Ibid.*, p. 13.
[289] *Gondibert*, Second Book, Canto II, verse 14, p. 126.
[290] *Ibid.*, Third Book, Canto VI, verse 8, p. 242.

and wrongs they harboured might at times be defended in the name of necessity:

Courts . . . are not the Schooles where men are bred to oppression, but the Temples where some times Oppressors take Sanctuary; a safety which our reason must allow them. For the ancient laws of Sanctuary . . . provided chiefly for actions that proceeded from necessity.[291]

There is a tone here in Davenant's argument that we have not detected before: an acknowledgement that politics might at times involve unethical actions for the sake of order or the preservation of the state. It is clear that the recognition and language of necessity, as the greater stress on the necessary ambition of rulers, reflect the experience of civil war. The experience of dislocation leads men to place a higher premium on authority. And the popular excesses of the 1640s led Davenant to a political cynicism concerning the place of the people: 'who can imagine lesse than a necessity of oppressing the people since they are never willing either to buy their peace or to pay for warre'.[292] The people were envious of courts. They believed them hostile to their liberties – but only because the mob equated their liberties with their purses. The people's idea of liberty was not the freedom of self-control but unbridled appetite and licence. Davenant depicts a populace unfit for freedom once again through the metaphor of corrupted nature and false love, as 'in a condition of Beasts whose appetite is liberty and their Liberty a licence of Lust'. The multitude, Davenant had come close to concurring with Hobbes, was a 'great beast' – in his own words, a 'monster'.[293] Such men, because they could not govern themselves, could only be left to the firm government of others. Power belonged to those endowed with nature's riches – to the wealthy and the beautiful whose outward qualities announced their inner virtues.[294] To such men was the epic poem directed; to their nature, poets, Nature's own apostles, might hope to appeal. The uncivil herd of men could not be reclaimed by Orpheus's harp. The 'common crowd (of whom we are hopelesse)' was 'rather to be corrected by laws (where precept is accompany'd with punishment)'.[295]

How then was the beast to be tamed, the people governed? Statesmen had employed as the instruments of the art of rule religion, arms, policy and law. Each had its uses, but each ultimately had failed. As for divines, 'their Christian meeknesse had deceav'd them in taming this wilde Monster the people'.[296] Armies subdued the bodies, but did not govern the minds of men.

[291] *Ibid.*, preface, p. 12.
[292] *Ibid.*
[293] *Ibid.*, p. 30.
[294] *Ibid.*, Third Book, Canto VI, p. 243.
[295] *Ibid.*, preface, p. 13.
[296] *Ibid.*, p. 30.

Statesmen and policies were subject to unstable flux and change. Offences 'are too hard for the lawes as some Beasts are too wylie for their Hunters'.[297] Besides, divines and soldiers, statesmen and legislators were often at odds with each other, and so (we may recall the poem to Richmond) 'how can these Pilots stedily maintain their Course to the land of peace and Plenty, since they are often divided at the Helme?'[298] Effective government required rulers to influence men's minds as well as order their bodies, to persuade as well as to constrain.[299] Authority, Davenant is saying, depends upon attitudes to authority and government rests upon the inculcation of desirable attitudes. And so he comes to reveal the intention behind his *Gondibert*, and the purpose of all his art: 'none are so fit aides to this important worke as Poets'.[300]

'The lastingnesse of government', Davenant concluded, 'is the principal work of art'.[301] Poets, as governors of the mind, had the responsibility for teaching patterns of virtue: 'To make great actions credible is the principall Art of poets'.[302] As the expositors of Nature, poets were best qualified to represent images of virtue.[303] The poets' world embraced not just particular men in time, but all men throughout and outside time, 'the general History of Nature'.[304] Not all forms of poetry, however, were suited to the education or reformation of all sorts of men. The heroic poem could not hope to appeal to the common man, for its comprehension required more perception than the ordinary people possessed. But qualifying his despair and fear of the mob, Davenant argued that

there are lesser forces in other kinds of Poesy, by which they may traine, and prepare their understandings; and Princes and Nobles being reform'd and made Angelicall by the Heroick, will be predominant lights, which the People cannot chuse but use for direction.[305]

Gondibert was written for such princes and nobles, for the present and future rulers of the realm. For this audience, as Hobbes acknowledged, the epic was the appropriate form: 'Great persons that have their mindes employed on great designes, have not leisure to laugh.'[306] And in such circumstances the didactic purposes of art might be effected by praise as well as criticism. 'Praise

---

[297] *Ibid.*, p. 34.
[298] *Ibid.*
[299] *Ibid.*, p. 38.
[300] *Ibid.*
[301] *Ibid.*, p. 40.
[302] *Ibid.*, p. 11. Cf. 'the wisdome of Poets, would first make the Images of Vertue so amiable that her beholders should not be able to looke off', *ibid.*, p. 39.
[303] 'Poets are of all moralists the most useful', *ibid.*, p. 41.
[304] *Ibid.*, p. 5.
[305] *Ibid.*, p. 38.
[306] Hobbes, 'Answer', p. 53.

is devotion fit for Mighty Mindes.'[307] But whether the form were comic, satiric or epic, whether the poet praised or criticized, the ethical and political function of his art remained the same: the representation of images of virtuous action.

The claims and powers of the poet lay in wit, the subject and title of earlier plays. In the preface to *Gondibert*, Davenant defines it:

Witte is not only the luck and labour, but also the dexterity of thought; rounding the world, like the sun, with unimaginable motion; and bringing swiftly home to the memory universall survays. It is the soules *Powder* . . .[308]

Wit, Davenant explains, was in divines humility, in statesmen gravity and vigilance, secrecy and patience. It was, in other words, those qualities appropriate to each man, the expression of those virtues necessary for his place. 'And it is in Poets a full comprehension of all recited in all these; and an ability to bring those comprehensions into action . . .'[309] Wit was not mere music, the empty rhetoric of words which the playwright had satirized in those who claimed to possess it: courtiers, Platonics, Trifle and Inland, Palatine and Thwack. Wit was the quality distilled by art – active virtue itself.

Discussing the preface to *Gondibert*, we may feel that we have come a long way from Davenant's plays. In some ways we have. There are allusions to and echoes of personal experiences and political upheavals which have coloured Davenant's values. We hear the language of necessity never voiced before. We sense a fear for the very survival of government and order. The danger of mob rule seems to concern him more than the idea of union between the ruler and the people. But the questions that Davenant has been examining remain constant: questions of human appetite and self-control, of virtue in private and public life, questions concerning the nature of the good ruler and of good government. And the metaphor of love and marriage through which Davenant discusses these questions forms the subject of his grandest literary venture, as of all his earlier plays.[310] Circumstances had changed and change dictated shifts of form but the artist's purpose remained unaltered.

Hobbes, who read Davenant's epic before it went to press, summarized all Davenant's work as well as his *Gondibert*. The poet's work, Hobbes argued, is 'by imitating humane life, in delightfull and measur'd lines to avert men from vice, and encline them to vertuous and honourable actions'.[311] In *Gondibert*, Hobbes read of 'settled valour, cleane Honor, calme Counsell,

---

[307] *Gondibert*, Second Book, Canto VI, Verse 89, p. 169.   [308] *Ibid.*, p. 18.   [309] *Ibid.*, p. 19.
[310] N.B. 'Mariage in Mankinde were as rude and unprepar'd as the hasty elections of other Creatures, but for acquaintance of Mindes, not of Bodys; and of the Minde, Poesy is the most naturall and delightfull Interpreter', *ibid.*, p. 42.
[311] Hobbes, 'Answer', p. 45.

learned diversion and pure Love'.[312] In order to distil virtue, poets needed to 'lodge' themselves in all the regions of mankind – in court, city and country.[313] Davenant's plays had done no less. And the fable of *Gondibert* too appeared to Hobbes 'not much unlike the Theater'.[314] During the 1640s, the theatres were closed and Davenant was off the centre of the stage. But *Gondibert* was fashioned, as Hobbes perceived, as a play. Not only had Davenant structured the books and cantos around the five acts and scenes of the play, his method of presentation throughout was that of the dramatist, disclosing scenes, drawing the curtain, standing aside, uttering a stage direction.[315] The interrelations of main plot and 'underwalks' are ordered towards a final 'untying of those particular knots which made a contexture of the whole'.[316] What better summary could there be of the author's own earlier drama? Davenant adopted the dramatic structure for *Gondibert* because, as he told Hobbes, 'I cannot discerne by any help from reading, or learned men . . . that any Nation hath in representment of great actions . . . digested Story into so pleasant and so instructive a method as the English by their *Drama*.'[317] Davenant saw a common purpose in his life's work from the tragedy *Albovine* to the heroic epic of *Gondibert*. The plays and the poems debate the issues of their age through the drama of love and passion.

[312] *Ibid.*, p. 50.   [313] *Ibid.*, p. 45.   [314] *Ibid.*, p. 50.
[315] *Gondibert*, preface, p. 16; see Gladish, 'Commentary', p. 294.
[316] *Ibid.*, p. 16.   [317] *Ibid.*, p. 15.

3

Thomas Carew and the poetry of love and nature

Of all the Caroline poets and playwrights few could claim a more intimate association with the court of Charles I than Thomas Carew.[1] For Carew was in the most exact sense a courtier: as gentleman extraordinary of the Privy Chamber and then as Sewer in Ordinary to the king he attended personally upon the king in the royal privy lodgings and so enjoyed a rare and familiar access to the monarch in a court otherwise characterized by rigid formality and privacy.[2] Carew's name on the Lord Chamberlain's roll of those entitled to lodgings and bouge of court – to daily diet and livery – would have released him from Davenant's need to dodge the bailiff for being in London out of season.[3] More importantly, it freed him from the necessity of earning a living. Carew could undoubtedly have been one of those courtly gentlemen who, in Pope's somewhat disdainful description, 'wrote with ease'. He was the epitome of the amateur court poet.

But if Carew was undoubtedly of the court, his biography does not read like that of a model courtier. Nor does his contemporary reputation reflect the image of the court of Charles I as ordered and regulated, ceremonial and chaste. Controversy surrounded Tom Carew from his earliest steps towards preferment. He did not want for valuable connections. Born in 1594 or 1595, the son of Sir Matthew Carew, a Doctor of Civil Law and Master in Chancery, Tom proceeded in 1608 to Merton College, whose warden, Sir

[1] There are two book length studies of Carew: I. Selig, *The Flourishing Wreath: A Study of Thomas Carew's Poetry* (Hamden, Conn., 1970), and L. Sadler, *Thomas Carew* (Boston, 1979). The best short life is to be found in the introduction to R. Dunlap, ed., *The Poems of Thomas Carew* (Oxford, 1949). See also B.L., Add. MS 24,489 (Hunter's Lives). This chapter is an expanded and revised version of my 'Cavalier critic? The ethics and politics of Thomas Carew's poetry', published in *Politics of Discourse*. I am grateful to Steven Zwicker and the University of California Press for permission to use it here.
[2] See Sharpe, 'The court and household of Charles I'.
[3] See 'The Long Vacation in London', lines 67–70 in Gibbs, *Sir William Davenant. The Shorter Poems*, p. 127.

Henry Savile, was related to the Carew family. His father intending him to
follow him in a legal career, Carew went on to the Middle Temple in 1612.
Within months, however, Sir Matthew was complaining that his son 'I feare
studieth the law very little'.[4] And the following year Tom travelled to Italy to
become secretary to Dudley Carleton, ambassador to Venice, who had
married Sir Matthew's niece. In Italy, Carew also made the acquaintance of
Thomas Howard, Earl of Arundel, heir to the dukedom of Norfolk, and scion
of the senior noble house of the realm, who was then travelling on the
continent, with Inigo Jones in his train.[5] Carew evidently impressed both
Arundel and Carleton, whom he subsequently accompanied to the Nether-
lands in 1615 when Carleton took up a post as envoy to the Hague. Carew's
very promising career, however, was here shattered by an indiscretion. The
details remain unclear.[6] But it appears that Carew had committed to paper
reflections which cast aspersions on Sir Dudley and Lady Carleton who, on
discovering the document, sent Thomas back to England in August 1616.
Carew tried to repair the damage to his fortune by making overtures for
favour first to another relative, his cousin Lord George Carew, Master of the
Ordnance, and then to Thomas Howard, Earl of Arundel, who had returned
to England in 1614, on the death of his great-uncle Henry, Earl of Nor-
thampton.[7] Arundel promised his assistance, but subsequently came to hear
through Edward Sherborne (to whom Carleton had reported the incident) of
Carew's disloyalty to his former patron. Such hopes as Tom might have
entertained of Arundel's support were dashed.[8] During the following months
Sir Matthew, whose own fortunes were in decline, attempted to atone for his
son's misdemeanours by a series of apologetic letters to Carleton. Tom
himself, however, remained unrepentantly stubborn, 'puffed up with to
miche pryde' as his father put it, and apparently drifted for some time into a
life of debauchery, on the fringes of the court.[9] It was evidently at this time
that he contracted syphilis, for in October 1617 Carew's long-suffering father
reports his son afflicted by 'a new disease com in amongst us, by the which I
pray God that he may be chastised to amend his lyfe . . .'[10] We do not know
for sure whether Carew amended his life.[11] But he evidently quite quickly
recovered his fortunes. For on 4 November 1616 Carew attended Charles at
his investiture as Prince of Wales, as squire to Lord Beaumont, and was

[4] Matthew Carew to Dudley Carleton, 25 Feb. 1612, P.R.O., S.P. 14/72/44, quoted in Dunlap,
Poems of Carew (hereafter Dunlap), p. xviii.
[5] On Arundel, see Hervey, *Thomas Howard, Earl of Arundel*.
[6] Dunlap, pp. xxi–xxii; Sadler, *Carew*, p. 13.
[7] Dunlap, p. xxiii; K. Sharpe, 'The Earl of Arundel, his circle and the opposition to the Duke of
Buckingham, 1621–8', *Faction and Parliament*, pp. 209–44.
[8] Dunlap, p. xxv.
[9] Matthew Carew to Carleton, 7 Nov. 1616, P.R.O., S.P. 14/89/10, quoted in Dunlap, p. xxvii.
[10] Matthew Carew to Carleton, 4 Oct. 1617, P.R.O., S.P. 14/93/112, Dunlap, p. xxvii.
[11] Sadler, *Carew*, p. 16.

singled out by that unrivalled clairvoyant of court fortunes, John Chamberlain, as one 'of high degree for cost and bravery'.[12] In May 1619, a year after the death of his despairing father, Thomas departed in the train of Sir Edward Herbert (later Lord Herbert of Cherbury), who was going as ambassador to Paris.[13]

Carew's shipwrecked career was relaunched. And Herbert, himself a poet as well as a philosopher, may have encouraged Carew's literary endeavours as much as he revived his fortunes. During his sojourn in France, a period of perhaps four or five years, Carew made the acquaintance of John Crofts, who wrote hymns set to music by Lawes, and was probably introduced to the literary circles of Paris. We know for certain that Carew wrote two poems at this time and the dating of manuscript anthologies might suggest several more.[14] Herbert was recalled from Paris in 1624 and then, if not before, Carew returned to England. Rumours that winter that he intended to marry a rich widow suggest the renewed quest for a living, and the suggestion is confirmed by Clarendon.[15] Thomas Carew, he informs us, 'returning from Travel, followed the court; which the Modesty of that Time disposed Men to do some Time, before They pretended to be of it'.[16] During this time Carew befriended the wits of the town and spent his time among the circles of Ben Jonson and John Selden, Thomas May and Sir Kenelm Digby, and of Edward Hyde (future Earl of Clarendon) himself, upon whose account we depend for our knowledge of Carew's activities.[17] Hyde, we recall, shared lodgings with William Davenant at the Temple in the late 1620s, so it is not surprising to learn that Carew was also introduced to Davenant and to Aurelian Townshend, to both of whom in the early 1630s he addressed verses which commend their friendship.[18] Carew's literary friends were indeed ones of 'eminent faculties'.

More importantly for his political fortunes, Carew also won friends in high places during the years after his return from France. In Clarendon's words, 'He was very much esteemed by the most eminent Persons in the Court, and well looked upon by the King himself.'[19] Such favour inevitably and eventually brought its reward. On 6 April 1630 Carew was granted a warrant for the place of 'A gent of ye Privy Chamber extraordinary' and soon after obtained the place of Sewer in Ordinary to the king, that is personal waiter to the royal

---

[12] John Chamberlain to Dudley Carleton, 9 Nov. 1616, P.R.O., S.P. 14/89/17.
[13] Dunlap, p. xxxi.
[14] *Ibid.*, p. xxxii, lxviii-lxxv.
[15] Sadler, *Carew*, p. 15.
[16] *The Life of Edward, Earl of Clarendon* (Oxford, 1761), p. 36.
[17] *Ibid.*, p. 36.
[18] Harbage, *Sir William Davenant*, p. 37; Nethercot, *Sir William Davenant*, p. 67; 'To my worthy friend M. D'Avenant, Upon his Excellent Play, The Just Italian', Dunlap, p. 95; 'In Answer of An Elegiacall Letter' (*ibid.*, p. 74).
[19] *Life of Clarendon*, p. 36.

table.[20] It was a mark of special royal favour, for Charles I took great care over appointments to his domestic service and promoted Carew in the face of a rival candidate put forward by the Scots, who were a powerful group within the privy lodgings.[21] The king, perhaps, had already got to know Carew well. If anecdote is to be trusted, Carew's position brought him early experience of court intrigue and hypocrisy. Among the papers of the Earl of Egmont, in a volume of characters, we find a story of Carew's lighting the king to his chamber one evening, only to discover Henrietta Maria in an embrace with her favourite, Henry Jermyn. Carew, the story goes, feigned a fall and, stumbling, extinguished the taper and so enabled Jermyn to escape in the dark. 'The Queen heaped favours on Carew,' we are told.[22] It is an enticing tale, but the story is supported by little else than the other rumours which surrounded Jermyn's relationship with the queen. True or false, however, the account is a vivid reminder of the intimacy which a man in Carew's position enjoyed with the king and queen, and an illustration of the importance of such a domestic post and of the delicate tact it might require. Despite his earlier failings on that score, Carew evidently passed the tests. As he followed the court, Carew formed a close friendship with Charles I, and evidently a personal bond of loyalty which transcended the duty of subject to sovereign. Carew attended the king on the expedition against the Scots in 1639 and it may be that the conditions suffered in 'the cold nights out by the banks of Tweed' hastened his death in March 1640.[23] Charles I personally grieved at Carew's death, as he had evidently admired him in life. The king, as well as other favours, had bestowed upon him the royal manor of Sunninghill in the forest of Windsor, having, in the words of Anthony Wood, the Oxford antiquary, 'always esteemed him to the last one of the most celebrated wits in his court'.[24]

Charles I's favourable evaluation of his servant was echoed by many of Carew's contemporaries. Clarendon believed that Carew's poems 'for the Sharpness of the Fancy, and the Elegancy of the Language, in which that Fancy was spread, were at least equal, if not superior to any of that Time'.[25] Aurelian Townshend, a friend and fellow poet, praised Carew's 'sweete' verses, which he contrasted with the 'Rough footed satires' of the age.[26] William Davenant, Thomas Randolph, James Shirley and his patron Lord Herbert all bore testimony to that 'excellent wit' which made Carew one of

[20] P.R.O., Lord Chamberlain's Dept., L.C. 5/132, pp. 180–1.
[21] *Life of Clarendon*, p. 36.
[22] H.M.C., *Seventh Report, Part I* (London, 1879), p. 244, manuscripts of the Earl of Egmont at St James's Palace.
[23] See 'To my friend G.N. from Wrest', below, pp. 128–30.
[24] T. Wood, *Athenae Oxonienses*, ed. P. Bliss, (2 vols., London, 1815), II, p. 658; *D.N.B.*
[25] *Life of Clarendon*, p. 36.
[26] 'Elegy on the death of the King of Sweden', lines 7–10, in C. Brown (ed.), *The Poems and Masques of Aurelian Townshend* (Reading, 1983), p. 48.

the most popular poets of his day.[27] Even Suckling, who in the '(The Wits) A Sessions of the Poets' denied Carew, along with all others, the crown of the Muses, paid him the backhanded compliment of acknowledging the 'trouble and pain' which Carew devoted to his art.[28] Critics since have been less appreciative. During the 1640s Carew appears to have represented all that the puritans disliked about the Caroline court; and he was remembered generally for his reputation as a profligate and particularly for his erotic poem, 'A Rapture'. Dismissed as one 'who pleas'd faire ladies with his courtly muse', Carew was charged with bringing

> Effeminate desires, and thoughts uncleane,
> To minds that earst were pure, and most serene.[29]

Carew's reputation since has never entirely escaped the taints of those charges, of frivolity, lightness and immorality. Even today, though there is a complete edition of his verse, Carew is more often sampled through the pages of poetic anthologies. And though F. R. Leavis argued powerfully for his superior intelligence and distinctiveness, Carew is more often studied as one of that indistinguishable quartet of 'cavalier poets' than investigated independently.[30]

The phrase 'cavalier poetry', as we have suggested, has all too often been employed to define and prejudge rather than to analyse the verse. Like 'cavalier dramatists', the 'cavalier poets', Carew and Herrick, Lovelace and Suckling, are dismissed as a court coterie, pandering only to court tastes, the last decadent echoes of an era of greatness. Where Jonson and Donne spoke substantially and forthrightly, their Caroline successors, it is argued, voiced slavishly the trivial concerns of the courtly gallants and flattery of their patrons and monarch. Amidst such general charges, Carew has been singled out for particular attack. Douglas Bush saw his strengths only in the bequests of his greater predecessors: 'Without Donne, Carew's best poems would have lost much but ... without Jonson he would not have been a poet at all.'[31]

---

[27] Dunlap, pp. xlvi–xlviii.
[28]   *Tom Carew* was next, but he had a fault
       That would not well stand with a laureat;
       His Muse was hard bound, and th'issue of 's brain
       Was seldom brought forth but with trouble and pain ...'
       ('(The Wits) (A Sessions of the Poets)', lines 33–6,
       The Non-Dramatic Works of Sir John Suckling, pp. 72–3).
[29] *The Great Assizes Holden in Parnassus by Apollo and his assessours* (1645), cited Dunlap, p. xlviii. Sir Edward Dering named Carew in the Long Parliament as a lascivious and idle poet, Sadler, *Carew*, p. 142. See J. E. Ruoff, 'Thomas Carew's early reputation', *Notes and Queries*, 202 (1957), pp. 61–2.
[30] F. R. Leavis, 'The line of wit', in *Revaluation* (London, 1962), pp. 10–41. Leavis writes of 'remarkable strength' in the 'light grace' of the verse, which entitles Carew to 'more distinction than he is commonly awarded' (pp. 15–16). Clayton, *Cavalier Poets*, introduction.
[31] Bush, *English Literature in the Earlier Seventeenth Century*, p. 120.

George Parfitt dismissed his verse, along with other 'cavalier poetry', as
poetry exhibiting 'a narrowing of range of reference and interest ... and a
consequent concentration upon relatively few areas of emotional experience'.[32] Even for Carew's editor, Rhodes Dunlap, 'admiration is still cooled',
not only by the offensive libertinism of the verse, but by 'an ethos circumscribed and corrupted by a hundred random influences of literary and social
fashion'.[33] The critical consensus, therefore, if it has not condemned Carew
to total exile, has confined him to those minor and barren territories, little
visited, uninviting and significant more as the satellites of greater powers than
for themselves.

Not until 1970 did an explorer search him out and make Carew the subject
of independent investigation. The title of E. I. Selig's monograph, taken from
Carew's poem to Sir George Sandys, *The Flourishing Wreath*, itself promised
a pioneering investigation, the metaphor expressing the antithesis of that
decadent and withering culture in which Carew had hitherto been placed.[34]
Indeed a better sense of historical context, Selig argued, might lead to a
greater appreciation rather than reinforced condemnation of Carew's poetic
genius. Making a distinction between form and treatment of form, Selig
argued for Carew's sensitivity to the conventions – of verse compliment for
example – and his skill in transcending and undermining whilst working
within those conventions. Subject and style, matter and tone in Carew's
poetry are as often in debate and in tension as in concord. And Selig argued
for a recognition of that playful irony through which the reader is invited to a
deeper and more serious contemplation of the subject than Carew is credited
with by those who read him deaf to its tone. *The Flourishing Wreath*
identified in Carew's poetry a tension passed over before, a tension which
Selig described as that between the singing voice and the speaking voice: 'the
singing voice of the poet in Carew's songs derives a certain vitality from its
being forced at all times to contend with the speaking voice, with the
recalcitrant world of statement'.[35] Tensions and debate are not the obvious
instruments of flattery, the object of which is to mirror an individual's own
vision of the world, or to represent reality as in harmony with the reader's
own voice. Not surprisingly, then, Selig attempted to prove Carew innocent
of servility by drawing a clear distinction between flattery, the discourse of
servitude, and compliment, the style of equals. Love poetry, whilst it may at
times employ the language of the former, expresses a relationship of equals.
And the voice of Carew's poetry, as we shall argue, was not a meek voice of
subservience but a voice of authority.

[32] Parfitt, 'The poetry of Thomas Carew', pp. 56–68.
[33] Dunlap, p. lii.
[34] Selig, *Flourishing Wreath;* 'To my worthy friend Master Geo Sands, on his translation of the
      Psalms', line 36; Dunlap, p. 94.
[35] Selig, *Flourishing Wreath*, p. 59.

The identification of more than one voice in Carew's poetry clearly caused some discomfort. For Selig himself it raised more problems than could be resolved, and it raises more than he acknowledged. Carew adopts a range of tones and voices: the complimentary and the gently satirical, the erotic and the Platonic, the frivolous and the intellectual. How are we to accommodate these ambiguities and tensions? When the poet speaks to us consciously denying a position or intention, do we hark more to the denial or to what is denied? And when a poem appears to sound with only one voice, do we appreciate the solo performance or harmony, or do we suspect our own insensitivity to another refrain, perhaps sung in different key or discord off-stage? Such questions and problems, of course, are normal to literary (and historical) criticism, but it is not customary to be concerned with them in a discussion of Carew or the Caroline poets. The temptation is to ignore them or alternatively to explain them away. And so have Carew's critics and recent biographer. Though she acknowledged the tensions 'between the subject matter and the poet's attitude towards it', Lynn Sadler found no room for such ambiguity in her final critical verdict on Carew: 'the poems mirror his age and the frivolity of Charles's court'.[36]

Carew's poems undoubtedly mirrored his age, but the metaphor should detain us for a moment. For, like so many looking glasses, Carew's poems presented a variety of images, not all of them reassuring, images which not only reflected men's self-perception, but the divorce between the self and self-perception. Carew's were mirrors which could please and displease, invoke pride or shame, support or undermine, present clearly or distort according to subject and to circumstance. We should never forget that they were glasses held by the poet and that the angle of vision which formed the image was determined by Carew himself. Carew, we shall argue, turned his glass this way and that to show the different aspects and faces of his subjects – to each other and to themselves. Held before subjects in private and in public, they were mirrors both for men and for magistrates. And in the private and public worlds Carew's mirrors educated and informed as they reflected values in different lights and from various perspectives. They became, that is, not the accoutrements of vanity but the mirrors of morality.

In the sphere of personal morality, it might be thought that Thomas Carew had little to tell anyone. He was evidently well known as a libertine in his own age and he has been remembered since most for 'A Rapture', a poem often read as a lover's erotic guide to the topography of the female anatomy – with

---

[36] Sadler, *Thomas Carew*, pp. 85–6. After this chapter was substantially completed, I was able to see M. Parker, '"Comely Gestures". Thomas Carew and the creation of a Caroline Poetic', Yale University unpublished Ph.D. thesis, 1979, which offers the beginnings of an important re-evaluation of Carew's poetry, though the argument that Carew takes only a '*ludic*' attitude to love is unhelpful. Cf. Parker, '"All are not born (Sir) to the Bay": "Jack" Suckling, "Tom" Carew, and the Making of a Poet', *Eng. Lit. Renaiss.*, 12 (1982), pp. 341–68.

nothing out of bounds. Carew's poetry *is* frankly erotic and seductive; the love the poems express is physical and sensual, not abstract and intellectual. This recognition alone should cause us to pause and reconsider the evidence of flattery, for Carew's eroticism would seem to be out of place in a court milieu devoted to the cult of Platonic love, the fashionable appeal of which he would have known well. At times the poetry seems clearly to express his irritated reaction to the cult: 'Let fooles thy mystique formes adore, / I'le know thee in thy mortall state.'[37] But to know Carew's poems only in their mortal state would be to misunderstand them, or to hear but one of the voices through which the poet articulated his views on love and morality. For there is an ambiguity about love and passion both between various poems and within them. The first thirty or forty lines of 'To A. L. Perswasions to Love', for example, read as the conventional rhetoric of seduction: as an incitement to a young girl to indulge the pleasures of the flesh before time robs her of her beauty. All the seducer's persuasive tricks and tropes are there: the pleasures that the maiden will herself enjoy, the responsibility to use Nature's stock of beauty with liberality, the point that lesser lights shine when the greater are hid under a bushel:

> Thus common beauties, and meane faces
> Shall have more pastime, and enjoy
> The sport you loose by being coy.[38]

These tropes are standard, but we note that it is precisely such persuasive eloquence that forms the subject of Carew's 'Good Counsel to a young Maid', in which, conscious of the seductive powers of (his own?) verse, he warns his pupil that:

> Netts, of passions finest thred,
> Snaring Poems, will be spred,
> All, to catch thy maiden-head.[39]

The young woman is warned to be on her guard, for the rhetoric of seduction is not to be confused with the reality of love. The seducer, she is advised in another poem of the same title, displays appetite rather than devotion. As a thirsty man once satiated by the stream,

> with disdainfull feet
> He kicks her banks, and from the place
> That thus refresht him, moves with sullen pace.

The parallel is made clear:

[37] 'Ingratefull beauty threatned', lines 15–16, Dunlap, p. 18. See below, p. 139.
[38] 'To A. L. Perswasions to love', lines 14–16, Dunlap, p. 4.
[39] 'Good Counsel to a young Maid', lines 10–12, Dunlap, p. 13.

> So shalt thou be despis'd, faire Maid,
> When by the sated lover tasted.[40]

The maiden is counselled to resist the powerful anguished overtures of the seducer's eloquence rather than purchase her shame by consent. Chastity, Carew tells her, is central to her honour and only honourable love should be allowed to conquer it. And this, for all the seductive opening, is also the point of 'Perswasions to love'. For, as we read on, it becomes clear that here the poet/lover offers not merely the sexual gratification of the moment, but love for life. Indeed A.L., like the young maid, is advised to select only such a suitor:

> Cull out amongst the multitude
> Of lovers, that seeke to intrude
> Into your favour, one that may
> Love for an age, not for a day;
> One that will quench your youthfull fires,
> And feed in age your hot desires.[41]

The conjunction that opens the last line quoted lends its force to the whole verse. The poem, as we read further, becomes not simply an act of seduction, but rather advice to use the gift of youthful beauty in order to purchase life-long love.

That love clearly involves physical passion, but mere lust is not the same as love. Carew debates the difference between them in one of four songs on the subject of love that he wrote for a court entertainment:

> *Quest.* By what power was Love confinde
> To one object? who can binde,
> Or fixe a limit to the free-borne minde?[42]

The question evokes the argument of Platonic lovers as expressed, for example, by Queen Atossa in *The Royal Slave*.[43] But the answer dismisses the implications of such a question and, before a court audience, denies the polygamous mode of Platonic love:

> *An.* Nature; for as bodyes may
> Move at once but in one way,
> So nor can mindes to more then one love stray.[44]

Unlike mere lust, love, Carew asserts, is faithful. Unlike mere lust it is also timeless. It is 'Eternitie of Love protested' in Carew's song, as in 'To A.L.' That which is not eternal cannot be called love:

[40] 'Good Counsell to a young Maid', lines 10–14, Dunlap, p. 25. The same title for two very different poems may suggest a playful irony.
[41] 'To A.L.', lines 55–60, Dunlap, p. 5.
[42] 'Incommunicabilitie of Love', lines 1–3, Dunlap, p. 62. See note, *ibid.*, p. 244.
[43] *The Royal Slave*, lines 1003–14, 1029–45 in Blakemore Evans, *Plays and Poems of William Cartwright*, pp. 231–3; see above, ch. 1, pp. 47–51.
[44] 'Incommunicabilitie of Love', lines 4–6, Dunlap, p. 62.

> True love can never change his seat,
> Nor did he ever love, that could retreat.[45]

We recall the traveller, his thirst assuaged, disdaining the stream. Such a figure never loves but expresses mere appetite and is ruled by it. Love's 'noble flame' has never fired his soul, for true love 'shall like a hallowed Lamp, for ever burne'.[46] The flame of love is more than the corporeal heat of hot lust or burning desire. To a 'cold' mistress at heart, 'she burning in a Feaver', Carew makes the distinction clear

> Love; let her know the difference
> Twixt the heat of soule, and sence.[47]

Love is physical and spiritual; unlike mere lust it is honourable, faithful and eternal.

Such an interpretation of Carew's position seems to be at odds with his most famous erotic ode. For in 'A Rapture' those qualities are dismissed. Honour is 'but a Masquer', a figure of show rather than substance; it is the 'nobler' lovers who refute it and act on their love, oblivious of reputation. There men sin only 'when loves rites are not done' and all is devoted to the free expression of sensual love. The poem is usually read as an incitement to total sexual licence, and it is easy to see why. For at one level the poem reads as a playful but sophisticated act of seduction, in which the poet attempts to answer all his mistress's and society's objections to the free vent of sexual passion. But to read the poem as only unrestrained hedonism or as a mere jeu d'esprit is to oversimplify it. For the context of Carew's sexual freedom is not society but an Elyzium where 'All things are lawfull', and, as Earl Miner has observed, the poem depends upon this location.[48] Sexual licence here is not at odds with social order. Carew writes of a world apart from society, a paradise, a land of innocence free of sin where men do not know the names 'of husband, wife, lust, modest, chaste or shame'.[49] In this Elyzium, men live virtuously by acting according to their natural instincts. Here what society has labelled sinful bears no such taint. In this Elyzian ground Carew playfully envisages Aretine's works, handbooks of sensuality, becoming 'divine' lectures of love, and Daphne surrendering to Apollo. Here where 'Beautie and Nature, banish all offence', the social labels of moral and immoral, honourable and dishonourable, have no place.[50] This is Carew's own rapture: an

---

[45] 'Eternitie of Love protested', lines 7–8, Dunlap, p. 23. Cf. below, p. 121.

[46] 'Eternitie of Love Protested', lines 9, 16.

[47] 'To her againe, she burning in a Feaver', lines 11–12, Dunlap, p. 35.

[48] 'A Rapture', lines 4, 6. For a recent discussion of this little-studied poem, see P. Johnson, 'Carew's "A Rapture": the dynamics of fantasy', *Studies in English Literature*, 16 (1976), pp. 145–55.

[49] 'A Rapture', lines 109–10, Dunlap, p. 52.

[50] *Ibid.*, lines 26, 115–16, 131–5.

Elyzium in which the tensions between man's natural appetites and social order are resolved. 'Only by casting erotic experience into such mythic terms can Carew purge it of numerous dissident elements.'[51] 'A Rapture' is, we might say, a laboratory in which Carew creates an ideal condition so that he may better explore an actual problem.

In Elyzium 'All things are lawfull ... that may delight / Nature, or unrestrained Appetite.'[52] From this location honour is seen to be only a social attribute, one at times in conflict with religion and with values natural to man. Where honour dictates that men kill, 'religion bids from blood-shed flye'; in Elyzium he enjoys 'steadfast peace'.[53] Society, necessarily perhaps, establishes codes that restrain men's natural instincts and so creates tensions beween natural and social behaviour. Carew envisions a paradise in which man's innocence removes the need for restraint, in which such contradictions are dissolved. 'A Rapture' is not only located in, it is Carew's dream, his vision of that world – a world of natural innocence, a world, as 'The Second Rapture' describes it, 'of lust and lovers', for in innocence they are reconciled.[54] Carew's quest for a reconciliation of sensual passion and virtue may lie behind 'The Second Rapture' as well as 'A Rapture'. For all the explicit eroticism of the imagined sexual union with a young girl, the imagery is religious and the maiden remains chaste. Lynn Sadler has suggested that the poem plays on the biblical story of the virgin presented to David 'that my lord the King may get heat'.[55] The maiden may not only arouse her suitor but 'renew the age' by a reunion, a reconciliation of 'lust' and 'blisse', a condition that man enjoyed before the Fall tainted him with sin.[56] From this perfect state man had fallen. But though he knew all too well that man was a creature of appetite. Carew seems to have believed in his potential for virtue and reformation. It may be then that Carew's hopes for mankind (and for himself) lay not in mere obedience to the social dictates of honour and reputation, but in striving for the natural innocence of man's first perfect state.

Society, however, was far from that state. In society, it would seem, Carew suggests that the best hope for reconciling love and passion, appetite and order, was found in marriage. The subject of his poem 'On the Mariage of T.K. and C.C. the morning stormie' is the resolution of tensions. Carew depicts marriage as the calm in a world of tempests. It puts an end to the winds and waters, the sighs and tears of unrequited love; it brings peace to the soul. And marriage can unite lovers in a physical union now that they are

---

[51] Miner, *Cavalier Mode*, p. 80.
[52] 'A Rapture', lines 111–12.
[53] *Ibid.*, line 163, Dunlap, p. 53.
[54] 'The Second Rapture', line 9, Dunlap, p. 103.
[55] See Kings 1.1, 1–5; Sadler, *Carew*, p. 69.
[56] 'Second Rapture', lines 17, 26. The rearousal of sexual passion is closely related in the poem to the idea of renewal.

joined by holy sacrament to each other. When the priest unites the bride and groom:

> From the misterious holy touch such charmes
> Will flow, as shall unlock her wreathed armes,
> And open a free passage to that fruit
> Which thou hast toyl'd for with a long pursuit.[57]

In society, outside matrimony, it had been forbidden fruit; within marriage it is the fruit of the garden of innocence to which, by partaking of it, the couple return. Marriage restores them to innocence. As a result, it removes them, like the lovers of 'A Rapture', from the values and language of society. The bride's exclamations of physical pleasure become 'pleasing shreekes'; the 'fight of love' has become peace; ''Tis mercy not to pity' the virgin for her blood spilt.[58] Their marriage reconciles contradictions rendering chaste what was impure, honourable what was otherwise shameful, moral what was immoral. Marriage, because it orders man's passions, because it raises man above his grosser senses to his higher nature, enables him to partake of sensual pleasure without being debased by it; it unites in harmony and order the elements of his own nature:

> So shalt thou relish all, enjoy the whole
> Delights of her faire body, and pure soule.[59]

The idea is developed more clearly in Carew's poem, 'A married woman'. Here marriage is specifically presented as a return to the Garden of Eden. Like the garden of innocence, marriage is not free from temptation. Man's fallen nature inclines him to 'furious rage' and 'hot lust', but 'man must in judgement sit, / And tame this Beast'.[60] This Adam failed to do, and so weakened and corrupted his heirs. But marriage strengthened men's will to virtue, by governing without denying their natural passions.

> For in habituall vertues, sense is wrought
> To that calme temper, as the bodie's thought
> To have nor blood, nor gall, if wild and rude
> Passions of Lust, and Anger, are subdu'd.[61]

In marriage man's sense and soul are reconciled. If, as Sadler points out, Carew writes with the most frank and free eroticism when he writes of married love, it is because in marriage pleasure is reconciled to virtue.[62]

---

[57] 'On the Mariage of T.K. and C.C. the morning stormie', lines 21–4, Dunlap, p. 80.
[58] *Ibid.*, lines 31–2, 36.
[59] *Ibid.*, lines 29–30. Once again, we note the force of the conjunction.
[60] 'A Married Woman', lines 22–3, Dunlap, p. 116.
[61] *Ibid.*, lines 11–14.
[62] Sadler found this a problem: 'It is strange that in some of his amorous lyrics to women not his wife, Carew tries to Platonize the erotic while in most of his celebrations of marriage, he blatantly declares for sexual fulfilment' (*Carew*, p. 115). But the contrast is central to Carew's whole poetic and morality.

Such an interpretation of Carew's verse, and especially of 'A Rapture', might seem to detach the poetry from the poet – a man who, we recall, was brought close to death, if not finally killed, by a life of licence and by syphilis. On the contrary, however, I would suggest that a strong personal sense of the ungoverned anarchy of his own appetite and passion, some internal quest for order and regulation, might have dominated Carew's life as well as his poetry. Evidently he contemplated marriage – there were rumours in 1624–5 that he might wed the rich widow of Sir George Smith.[63] And though cynicism might incline us to suspect that economic motives were to the fore, Carew's correspondence with Sir John Suckling concerning his plans would support the suggestion of the poet's search for regulation in his life as well as his art.[64] Suckling attempted to dissuade his friend from matrimony. With more than a hint of irony induced by the prospect of his pox-ridden friend taking the marriage vows, Suckling ribaldly urged him to consider that fruit trees only multiplied when transplanted. 'Do but make love to another', he counselled, and the 'homely meal' of marriage would soon pale before the varied dainty dishes available to the lover's palate.[65] Carew, significantly, remained adamant in his reply. Love, he agreed with Suckling, was natural, but 'if *Love* be *natural*', he added, 'to *marry* is the best *Recipe* for living honest'.[66] For marriage he defined as the expression of love which was fixed and immutable; and, as we have seen, Carew maintained that there was no other love: '*Love* and *change* are incompatible.'[67] In marriage alone, love seeded, bore fruit and multiplied. Carew responded to Suckling in his friend's own coin: the tone of his answer is jocular, bawdy and coarse. To us, perhaps, Carew's argument for sexual fidelity is couched in less than appropriate language: '*one Steed* shall serve your turn as well as twenty more'.[68] But, as often with Carew, the language and the tone should not be simply equated with the meaning. As he himself told Suckling, ''Tis not the want of *Love* . . . if every day afford not *new-language*, and *new waies* of expressing affection.'[69] Carew's coarse language also has a point to make: it is itself a frank acknowledgement of those physical, those animal urges to which marriage may give vent. The sensual and the physical are as significant in Carew's reply

[63] Dunlap, *Poems of Carew*, p. xxxii; Sadler, *Carew*, p. 15.
[64] The correspondence is printed as an appendix in Dunlap, pp. 211–12. T. Clayton has suggested that the 'Answer' to Suckling is not by Carew, but also by Suckling himself (Clayton, *The Non-Dramatic Works of Sir John Suckling*, pp. lxxxvi, 332). There can be no final conclusion, since manuscript copies are found subscribed 'T.C.', as well as 'J.S.'. *If* Carew did not write the letter, evidently Suckling thought it a fair representation of views held by Carew and quite at odds with his own.
[65] 'A Letter to a Friend', lines 35, 44; Dunlap, pp. 211–12.
[66] 'An Answer to the Letter', lines 21–3; Dunlap, p. 211.
[67] 'An Answer to the Letter', lines 13–16; Dunlap, p. 211; cf. 'Eternitie of Love protested', p. 23.
[68] 'An Answer to the Letter', lines 31–2.
[69] *Ibid.*, lines 44–5.

as in Suckling's letter. But his final conclusion is not the same: 'I know what mariage is, and know you know it not.'[70] For Carew believed that, in condemning marriage, Suckling denied what was natural, in the sense of that which might restore man to his higher nature, the original innocency of his uncorrupted nature. In the words of the Book of Common Prayer, marriage was 'instituted of God in paradise in the time of man's innocency' and 'ordained for a remedy against sin'. Marriage for Carew, as for Davenant, was the literal and metaphorical expression of the poet's 'attempt to impose a civilized order upon the desperate chaos of man's inner realities'.[71] It accommodated the physical and the spiritual nature of man, natural appetites and social order.

It is these tensions and the search for a reconciliation of these tensions, I would suggest, that dominate Carew's life and poetry. Once we see that there is more to Carew than the libertinism of 'A Rapture', we may also begin to appreciate that there was more to his love lyrics than the celebration of court love games played by the precieux. We may come to see that while he wrote within the conventions of Petrarchan love poetry, Carew re-employed, adapted and even subverted them as he brought to them the concerns and problems of his age. Through a poetry of beauty, love and nature, as we shall see, Carew did not retreat from contemporary issues and problems; rather he examined not only amorous, but social and political relationships.

THE PERFECTION OF NATURE

The celebration of beauty is a raison d'être of the love poem. The equation of a lover's physical attributes with the features of the natural or celestial spheres was conventional in the poetry of the Renaissance. Carew's most famous and most delightful love song, 'Aske me no more', places him firmly within the convention. But even in this poem, apparently sung simply in the key of celebration, the refrain transcends the mere flattery of a mistress.[72] For Carew does not only compare the hair of his mistress to the sun, her voice to the nightingale, her eyes to the stars. The lady's beauty is not simply compared to roses; it becomes the very essence or idea of roses, and so captures the very essence of perfect nature.[73] In the final forcefully surprising lines her beauty emerges not as the reflection of nature but the home of nature, the place in which nature finds its greatest peace and resting place:

[70] *Ibid.*, lines 24–5.
[71] The phrase is B. King's, 'The strategy of Carew's wit', *Review of English Literature*, 5 (1964), pp. 42–51.
[72] Whilst Carew writes within the conventions of Petrarchan love poetry, he reveals an ambivalence towards it.
[73] 'A Song' ('Aske me no more . . .'), Dunlap, p. 102, lines 1–4; see Dunlap's commentary, p. 265.

> Aske me no more if East or West,
> The Phenix builds her spicy nest:
> For unto you at last shee flies,
> And in your fragrant bosome dyes.[74]

Like the mythological phoenix, nature, though it 'dyes', is renewed and reborn. The beauty of Carew's mistress is that of nature itself.

This is not the conventional comparison of a lover's physical features with natural phenomena. In 'The Comparison' Carew boldly eschews such convention:

> Dearest thy tresses are not threads of gold,
> Thy eyes of Diamonds, nor doe I hold
> Thy lips for Rubies . . . [75]

For Carew beauty does not reside in his mistress's fair hair (though 'threads of lawne'), her coral lips, her 'teeth of pearle', nor even her wit (though 'pure and quicke').[76] The poet loves 'for all', and it is 'The Complement' of each part to the other rather than the compliment of a suitor that gives that poem its title.[77] Beauty expresses the harmony of *perfect* nature, not its earthly manifestations. And so 'The Comparison' is that of the maiden with the purest essence of nature: her cheek is of 'perfect crimson'; her lips are 'Nectar'. Such beauty, as the language makes apparent, is an expression of the divinity of nature: the lover's skin is 'heavenly and immortall weede'; her breath is 'frankincense'; her cleavage is a 'Paradise'; her body a 'sacred land'. Celia's beauty 'Holds nothing earthly, but is all divine'. She is a 'Faire Goddess' to be worshipped: the goddess Nature herself.[78] Nature, as here employed, does not describe the material world, but an ideal, perfect state and a moral force.

As nature's legate, beauty influences men with all the might of nature's sway. The beauty of nature leads men necessarily to love: 'Love flow from Beautie as th'effect.'[79] It has a 'magique' which enchants men so that the greatest beauty most attracts. Such a power needs to be exercised with responsibility. Those endowed with nature's gifts must come to acknowledge it – 'Confesse thy beauty' – and to attune their behaviour to their outward appearance: ''tis fit thou thine owne value know'.[80] For she who, possessed of beauty, denies her own divine appearance becomes a 'heretique' and denies her own nature, indeed nature itself. The beautiful, those endowed with the

---

[74] Lines 17–20, Dunlap, p. 103.
[75] 'The Comparison', lines 1–3, Dunlap, p. 98; cf. Shakespeare's sonnet no. 130.
[76] 'The Complement', lines 9, 20, 21–55; Dunlap, pp. 99–100.
[77] Cf. 'Epitaph on the Lady S.', Dunlap, p. 55.
[78] 'The Comparison', lines 13, 24, 25, Dunlap, pp. 98–9; 'On a Damaske rose sticking upon a Ladies Breast', line 6, *ibid.*, p. 108.
[79] 'To A.D. unreasonable distrustfull of her owne beauty', line 35, Dunlap, p. 85; cf. 'Incommunicabilitie of Love', lines 10–15, *ibid.*, p. 62.
[80] 'To A.D.', lines 54, 60.

quintessence of nature, must lead the life of the beautiful, that is the virtuous life, so that their outward divinity expresses, as it should, the inner virtue of perfect and uncorrupted nature. For beauty's authority is legitimate only when founded upon virtue. In his 'Epitaph on the Lady S.' Carew offers an encomium on the union of beauty and virtue to her:

> Whose native colours, and purest lustre, lent
> Her eye, cheek, lip, a dazling ornament:
> Whose rare and hidden vertues, did expresse
> Her inward beauties, and minds fairer dresse.[81]

Such a fusion of outer beauty and inner virtue represented (and restored) the divine image in which men were moulded before the fall of nature. But, like the first man and woman, not all endowed with such beauty recognized their divinity or lived according to their divine image. The mistress of Carew's 'The Comparison', for instance, is a 'Faire Goddesse' only in outward appearance. 'The Comparison', it becomes clear, is not only (or primarily) between the woman's beauty and the hues and features of nature which it transcends; it is a comparison, or rather an unfavourable but forceful contrast, between the divinity of appearance and an inner personality which fails to live up to it. So the mistress is exhorted:

> Faire Goddesse, since thy feature makes thee one,
> Yet be not such for these respects alone;
> But as you are divine in outward view
> So be within as faire, as good, as true.[82]

The commandment of the last powerful line emphasizes the didacticism of Carew's poetry of love. Thomas Carew, here as elsewhere, works within and through the conventions of the poetry of compliment. But, like Jonson, he instructs whilst seeming to flatter. And whilst appearing to describe the charms of a mistress, he posits a view of beauty that implies a morality.

Beauty is depicted in some of Carew's poems as vulnerable to the ravages of time. And this, perhaps more than anything else, has led us to reading his verse in conventional *carpe diem* terms, as pieces of the moment hedonistically urging men and women to seize the pleasures of the hour. 'A Rapture' opens with a line redolent with the hot impatience as well as physical force of sexual passion:

> I will enjoy thee now my *Celia*, come.[83]

'Perswasions to Enjoy' too warns Carew's Celia of the pressing need to 'reape our joyes / E're time such goodly fruit destroyes', just as A.L. had been

---

[81] 'Epitaph on the Lady S.', lines 7–10, Dunlap, p. 55.
[82] 'The Comparison', lines 25–8, Dunlap, p. 99. A classic illustration of 'that wrenching final couplet for which Carew should be better known', Sadler, *Carew*, p. 52.
[83] 'A Rapture', line 1, Dunlap, p. 49; see Johnson, '"A Rapture"', p. 149.

reminded that 'that lovely face will faile,' that fragile beauty ''Tis sooner past, 'tis sooner done / Then Summers raine, or winters Sun'.[84] Before we confine Carew to such convention, however, the last lines must lead us to recollect that 'To A.L. Perswasions to love' concludes *not* as advice to seize the moment, but as an exhortation to secure the long term, rather than merely to indulge immediate sexual urges. This offers us an important insight into Carew's perhaps more serious preoccupation. Time, the eternal enemy of mankind, was the threat which Renaissance man feared most. In the battle against time, Carew's weapon is love. For love is shown to transcend the externals of beauty and so to be free of that decay natural to physical substance. Carew's Cleon reassures his fearful mistress: 'Though beautie fade, my faith lasts ever.' [85] For Cleon dotes not only on Celia's 'snow white skin' but on 'Thy purer mind', and that is incorruptible.[86] When the two exchange their tokens of a love so founded, they know that they have won the victory over time and their fears: 'Thus we are both redeemed from time.'[87] And the poet, by celebrating their love, or any true love, may redeem others. The publicizing of conquering love by the poet/lover clinches the victory and guarantees immortality. Celia learns it too:

> Ce. And I
> Shall live in thy immortall rime,
> Untill the Muses dye.[88]

What Celia comes to understand in dialogue with Cleon, the poet/lover, the shepherd and the nymph in another poem evidently know instinctively. The lovers are reluctant to part as dawn approaches, announcing with the first light of day the passage of all time. The nymph knows the power of love to arrest it:

> Then let us pinion *Time*, and chase
> The day for ever from this place.[89]

They part. But he is her 'soule', she 'My Paradise'. Their love is 'for ever'. We must note that both these poems share a common title. Cleon and Celia, the shepherd and the nymph, are the speakers in 'A Pastorall Dialogue'.[90] It is a dialogue not only between themselves, but among time, love and, as the title suggests, nature. For nature, though it expresses the passage of time in the seasons, is yet eternity itself. Men conquer time then when they accord and

---

[84] 'Song Perswasions to Enjoy', lines 5–6, Dunlap, p. 16; 'To A.L.', lines 31, 33–4, *ibid.*, p. 4.
[85] 'A Pastorall Dialogue', line 19, Dunlap, p. 43.
[86] *Ibid.*, lines 21–2.
[87] *Ibid.*, line 45, Dunlap, p. 44.
[88] *Ibid.*, lines 46–8.
[89] 'A Pastoral Dialogue. Shepherd Nymph Chorus', lines 29–30, Dunlap, p. 46.
[90] That is to say the two poems have the same title.

act with nature. Only by returning to a life in accordance with perfect nature, only, in other words, by the good life of man's uncorrupted nature, may man triumph over his enemy, Time.[91]

Man, Carew suggests, returns to nature through love. Metaphors drawn from nature are a commonplace of Renaissance, perhaps most, love poetry. In Carew's poetry, however, naturalistic imagery is employed with unusual freshness and vigour to articulate a real and philosophical rather than allegorical and metaphorical relationship between nature and love. In 'A Prayer to the Wind', for example, the wind, that is nature's messenger, becomes the ambassador of love, an effective envoy, capable of infusing love in women as of turning weeds into flowers.[92] In Carew's poems love's language and tactics are the voices and movements of nature. The response of a mistress to entreaty may come from 'The Torrid, or the frozen Zone'; the mistress of a 'cold heart' is depicted as 'frozen', unwarmed by the beams of love.[93] The bold lover, by contrast, is indeed himself a sun whose rays cannot be resisted by the most unyielding of nature's flowers:

> Marke how the bashfull morne, in vaine
> Courts the amorous Marigold,
> With sighing blasts, and weeping raine;
> Yet she refuses to unfold.
> But when the Planet of the day,
> Approacheth with his powerfull ray,
> Then she spreads, then she receives
> His warmer beames into her virgin leaves.
> So shalt thou thrive in love, fond Boy.[94]

That 'So' transcends mere simile. Nature *is* a lover and love is natural. In the Elyzium of 'A Rapture' nature provides the lovers' bed and pillows from her stock of roses and of down.[95] The woman's body is itself a garden through which the lover wanders, partaking of the 'warme firme Apple, tipt with corall berry', the 'vale of Lillies', 'the swelling *Appenine*' and 'grove of Eglantine' into which the lover/bee flies to extract the nectar of love/nature that gives life.[96] This is eroticism *and* innocence. 'A Rapture' is a vision of an ideal in which, because nature and love are both pure, innocence and passion are one.

In society, nature no less than love has become corrupted and disordered.

---

[91] Several of Carew's poems, including 'A Rapture', are concerned with appropriate time. See, for example, 'The Spring', Dunlap, p. 1. Cf. A. Long and H. Maclean, '"Deare Ben", "Great Donne" and "my Celia": the wit of Carew's poetry', *Studies in English Literature*, 18 (1978), pp. 75–94. Miner observes that in cavalier poetry the remedy against time is not the enjoyment of the happy life as much as the virtue of the good life, *Cavalier Mode*, p. 154.

[92] 'A Prayer to the Wind', Dunlap, p. 11.

[93] 'Mediocritie in Love Rejected', lines 1–2, Dunlap, p. 12; 'A Looking-Glasse', line 16, *ibid.*, p. 19.

[94] 'Boldnesse in Love', lines 1–9, Dunlap, p. 42; cf. 'A Prayer to the Wind', *ibid.*, p. 11.

[95] 'A Rapture', lines 35–40, Dunlap, p. 50.

[96] *Ibid.*, lines 66–76, Dunlap, p. 51.

Passion and lust manifest the chaos of a wild, unruly nature, as we recall they do in Davenant's *Gondibert*. Carew has suggested that perfect, faithful, ordered love may restore men to innocence. So, as perfect nature instructs lovers, love, in its turn, might order and rule the chaos of fallen nature. The beauty and love of Carew's mistress might then calm the unruliness of wild nature. As Celia sings, the poet tells us, she

> Stills the loude wind; and makes the wilde
> Incensed Bore, and Panther milde![97]

As the ode 'To the Queen' makes clear, the 'great Commandresse' who orders love and tames lust also disciplines nature. Her example

> shews us the path
> Of Modestie, and constant faith,
> Which makes the rude Male satisfied
> With one faire Female by his side.[98]

The power of love's example subdues even the 'wilde / Satyr' to its regimen. Ultimately love's law will rule the flood and 'free' man through the 'deepe divinitie' of love from the Fall.[99] The love that may order nature must itself be ordered: true love expresses the peace, order and eternity of nature. Mutability and infidelity are not the attributes of love but of the chaos and anarchy of lust. Lust is – the word is used often – 'wilde', the behaviour of man cast into the wilderness because he fell slave to his appetite.[100] Legitimate love, by contrast, manifests 'calm desires' and displays 'milde aspects'.[101] Love distils the harmony of nature; it reconciles body and soul, appetite and order, the fiery red of passion with the pale white of innocence in a harmony of heat and hue.[102] In society, the love that unites them is the marriage union. And marriage, we may see, might not only calm the tempests of man's personal turmoil, it might restore too the harmony and order of nature and so effect the reformation of society.

The state of perfect nature and reformation of society are the subjects of two of Carew's poems, usually described as 'country house poems'.[103] I refer, of course, to 'To Saxham' and 'To my friend G.N. from Wrest'. At one level,

---

[97] 'Song *Celia* singing', lines 3–4, Dunlap, p. 38.
[98] 'To the Queene', lines 13–16, Dunlap, p. 90; see below, p. 144.
[99] *Ibid.*, lines 20, 28, Dunlap, p. 91.
[100] E.g. 'Love's Force', line 1, Dunlap, p. 116; 'Song *Celia* singing', line 3, *ibid.*, p. 38; 'Incommunicabilitie of Love', line 9, *ibid.*, p. 62; 'To G.N. from Wrest', line 7, *ibid.*, p. 86.
[101] 'Disdaine Returned' ('Hee that loves a Rosie cheeke . . .'), line 8, Dunlap, p. 18; 'To one that desired to know my Mistris', lines 3–6, *ibid.*, p. 39.
[102] On the significance of images of heat and hue in the verse, see Selig, *Flourishing Wreath*, ch. 3.
[103] See, for example, G. R. Hibbard, 'The country house poem of the seventeenth century', *Journ. Warburg & Courtauld Inst.*, 19 (1956), pp. 159–74; W. Maclung, *The Country House in English Renaissance Poetry* (Berkeley, 1977); M. A. C. McGuire, 'The cavalier country house poem: mutations on a Jonsonian tradition', *Studies in English Literature*, 19 (1979), pp. 93–108.

these poems, like 'To Penshurst', are undoubtedly charming celebrations of
the pleasures Carew enjoyed at the country seats of two friends and patrons –
Sir John Crofts and Henry de Grey, Earl of Kent.[104] But, like 'To Penshurst',
there is more to them than that. Like Jonson's, Carew's poems transcend their
particular circumstances; they are representations of an idealized nature
which was central to Carew's ethics and social values.

'To my friend G.N. from Wrest' opens with a contrast – between the
'temperate ayre' of Wrest and the 'raging stormes' of the 'cold nights out by
the bankes of Tweed'.[105] Carew has just returned from the king's campaign
against the Scots and the discomforts of the royal camp near Berwick upon
Tweed.[106] He has also returned to a garden of peace and order from a
wilderness of disorder.[107] Wrest is described as a haven of nature, of an
idealized, perfected nature: the garden is pregnant with nature's seed and
fertile with her fruits. It is a world free of social artifice: there are no
compounds, nor 'forraigne Gums' but 'pure and uncompounded beauties'
expressing all the gifts of a fecund, ordered and uncorrupted nature.[108]
Where by the Tweed there were 'bleake Mountains', 'fierce tempests',
'everlasting winter', Wrest caresses its guest with 'balmie dew', 'odours
sweete' and 'with the warme Suns quickning heate'.[109] Wrest symbolizes the
harmony of perfect nature. And so, in Carew's hands, it becomes, like nature
itself, a model of behaviour. Everything at Wrest follows nature's dictates and
is good. The virtues of natural activity are found within the house as well as its
fruits outside. Wrest offers the warm hospitality of 'cheerfull flames' to all
strangers; its ornaments are 'living men'.[110] Hierarchy is respected here
because it too is natural: 'Some . . . spun of a finer thred' are fed with daintier
fare, but there is plenty for all and all live together there in harmony.[111] A
natural hierarchy does not preclude the natural community of men. At Wrest
nature is not merely represented in images – in statues or marbles of gods.

[104] Dunlap points out that the manor of Wrest Park, Bedfordshire 'with the title of the Earl of
Kent had passed in 1631 to Anthony de Grey who died in 1643'. This is erroneous. The title
passed in 1624 to Henry de Grey who died in 1639, and only then to Anthony, who succeeded
aged 82.

[105] 'To G.N. from Wrest', lines 1–3, Dunlap, p. 86. For an interesting discussion of this poem, see
M. P. Parker, '"To my friend G.N. from Wrest": Carew's secular masque', in C. J. Summers
and T. Larry-Pebworth, eds., *Classic and Cavalier: Essays on Jonson and the sons of Ben*
(Pittsburgh, 1982), pp. 171–92. Cf. below, ch. 5, pp. 242–3.

[106] Dunlap, p. xli.

[107] Compare Carew's opening lines with the first scene of *Salmacida Spolia*, Davenant's masque,
performed at the time of the Scots war on 21 January 1640: 'A curtain flying up, a horrid
scene appeared of storm and tempest. No glimpse of the sun was seen, as if darkness,
confusion and deformity had possessed the world,' lines 111–14 in Orgel and Strong, *Inigo
Jones*, II, p. 731. Cf. sketch on p. 201 and below, ch. 5, pp. 251–5.

[108] 'To G.N. from Wrest', lines 15, 19, Dunlap, pp. 86–7.

[109] *Ibid.*, lines 9, 11–12.

[110] *Ibid.*, lines 28, 34.

[111] *Ibid.*, lines 35–46.

And Carew wishes us to appreciate that the natural imagery of his poem is more than poetic conceit or 'gay Embellishment'.[112] Wrest *is* a vision of perfected nature. Ceres and Bacchus do not stand as stone figures in niches there, nor are they useless decorations for Carew's poem:

> We offer not in Emblemes to the eyes,
> But to the taste those usefull Deities.
> Wee presse the juycie God, and quaffe his blood,
> And grinde the Yeallow Goddesse into food.[113]

Those who 'presse the juycie God' are not only making wine; they are extracting nature's essence. And it is this that Carew too wishes to distil through his poem. His readers are being urged not to live with the images of nature (nor with a poetry concerned with them) but to return to nature itself.

Grey's house, of course, was built by man's art, but in it we find the gifts and attributes of nature. Outside in the garden, in the world of nature, 'we decline not, all the worke of Art'. Here the lake and winding stream represent man's capacity to order nature's wilderness and to perfect her as in the house nature perfects man's art. Wrest 'directs' the 'course' of nature and so enjoys 'fertile waters', fecundity and fruit.[114] Religious imagery pervades the poem, suggesting a garden paradise. Nature, we are told, doth 'blesse / this Mansion'.[115] Here all men 'freely sit / At the Lords Table'. False gods are banished in

> This Island Mansion, which i'th' center plac'd,
> Is with a double Crystall heaven embrac'd.[116]

In this garden of innocence, as in 'A Rapture', erotic love has full rein – '*Vertumnus* sits, and courts / His ruddie-cheek'd *Pomona*' on the bank.[117] To this 'blest Place' Carew has come – perhaps from his own personal wilderness as well as the raging storms of the Scottish border. 'Thus', he announces to his friend G.N., 'I enjoy myselfe.' The simple half-line has an unusually quiet force. Carew does enjoy *himself*; that is he finds himself in this perfect state of nature and so finds calm. His friend, hunting, by contrast strives against nature and so toils (the word is Carew's own) in the wilderness.[118] Wrest

---

[112] *Ibid.*, line 54.

[113] *Ibid.*, lines 65–8, Dunlap, p. 88.

[114] *Ibid.*, lines 69–80.

[115] *Ibid.*, lines 19–20, 42.

[116] *Ibid.*, lines 79–80.

[117] *Ibid.*, lines 93–6. See A. B. Giametti, *The Earthly Paradise and the Renaissance Epic* (Princeton, 1966); H. Levin, *The Myth of the Golden Age in the Renaissance* (Bloomington, Ind., 1969).

[118] 'To G.N. from Wrest', line 107, Dunlap, p. 89. The bucks and stags chased by Carew's friend are the 'emblemme of war': they signify, perhaps, both the war against nature and that war on the borders from which Carew has just escaped to nature's haven, lines 107–10.

beckons all men who strive in the wilderness to return to the garden of innocence.

Saxham too is the shrine of nature. Where outside the house the inclement season bore little fruit, 'thou hadst daintyes, as the skie / Had only been thy Volarie'. Nature's sweets 'blesse' Saxham; animals come thither 'as to the Arke' – that shrine that saved the world from the flood.[119] At Saxham there is no striving in the wilderness, for here animals freely offer themselves as sacrifice on this altar of nature:

> The willing Oxe, of himselfe came
> Home to the slaughter, with the Lambe,
> And every beast did thither bring
> Himselfe, to be an offering.[120]

Even the elements paid 'tribute to thy fire'. Here is a paradise again. At Saxham it is 'endlesse day'. The shrine of nature welcomes every 'weary Pilgrim' come to worship. Its 'chearfull beames send forth their light', beckoning all who travel in darkness.[121] He who saw the light might, like the lamb, 'bring Himselfe' and so find, by worshipping at nature's shrine, that 'inward happinesse' he seeks.

'To my friend G.N. from Wrest' and 'To Saxham' are usually studied as country house poems. In this context, one critic has dwelt upon Carew's 'Mutations' of the Jonsonian mode, pointing to the relative isolation of Saxham, compared with Jonson's 'Penshurst', and to a sense of the Crofts' house as a retreat. So far, we would not dissent. But to M. McGuire Saxham thus becomes a 'cavalier justification of the country house as a private stronghold, within which aristocratic comforts and powers can be preserved against the rising tide of opposition'.[122] Such an interpretation reveals an extraordinary ignorance of the historical circumstances, and, I would suggest, a misunderstanding of Carew's poetry and values. It is not clear who in the 1620s (when 'Saxham' was evidently written) was 'rising' in opposition to aristocratic comforts and powers: ideological challenge to aristocratic privilege was virtually non-existent. Besides, whilst Saxham and Wrest are undoubtedly portrayed as retreats, they are not socially exclusive. Both households, it is stressed, open their doors and offer unlimited hospitality to the poor and strangers as well as those of 'finer thred':

> Thou hast no Porter at the doore
> T'examine, or keep back the poore;
> Nor locks, nor bolts; thy gates have bin
> Made onely to let strangers in.[123]

---

[119] 'To Saxham', lines 18–19, 22, Dunlap, p. 28.   [120] *Ibid.*, lines 23–6.
[121] *Ibid.*, lines 35, 38.   [122] McGuire, 'The cavalier country house poem', pp. 93–4.
[123] 'To Saxham', lines 49–52, Dunlap, pp. 28–9; cf. the implied 'open house' at Wrest, 'To G.N.

Nature does not, as McGuire would argue, support only aristocratic society. It offers its fruits to all societies that live in accordance with its dictates. Saxham and Wrest are models of how men might in society return to nature: they are, in some ways, poetic parables. They offer the pattern of a peaceful, ordered, hierarchical yet communal life which might bring men closer to the perfection of that ideal commonweal: the kingdom of nature and love.[124]

Our language, like Carew's own in his discussion of nature, has, almost unconsciously, become religious. It is undoubtedly tempting to think of nature as Carew's religion and so to ally him closely with his friend Sir John Suckling (and perhaps, as we have seen, Sir William Davenant), who espoused a deistic or naturalistic theology. Such a suggestion, however, attractive though it is, encounters problems both in Carew's biography and his verse. Clarendon, for example, upon whom we rely for much of what we know of Carew's life, closed his short biography with this epitaph:

But his glory was that after fifty years of his life spent with less severity or Exactness than it ought to have been, He died with the greatest Remorse for that licence, and with the greatest Manifestation of Christianity that his friends could desire.[125]

Carew also translated several psalms, which some commentators have viewed as evidence of that conversion.[126] Carew's editor has cast doubt on the reliability of any story of a deathbed conversion, and has demonstrated that at least two of Carew's psalms can be dated to the 1620s, some fifteen years at least before his death and in the period in which he wrote 'A Rapture'. Clearly there is a problem.[127] But Rhodes Dunlap's correctives cannot, I believe, entirely explain away Carew's religious sensibilities nor completely discredit (the usually reliable) Clarendon's account of Carew's conversion late in life. In general, we have discussed tensions in Carew – between the body and the spirit, between human appetite and order. More particularly, the poetry offers suggestions that Carew had for long grappled with Christianity, and found himself at times drawn towards it.[128] Further, it

---

from Wrest', lines 34–45, 60. For a discussion of early seventeenth-century concern about hospitality, see F. Heal, 'The idea of hospitality in early modern England', *Past & Present*, 102 (1984), pp. 66–93. Dr Heal argues that the decay of hospitality was a special concern of the 1620s and 1630s.

[124] Giametti points out the connections between the Garden of Eden tradition and that of the secular garden of love, *Earthly Paradise*, ch. 7.

[125] *Life of Clarendon*, p. 36.

[126] See Dunlap, pp. 135–50; R. G. Howarth, *Minor Poets of the Seventeenth Century* (London, 1953), p. xiii.

[127] Dunlap, pp. xxxix–xlii.

[128] Cf. Sadler, *Carew*, p. 123.

provides indications too that there were religious as well as secular dimensions to his love poetry that were never fully reconciled.

Carew's love poetry is often in the most general sense religious and at times seems specifically Christian. Let us consider 'A Married Woman', which, it has been suggested, represents Carew's youthful work. On one level the poem is about the desirable qualities in a bride. But, significantly, given Carew's attitude to marriage, the poem is more broadly concerned with man's nature, with the questions of free will and sin. Carew, perhaps wrestling with his own turbulent nature, portrays man as a creature of appetite as well as reason, of the flesh as well as the spirit. If then his animal nature leads him to 'wild and rude / Passions of Lust, and Anger', might he not ask

> Will it suffice to say my sense, the Beast
> Provokt me to 't . . .[129]

The answer is no. And it is no because man has spirit as well as flesh and is by that separated from the animal world.

> could I my soule devest,
> My plea were good, Lyons, and Buls commit
> Both freely, but man must in judgement sit,
> And tame this Beast, for Adam was not free,
> When in excuse he said, Eve gave it me:
> Had he not eaten, she perhaps had beene
> Unpunisht, his consent made hers a sinne.[130]

Man's soul may order his own nature and nature too. Adam disrupted nature, the paradise of the garden and the innocence of man, when he harked not to the voice of his spirit. Carew's language is often sacred.[131] But this poem is unusually explicitly biblical and Christian in its subject and treatment, unusually unsecular. Elsewhere in the poetry Carew appears much more in and of this world; his ethics depend less upon an acknowledgement of Christianity.

The tensions between the secular and the spiritual may have always been with him; the differences of tone may echo inner voices that spoke to Carew at different periods of his life or contrary voices that he always strove to reconcile. Because we know little of the details of his life, and because we cannot assign dates to most of the poems, we cannot be sure how Carew's beliefs changed or developed.[132] But it is of particular interest that in one poem written shortly before his death Carew both confessed the secular

---

[129] 'A Married Woman', lines 13, 19–20, Dunlap, p. 116. Dunlap suggests that the poem, though not included until the 1642 edition of Carew's verse, represents youthful work, p. 271.

[130] 'A Married Woman', lines 20–6.

[131] See Sadler, *Carew*, pp. 122–3.

[132] Dunlap, pp. lxviii–lxxv.

priorities of his muse *and* hinted at a restlessness of a spirit unfulfilled by
religious faith. Carew's commendatory ode 'To my worthy friend Master
Geo. Sands, on his translation of the Psalmes' appeared in 1638 in the second
edition of Sandys's translation of the psalms, *A Paraphrase Upon the Divine
Poems*.[133] It was a poem appropriate to the occasion and the recipient and
hence must be read with caution before we conclude that it was a statement of
Carew's personal convictions. Yet there is a personal, even confessional tone
to the poem that insists upon a hearing – and no less so because Carew would
seem to discount any involvement with religion:

> My unwasht Muse, polutes not things Divine,
> Nor mingles her prophaner notes with thine.[134]

For in so saying, of course, the poet performs what he denies: he does mingle
his own prefatory verse with Sandys's divine poems, and, moreover, he
evaluates his own poetry by the standards and styles of more pious lines.
Carew's poem stands at the entrance to Sandys's volume, observing, listening, and ushering in the reader. And it is in this position as a person and poet
in general that Carew finds himself – like a penitent of old, as he puts it,
waiting at the church door, 'to stand and heare the Churches Liturgies, / Yet
not assist the solemne exercise'.[135] The poet, like the penitent, sees the
possibility of, perhaps he even hopes for, that sudden conversion which will
change his life and his art – for 'A pure flame' which 'shot by Almighty power'
may 'the earthy flame devoure'.[136] Then, Carew foresees,

> My eyes, in penitentiall dew may steepe
> That brine, which they for sensuall love did weepe.[137]

The poet bares his 'restlesse soule, tyr'de with persuit / Of mortall beauty' and
even admits the possibility that his 'vaine search below' may have been the
worship of a false idol to the neglect of that 'immortall love', to be found
'Above'.[138]

The poem is arresting because Carew foresees himself renouncing, even
hopes that he will renounce, his more secular preoccupations as a consequence of a spiritual conversion. But the poem in the end stops short of that
revelation and commitment: the tensions remain; they are not resolved. The
celestial fires of his vision Carew describes as ''gainst Nature's course'.[139]

---

[133] *Ibid.*, pp. 93–4, 259.
[134] 'To my worthy friend Master Geo. Sands, on his translation of the Psalmes', lines 3–4,
Dunlap, p. 93.
[135] *Ibid.*, lines 9–10, Dunlap, p. 94.
[136] *Ibid.*, lines 14–15.
[137] *Ibid.*, lines 19–20.
[138] *Ibid.*, lines 24–7.
[139] *Ibid.*, line 21.

Even in the lines in which he envisions a more spiritual life, the language reveals an enduring ambivalence about that commitment:

> Then, I no more shall court the verdant Bay,
> But the dry leavelesse Trunke on *Golgotha*;
> And rather strive to gaine from thence one Thorne,
> Then all the flourishing wreathes by Laureats worne.[140]

Christianity begins to seem barren and sterile beside the 'flourishing wreathes' worn by poets dedicated to the world of nature, and dedicated too, for all their frustrations, their own crosses, to a search *in the world* for the 'immortal love'. Carew's soul perhaps remained restless. His search for contentment perhaps continued 'without fruit'. But, in the end, it was through the poetry of beauty, love and nature, the world of sense *as well as* spirit, rather than in Christianity that he continued to seek for that contentment – for himself and for the world.

THE POLITICS OF NATURE

Nature and love are the basis of Carew's attitudes to politics as well as ethics. This should in no way surprise us. For all Carew's poetry was public poetry, even (perhaps especially) that love poetry that we conceive of as the most private.[141] The interrelationship between love and politics pervades Carew's language and metaphors. Carew's lover may be now subject, now monarch, but his relationship with his mistress is most often expressed in political terms. The lover acknowledges his duty to a mistress who commands him to return her letters: 'so powerfull is your sway / As if you bid me die I must obey'.[142] Her letters have been but her ambassadors which now return to their 'soveraigne', leaving the lover's 'vassall heart' 'ever hon'ring her', as a 'true Servant and subject to her self'.[143] In 'A deposition from Love', by contrast, the lover is a conquering prince rather than servant, waging a war against 'your rebell sex' in order to take the citadel of his mistress's heart. The victory, however, is short lived and Carew's abandoned lover

> he that is cast downe
> From enjoy'd beautie, feeles a woe,
> Onely deposed Kings can know.[144]

This is the language of politics employed as the discourse of a common world of lovers and kings, a world which does not rigidly distinguish what we would

---

[140] *Ibid.*, lines 33–6.
[141] For an incisive comment on the interdependency of love and government see Goldberg, *James I and the Politics of Literature*. Cf. below, ch. 6, *passim*.
[142] 'My mistris commanding me to returne her letters', lines 5–6, Dunlap, p. 9.
[143] *Ibid.*, lines 15, 24, 70, Dunlap, pp. 9–10.
[144] 'A Deposition from Love', lines 28–30, Dunlap, p. 17. Cf. below, p. 142.

call the private and the public domain. As Carew himself put it, 'Service in prose, is oft call'd love in verse.'[145] The relationships of men and women are described in political language because they are public and political relationships. No less, by corollary, political relationships may be examined through the language of love. Charles I and Henrietta Maria expressed their political ideas and values in the language of Platonic love, representing through their marriage the regulation of passion by higher understanding, the rule of the soul over the senses. In his love poetry, then, Carew employed and articulated a discourse that was intrinsically political in Renaissance England and a language through which in the 1630s the monarch directly expressed his political values. Carew's poetry of love and nature should not therefore be read as mere amorous banter, nor as an escape from political realities and problems, but as a discourse through which he examined political relationships and offered counsel and criticism to the court and the king.

Carew is usually depicted as one of the court lackeys whose poetry celebrates uncritically the virtues and values of the Caroline court.[146] But once we have appreciated his attitudes to nature and ethics, we may come to see that Carew's verse was independent and critical of the court. Let us consider 'To the King at his entrance into Saxham', written by Carew as a poem to be delivered to Charles I by John Crofts.[147] Saxham, as we have seen, enshrines the virtues and gifts of nature. And here, as the king enters the house, his host welcomes him to plain entertainment: the fruits and beasts of the local countryside rather than the 'rarities' or 'dainties' (compare the 'forraigne gums' of Wrest) 'that come from farre', but that are found too, of course, at court.[148] At Saxham, along with simple fare the king is offered plain entertainment, a country dance, and with it the plain language of loyalty, love and 'pure hearts'. Here Crofts and his family are devoted to their country and to nature as well as to their monarch; they pay their 'pious rites' to 'our household Gods' as well as to their king.[149] Their tone is loyal and loving, but not flattering or sycophantic. For the king himself is also expected to adjust to their world – to bring the mercy, 'not the greatnesse' of his majesty and to appreciate their endeavours.[150] In Saxham, and at Wrest of course, the king himself may find the greatness of the state of nature which may lend lustre even to his rule. Implicitly the richness and honesty of this

[145] 'My mistris commanding', line 28, Dunlap, p. 9.
[146] Parry, *Golden Age Restor'd*, p. 211; Parfitt, *Poetry of Carew*, p. 56; Sadler, *Carew*, p. 85.
[147] 'To the King at his entrance into Saxham, by Master Io. Crofts', Dunlap, pp. 30–1. For suggested dates of the poem, see *ibid.*, p. 226.
[148] 'To the King', line 25; 'To G.N. from Wrest', line 15.
[149] 'To the King', lines 3–4, 6.
[150] *Ibid.*, lines 37–9. There is almost a tone of reciprocity in the language and structure of the poem.

world are contrasted with the superficiality and deception of the court. Wrest, for instance, boasts no outward finery, but offers sincere hospitality:

> No Dorique, nor Corinthian Pillars grace
> With Imagery this structures naked face,
> The Lord and Lady of this place delight
> Rather to be in act, then seeme in sight.[151]

At Wrest, we recall, Bacchus and Ceres are not merely represented in statuary; at Saxham there is no porter to exclude the poor. Pillars, porters and statues, 'Emblemes to the eyes', 'outward gay Embellishment', the images evoke the Caroline court, its paintings and marbles, and perhaps too the images which they in turn portrayed.[152] They also suggest a society which would seem what it is not, an unnatural society beside Saxham and Wrest where 'we presse the juycie God'.

Criticism of the insincerities of the court is made more explicit in other poems. Carew's 'Obsequies to the lady ANNE HAY' opens with the powerful shock of a death that has changed the normal course of all behaviour: 'I saw the sleeke / And polisht Courtier, channell his fresh cheeke / With reall teares.'[153] Sincerity beneath the polish is evidently exceptional at court, where everything is unreal, a veneer which covers a less attractive fabric. From such a world the most honest men were inclined to withdraw. The Earl of Anglesey (Carew reminded his widowed countess) 'chose not in the active stream to swim'. Like Davenant's Earl of Rutland, Anglesey 'retir'd from the tumultuous noyse / Of Court, and suitors presse'.[154] Living apart from the court, and only by so doing, Anglesey enjoyed 'freedome and mirth, himselfe, his time, and friends'; 'all his actions had the noble end / T' advance desert'.[155] At court, by contrast, there was only dependence and hollow laughter, rivals rather than friends. At court a man must deny himself and his nature for falsehood and deception. And at court, Carew indicates, noble ends and desert find little place.

The court was expected to prescribe models for behaviour and values to be emulated.[156] Carew shares that expectation but sees that the court fails to fulfil it. Carew *contrasts* the values of the court with those of the virtuous life. The court is concerned with honour and reputation. Honour to Carew,

---

[151] 'To G.N. from Wrest', lines 29–32, Dunlap, p. 87. Cf. Ashton's comments on the similar lines of 'To Penshurst', *Civil War*, p. 35.

[152] On Carew's attitude to the plastic arts see below, p. 149.

[153] 'Obsequies to the Lady Anne Hay', lines 1–5, Dunlap, p. 67.

[154] 'To the Countesse of Anglesie upon the immoderatly-by-her lamented death of her husband', lines 57, 65, Dunlap, p. 70. Cf. above, ch. 2, p. 91. Like Jonson and Davenant, Carew turns an epitaph on an individual into a critique of court society.

[155] 'To the Countesse of Anglesie', lines 66–7. Cf. 'himselfe' with the 'myselfe' of 'To G.N. from Wrest', line 107, above, p. 129.

[156] Above, ch. 1, pp. 19–20.

however, is 'but a Masquer' which deludes 'baser subjects' but is disdained by
'the nobler train'.[157] This appears to be self-contradiction. But Carew's point
is that honour as traditionally understood is a mere appearance – a concern
with reputation in society rather than with true virtue, irrespective of public
estimation. And society and reputation, he makes clear, may often be at odds
with the truth:

> malice can on vestals throw
> Disgrace, and Fame fixe high repute
> On the close shamelesse Prostitute.[158]

When morality is so overturned, all order is subverted.

> Who may know
> Rebels from subjects that obey.[159]

True virtue lies not in potentially false reputation but in personal integrity, in
a return to that innocence of man's first existence:

> Vaine Honour! Thou art but disguise,
> A cheating voyce, a jugling art,
> No judge of vertue, whose pure eyes
> Court her own Image in the heart.

Carew's lines come from a chorus he wrote to the court performance of a
play.[160] And that powerful 'Court' of the last line quoted may be intended to
reinforce the point: virtue courts her own image in the heart, but the image of
the court, honour, is but a disguise for the 'jugling art' there practised. The
court continues to boast and advocate a virtuous code of conduct, but in
reality courtly values have become detached from virtue and so the court has
lost its claim to prescribe morality.

During the 1630s, as we know, the ethical and political values of the court
were expressed through the idea of Platonic love, 'a love', in James Howell's
words, 'abstracted from . . . sensual Appetite', consisting in 'Contemplations
and Ideas of the Mind, not in any carnal fruition'.[161] Some critics have
dismissed its importance for Caroline poetry.[162] But there can be little doubt
that Carew recognized the importance of Platonic love for courtly values and
addressed some of his verse directly to the subject. Some poems indeed appear
to be a critical response to it. Carew himself, as we have seen, writes of a
spiritual love which transcends the merely physical. In 'A Pastorall Dialogue',

---

[157] 'A Rapture', lines 4–6.
[158] 'Feminine Honour', lines 16–18, Dunlap, p. 61.
[159] *Ibid.*, lines 14–15. A breach of love is identified in one poem with the disruption of all nature.
See 'The protestation, a Sonnet', Dunlap, p. 109. See ch. 5, *passim.*
[160] 'Feminine Honour', lines 19–22, p. 61; Dunlap suggests the date was 1633, p. 244.
[161] Above, p. 24.
[162] Miner, *Cavalier Mode*, p. 110.

Cleon dotes not on Celia's pure white skin, 'but on thy purer mind'.[163] Carew
tells his Celia that lovers whose spirits are joined taste

> a sweet, and subtle blisse,
> (Such as grosse lovers cannot know,
> Whose hands, and lips, meet here below;)[164]

But in Carew's poetry the spiritual relationship never supplants or negates the
physical. Nor can the one be divorced from the other. In the famous 'Disdaine
Returned' ('Hee that loves a Rosie cheeke . . .') Carew loves not with the spirit
or body alone: he seeks in his mistress both 'a smooth and steadfast mind' *and*
'lovely cheekes, or lips, or eyes'.[165] The union of body *and* spirit is the
ultimate expression of love, besides which all else is second best. So, Carew's
lines to his mistress 'in absence', describing their closeness while apart,
emerge in the end as a device to pass the time before they may come together
again in flesh as well as in spirit:

> Wee'le cheat the lag, and lingring houres,
> Making our bitter absence sweet,
> Till soules, and bodyes both, may meet.[166]

That 'both' unites them all – soul to soul, body to body, and, perhaps most
significantly, body to soul. There is a suggestion that Carew believed in a
progress of perception from the world of sense to the sphere of spirit. Physical
love in the poetry does elevate men and women to a spiritual union. So, in 'A
Rapture'

> our soules that cannot be embrac'd,
> Shall the embraces of our bodyes taste.[167]

But, in turn, spiritual love is shown to require that life and rejuvenation of the
senses that first fired it. As Carew put it in a song to a court entertainment,
'Separation of Lovers':

> For the sense not fed, denies
> Nourishment unto the minde.[168]

It is love's 'hand' that unites souls. Spirit and sense feed each other and love is
the union of body and soul both within the lover and between the lover and
his mistress. Carew's position then is quite different from the philosophy of

---

[163] Above, p. 125.
[164] 'To my Mistresse in absence', lines 18–20, Dunlap, p. 22.
[165] 'Disdaine Returned', lines 7, 12 of a stanza carefully balanced to enfold both a steadfast mind
     and lovely cheeks, Dunlap, p. 18.
[166] 'To my Mistresse in absence', lines 32–4, Dunlap, p. 22. Once again the final couplet turns the
     sense of the poem from a celebration of a purely spiritual to the eager contemplation of also a
     physical relationship.
[167] 'A Rapture', lines 43–4, Dunlap, p. 50.
[168] 'Separation of Lovers', lines 21–2, Dunlap, p. 62.

Platonic love and the court masques in which the world of spirit and idea *transcends* the physical universe, as masque dispels antimasque.

It is noteworthy that Carew's 'Separation of Lovers' was one of four songs, all on the subject of love and honour, which he wrote for 'an entertainment of the King and Queene' evidently in 1633.[169] It may be that the songs were intended as a commentary upon, and to some extent a criticism of, the cult of Platonic love which had just taken the court by storm in the production of Walter Montagu's *The Shepherd's Paradise*.[170] Carew would have seen the play and Rhodes Dunlap has drawn attention to the close echoes in lines 9–12 of 'To My Mistresse in absence' of the speech by Melidoro, Montagu's Platonic lover.[171] Beyond that, we cannot be sure. But what is clear is Carew's awareness of Platonic love and his (rare) expression of irritation at the cult:

> Let fooles thy mystique formes adore,
> I'le know thee in thy mortall state.[172]

For Carew courtly Platonism was an abstraction which denied the senses, and thereby negated what Carew lamented the absence of in 'A divine Mistris' – the 'humanitie' of man, his nature.[173] If so, we may understand how he might have regarded it as an affront to his beliefs. The criticism, however, goes further, because Platonic love was the metaphor through which the court articulated a political philosophy as well as an ethical code. Carew may well have been more optimistic than Charles I about the capacities of men to regulate themselves, and so may have been less attracted to an ethical and political philosophy that enshrined the king as the soul of the commonwealth, ruling over creatures of appetite. Carew's criticism of courtly Platonism, as we shall see, questioned the political ideology of the court and its understanding of the relationship between the king and his people.[174]

The description of the commonweal as the 'body politic', with the king the head and his subjects the members, is a commonplace Renaissance image. In Carew's poetry, however, the idea of the 'body' takes on a literal as well as metaphoric reality. The king and people Carew presents with freshness as literally conjoined so that sensations in one part of the body rapidly affect the other. When sickness befalls the monarch:

> Entring his royall limbes that is our head,
> Through us his mystique limbs the paine is spread,

[169] Dunlap, p. 244.
[170] *The Shepherd's Paradise*, we recall, was acted on 10 January 1633. See above, ch. 1, pp. 39–44 and for the court reaction to the cult of Platonic love, Beaulieu to Puckering, 10 Jan. 1633, Birch, *Court and Times of Charles I*, II, p. 216, and the letter of James Howell.
[171] Dunlap, p. 224.
[172] 'Ingratefull beauty threatned', lines 15–16, Dunlap, p. 18.
[173] 'A divine Mistris', line 16, Dunlap, p. 7.
[174] See below, ch. 6.

> That man that doth not feele his part, hath none
> In any part of his dominion.[175]

The language of feeling and pain imparts a physicality which transcends metaphor. The king and his people are one body physically as well as theoretically united, just as Carew's lovers are joined in body as well as soul. And it is just such a love, physical as well as spiritual, of the people for the king that afflicts them too with his pain.

> This griefe is felt at Court, where it doth move
> Through every joynt, like the true soule of love.[176]

Such a grief 'shewes a good King is sick, and good men mourne'.[177] The repetition of the epithet underlines the fact that Carew is prescribing an ideal relationship, whilst describing an actual one. The best relationship between a *good* ruler and *good* subjects is like the perfect union of true lovers: it is a physical togetherness as well as spiritual; it unites ruler and ruled, virtue and government. And so sickness, which threatens the good monarch, is a 'Tyrant' ruling by arbitrary will that king who has governed in conjunction and love with his people.[178] It is 'the minister of death', the most arbitrary of all rulers who knows no regimen but merciless conquest.[179] The union of king and subjects, and mutual love between them, Carew is saying, is essential to the health, indeed the very life, of the body politic. And the good king of this ideal polity is not only God's lieutenant on earth, but is possessed too, as was Carew's ideal mistress, of 'humanity'; he is the 'Darling of the Gods and men . . .'[180]

For, to Carew, kings are not gods who may decree what is virtuous and what is vicious. They too live in and are of a society which has fallen from virtue and so may themselves be susceptible to the corruptions of fallen nature. Absolute authority is beyond them. Carew tells his mistress who commands the return of her letters that, though a monarch, she too has to account for her actions and heed his wishes:

> If she refuse, warne her to come before
> The God of Love, whom thus I will implore.[181]

Monarchs, Carew informs a lady resembling his mistress, may establish by their own authority values in their own kingdom, but there remains an absolute morality, a universal virtue to which they too are subject. The poet

---

[175] 'Upon the Kings sicknesse', lines 19–22, Dunlap, p. 35. See note p. 229. The date must remain uncertain; I incline to 1633, on account of the reference to youth.
[176] 'Upon the Kings sicknesse', lines 25–6.   [177] *Ibid.*, line 42.
[178] *Ibid.*, line 17. Cf. the 'government Tyrannicall / In Loves free state . . .' cited below, p. 142.
[179] *Ibid.*, line 1.   [180] *Ibid.*, line 37.
[181] 'My mistris commanding', lines 31–2, Dunlap, p. 9. The passage is a nice reminder that divine right theory involved a responsibility of the king to God, as well as power derived from Him.

explores the idea, with unconventional implications, through the disarmingly familiar metaphor of the coin that bears the king's stamp:

> To Lead, or Brasse, or some such bad
> Mettall, a Princes stamp may adde
> That valew, which it never had.
>
> But to the pure refined Ore,
> The stamp of Kings imparts no more
> Worth, then the mettall held before.
>
> Only the Image gives the rate
> To Subjects; in a forraine State
> 'Tis priz'd as much for its owne waight.[182]

A debased coinage was regarded in early Stuart England as the currency of an ailing kingdom. Here, of course, it is a kingdom falling from virtue and, incidentally, one in which outward values have become detached from intrinsic qualities. A good currency was that which most nearly reflected intrinsic (metallic) value, and so, Carew is arguing, a good king is he who comes closest to nature and stamps its values with his image, so that society takes by his authority nature itself as its currency. The good ruler's responsibility is to return society to those inherent, natural values of its first pure unpolluted condition – that of man before society (and its sham concern with reputation) in the garden of innocence. A vision of nature, then, is central to Carew's political as well as his ethical system. The function of government he still perceives as the rule of virtue: politics and morality are not divorced; government and love are not distinct. Rulers indeed, like lovers, ought to renounce the empty considerations of honour and reputation by which princes like all men were evaluated in a fallen world. They were to take their standards of government from uncorrupted nature, to exemplify nature's first innocence in their persons, and to codify nature's dictates as the maxims of their rule.

We have suggested in discussing Carew's ethics that men and women rediscover their nature through a pure and eternal love, a love sealed in society by the physical and spiritual union of marriage. I would like to suggest that for Carew it is through the marriage of ruler and ruled, of the king and his people, that the commonweal too comes nearest to the kingdom of virtue. Carew's lovers, as we have seen, are political beings – sometimes monarch, sometimes subject. The lover is unfulfilled, however, in either rôle if, in the one case, his sovereign mistress spurns his 'vassall heart' or when, as a conquering prince, his power does not secure him her love.[183] Whether ruler or subject, man as lover is only complete and fulfilled when love is physical

---

[182] 'To T.H., a Lady resembling my Mistresse', lines 16–24, Dunlap, p. 27.
[183] Above, p. 134.

and spiritual, mutual and reciprocated. So, a king who conquers but rules without love is no king at all: he is, as 'A Deposition from Love' makes clear, 'deposed'.[184] And so in the commonweal as in the polity of love (for the two are really one), true kingship depends upon reciprocal love. Monarchy is the marriage of ruler and ruled that conjoins authority and love and so leads society, as it does man, to the virtue of nature.

The place of love and marriage in Carew's political thought may be understood most clearly from his poem 'Upon my Lord Chiefe Justice his election of my Lady A.W. for his Mistresse'.[185] Law and love are here betrothed. In consequence the 'government Tyrannicall' (compare the 'tyrant Mistresse' of 'An Elegie on the La-PENN') of 'Usurping Beauties' is to be brought under the rule of law.[186] Law controls the passions by governing them. But law and government in their turn are to lie 'In Love's soft lap' exchanging rigour and coercion for love and union:

> Harke how the sterne Law breathes
> Forth amorous sighs, and now prepares
> No fetters, but of silken wreathes, . . .
> Love hath fi'lde
> His native roughnesse, Justice is growne milde.[187]

Their union improves both potentially arbitrary love and over-rigorous law. In their union 'The golden Age returnes' – that is an age in which outward appearances and inner virtues become one ('the fayre shall all be kind'); in which love is reciprocal ('who loves shall be belov'd'); in which men find their true and perfect nature (only the 'froward mind' is 'To a deformed shape . . . confin'd').[188] This is Carew's state of nature and perfect commonweal; it is the ideal vision of his politics of love: heavenly justice has now come to earth, as Astraea returns to rule.[189]

Carew's poem, however, is addressed to a specific person and has too a more particular application. The Chief Justice of the verse is Sir John Finch, who became Lord Chief Justice of the Court of Common Pleas on 16 October 1634. Finch was close to the court and a vigorous upholder of the royal prerogative; in 1637 he was the leading spokesman for the crown in the ship money case.[190] Finch then stands not only for justice in the abstract or in general but for royal justice and the exercise of royal justice during the years

---

[184] 'A Deposition from Love', line 30, Dunlap, p. 17.

[185] Dunlap, pp. 83–4.

[186] *Ibid.*, lines 2–3; 'An Elegie on the La-PENN', line 1, Dunlap, p. 19.

[187] 'Upon my Lord Chiefe Justice', lines 8–14, p. 83. We recall how Carew employed the term 'milde' to describe the havens of nature and the condition of the love.

[188] *Ibid.*, lines 19–21. The 'deformed shape' of the forward lovers evokes the antimasques of the 1630s, especially the depraved lovers of *Tempe Restored*. See below, ch. 5, pp. 184, 201–2.

[189] 'Upon my Lord Chiefe Justice', lines 22–3.

[190] See W. H. Terry, *The Life and Times of John, Lord Finch* (London, 1936); F. Hargrave, ed., *A Complete Collection of State Trials* (11 vols., London, 1776–81), VII, pp. 506–719.

of the personal rule of Charles I. Finch's mistress, 'my Lady A.W.' is Anne Wentworth, niece to Sir John Crofts, whose country home, Saxham, Carew regarded, as we have seen, as a haven of nature and virtue. In Saxham there is no crime because men cannot steal what is given freely: 'And as for theeves, thy bounties' such / They cannot steale, thou giv'st so much.'[191] The rigour of justice has no place in this perfect society, as there is no sin in 'A Rapture'. Even in society, Carew tells us, men are not mere wild beasts to be tamed by 'dreadfull Rods' of 'sterne law', but have the potential for virtue in their nature.[192] And so in society and in the polity men should be ordered by love as well as authority so that they might rediscover their own higher nature and so achieve that self-regulation which is the best government of all. If marriage regulates the sexual passions without denying man's sensual appetite, so in government the marriage of love and justice may order society without denying the humanity and good of man. There is then in a poem that might appear to be a conventional celebration of courtly romance more than a hint of criticism – that justice needs to be softened and government should woo with 'silken wreathes' not 'fetters'.[193] The reference to Astraea (Justice) 'new enthron'd' could not but have evoked memories of a Queen Elizabeth under whose rule love had in rhetoric and perhaps in reality softened the harshness of government.[194] Carew's 'Upon my Lord Chiefe Justice' perhaps then argues for in general what it celebrates in particular: a union of love and justice as the best form of government.

Charles I, as we have seen, communicated his vision of the best government through his marriage represented as a Platonic union of souls. Significantly the royal marriage is the central subject of the poetry that Carew addressed to both the king and the queen, but Carew's depiction of that marriage is very different from the king's. Love and government are intertwined in a verse which wishes for the monarch as 'A New-yeares gift' the physical joys and fertile fruits of marriage:

> Season his cares by day with nights
> Crown'd with all conjugall delights,
> May the choyce beauties that enflame
> His Royall brest be still the same,
> And he still thinke them such, since more
> Thou canst not give from Natures store.
> Then as a Father let him be
> With numerous issue blest, and see

---

[191] 'To Saxham', lines 57–8, Dunlap, p. 29.
[192] 'Upon my Lord Chiefe Justice', line 12. It is this optimistic belief in the intrinsic and potential good of human nature that is central to Carew's ethics and politics. See below, ch. 6.
[193] 'Upon my Lord Chiefe Justice', line 10.
[194] F. Yates, *Astraea: the Imperial Theme in the Sixteenth Century* (London, 1975).

> The faire and God-like off-spring growne
> From budding starres to Suns full blowne.[195]

In this important extract many of the strands in Carew's ethical and political thought are interwoven. Love ameliorates the cares of government. The king confirms his title through a love that is pure and constant, yet physical as well as spiritual. Such a love, such a marriage is indeed 'from Nature's store'. In this physical and spiritual union, the king not only lives and rules virtuously, he seeds and sires virtue as his offspring, giving birth to 'God-like' children, made like the first man in God's image, 'Suns' who, as nature's light and God's own Son, may rescue a fallen world from darkness. The perfect ruler is become the true lover. And in fashioning his government by his marriage the king may secure 'loyall hearts' and 'conjugall delights' too with his subjects. This marriage – between the king and his people – would see 'one great continued festivall' of joy, that golden age of love and justice united.[196] It is the prescription of this perfect polity that is Carew's 'New-yeares gift. To the King'.

It is, as it were, the other side of the government–love equation that Carew addresses to the queen. If the good ruler is, in Charles's case, the right lover, then here, Carew maintains, the true lover may have the best claim to rule. The queen, who exemplifies love, is a 'great Commandresse' who has ordered the unbridled excesses of 'wilde lust'. Her government flows directly from her love by example rather than coercion. She teaches men that love is constant and fruitful and as a result of her influence disordered nature itself submits to her government willingly. The 'rude male' becomes satisfied with one partner; the very Satyr is 'reconciled' to order.[197] But the queen in Carew's poem is not the Platonic lover of the masques. Like the 'numerous issue' of 'God-like off-spring' wished for the king, the queen's example and love are a 'pregnant fire', which will engender virtue and order throughout the natural world. In both poems Carew's message is the same: true love is the government of nature, and the only true government is that which is founded on love.

Carew's position on love and the politics of love, then, is very different from the tone and stance of the courtly Platonic love cult. The subject and images of Carew's love poetry are more physical, his language more explicitly erotic than the abstractions of courtly Platonism. But we should not conclude that his poetry is less philosophical, less serious, or less political. Language and tone reinforce Carew's argument. For Carew believes strongly in the

---

[195] 'A New-yeares gift. To the King', lines 17–26, Dunlap, p. 90.

[196] The intertwining of the subjects of love and nature, rich in a language of fecundity, in a poem addressed to the monarch, encapsulates the argument of this chapter.

[197] 'To the Queene', Dunlap, pp. 90–1. Perhaps significantly in the 1640 edition of Carew's poetry this poem follows 'A New-yeares gift. To the King'.

potential for virtue in man's nature, and so advocates not the transcendence
or denial of the potentially wild manifestations of nature, but insists upon
that marriage of the senses and the spirit, or the reason, in which alone man
may fulfil his nature. Accordingly, Carew sees right government not as the
suppression of man's anarchic natural appetite by abstract authority ruling
by coercion. Rather he prescribes as the purpose of government that reorder-
ing of men's natures so as to restore them to the purer condition of their
original state of nature in which no government was necessary. Such a
regimen must be founded upon love. And in the commonweal as well as in the
world of ethics (the distinction would have meant much less to him than to us)
Carew advocates marriage – here the union of the ruler and the ruled in love
and virtue – as the mean between the anarchy of unordered appetites and the
sterility of denial, or of an authority which in suppressing the sensuality of
man denied his nature and nature itself.[198]

Marriage, we recall, Carew described as a condition of peace in a polity of
love beset by the tempests of tears and sighs of wild or unsatisfied passion.[199]
Love, illicit, unrequited or lost, is often depicted in Carew's poetry in
Petrarchan martial imagery, as a struggle or battle. In returning his letters to
the mistress who now spurned him, Carew recalled in defeat his 'former
fights, 'gainst fiercer foes, then shee / Did at our first incounter seeme to
bee'.[200] 'A Deposition from Love' compares the conquest of a mistress to a
siege; it is 'Truce in Love entreated' by he who has in his heart 'No voyd place
for another Dart'.[201] Constant and mutual love, by contrast, secures, as
Carew describes it in 'A Rapture', 'steadfast peace' where 'no rude sounds
shake us with sudden starts', that 'Halcion calmnesse' of the Elyzium in
which the poem is located.[202] It may be that it is this peace and calmness –
that of a paradise located outside time and history – that Carew wished for
society and the commonweal as well as for individual men in prescribing a
politics of marriage as the best mode of government.

It may be in this context that we can begin to understand Carew's most
difficult and most obviously political poem, his 'In Answer of an Elegiacall
Letter upon the death of the King of Sweden from Aurelian Townshend
. . .'[203] During his personal rule Charles I, it is often said, was dedicated to a
policy of peace, in order to avoid resummoning parliament. Cavalier poetry
celebrating the 'halcyon' days of the 1630s is accordingly read as uncritical
idealization of the king's ignoble and enforced withdrawal from European

[198] See below, ch. 6.   [199] Above, p. 119.
[200] 'My mistris commanding', lines 37–8, Dunlap, p. 10.
[201] 'A Deposition from Love', Dunlap, pp. 16–17; 'Truce in Love entreated', *ibid.*, p. 41.
[202] 'A Rapture', lines 97–9, 110.
[203] Dunlap, pp. 74–7. Townshend's 'Elegy on the death of the King of Sweden: sent to Thomas
    Carew' is printed in Brown, *Poems and Masques of Aurelian Townshend*, pp. 48–9, and is
    discussed below, ch. 4, pp. 174–6.

affairs, as, once again, the sycophantic celebration of a royal policy which was not for the good of the realm. Carew's poem is usually regarded as the classic example of this flattery of Caroline foreign policy, and it is not hard to see why.[204] The poem at one level exemplifies that retreat from European engagement that characterized Charles I's foreign policy and alienated some of his subjects. In reply to Townshend's exhortations 'inviting me to write' on the death of Gustavus Adolphus, Carew counsels his friend:

> But let us that in myrtle bowers sit
> Under secure shades, use the benefit
> Of peace and plenty, which the blessed hand
> Of our good King gives this obdurate Land.[205]

The poet's place, Carew argues, is to celebrate this peace rather than to dwell upon the ravages of a European war from which England is fortunately free. Townshend's own court masque, *Tempe Restored*, is held up as a more fitting subject for his muse:[206]

> These harmelesse pastimes let my *Townsend* sing
> To rurall tunes; ...
>   these are subjects proper to our clyme.
> Tourneyes, Masques, Theatres, better become
> Our *Halcyon* dayes; what though the German Drum
> Bellow for freedome and revenge, the noyse
> Concernes not us, nor should divert our joyes.[207]

And yet, for all his disclaimer (let us recall Carew's poem to George Sandys on his translation of the psalms), the subject does concern Carew – for one of his longest poems of 104 lines! There is a suggestion of irony too, or at least of some divorce between words and meaning, in these lines. The forcefulness of 'Bellow for freedome' is a noise that must awake the reader as Townshend's 'shrill accents' sounded an alarm to Carew's 'drowsie eyes'.[208] Gustavus Adolphus forces himself upon the stage of Carew's poem – as a figure

---

[204] Wedgwood, *Poetry and Politics under the Stuarts*, p. 44.

[205] 'In Answer of an Elegiacall Letter', lines 45–8, Dunlap, p. 75. The recognition of the obduracy of Charles I's subjects in 1632 indicates a greater awareness of political reality in Carew than Wedgwood and others have allowed. The poem indeed may be ironic, see L. Marz, *The Wit of Love* (Notre Dame, 1969), p. 78.

[206] 'In Answer', lines 52–8, Dunlap, p. 76. Carew refers to 'The beauties of the SHEPHERDS PARADISE', but it is clear that the masque of Townshend's which he is describing is *Tempe Restored*. See below, ch. 5.

[207] 'In Answer', lines 94–8, Dunlap, p. 77. Cf. Jonson's comment:
> What is't to me whether the French designe
> Be, or be not, to get the Val'telline
quoted by R. S. Peterson, *Imitation and Praise in the Poems of Ben Jonson* (New Haven, 1981), p. 144.

[208] 'In Answer', lines 2–3, 96–7, Dunlap, pp. 74, 77. Compare the 'drowsie eyes' with the 'slumbers' and 'amorous languishment' of 'A Rapture', lines 41, 52.

'mightie', 'victorious', 'majesticke'.[209] Carew's obvious praise for the King of Sweden appears inexplicably at odds with his advice to Townshend about the appropriate subjects of his art. There is a tension within the poem that may reflect Carew's ambivalent attitude to royal foreign policy. But the discrepancy may also be understood otherwise. For Gustavus is presented as a figure above conventional poetic celebration:

> His actions were too mighty to be rais'd
> Higher by Verse, let him in prose be prays'd,
> In modest faithfull story, which his deedes
> Shall turne to Poems.[210]

He is, for Carew, a figure outside poetry. Gustavus represents the flux and change, victories and defeat of action in the world – a world of noise, of time and events, of death, of fate, of history. It is this world rather than Gustavus Adolphus that Carew rejects as a subject for his muse:

> Let us to supreame providence commit
> The fate of Monarchs, which first thought it fit
> To rend the Empire from the *Austrian* graspe,
> And next from *Swedens*.[211]

Carew then does not reject Gustavus Adolphus specifically. He wishes to distance his verse from history and chronicle – from the relation of events, the rise and fall of states. And he does so because poetry, as Sidney had claimed, may express higher truths than history. Carew's poetry 'of Love and Beautie' has a more sublime purpose and engagement than with the flux of European power politics: it is concerned with reformation, the restoration of a golden age of innocence beside the calm of which the battles of Germany seem but a noise in time. So half-way through his 'answer' Carew commends to his friend Townshend's own poetry of love and nature as a more fitting subject for his muse. For Townshend's 'past'rall pipe' and 'Angel-shapes', in his masque for the queen, 'brought us from above / A patterne of their owne celestiall love'.[212] Townshend's masque had risen above the world of events: its 'ravishing sounds' did 'dispense / Knowledge and pleasure to the soule, and sense'.[213] Poetry could do no more. Townshend's had instructed in that pure love that might lift men and monarchs beyond the noise of time and events to the calm of an earlier condition of innocence. All man's strivings in the world could secure no more. The 'Halcyon days' Carew celebrates is that 'Halcyon

---

[209] 'In Answer', lines 5, 9, Dunlap, p. 74.
[210] *Ibid.*, lines 15–18, Dunlap, p. 75.
[211] *Ibid.*, lines 35–8. Cf. Carew's masque, *Coelum Britannicum*, lines 684–760, where Fortune presents an antimaque, 'the representation of a battle'. Orgel and Strong, *Inigo Jones*, II, p. 576; below, ch. 5, p. 204.
[212] 'In Answer', lines 52, 60, 63–4, Dunlap, p. 76.
[213] *Ibid.*, lines 75–6.

calmenesse' of the lovers in the Elizium of 'A Rapture'.[214] It is far from clear whether Carew believed that those days had come to England during the 1630s: he acknowledges that England is not the land of perfect peace and harmony but an 'obdurate' country, resistant to reformation. But we may be sure that the securing of such a condition was for Carew the purpose of poetry. If Carew believed that the restoration of uncorrupted nature might be attained by the poetry of love, then we may more clearly understand his disclaimer that the noise of strife and battle (the antithesis of love) 'concernes not us'.[215]

THE PURPOSE AND POWER OF POETRY

If we are to argue that Carew's poetry expounded ethical and political beliefs, if we are to suggest that Carew believed in the power of poetry to effect important change, then we must withdraw Carew from Pope's company of gentlemen that wrote with ease. It is right that we do so, for too many since Pope have been led into the assumption that because Carew was a courtier, because his lines often read with effortless simplicity, Carew did not take his poetry seriously, or have anything serious to say. His contemporaries, however, did not make the same mistake. Suckling, for example, rejected, probably with tongue in cheek, Carew's claims to the crown of the wits because

> His Muse was hard bound, and th'issue of's brain
> Was seldom brought forth but with trouble and pain.[216]

Carew himself acknowledged his painstaking industry in a less scatological metaphor, spurning what he called the 'unkneaded dowe – bak't prose' or ballad rhymes of his contemporaries. Carew worked at his poetry and admired others who laboured to refine their verse.[217] 'Thy labour'd workes', he assured Ben Jonson, 'shall live, when Time devoures / Th'abortive offspring of their hastie houres.'[218] Such labour did not always guarantee appreciation. But poets, Carew reminded his mentor, wrote not for their reputation in a 'dull age', but for 'after dayes', 'immortall Bayes' that placed

---

[214] *Ibid.*, line 96, Dunlap, p. 77; cf. 'A Rapture', line 97, *ibid.*, p. 51.

[215] 'In Answer', line 97, Dunlap, p. 77. For different interpretations of this poem, see M. P. Parker, 'Carew's politic pastoral: Virgilian pretexts in the "Answer to Aurelian Town-shend"', *John Donne Journal*, 1 (1982), pp. 101–16, and R. A. Anselment, 'Thomas Carew and the "Harmelesse Pastimes" of Caroline Peace', *Philological Quarterly*, 62 (1983), pp. 201–19.

[216] '(The Wits) (A Sessions of the Poets)', lines 35–6, *The Non-Dramatic Works of Suckling*, p. 73.

[217] 'An Elegie upon the death of the Deane of Pauls, Dr. John Donne', lines 4, 69, Dunlap, pp. 71–3.

[218] 'To Ben Jonson', lines 45–6, Dunlap, p. 65. Cf. Carew's remark in his letter to Suckling: 'Second thoughts (which are by all allowed the Best) . . .', *ibid.*, p. 211.

them, as their poetry, beyond reputation and time. Jonson, unlike the rhymsters, struck 'soules' in his verse and so wrote not for an age but for all time.[219]

Carew took his own poetry seriously because he appreciated and made claims for the importance, indeed the power, of poetry. The claim to poetic power is conventional, but Carew asserts it with particular force to remind the lover of his authority. And given the political freighting of love poetry, this was also to argue, in the 1630s, for the power of poetry in the commonweal. When the poet speaks, often through the lover, in Carew's lines, he assets the power of his art. Though she spurns him, Celia is forcefully reminded of the poet's power in the aptly titled 'Ingratefull beauty threatned':

> Know *Celia* (since thou art so proud,)
> 'Twas I that gave thee thy renowne:
> Thou hadst, in the forgotten crowd
> Of common beauties, liv'd unknowne,
> Had not my verse exhal'd thy name,
> And with it, ympt the wings of fame.[220]

Celia's 'killing power' is the gift of the poet – and the poet may as easily take it away. The power to create and to 'uncreate' remains in the poet's hands.

Herein lay the power of poetry: the power of creation and of immortality. Celia recognizes it when she tells Cleon in 'A Pastorall Dialogue', 'I / Shall live in thy immortal rime.'[221] Her lover is a poet and both love and poetry will redeem her from time, re-create her for all time. The poet's power to create and to immortalize derived from a treasury of which the poet was the beneficiary. And that treasury, Carew tells us, is nature. Carew offers to a mistress in return for her favours 'Rich Nature's store (which is the Poet's Treasure)'.[222]

The best poetry, the only true poetry, distributed nature's wealth in order to give life. Jonson's poems were 'births', as Donne 'kindled first by thy Promethean breath'.[223] For to Carew poetry alone offered images of virtue which could effect man's reformation. Pictorial images, Carew makes clear, could not represent nature, for they are concerned with surface appearance, not inner qualities. 'Canst thou . . .', Carew asks in 'To the Painter', '. . . tell how / To paint a vertue?' The answer is already clear: 'your Artifice hath mist'. For 'artifice' is not nature and so the painter must desist when he cannot present emotions or virtues. But the perfection of nature can be represented faithfully in love and in the virtuous offspring of love:

[219] 'To Ben Johnson', line 17, Dunlap, p. 65.
[220] 'Ingratefull beauty threatened', lines 1–6, Dunlap, p. 17.
[221] 'A Pastorall Dialogue', lines 46–7, Dunlap, p. 44.
[222] 'To a Lady that desired I would love her', line 31, Dunlap, p. 82.
[223] 'An Elegie upon . . . John Donne', line 23, Dunlap, p. 72; 'To Ben Jonson', line 17, Dunlap, p. 65.

> Yet your Art cannot equalize
> This *Picture* in her lovers eyes,
> His eyes the pencills are which limbe
> Her truly, as her's coppy him,
> His heart the Tablet which alone,
> Is for that porctraite the tru'st stone.
> If you would a truer see,
> Marke it in their posteritie.[224]

Love is perfect nature's expression. And so the poet who writes of love does what the painter cannot: he distributes nature's treasure – virtue – where the painter may only represent nature in images.

The inculcation of virtue through a poetry of love and nature was Carew's contribution to his age. He believed it also to be the function of government. We have seen how Carew's lover is depicted in political language. No less the poet, nature's lover, is presented as a monarch. Jonson, for example, is advised to dispel any concern for criticism of his verse, because his less good is judged by the standards of his best: 'the quarrel lyes / Within thine own Virge'.[225] The virge, of course, is the boundary of the king's domain: poetry is Jonson's court and he its monarch. The parallel is succinctly made in Carew's famous epitaph on Donne:

> Here lies a King, that rul'd as he thought fit
> The universall Monarchy of wit.[226]

Wit Carew defines for us as the didactic content of art:

> A sence that can enforme the mind;
> Divine, or moral rules impart.[227]

The monarch of wit, then, is a king indeed, leading men to knowledge and establishing rules for behaviour. For Carew, that knowledge and those rules come from nature and the poet's claim to rule stems from his rôle as a tutor of nature's divine and moral rules to his age. For Carew, government and authority should be didactic rather than coercive; their purpose is to make each man his own ruler by restoring him to the innocence of his first nature. Poets and kings share this responsibility and this power. And so for Carew as for Davenant the poet is a principal aid to government.

Like Davenant, Carew appreciated that not all men would be led to virtue by the poetry of nature. The age which had fallen from the virtues of nature had become, too, more stubbornly committed to its own distorted values and so more unwilling to heed nature's dictates, or the words of her ambassadors, the muses. The arts themselves revealed the taints of that degeneration.

[224] 'To the Painter', lines 12–14, 43–50, Dunlap, pp. 106–7.
[225] 'To Ben Johnson', lines 47–8, Dunlap, p. 65.
[226] 'An Elegie', lines 95–6, Dunlap, p. 74.
[227] 'A Fancie', lines 16–17, Dunlap, p. 117.

Poetry had descended to mere 'ballad rime' without 'fire' or 'soul', whilst in the theatre the audience clamoured for empty spectacle and burlesque rather than 'characters of vertue'. Artificial action on the stage, Carew argues, reflected a life of artifice (divorce from nature) off the stage. In an age devoid of virtue and wit, men throng

> To that adulterate stage, where not a tong
> Of th'untun'd Kennell, can a line repeat
> Of serious sence: but like lips, meet like meat;
> Whilst the true brood of Actors, that alone
> Keepe naturall unstrain'd Action in her throne
> Behold their Benches bare, though they rehearse
> The terser *Beaumonts* or great *Johnsons* verse.[228]

Such a disease, Carew suggested, not only infected the arts: 'perhaps the State / Hath felt this rancour'.[229] Because poets and princes have a common goal it is not surprising that they are both misunderstood and resisted when an ignorant age confuses judgement and taste, reason and appetite. Carew appears to have feared that his own verse might be misunderstood. But in politics and in poetry there were still men of discrimination and knowledge. 'Wisemen, that governe fate', Carew assured Davenant, would appreciate his 'loftie straine'.[230] And it is these men who understand his verse who Carew hopes will perform upon the public stage of the commonweal, like the 'true brood of Actors', to keep there, as in the theatre, 'naturall . . . Action in her throne'.[231] Through right rulers subjects might be led to virtue and their higher nature. To rulers the poet imparts the values of nature as their guide to governance. Carew's purpose could not have been loftier or more serious. We should not read his love poetry as light or superficial

> cause you underneath may find
> A sence that can enforme the mind;
> Divine, or moral rules impart
> Or Raptures of Poetick Art.[232]

[228] 'To my worthy friend, M. D'Avenant', lines 26–32, Dunlap, p. 96.
[229] *Ibid.*, lines 34–5.
[230] *Ibid.*, lines 37–8.
[231] Cf. the 'heroic virtue' of *Coelum Britannicum*, line 670, Orgel and Strong, *Inigo Jones*, II, p. 576.
[232] 'A Fancy', lines 15–18, Dunlap, p. 117. Cf. Carew's poem in praise of Davenant, above, p. 87.

4

Aurelian Townshend and the poetry of natural innocence

For one who rose to become the author of two masques for the court and perhaps even to personal acquaintance with the queen or king, Aurelian Townshend has left little trace in the records of early Stuart England. Born about 1583, the son of John Townshend of West Dereham, Norfolk, Aurelian came from a family that had established its fortunes under the Tudors by successful careers at law.[1] His cousins, Sir Roger Townshend of Raynham and Hayward Townshend, had made their mark on the Elizabethan age, the one as a hero of the battle against the Armada, the other as a famed orator and diarist of the later parliaments of Elizabeth's reign.[2]

It was probably such connections that brought the young Aurelian, about 1600, to the notice of Sir Robert Cecil, the queen's secretary, who all but monopolized the control of royal patronage during the last years of her reign. Cecil was impressed by Townshend's linguistic talents and, evidently intending to place him as a servant to his own son who was at university, Cecil sent Aurelian to Paris, commending him to the care of Sir Henry Neville, the ambassador to France. Townshend, who had 'by his owne industrie attayned to a good superficiall knowledge in the French and Italian tongues', was to perfect his skills in Paris so that 'his tongue may be pure'.[3] Neville, heeding Cecil's exhortations to keep a watchful eye on the manners and morals of his young charge, lodged Townshend at a minister's house in the capital. Townshend remained in Paris about a year, regularly writing letters of gratitude to Cecil for his patronage, in French in order to display the fruits of his studies.[4] Evidently well satisfied with this stage of his progress, Cecil sent

[1] The following brief life is taken primarily from E. K. Chambers, ed., *Aurelian Townshend's Poems and Masks* (Oxford, 1917), introduction (hereafter Chambers).
[2] H. Townshend, *Historical Collections, an Exact Account of the last four Parliaments of Elizabeth* (London, 1680).
[3] Sir Robert Cecil to Sir Henry Neville, in Sir Ralph Winwood, *Memorials of Affairs of State*, ed. E. Sawyer (3 vols., London, 1725), I, p. 167.
[4] Chambers prints some of these letters in an appendix to the introduction.

Townshend on to Italy, providing for all his needs and, it would seem, with a promise of empolyment within his household on his return.

Townshend's first letter to Cecil from Venice is dated July 1601.[5] From this and later letters we may infer that this time it was not only for his further education in languages that Cecil had sent him to Italy. Townshend reports political news – the sacking of Baffa in Cyprus, the size and location of the Spanish fleet then at sea – and makes it clear that this is his purpose. Asking his patron 'to excuse me if my speech is not Tuscan and polished', Townshend reminded Cecil that 'That is not proper to this place . . . I am at Venice for other matters.'[6] Cecil certainly had important matters in Italy, keeping a watchful eye on the manoeuvres of Spain at a time when the queen was old and nearing her end, when the succession was not determined and when the Habsburgs, through the marriage of Philip and Mary, had a distant claim to the English throne. But a more experienced agent, Dr Thomas Wilson, was already placed in Venice and it is highly improbable that Cecil employed the youthful Townshend in any important or sensitive intelligence rôle.[7] It may well be that the sojourn in Venice was intended to further train Aurelian and to assess his suitability for the world of diplomacy for which his languages already equipped him. If this is the case, the experiment proved unhappy and Townshend failed the test. Within weeks of his arrival, Aurelian apologized to 'my Mr.' for what might have been a misleading report based on insufficient knowledge.[8] Time and experience brought little improvement in Townshend's diplomatic skills, but rather added indiscretion to ignorance. In the summer of 1602, Townshend recommended warmly to Cecil Dr John Thornhill, an English Canon of Vicenza, with whom he had travelled from Bologna to Florence, and from whom he had gleaned the information that had informed his recent despatches.[9] Thornhill proved a singularly unsuitable candidate for Cecil's protection and for Townshend's acquaintance; when he came to England in 1605 it was as a Catholic missionary who assisted in harbouring Catholic dissidents who came over from Italy to plot. Worse still, by the autumn of 1602, Townshend had entered into friendship with Sir Anthony Shirley to whom he had lent 200 scudi of Cecil's money. Not only was Shirley unreliable for his debts, he was, at that very time, intriguing for Spain, as Cecil knew from reports sent by Thomas Wilson.[10] Townshend came to learn of his blunder. Expressing his fear 'that your honour should be angered with me', he asserted the sincerity of his intentions.

[5] Chambers, p. xli. This letter is not calendared in H.M.C., *Salisbury MSS*.
[6] Townshend to Cecil, 17/27 July 1601; Chambers, pp. xlii–xliii; H.M.C., *Salisbury*, XI, p. 289.
[7] Chambers, p. xiii.
[8] *Ibid.*, p. xliii.
[9] Townshend to Cecil, June 3/13, Chambers, pp. xliii–xliv; H.M.C., *Salisbury*, XII, p. 195; where the date is given as 15 June.
[10] Townshend to Cecil, 24 Oct. 1602, Chambers, pp. xlv–xlvi; H.M.C. *Salisbury*, XII, pp. 454–5; Chambers, p. xiv.

But good intentions do not go far in the world of intellegince. Cecil summoned Townshend home. Accident and illness delayed his return; Townshend wrote from Paris in February 1603 to appeal for funds to his patron.[11] He was back in England by April, when, for all his blunders, he received payment for his services as a messenger from the Treasurer of the Chamber, 'upon a warrant signed by Mr. Secretary', that is by Cecil himself.[12] But there is no firm evidence, nor much likelihood, that Townshend entered Cecil's service or employment and the silence of the Cecil manuscripts confirms the impression that Townshend was left to pursue his fortunes elsewhere.

Like Carew, however, with whose equally undistinguished and indiscreet early career Townshend's biography compares, Aurelian enjoyed a second chance. And even more coincidentally he was offered his second opportunity by Sir Edward Herbert, future Lord Herbert of Cherbury. Thanks to his reputation as a gifted linguist Townshend joined Herbert's entourage to France in 1608, as Carew was to do a decade later.[13] He stayed for about a year. Townshend's fortunes on his return in 1609 remain uncertain. It is possible that he re-entered Cecil's service, for Dr John Bowles's account of the Earl's fatal illness in 1612 mentions one Townshend as an intimate acquaintance during Cecil's last hours.[14] Equally it may be that Townshend continued to be employed by Sir Edward Herbert, who disbursed money for a 'Mr Townsend' as late as 1615.[15] Such suggestions must remain mere conjecture, for there is nothing to associate Aurelian Townshend firmly with either Cecil or Herbert after his return from France, nor are there any other mentions of his name among their surviving papers or memoirs. Townshend wrote a poem to the wife of Cecil's son, but his reference to his wearing the 'privy coat' of another might possibly indicate service outside the family, as well as romantic pre-engagement.[16] After 1609 the life of Townshend, who had once been connected to the most powerful figure in England, is lost in obscurity.

When Townshend re-emerges in the historical record, twenty years later, it is again as the beneficiary of favour and powerful connections. In May 1629 Aurelian successfully petitioned the king for a grant of the wardship of Philippa Ivatt, the lunatic widow of Thomas Ivatt, searcher (or customs officer) of the port of London. It may be significant that the petition is

[11] Townshend to Cecil, 7 Feb. 1603, Chambers, pp. xlvi–xlvii; H.M.C., *Salisbury*, XII, p. 621.
[12] P.R.O., Pipe Office Declared Accounts, Roll 543, m. 94, quoted in Chambers, p. xlvii.
[13] S. L. Lee, ed., *The Autobiography of Edward, Lord Herbert of Cherbury* (London, 1886), p. 90, Cf. pp. 93, 100.
[14] Chambers, p. xvi.
[15] *Ibid.*, p. xv.
[16] 'To the Countesse of Salisbury', Chambers, pp. 4–5; Brown, *Poems and Masques of Townshend*, p. 19. Hereafter I give references to both the editions since Chambers is rare and Brown contains extra material.

underwritten, as granted by the king, by the Earl of Holland, who evidently acted as intermediary.[17] Henry Rich, Earl of Holland, had negotiated for Prince Charles the marriage with Henrietta Maria and had become a favourite of the French queen upon her arrival in England. In December 1629 he was appointed the queen's High Steward. It may be that with the arrival of the French princess, Townshend had seen a new source of patronage for his linguistic talents and attached himself to her circle. We cannot be sure. But some close contact with the court, and perhaps with the queen, would seem to be necessary in order to explain Townshend's appointment, early in 1632, as the author of the first court masques in nearly twenty years which were not written by Ben Jonson.[18] According to the newswriter John Pory, in a letter to his friend Sir Thomas Puckering on 12 January 1632:

The last Sunday at night the Kinges masque was acted in the banquetting house . . . The Inventor or Poet of this masque was Mr Aurelian Townshend sometimes towards the lord Treasurer Salisbury, Ben Jonson being for this time discarded, by reason of the predominant power of his Antagonist, Innigo Jones . . .[19]

Townshend tells us himself that he collaborated with Jonés – for the 'Invention' or subject as well as for the verse of the masque *Albion's Triumph* which was performed on 8 January and followed a month later by a Shrovetide masque for the queen.[20] But precisely how Townshend had recommended himself to Jones, to the king or the queen we cannot, any more than Pory, finally say.

During the years after 1632, Townshend appears to have remained in contact with the Caroline court. He penned a verse to Charles I in 1632 or 1633;[21] he heard Henrietta Maria sing;[22] he mourned the death of Venetia Stanley, a famous court beauty who died in May 1633;[23] in 1636 he wrote a funeral elegy for the Countess of Bridgewater, whose husband was Lord President of the Marches.[24] Recent evidence adds force to the suggestion that

---

[17] 'Petition of Aurelian Townshend to the King', May 1629, *Cal. Stat. Pap. Dom. 1627–9*, p. 560; grant, *ibid.*, p. 567.

[18] Chambers suggests (p. 107) that the Lady May of the poem 'Your smiles are not' (p. 17, Brown, p. 23) was the wife of Sir Humphrey May and one of the masquers of the planned masque of Amazons. This would indicate acquaintances in court circles. Sir Humphrey May became Vice-Chamberlain of the Household in 1629. Chambers suggests that Townshend may have been reintroduced to court by Edward Taverner, who in 1608 had been in the train of Sir Edward Herbert and who in 1632 was secretary to Philip, Earl of Montgomery, Lord Chamberlain (pp. xvii–xviii).

[19] John Pory to Sir Thomas Puckering, 12 Jan. 1632, B.L., Harl. MS 7000, f. 318.

[20] A. Townshend, *Albion's Triumph*, line 3, Orgel and Strong, *Inigo Jones*, II, p. 454; see below, ch. 5.

[21] ''Tis but a while . . .', Chambers, pp. 36, 112; Brown, p. 50.

[22] 'On hearing her majesty sing', Chambers, p. 13; Brown, p. 47.

[23] 'An Elegie made by Mr Aurelian Townshend In remembrance of the ladie Venetia Digby', Chambers, p. 38; Brown, p. 52.

[24] 'A funerall Elegie', Brown, pp. 54–6. This poem is not included in Chambers. *Comus*, of course, was performed for Bridgewater's induction as President.

in December 1635 Townshend devised a masque to follow the performance by the queen's ladies of the French pastoral *Florimene*.[25] During the early 1620s, Townshend evidently befriended the other poets and wits of the court. We know he knew Carew and Suckling and most probably Davenant and through them the wider circles of their own associates.[26] But Townshend has left far fewer traces than his literary colleagues in the letters and memoirs of the 1630s and, unlike Carew and Davenant, he may never have secured a place at court.

It has recently been suggested that he may have scotched his own chances of preferment by the outspokenness of his 'Elegy on the death of the King of Sweden: sent to Thomas Carew' at the end of 1632. It is argued that Carew in his answer to the letter warned Townshend of the risks he took in dabbling in the sensitive area of England's foreign policy and in criticizing the king's failure to support Gustavus Adolphus.[27] It may be that Townshend's poem, if it circulated in manuscript, caused offence and that in consequence any hope that he harboured of royal favour or place was dashed. But, if there is any substance to such a suggestion, we should recall that it would be surprising if Townshend had not himself been aware of the consequences of his poem. More importantly, we should recollect that if Charles I remained more committed to a policy of peace, there were many at court who shared Townshend's implied criticisms of English non-involvement, most notably the queen. As we have seen, the queen's circle – the Earls of Holland, Hamilton and Northumberland especially – were committed to a French alliance and active involvement in the Thirty Years War on behalf of the elector Palatine. Townshend may have felt political affinity with and pursued whatever ambitions he nurtured through this circle. Though he was not called upon to write a masque for the king after 1632, his masque to follow the queen's presentation of *Florimene* suggests that he had not lost the favour of Henrietta Maria.

A more intimate and personal connection with the queen's circle and with the cause of the Elector Palatine is indicated by a note, in the hand of Philip Earl of Pembroke, Lord Chamberlain to the king, in his copy of William Roper's *Life of Thomas More*:

Mr Aurelian Townshend, a poore & pocky Poett but a marryed man & a housekeeper

[25] Brown, *Poems and Masques of Townshend*, pp. 109–14. See below, ch. 5.
[26] He penned a poem to Carew (see below, p. 174); Suckling referred to him disparagingly in 'A Sessions of the Poets', line 11, *The Non-Dramatic Works of Sir John Suckling*, p. 72). Carew, Suckling and Davenant knew each other. See also 'To the Right Honourable the Lord Cary . . .', line 11, Brown, p. 121.
[27] See Parker, 'Carew's politic pastoral: Virgilian pretexts in the "Answer to Aurelian Townshend"', pp. 101–16; R. A. Anselment, 'Thomas Carew and the "Harmelesse Pastimes" of Caroline Peace', *Philological Quarterly*, 62 (1983), pp. 201–19. For a discussion of the poem, see below, pp. 174–6.

in Barbican hard by ye now Earl of Bridgewater's. He hath a very fine and fayer daughter, Mrs. to the Palsgrave first, and then afterwards ye noble Count of Dorset, a Privy Counceolour & a Knight of ye Garter.[28]

The note is important. Chambers, Townshend's first editor, argues convincingly that if there is substance to this statement concerning an affair between Mary Townshend and Charles Louis, Elector Palatine, then the occasion of their liaison cannot have predated the elector's second visit to England in 1641 at which time Mary was still only fifteen. Her acquaintance with Charles Louis might reinforce the suggestion of Townshend's own commitment to the Protestant cause and the queen's party, especially if we observe that her second lover, the Earl of Dorset, had himself fought at the battle of Prague and was Lord Chamberlain to the queen.[29] Certainly Mary's liaison with them both must lead us to question whether, despite his poverty, Townshend had lost his contacts with the court. For Mary was evidently then and continued to be well connected. When in 1646 she married George Kirke, one of the grooms of the King's bedchamber, Charles I not only gave her away, he settled upon her a jointure from the rental of crown lands.[30] We do not know whether Townshend held any post or enjoyed any pension from the king. But though a 'poore & pocky' poet in the 1640s, if not before, Townshend appears to have remained within the compass of the court perhaps until the grave.

The date of Aurelian's death remains uncertain. The *Dictionary of National Biography* suggests '?1643', which is certainly too early. Townshend's elegy 'upon the untymely death of the right honourable Edward Sackvile' is conclusive evidence that the poet was alive and active in 1645 when Sackville, son of the Earl of Dorset, died, and incidentally confirms the connection with Dorset's family suggested by Pembroke's report of the affair between Mary and the earl.[31] A commendatory verse by Townshend to the book of *Choice Psalms . . . Composed by Henry and William Lawes*, printed in 1648, offers circumstantial evidence that might lead us to prolong the poet's life further.[32] Fortunately there seems to be all but conclusive proof that the poet survived his king. For, in a second edition of *Knole and the Sackvilles* published in 1947, Vita Sackville West quoted lines from a poem by Townshend on the death of Charles I then in the Sackville manuscripts.[33]

[28] Quoted in Chambers, p. xxiv.

[29] *D.N.B.*

[30] Chambers, pp. xxv–xxvi.

[31] Brown, *Poems and Masques of Townshend*, pp. 68–9. The poem was not known to Chambers.

[32] 'To The Incomparable Brothers, Mr Henry, and Mr. William Lawes (Servants to His Majestie) upon the setting of these Psalms', Chambers, pp. 44–5; Brown, p. 122. Chambers suggested that because the poem made no reference to the death of William Lawes in 1645 it predated that time.

[33] Brown, p. 70.

The existence of these verses was independently announced in the *Times Literary Supplement* for 1924 by G. C. Moore Smith, who added the suggestion that Townshend was living at this time under the protection of Dorset, 'a devoted though liberal minded Royalist', and that the two men had been acquainted for some time.[34]

The suggestion – for such it must remain – is persuasive. It is most likely that from his youth to old age, Townshend lived on the fringes of the court, receiving patronage from successively Cecil and Sir Edward Herbert, and probably the Earl of Dorset. Apart from his two masques of 1632, however, there is little evidence that he was close to the king or well known at court and his poverty in the 1640s might refute any suggestion that he held a profitable office. Unlike Davenant and Carew, Townshend could not write from a position of ease, whatever the style of his poetry.

If the details of Townshend's life remain obscure, his poetry is little better known. Though his verses have survived in manuscript commonplace books, neither he nor his contemporaries sought to publish them, and no edition of his verse appeared until Chambers printed his poems and masques in 1917. Aurelian Townshend never attracted a following like Carew or Suckling and it is by no means clear that he sought one. Whilst he wrote several commendatory verses to courtiers with whom he was connected, there is not much evidence to indicate that Townshend regarded his muse as his means to favour and place; his skill in foreign languages remained his best qualification for office. If what has survived is a fair guide to his poetry, Townshend wrote relatively little, and significantly wrote most during the decade of the 1630s when he apparently enjoyed more than at any other time such fruits or benefits as patronage brought him. The Earl of Pembroke suggested that in the penury which he suffered in the 1640s, 'Aurelian would be glad to sell an 100 verses now at sixpence a piece . . .',[35] But, if surviving manuscripts are a reliable pointer, there is no evidence that he wrote them. Townshend's poetry may here and there reflect his court career and fortunes, but there is no reason to believe that it decided them nor, more importantly, that his verse was directed towards or dictated by ambition or pursuit of favour. Aurelian's comment on himself – 'I that delight most in unusuall waies'[36] – *may* express, as well as a conventional statement of novelty or a pride in cosmopolitan sophistication, an assertion of his independence from the poetic conventions of his age; or a claim that he expressed his own views rather than pandered to the tastes or values of the Caroline court.

Critics have been harsh in their evaluations of his verse. In his 'A Sessions of

[34] *Times Literary Supplement*, 23 Oct. 1924, p. 667.
[35] Chambers, p. xxiv.
[36] 'An Elegie . . . in remembrance of the Lady Venetia Digby', line 45, Brown, p. 53; Chambers, p. 40. Cedric Brown has reminded me that Jonson had spoken of his own 'strange' poems.

the Poets', Suckling implies a low place for Townshend among those candidates for the laurel of the poets.[37] In T. S. Eliot's famous phrase, Townshend's poetry was the 'faint, pleasing tinkle' of a metaphysical score which had sounded before him with the 'massive music' of Donne.[38] Graham Parry is even more condemnatory, scorning Townshend as 'the hired admirer, the grateful uncritical mind favoured by the atmosphere of Charles's court'.[39] The charge is not entirely denied by Townshend's recent editor. Cedric Brown confesses to finding much of the verse 'dully dutiful' or 'a conceited expression of the obvious' and the poet adopting a posture 'that was a little too obvious in its obsequiousness'.[40] It is not my purpose to make great claims for Townshend nor to act as his defence counsel against these charges. But it is my intention to suggest that to ignore him or to regard his poetry as merely dutiful compliment would be to deny a hearing to one on the fringes of the court who regarded himself as speaking with a distinctive voice to his age. For, though a friend of Carew and Suckling, and evidently one who appreciated Carew's poetry, Townshend asserted his independence from them and from convention.

The subjects of Townshend's poetry, like Carew's, are the themes of beauty, love and nature, and the relationship between them. Like Carew, Townshend believes in beauty as a necessarily effective force. That is to say, beauty literally attracts men, in the manner of a magnet, and the greater beauty perforce draws men from the lesser. Her beauty, Townshend tells the Countess of Salisbury, may 'subdue an hoste' and the poet himself is 'charmed' by its magical power.[41] The beauty he discusses is not merely the outward appearance of a mistress, nor is it subject to physical decay. Townshend presents beauty as a condition of the mind which is reflected in but not dependent upon the physical features. This is poetically conventional, but is not, it is implied, the judgement of the world. Townshend contrasts the 'faire forme' of beauty which he praises with the more superficial considerations of his age, in his 'A Funerall Elegie' for Frances, Lady Bridgewater, whom he may have known well:

> The Courte hath lost a Beautie, in her prime,
> Scarce paralel'de; and when the hande of Time
> In spight remov'd it from her lovelie face,
> Her Beautie settled in a safer place,
> I meane her Minde; so her faire forme noe doubt
> Did but sinke in, not (as in some) weare out.[42]

[37] Above, p. 156 n. 26.
[38] T. S. Eliot, 'The Metaphysical Poets', in *Selected Essays* (London, 1969), p. 291.
[39] G. Parry, *Golden Age Restor'd*, p. 191.
[40] Brown, *Poems and Masques of Townshend*, pp. 13–14.
[41] 'To the Countess of Salisbury', lines 2, 9, Brown, p. 19; Chambers, p. 4.
[42] 'A Funerall Elegie', lines 57–62, Brown, p. 55.

The double meaning of that last phrase makes the point sharply: those who wear their beauty only in their face, not in themselves, will find that such beauty indeed wears out, decays. The beauty of the mind celebrated by Townshend is virtue, virtue which unlike physical beauty survives and even defeats time, as Lady Frances's virtuous reputation triumphs over the grave.

Townshend's beauty of the mind, or virtue, is, as his other poetry makes clear, an expression of perfect nature, which is timeless; it is the expression in fact of the 'faire forme' of Nature itself. Townshend contrasts the beauty of nature expressed in his mistress, 'lovely Maye', with the looks of other women which are the product of artifice.

> Your smiles are not as other womens bee
> Only the drawing of the mouth awrye.

Beauty lies not in coy and calculated gestures, nor in particular physical attributes, but in the expression of the whole self:

> For breasts and cheekes and forehead wee may see,
> Parts wanting motion, all stand smiling by.[43]

In the beauty of her whole person, Townshend's lover expresses Nature:

> Noe sympering lipps nor lookes can breed
> Such smyles, as from your Face proceed.
> The sunn must lend his goulden beames,
> Soft windes their breath, green trees their shade,
> Sweete fields their flowers, cleare springs their streams,
> Ere such another smyle bee made.
> But these concurring, wee may say,
> Soe smiles the spring, and so smyles lovely Maye.[44]

The name of Townshend's mistress describes what she *is* – May, the spring, nature. And her beauty is all such beauty as expresses the inner virtue of perfect nature. The whole person of Townshend's mistress is a microcosm for the harmony of nature, its part like hers 'concurring' in fruitful co-operation. The point is made more explicitly in Townshend's elegy to a renowned court beauty, Lady Venetia Stanley, wife of Sir Kenelm Digby:

> Thou were't eye-Musike, and no single part,
> But beauties concert; not one onely dart,
> But loves whole quiver; no provinciall face,
> But universall; Best in every place.[45]

Venetia Digby's beauty is a form beyond imagination because it is the harmony of universal nature. The subjects of Townshend's verse compli-

---

[43] 'Your Smiles are not', lines 1–2, 3–4, Brown, p. 23; Chambers, p. 17.
[44] *Ibid.*, lines 9–16.
[45] 'An Elegie ... in remembrance of the Ladie Venetia Digby', lines 9–12, Brown, p. 52; Chambers, p. 38.

ments and elegies are not only the particular women to whom they are addressed; they are the representatives and embodiment of an idealized perfected nature.

If the 'Magniticke' beauty of Venetia attracted men to the nature of which it was an expression, Townshend is saying that it is love that joins man in a relationship with nature and so to a realization, a fulfilment of himself. The pursuit of love in the seventeenth century, perhaps in any age, was closely related to the search for the self; it was, and is, a quest for spiritual and physical fulfilment, the realization of one's humanity.[46] When Townshend asked, 'Where may I find my Shepheardess', he posed a universal, a metaphysical question, as concerned with the internal quest for self of the created man as with the pursuit of a lover.[47] It is 'Thou Shepheard' who is addressed and who replies:

> With that he smiling sayd, I might
> Of Chloris partly have a sight,
> And some of her perfections meet
> In ev'ry flow'r was fresh and sweet.
>
> The growing Lilly bears her skin,
> The Violet her blew veins within.[48]

Townshend's restless lover in search of 'my shepheardess' is directed to no individual or particular mistress:

> For Heav'n and Earth, and all we see
> Dispersed, collected is but shee.[49]

He is directed, that is, to nature and so to a relationship with nature herself. The shepherd – the good shepherd who watches over 'ev'ry lamb' – asks, 'How can that Jewell stray from thee?'[50] And Townshend asks his age how men can so far depart from the purity of nature and yet search restlessly for the peace and fulfilment of being that only a life lived according to pure nature may provide. Something in each man knows it too. For nature's 'Image', virtue, Townshend's enquirer acknowledges, is printed in his heart; it is his 'fond eyes' that cannot discern what he is seeking.[51] The concerns of the world, trust in the foolish senses before the wise heart, have closed men's eyes to the perception of nature and so divorced them from a life in communion with nature. Men may return to perfect nature, to virtue, through an understanding of love, the expression of nature's 'Image' in men's hearts. The

---

[46] See below, ch. 6.
[47] 'Thou Shepheard . . .', line 4, Brown, p. 57; Chambers, p. 9.
[48] *Ibid.*, lines 13–18.
[49] *Ibid.*, lines 27–8.
[50] *Ibid.*, line 6.
[51] *Ibid.*, lines 11–12.

shepherd advises that man take nature as his mistress because love is nature. Love, like nature, regenerates, and cures the blindness of men:

> Restoringe life to leaves that fall,
> And sight to Eyes that hardly see.[52]

The love that restores man must itself be pure and untainted. True love triumphs over distance, separation and time. Like nature, it works wonders 'As far as East from West'. It is 'Rock Constancy', an attribute as well as constituent of nature.[53] Changeability and infidelity are no more the marks of love than of harmonious nature; they are the corruptions of love:

> There is no Lover, hee or shee,
> That ever was or can bee false.
> 'Tis passion . . .[54]

And Townshend identifies man's fall from nature with such corruptions of love. The poem 'Come not to me', for example, rejects the 'love' born of a society that prizes the vanities of the world, the mark of its departure from nature. Townshend wants no mistress drawn by what passes as tokens of love, nor one attracted by the plumes and perfumes, lead and marble of a polite society which sang of love in courtly airs, but tainted it in practice. True love the poem locates in the world of perfect nature, here represented by the simplicity of the countryside:

> Our roofes are low, our cabins small,
> Our loves as well as loaves are browne,
> Yet soe contented there withall,
> . We seeke no finer in the towne;
> For thach and mudd
> Sometimes have stood,
> When lead and marble weare blowne downe,
> And love, they say, as often rests
> In sunnburnt, as in snowy breasts.[55]

In the country, "Tis love alone, thou com'st to seeke',[56] love, that is, untainted by social trappings, learned discourses or finery.

References to lead and marble and to snowy breasts might lead us to suspect an implicit criticism of the court. And the contrast between shepherds who love naturally and learned 'doctors' who discuss and theorize about love but 'misse' the truth reinforces the suspicion.[57] Townshend is contrasting

---

[52] 'Thou art soe faire', lines 3–4, Brown, p. 63; Chambers, p. 5. For all the difference of tone, the point of this poem is close to Carew's 'The Second Rapture'.
[53] 'Through Regions Farr', lines 6, 35, Brown, pp. 24–5; Chambers, pp. 18–20.
[54] 'A Paradox', lines 1–3, Brown, p. 30; Chambers, p. 33.
[55] 'Come not to me', lines 19–27, Brown, p. 26; Chambers, p. 21.
[56] *Ibid.*, line 29.
[57] *Ibid.*, line 36.

love with the artifices and conventions of society, most evident at court.
Morality, he is saying, is not to be confused with *reputation* in the world.

True love for example must be chaste, but chastity rests not in abstinence
nor a (sometimes false) reputation for innocence, but in an eternal devotion to
a lover. Townshend may be thinking of the devotees of the courtly Platonic
love cult, in asserting:

> They need not studie to disguise
> Actions, or eyes,
> Whose justifying thoughts be pure;
> Though most are masquers now-a-dayes,
> Wee'le followe Natures barefast wayes.[58]

The difference between true love and that of the court is drawn in that
condemnation of masquers – men who disguise the truth as well as those who
perform in court entertainments which, of course, celebrate Platonic love.
The love proclaimed at and by the court is shown not to be love at all: it is in
fact a mask, a fashion, changeable where love is constant and, for all the
rhetoric, promiscuous where love is faithful. Townshend paints it as the
antithesis of love in nature:

> Att court new fashions are not strange,
> But heere we ever keepe our old;
> There love (they say) consists in change,
> Heere, after one, all ours are told.
> The first is last,
> Because wee cast
> One hand can but another hold;
> But they have loves, wee understand,
> For every finger of the hand.[59]

The parentheses and asides add the force of irony to Townshend's contrast
and criticism. 'They say' at court when the truth is quite the opposite; and the
'loves' they have in the plural, 'we' do *not* understand as love at all because
they are not love.

Townshend makes clear his belief that the court has corrupted love. And in
corrupting love, the court has rejected innocent nature, for Townshend
regards the perversion of love and the departure from the perfection of nature
as one common malady of man's condition in society. The court is depicted as
the epitome of that condition. So Townshend's mistress who is summoned to

---

[58] 'Hide not thy love', version 2, lines 44–8, Brown, p. 39. (On the editorial problems of this
poem, see *ibid.*, pp. 32–3.) Cedric Brown has suggested to me that the poem may be read, at
one level, as a teasing strategy of seduction, or as the court playing at the pastoral, but
Townshend seems to me to have a more serious purpose, not least because of the poem's
emphasis on fidelity.
[59] 'Come not to me,', lines 100–8, Brown, p. 28.

the world of nature in order to express her love will, she is advised, there come
to see how society and the court have both corrupted love and abused nature:

> Take but the country aire a while,
> And if thou wilt descend soe lowe,
> To please thyne eare, wee'll raise our stile,
> Which soe refind perhaps may grow,
> Thy hearing sence
> Shall not stirr hence,
> Admit thyne eyes from court doe goe.[60]

Once her sense of hearing is attuned to the harmony of nature, Townshend's
mistress, and his age, may again hear and see sense, that is may come to see the
emptiness of the sham accoutrements and vanities of society beside the real
riches of nature. In the world of nature, Townshend promises, his lover will
be a queen:

> A mountaine toppe shall be thy throne,
> Thy Percian carpetts flowry fieldes.[61]

Lead and marble pale by comparison.

Townshend's verse reads like a full-blown criticism of the court from the
standpoint and values of the country. Indeed 'Come not to me' expresses
many of the attitudes which, Professor Stone has argued, make up the
ideology of the country: constancy as opposed to change; chastity as opposed
to promiscuity; plainness as opposed to fashion or foppery; honesty rather
than deception; simple rural life as opposed to urban sophistication and
sophistry.[62] To observe this is to make an important point: that the expressions of such positions and criticisms may be found within the circles of the
court as well as beyond. It is a reminder that, as we suggested in chapter 1,
idealizations of the country as a model for private and public life were part of
the common world of Renaissance values, and were expressed at court no less
than in the country. But it would be wrong to limit Townshend's purpose or
poetry to this context. For nature in his verse is not merely 'the country' either
as a place (the countryside) or as an ideal (the pastoral). Nature for
Townshend, as with Carew, is also the state of perfect nature, that is the
condition of man before and outside society, before the fall, a golden age – in
Christian belief, the garden of innocence. In 'Come not to me', nature
becomes the location of a love that is a religious experience. 'Heaven itselfe',
Townshend's mistress is assured, will be 'thy canopy'.

---

[60] *Ibid.*, lines 46–52. Note how the ideas of refinement and being raised are here applied against
the court, as it indeed has overturned the values of nature which is the true height to which
man should aspire. 'Hearing sense' may mean of course listening to reason as well as aural
capacity.

[61] *Ibid.*, lines 55–6; cf. Carew's 'To G.N. from Wrest', above, ch. 3.

[62] Stone, *The Causes of the English Revolution*, p. 106.

> A larke shall call thee from thy rest,
> And sing thee mattens every day;
> The nightingall that warbells best
> Shall vespers every evening saye.[63]

This is a holy state and in that state what society condemns may be enacted in innocence. 'Hide not thy love', the poet exhorts his mistress. For in this golden world of natural innocence, Townshend tells her what the Lord told Eve in Eden: there is no shame in nakedness. In the garden, before any example of evil, love knew no right or wrong: it was innocent and faithful.[64] Townshend acknowledges that this state of innocence is an ideal condition:

> How golden was that age that lett,
>   When Couples mett,
> Their lips and hands doe what they woulde.[65]

For now, in the world after the fall, men are perceived as sinful by nature and so 'when twoe / Maie doe amisse, tis thought they doe'.[66]

But Townshend stops short of this fatal pessimism. He asserts that, though man has lost his direction, 'there bee some people still, / That meane no ill, / The worlde is not so full of sinne.'[67] Man has the potential still within him for the virtuous life of his first uncorrupted nature.[68] And he may realize that potential through love. It is through the experience and expression of love that man may return to the innocence of the state of nature. Moreover, love may enable him to resist temptation and so preserve that innocence by endowing him with power over evil. The lovers of 'Hide Not thy love' know that:

> Had we been that created paire,
>   Eve halfe soe faire,
> Or Adam lov'd but half so well,
> The Serpent could have found no charme
>   To doe us harme.[69]

Temptation exists in the condition of love (let us recall Carew's 'A Married woman')[70] as it did in the garden of Eden. Lust may lead the lover into an illicit purely physical passion; sexual immorality may lead to the fall. But true

[63] 'Come not to me', lines 64–7, Brown, p. 27.
[64] 'Hide not thy love', Brown, pp. 34–40 (2 versions); Chambers, pp. 28–32. Cf. 'A Rapture', ch. 3, pp. 118–19.
[65] 'Hide not thy love', version 1, lines 57–60, Brown, p. 35. This is a conventional 'golden age' topos, but Townshend *adapts* the convention for a more religious treatment.
[66] *Ibid.*, lines 63–4.
[67] *Ibid.*, lines 65–7. Cf.
   For no example can infect
   Thyne innocence or my respect. (*ibid.*, lines 39–40).
[68] See below, ch. 6.
[69] 'Hide not thy love', version 1, lines 17–21, Brown, p. 34.
[70] Dunlap, *Poems of Carew*, pp. 115–16; above, ch. 3, pp. 120, 132.

love enables men to resist temptation and to remain constant – in love and in virtue, and so he who loves truly need not fear that he will sin:

> Yett hee that meanes not to transgres,
> Needes fear the lesse.[71]

Through love innocence may triumph. And so by conquering sin the lovers may together engender a new age of virtue, seeds not of Adam's fall but of love's innocence uncorrupted by society or example:

> little babies, which shall bee
> Our unpolluted progenee.[72]

Love by restoring men to innocence might lead society back to virtue.

For Townshend love is a religious experience that might redeem men from the consequences of the fall. In contrast to predestinarian theology and the puritan insistence upon the absolute sinfulness and depravity of man after the fall, Townshend asserts the innate goodness of humanity.[73] Man after the fall is still a creature made in the image of God; he has, we recall, that 'Image' in his heart and it may be rekindled by love, the cleansing flame of salvation. Lovers need not disguise their actions when their 'justifying thoughts be pure'.[74] Their love and sincerity justify their physical passion. But Townshend's meaning is that their love 'justifies' too in the theological sense; it is that faith which may effect their salvation. In 'Come not to me' he assures his mistress of eternal life: through love 'after death the lowly mynde / And humble spirite raysed by grace / A place in glory sooner finde'.[75] For their love returns them to the original state of unfallen nature and so brings them close to God. God is love. And love is nature and God. Let us take Townshend's 'A Dialogue betwixt Time and a Pilgrime'. Like the lover in search of his shepherdess the pilgrim has come in search of himself. But as his title 'a pilgrim' implies, he has come with faith to that 'sweet Pasture' where he may find himself. That 'pasture' is nature, love and God. Accordingly when he asks 'where am I', Time provides the answer:

> *Time* In Love.
> *Pilgr.* His Lordship lies above?
> *Time* Yes and below, and round about,
>   Wherein all sorts of flow'rs are growing.[76]

Through love others too may find themselves, nature and God.

Townshend explicitly describes love as a religious faith, and one of

---

[71] 'Hide not thy love', version 1, lines 33–4, Brown, p. 35.
[72] *Ibid.*, lines 79–80.
[73] Below, ch. 6.
[74] 'Hide not thy love', version 2, line 46.
[75] 'Come not to me', lines 118–20, Brown, p. 29; Chambers, p. 27.
[76] 'A Dialogue betwixt Time and a Pilgrime', lines 5–8, Brown, p. 43; Chambers, p. 6.

monastic severity. Where love lyrics only sing of men dying for their mistress, true love must really last to the grave. Indeed it lasts beyond the grave, for in dying constant the lover acquires 'This crowne of thornes' which, like Christ's crown of thorns, may redeem men from sin for eternal life. True love that secures eternal union triumphs over time and over death:

> 'Tis much to dye, 'tis more to finde
> Two of my minde.[77]

Townshend's love is that love, that faith which may secure man's salvation by restoring him to the innocence of the state of nature.

The state of nature is the ideal through which Townshend instructs his age and the ideal against which he criticizes the social and political failings of his society. Love and nature in his verse prescribe patterns of morality and government. In 'Come not to me', Townshend's mistress will learn religion and rule from nature herself, among the thatch and mud far from court.

> The wise ant preach,
> And bees shall teach
> Us, how to rule, and to obaye;
> A crane the watch and ward shall keepe,
> And noe lambe bleat, to breake thy sleepe.[78]

In the harmony of nature, in the state of innocence, of course, there was no need for government, because men knew no sin. So love's kingdom, which is the state of nature, requires no government either:

> For what hath Justice heare to doe
> But with her scales? Her sword may lye
>   As Useles by,
> When shee comes downe to Judge us twoe.[79]

Innocence is its own rule. Townshend believed, as we have argued, in the potential good of man to recover his first condition of virtue. Love, he argued, restored man to innocence. The best government, therefore, he believes to be the rule of love through which men might be not forced into obedience, but wooed into virtue and so to a self-regulation in which the sword of justice need never be wielded.[80]

In Townshend, as in Carew, the poetry of love is freighted with political language and values. True and false love, love and passion, stand in Townshend's verse, as in Davenant's *Gondibert*, for right and improper forms of government. Love is a political relationship or, as Townshend puts it

---

[77] 'A Paradox', lines 65–6, quoted Brown, pp. 30–1; Chambers, pp. 33–5. The whole poem pursues the idea of the lover as member of a strict religious sect. It may be intended as an ironic retort to puritanism.
[78] 'Come not to me,' lines 68–72, Brown, p. 27.
[79] 'Hide not thy love', version 1, lines 35–8, Brown, p. 35.
[80] See my discussion of Carew's poem 'Upon my Lord Chief Justice', above, ch. 3, pp. 142–3.

in his poem to the Countess of Salisbury, a form of allegiance, the cynosure of the relationships that constituted medieval and early modern government. Allegiance could not be broken. Allegiance involved a reciprocal relationship, an acknowledgement by patron as well as client of the bond between them and a sense of responsibility for the partner in that allegiance. It is for breaking precisely these rules that Townshend upbraids a mistress in 'When we were parted'. For she looks not to acknowledge or return his love but 'Looks for love custome free'. As such she dissolves the relationship and her lover's very being expressed through it:

> 'Tis then noe Merveile
> My state should decaye,
> Brought to be servile
> And kept from my paye.[81]

Servility is no condition for man and Townshend's 'paye' is his right. His mistress therefore is recalled to her responsibilities and reminded of her accountability in a metaphor which is explicitly political. Small streams, she is told, are 'part of your traine', but there are greater

> Know the sea as your kinge
> Can as well exhaust a river,
> As you sucke up a springe.[82]

Her beauty, though powerful, is subject to a higher authority. The political point becomes obvious. Her need to acknowledge a power beyond her own and her responsibility to one who serves her stand for the monarch's obligation to think always of his king, the lord of lords, and of his subjects whom he must 'use . . . gently'.[83] True love and true government are one: a reciprocal relationship based upon lasting mutual affection. Love's kingdom is not arbitrary government; it is a mixed polity, a union between ruler and ruled. The 'Delicate Beauty' who disdains her admirer without cause rules the kingdom of love by 'Will and not Reason'.[84] And that is to rule – in the commonweal as in love – tyrannically.

Love is a relationship of equality and respect. Neither disdainful pride nor fawning sycophancy have a place in love's polity. True love, as nature's expression, prescribes modes of government and so dictates that king and subjects should live together in reciprocal love. This interconnection between

[81] 'When we were parted', lines 8, 9–12, Brown, p. 61; Chambers, p. 12.
[82] *Ibid.*, lines 14–16.
[83] *Ibid.*, line 21.
[84]   Delicate Beauty, why should you disdaine
       With pity at least to lessen my pain?
       Yet if you purpose to render no cause,
       Will and not Reason is Judge of those Lawes.'
       ('Delicate Beauty, lines 1–4, Brown, p. 65; Chambers, p. 11).

love and government is, for all their differences, the motif of Townshend's, as of Carew's and Davenant's, poetry. And it is an interrelationship that must have struck the poet with particular personal force in the love affair between his daughter Mary, renowned for her beauty as a young teenager, and the Elector Palatine, nephew to Charles I. Townshend instructs Mary on the need for the responsible exercise of that power which her beauty has conferred upon her. But he prescribes too the style of government which a prince, sensible of the powers of love and nature beyond his own, should adopt. 'Let not thy beauty make thee proud,' the poem opens by way of commandment from the laws of the kingdom of love, 'Nor be not shy.' In love and in government, the best course lies in between, in the mean and in moderation:

> A state in evry princely brow
> As decent is required,
> Much more in thyne to whom they bow
> By Beauty's lightning fired.
>
> And yet a state so sweetly mixd
> With an attractive mildness,
> It may like Vertue sit betwixt
> Th' extremes of pryde and vildness.[85]

Virtue lies, as Aristotle had said in the *Ethics*, in the mean. A prince's claim to rule rested upon his virtue. Mildness therefore was the fit course for princes in government as in love the best state was 'sweetly mixd'.[86] Such mildness was 'attractive'; like beauty it perforce led men to love and to virtue and so was the best form of government: the guidance of men to self-government. Let us recall the circumstance in which the poem was written, which Townshend's editors have convincingly argued was the second visit of the elector in 1641.[87] In that year, Charles I faced the Long Parliament after eleven years of personal rule. In that year Davenant had delivered his poetic plea to the queen to ameliorate the rigours of prerogative by love.[88] Others of the queen's entourage pursued conciliation and settlement, counselling moderation rather than the rigidity urged by some royal advisers. In that year, we might suggest, Townshend had advice to give not only to his daughter, but to the elector, the queen and the king. It was not pride which led to love. But an attractive mildness, a state 'sweetly mixd' between authority and anarchy, might reunite king and people in that true love which was the best government.

The king and queen expressed their political values through their love and

---

[85] 'Let not thy beauty', lines 9–16, Brown, p. 67, Chambers, p. 3.
[86] See below, ch. 6.
[87] Chambers, p. xxv.
[88] Above, ch. 2, pp. 98–9.

marriage. And to the royal marriage Townshend, like Davenant, turns for a model of the right form of government. The theme of Townshend's masque for the queen, *Tempe Restored*, is the triumph of love over desire. Circe, the queen of desire, lives with her entourage 'in all sensuall delights'. She turns one man, who resists her, into a beast, the fit condition of one she wishes to subject to base desire: but when retransformed into a man he flees her magic. The very condition of his humanity, the 'Promethean fire' within him, knows that difference between passion and love, and the distinction between the anarchy of the senses and the order of reason. He flees 'to Vertue' and though he is pursued by Circe, her powers and charms are dispelled by love, by divine beauty and heroic virtue. At the end of the printed edition of his masque (to which we must return to examine more closely) Townshend goes to some lengths to explain the allegory and the particular application to the king and queen.

In Heroicke vertue is figured the king's majesty . . . he truly being the prototype to all the kingdoms under his monarchy of religion, justice, and all the virtues joined together.[89]

But it is his union with Divine beauty and their love that dispels the corrupt regimen of desire and restores Circe's slaves to the innocence of their nature. The union of beauty and heroic virtue is presented as the pattern of government. And in that marriage the queen had an equal rôle to play. Townshend, who we have suggested was attached to the queen's circle, may have wished to claim for Henrietta Maria greater power and influence in government. What is clear is that if love in Townshend's thought might teach the best form of government, then the queen by her very place had an important part to play as an example of love and innocence. It may be that in the second, revised version of his poem, 'Hide not thy love', Townshend exhorted the queen to play it:

> By acting in our modest play,
> Teach Psyche courtship . . .[90]

Courtship is the strategy both of love and government. There were those in Caroline England who were critical of the government and the queen's part in it. The puritans in particular objected to her taking that part on the stage which Townshend may be advocating. We recall that William Prynne's attack on 'women actors' as 'notorious whores' had appeared within weeks of the queen's performance in *The Shepherd's Paradise*, a play which debates the true form of love.[91] Townshend appears to be answering the puritans' objections and charges in urging:

[89] *Tempe Restored*, lines 356–60, *Inigo Jones*, II, p. 483. For a fuller treatment of the masque, see below, ch. 5, pp. 227–9.
[90] 'Hide not thy love', version 2, lines 78–9, Brown, p. 40.
[91] W. Prynne, *Histrio-Mastix*, index; above, ch. 1, pp. 40–4.

> Let not the abuces of this age
>> Barre thee our stage,
> But grace us with thy spotless part,
>> Whose presence brooks no act obseane,
> For where thow art all things are cleane.[92]

These lines suggest a refutation not only of the puritan objection to the stage, but a rejection too of their theology. For the words 'grace us' have a theological as well as social meaning. The phrase recalls the 'justifying thoughts' of Townshend's lovers and the point here is the same. By her example of love the queen may lead men back to the state of grace in the garden of Eden.

The royal marriage, like that of 'Hide not thy love', may through love engender virtue. But that marriage is not a Platonic union. In his verse epistle to Charles, Townshend dwells upon the fecundity of the royal marriage, upon the children – 'hopefull' Charles and '*Mary* full of Grace'. He wishes for the king a race of sons, but not only sons: 'gett each land else a Queene / Lovely, and loving, as your *Machless Bride*'.[93] It is not the king alone, but the royal marriage that expresses for Townshend the virtue of government in Caroline England – the union of 'Active vertue' and 'passive Grace'.[94] Love is the true mode of government. It is a king who loves who governs virtuously. Such is Townshend's message to the king as well as the realm. It is not easy to determine whether it was intended as praise or criticism. Indeed the distinction may have meant less to Townshend, as it did to Jonson, than it does to us: praise could make men realize what they should be but were not.[95] Townshend's epistle to Charles I may be dated between 1631 and 1633, most likely in 1633.[96] Perhaps by then Townshend had come to think that Charles too might learn those virtues of 'attractive mildness' from love's polity, and thought (as did Davenant) that the queen might soften the rigour of government. We cannot say. But many years later, after the very different circumstances of civil war, disorder and the execution of the king, Townshend catalogued the virtues of Charles I:

> pious, temperate, and grave,
> Just, gentle, constant, merciful, and brave.

[92] 'Hide not thy love', version 2, lines 87–8, Brown, p. 40.
[93] 'Verse Epistle to Charles I: "'Tis but a while"', lines 18–19, Brown, p. 50; Chambers, p. 36.
[94] *Ibid.*, line 25; cf. the 'Heroic vertue' of the masque, *Tempe Restored*.
[95] See below, ch. 6.
[96] Brown and Chambers point out that the poem must date from after the birth of Princess Mary on 4 November 1631 and before the birth of James on 14 October 1633 because he is not mentioned. Brown suggests that it may have been written in 1633 in anticipation of his birth (Brown, p. 51). Cf. Carew's poem of *c*.1631 which places similar stress on the hoped-for fecundity of the royal marriage, ('A New-yeares gift. To the King', *Poems of Carew*, pp. 89–90; above, ch. 3 p. 144); and Townshend's masque, *Albion's Triumph*, lines 368–78, *Inigo Jones*, II, p. 457.

> All this, and more, he was not pleased to be,
> Without the woman's virtue, Chastity.[97]

It cannot escape us that the qualities praised are those of man *and* woman.

Townshend's love poetry, no less than Carew's then, addresses itself to the ethical and political issues of his age. The state of nature is an ideal and idealized past against which the failings of the age are exposed. But, as we have seen, the perfections of nature are not a mythical or unobtainable past; they dwell, at least in image, within the heart of man. In his elegies and verse compliments, therefore, Townshend not only conventionally praises the qualities of particular men and women – the Earl of Dorset or the Countess of Salisbury – he also presents models of that life of virtue for which all men had the potential and to which all should aspire.[98] Townshend himself connects his visions of a state of innocence with his poetry of praise in 'An Elegie upon the untymely death of the rightly honorable Edward Sackvile':

> There was a Tyme and that not long agoe,
> Most men were good or laber'd to seeme so.
> He that was bad, strove to avoyde the name;
> Lost Innocence cover'd it selfe with shame.[99]

In this fallen world, however, Sackville remained a 'Type of Honor', a pattern for virtue.[100] His death robbed those that knew him of part of their humanity as it deprived them of his virtuous example. For Sackville had been a redeemer who might have restored a fallen world through his example to its earlier innocence. His murderer was 'a second Herod' whose bloody hand, like that of the first Herod, increased the sorrows of the land – 'And the sinnes too'.[101] Sackville's murder was a mark of a fallen world and he not only in life 'a Worthy among men' but also in death, a 'Saint'.[102] Townshend's poem of praise for the son of a patron becomes a celebration of the virtues which the poet wished to present as models for all men. The same device is employed more explicitly in Townshend's recently discovered poem, 'A Funerall Elegie' on Frances, Countess of Bridgewater, who died in 1636. The poem opens by an announcement of its universal purport:

> Dismisse thy private greife, and for a time
> Helpe to bewaile a publike losse in rime.[103]

[97] 'Fragment of a poem on the death of Charles I', lines 5–8, Brown, p. 70.
[98] See below, ch. 6.
[99] 'An Elegie upon the untymely death of the rightly honourable Edward Sackvile', lines 1–4, Brown, p. 68. The poem is not in Chambers.
[100] *Ibid.*, line 9.   [101] *Ibid.*, lines 17–21.
[102] *Ibid.*, lines 32, 36.
[103] 'A Funerall Elegie', lines 1–2, Brown, p. 54. The poem, not in Chambers, was discovered by Cedric Brown.

Townshend proceeds to a catalogue of Lady Frances's virtues, a catalogue which becomes a lament for standards of behaviour that have lapsed and a prescription for patterns of behaviour to be emulated, in private and in public.[104] Unlike her age the Countess was charitable, liberal and hospitable to rich and poor, to strangers and to neighbours. An epitome of good housekeeping, she lived plainly, well and free of debt. As a friend she was constant, 'just and true'. She 'Could give good counsell, and would take it too'. Lady Frances exemplifies the virtues expounded in Townshend's love poetry. Her beauty, because it was her virtue, did not (we recall) 'wear out'. Nor were her virtuous actions mere display – 'shee did not good for shewe' – but the natural expression of her innate virtue.[105] As a perfect wife, she 'Thought female valour, spotlesse Chastitie'.[106] Such virtues of nature and love made her the perfect governor of her household

> Ruling them all with such a gentle hande,
> Obedience seem'd as easie as command.[107]

Replete with virtue, Lady Frances brought 'grace' to every world she inhabited, as her virtue led others to their own salvation. Raising her children by the pattern of her own virtuous example, she made them 'Abraham's seede, / As well as Adams; naturall and kinde,'[108] God's chosen children as well as the offspring of the fall. For through the virtues of Frances, Lady Bridgewater, all who knew her might become the children again of innocence, made in God's image. In her death 'The Worlde hath lost . . . One of its propps that held up righteous handes.'[109] Townshend's funeral elegy has recently been dismissed by his editor as 'dully dutiful'.[110] But whatever its literary merits, it is important that we do not read it as mere compliment to a patron, but, through reassertion and adaptation of convention, as an exceptionally clear statement of Townshend's social criticism and of the values which it was the purpose of his poetry to impart.

Though Townshend's love poetry debates important and universal issues of morality and authority, for one who lived on the fringes of the court and experienced perhaps the personal hardships of civil war his poetry contains

[104] The poem nicely integrates the loss suffered by court, country, city and the Countess's family, friends and neighbours, underlining the interpenetration of those worlds, as well as the public and private loss occasioned by the death of a good person who by her goodness was also a model citizen.

[105] 'A Funerall Elegie', lines 8, 29. Cf. 'The Lord and Lady of this place delight / Rather to be in act, then seeme in sight', 'To G.N. from Wrest', lines 31–2, *Poems of Carew*, p. 87; above, ch. 3, p. 129.

[106] 'A Funerall Elegie', line 38.

[107] *Ibid.*, lines 19–20. Cf. *Salmacida Spolia*, lines 473–4, *Inigo Jones*, II, p. 734.

[108] 'A Funerall Elegie', lines 40–1. Townshend may be using the Old Testament promise to Abraham against the puritan emphasis upon the irredeemable sin of fallen man.

[109] *Ibid.*, line 9, Brown, p. 55.

[110] Brown, p. 13.

few specific allusions to political events or circumstances. To this generalization, however, one fascinating poem stands out as an exception: Townshend's 'Elegy on the death of the King of Sweden: sent to Thomas Carew'.[111]
The address to Carew itself announces Townshend's unusually public
purpose, as it summons the fellow poet to his public responsibility – to sing
the praises of Gustavus Adolphus, killed in November 1632 at the battle of
Lützen. Townshend acknowledges Carew's genius and admires his love
poetry. But the death of the King of Sweden commands the poet's attention,
for it marks the end of one world and the dawn of another. Like Christ,
Gustavus, is a 'dead conquering King'. Like Christ, his death may also enable
man to be reborn by washing away the sins of the fall, as the flood cleansed
the sins of Israel. Carew is called as an apostle to testify to Gustavus's
apotheosis and man's hope:

> Let our land waters, meeting by consent
> The showers discending from the firmament,
> Make a new flood; on whose teare swelling face,
> Clos'd in an Arke of fatal Cypresse, place
> Gustavus body, wound about with bayes.[112]

Celebrated by the poets, Gustavus's fame might, like the ark, remain as the
light and hope of the world until another may come to carry that torch.
Townshend's language is not merely biblical; it is explicitly apocalyptic:

> His sword shall like a fiery pillar stand,
> Or like that graspt in th' angry Angells hand,
> Before his herse, needing no other light
> But what he gave it, to make day of night.[113]

Gustavus, like Christ, was a monarch over all nature; his death like Christ's
has brought darkness. But his fame may see nature regenerated, reborn, 'like
a Phenix from his ashes rise'. The world now awaited a successor who,
inspired by Gustavus, might be monarch of 'Christendome', of a holy
kingdom which the lion of the north had purged of the monsters and snakes
of the bottomless pit:[114]

---

[111] See above, p. 156 and n. 27 of this chapter; ch. 3, pp. 145–8
[112] 'Elegy on the death of the King of Sweden: sent to Thomas Carew', lines 19–27, Brown, p. 48.
[113] *Ibid.*, lines 29–32; cf. Revelations 1, verses 14–16. I am grateful to Andrew Johnston for
discussions of this poem.
[114] *Ibid.*, line 47. And note:
    And when each spring to his exhausted head
    Is back retyr'd, if out of slime be bred
    Any foule monster overcharged with gall,
    One beame of his will make the Pithon fall;
    For though this Lion can no more prescribe
    Detraction boundes, then that of Judas tribe, (lines 49–54; cf. Revelations 5, verse 5).

> Princes ambitious of renowne shall still
> Strive for his spurres to helpe them up the hill;
> His glorious gauntlets shall unquestiond lie
> Till hands are found fit for a Monarchie;
> Minerva may without her Gorgon come
> To beare his shield, the shield of Christendome.[115]

Townshend's poem evokes the tone and the message of the sermons extolling Gustavus as the champion of Protestantism against the whore of Babylon. In the circumstances of November 1632, it is an extraordinarily outspoken comment. For the King of Sweden had stood in the eyes of the 'hotter' Protestants of England and Europe as the hope for the defeat of the Habsburg Antichrist and for the triumph of the Protestant cause. In England he was heralded as the potential saviour too of Frederick the elector and Elizabeth of the Palatinate, the son-in-law and daughter of James I. Since 1621, when they had been driven from their ancestral lands in the Palatinate, James I and Charles I had repeatedly been urged to take up their cause.[116] James had remained reluctant to involve himself in European war, especially a religious crusade; after the military debacles and defeats of 1625–8, Charles I determined upon peace. To many, English isolationism stood in marked and pusillanimous contrast to the victories of the lion of the north who, entering the war against the Habsburgs, was heralded as the deliverer of Protestantism from popery. Elizabeth of Bohemia and Sir Thomas Roe urged the king to join the crusade. Gustavus several times approached Charles I for assistance. News of his triumphs circulated in corantos, avidly purchased and read by a public critical of English inactivity. But apart from some small grants of money and permission given to the Marquis of Hamilton to raise volunteers for the Swedish army, Charles did nothing, preferring to pursue the option of negotiations with Spain.[117] Townshend's poem then must be read as a forthright criticism of Charles I's neutrality. In his verse epistle to the king written about the same time, Townshend reminded the king – rather unnecessarily in a poem about Charles I's own progeny – of the virtues of his sister, or niece, the *'pure Golden Princesse Pallatine'*, then in exile at the Hague.[118] The poet spurs Charles to bear Gustavus's shield, 'the shield of Christendome' and so to succeed to the King of Sweden's fame and immortality. Princes ambitious of fame, Townshend proclaims, will strive for

---

[115] 'Elegy', lines 33–8, Brown, p. 48.
[116] See S. L. Adams, 'The Protestant cause: religious alliance with the West European Calvinist communities as a political Issue in England, 1585–1630', Oxford University D.Phil. unpublished thesis, 1973.
[117] S. R. Gardiner, *History of England*, VII, ch. 70; VIII, ch. 80. There is no study of English foreign policy during the 1630s.
[118] 'Verse epistle to Charles I', line 22, author's italics, Brown, p. 50. Conrad Russell has suggested that the reference may well be to Elizabeth, eldest daughter of the Queen of Bohemia, since the latter would not have welcomed being referred to as 'princess'.

Gustavus's spurs 'to helpe them up the hill' – the hill of fame. The reference may be particular and important, for only a year earlier Charles I had appeared in Jonson's last masque *Chloridia* seated upon the hill of fame.[119] Townshend, who earlier in 1632 had, we recall, himself provided the verses for two court masques, cannot but have known of it. The masque as a genre equated the glory of Charles's reign with peace. But in his elegy on Gustavus, the hands 'fit for Monarchie', Townshend asserts, take up the 'glorious gauntlets' of the Swede. The poem is an implicit critique not only of royal policy, but also of a court culture which underpinned and in masque celebrated that policy.

Such criticism did not elude Townshend's contemporaries. Carew, to whom the elegy was addressed, counselled his friend both to eschew such dangerous public outbursts and to pursue his more lyrical muse in poems of love.[120] Significantly he praised masques as a form and Townshend's own in particular, aware perhaps of Townshend's implied denunciation of such entertainments. It may be that Townshend paid the price of penury for his outspokenness. It may be that he articulated his views on behalf of that circle around the queen committed to a war policy. But what is most important is that though of the court, though the author of two court masques, Townshend was, and felt able to be, directly and frankly critical of royal policy in an important area of the royal prerogative – foreign affairs. Such a realization must lead us to challenge any suggestion that common to Townshend's verse was 'a posture that was a little too obvious in its obsequiousness'.[121]

Townshend's elegy on the death of the King of Sweden demonstrates too his belief in the public responsibility of the poet, and the public rôle of poetry. Love poetry, as we have seen, is public poetry. And Townshend expresses his admiration for Carew's poetry to his mistress Celia because he recognizes that it 'Contains a spirit that full mans it all' – that is a moral, even religious dimension that gives the poetry life and perhaps through the poetry leads men to life.

> I love thy wit, that chooses to be sweet
> Rather than sharpe, therfore in lyrique feet
> Steales to thy mistris, letting others write
> Rough footed Satyres that in kissing bite.[122]

Such poetry, Townshend continues, feeds the reader with manna, the bread of heaven. His own poetry has done no less. But – and this is the point of the address to Carew – there were times when public affairs demanded a direct

---

[119] B. Jonson, *Chloridia* (22 Feb. 1631), lines 228–33, *Inigo Jones*, II, p. 422.
[120] 'In Answer of an Elegiacall Letter upon the death of the King of Sweden from Aurelian Townsend', *Poems of Carew*, pp. 74–7; above, ch. 3.
[121] Brown, Introduction, p. 14.
[122] 'Elegy', lines 7–10, Brown, p. 48. Townshend's lines suggest that Carew chooses a different style, but is not concerned with a different or less serious purpose than his own.

and explicit statement from the poet, just as there were times when the age required not sweet wit but, as Carew himself had told Davenant, a satire.[123] And on such occasions it was the duty of the poet to tune Orpheus's harp accordingly. For Townshend believes implicitly, with Carew, that the poet was possessed of power, of the stocks of nature, of the capacity to impart immortal fame and to reform. Poetry therefore might not only influence but effect events. The right form of government might come down to the right form of poetry. It was therefore the poet's duty to counsel kings, and for kings, like Lady Bridgewater, to 'take it too'. For Townshend art and politics were one. In his poem to the 'Incomparable brothers' Henry and William Lawes, he identifies the harmony of their songs with the constancy of their allegiance.[124] The subjects of their songs, music and love, were the expressions of nature's harmony and beauty. Naturally, therefore, understanding nature, they exemplified the virtuous self-government of man's higher nature:

Lawes of themselves, needing no more direction.[125]

Through their art, their songs 'both they and we / May singing rise to immortalitie'.[126] It was an art that was 'the life of lovers pens'; in the music for the psalms of David that art 'soar'd up to that Prophet and that King, whose Love is God'.[127] And through the poetry of love, nature and innocence, men, society and government might too regain the immortality of their first perfection.

This is not a poetry confined by merely conventional tropes or by 'the more refined manners of the Caroline court'.[128] Townshend admired Donne and Jonson; he admired poetry with 'spirit', as he told Lord Cary, a spirit that 'full mans it all'.[129] That spirit required the poet obey none but his Muse. In asserting this both in theory and in practice, Townshend's verse makes good his claim to independence, as the poet 'that delight most in unusuall waies'.[130]

Our brief examination of Townshend's poetry has introduced us to the last

---

[123] '. . . the sullen Age / Requires a Satyre . . .'; 'To my worthy friend, M. D.'Avenant . . .', lines 4–5, *Poems of Carew*, pp. 95–6.
[124] 'To the Incomparable Brothers, Mr Henry, and Mr William Lawes . . .', Brown, p. 122; Chambers, pp. 44–5. Townshend writes of the music they 'Compos'd *and Acted*,' line 3 (my italics).
[125] *Ibid.*, line 8.
[126] *Ibid.*, line 22.
[127] *Ibid.*, lines 19–20. The lines nicely illustrate Townshend's integration of religion, art and nature, love and government.
[128] Brown, p. 14.
[129] 'To the Right Honourable, the Lord Cary', line 5, Brown, p. 121.
[130] 'An Elegie in remembrance of the Lady Venetia Digby', line 45, Brown, p. 53.

and least known of our triumvirate – the three poets who succeeded Ben Jonson as authors of the Stuart court masque. They have been spurned as unworthy of his laurels and their masques have been dismissed as spectacular, self-congratulatory and sycophantic. Our study of Davenant's poetry and drama, of Carew's and Townshend's verse, has led us to different conclusions. Each of our writers engaged the fundamental ethical and political questions of his day, rather than attempted to escape from them. Each had independent values against which the failings of society were measured and judged. Each author asserted his independence of conventions and authorities. And we have seen them make good those assertions in their counsel and through implicit and at times outspoken criticisms of the court and even of the king. We have heard outward appearance contrasted with inner truth, representation with reality. Finally, for all their differences, each of our authors has debated issues, alluded to criticisms and offered counsel through a poetics of nature and love, and through an ethics and politics of nature and love which rejected the courtly Platonic love cult.[131]

But the masque, we are told, is inspired by Platonic love; the masque is representation divorced from reality, a spectacle through which the court escaped from engagement with the political issues and questions of the age. The masque, it is said, is the ultimate form of flattery, its raison d'être is to justify royal policy and to reassure doubters; it expresses the king's mind rather than criticisms of his policy. How are we to resolve this dilemma? Did Carew, Davenant and Townshend, once called upon to write court entertainments, subscribe to form and so suspend that independent and critical spirit that 'full manned' their poetry and drama? Did they in the masques celebrate the Platonic love which in their poetry and drama they had criticized? Did they abandon the serious purposes of their art for the frivolous and spectacular shows they had condemned? Or – and the alternative possibility must draw us up with a halt – does the Caroline masque itself express the questions and tensions, criticisms and counsels, substance and seriousness of the authors' other literature?

Once we have posed the question we have raised the possibility – indeed a number of possibilities, possibilities that some would argue could not find expression within the very form of the masque. We have seen enough, however, to suspect that generalizations based upon preconceptions do not do justice to the potential for independent statement within conventional genres. We turn to the Caroline masque with such suspicions fully aroused.

[131] See for a concluding discussion, ch. 6.

$$5$$

The Caroline court masque

THE NATURE OF MASQUE

In order to examine the court masque, it is necessary to define clearly what it is we are discussing. We must, that is, be clear in our minds what features make the masque recognizably different from other court festivals and entertainments and what common characteristics distinguish masques as a genre. Almost any definition, as we shall see, is susceptible to blurring at the edges, but we may begin by rules of thumb that may serve to identify the genre.[1] First, the masque was a distinctive courtly mode. It was not just a form of entertainment presented at court, but a performance by the court for the court. Although actors were usually employed for the speaking parts of the antimasque, the masquers themselves were courtiers, and despite their (transparent) disguises were recognizable as courtiers. In a masque, the relationship between performer and audience was quite different from that of other entertainments. Not only did courtiers perform before the court, the conclusion and raison d'être of the masque, the revels, involved the participation of the audience as well as the performers. In emerging to lead the spectators in the dances that took up much of the night, the masquers eroded that barrier of the stage that characterizes the drama as a form of entertainment. And this leads us to the second distinctive feature of the masque: the architecture of setting and performance. Court masques seem never to have been performed in the royal theatre, the Cockpit-in-Court, but (at least until 1635) in the public rooms of the royal palaces, most usually in the Banqueting House at Whitehall. The 'stage' of the court masque, then, was the court itself, that very same stage on which the monarch and his attendants performed the daily rituals of court ceremony and government. On the occasion of a court masque, the king's public audience chamber became a

---

[1] For the following paragraph, I draw principally on E. Welsford, *The Court Masque* (London, 1962); S. Orgel, *The Jonsonian Masque* (Cambridge, Mass., 1967); Orgel, *The Illusion of Power*; Orgel and Strong, *Inigo Jones*; M. Lefkowitz, *Trois Masques à la Cour de Charles Ier d'Angleterre* (Paris, 1970); Lindley, *The Court Masque*.

theatre, but for many in attendance the performance was doubtless not as distinguished from the other presentations of ordinary court life – receptions, ceremonies and banquets – as in our perception is the distance between theatre and life. The very location of the masque eroded that distance between the real and the represented which is achieved in the drama by the theatre as a place and by the stage as a barrier. Masques of course were performed on a stage, a stage especially erected for the occasion, and much of the action took place behind and framed by the proscenium arch. The proscenium arch was usually reserved for masques or masque nights.[2] The arch provided a border between performer and audience, illusion and reality, necessary for aspects of the entertainment. But the arch was not a barrier: it is an avenue of communication.[3] Perspective scenery drew the spectator through the arch into a new reality effected by illusion; and the masquers emerged from the arch to lead the courtiers in the revels. The proscenium arch exemplifies the purpose of the masque as the transformation of the spectator. The drama presents action to an audience. In the masque, as Stephen Orgel put it, what the spectator saw he became.[4]

The arch too is a symbol of triumph and of government, a monument to the victories of kings. And it is the royal presence that gives life to the masque. Though the king attends the performance, whether he takes part in the masque or not, masquers and spectators both are in attendance before the king. This should reinforce our sense that for those present the masque could not be perceived as theatrical occasion separate from public life. For most courtiers, the most powerful experience at a masque was still that of their daily reality – the majesty of the king's presence. The masque then was indeed a celebration of the monarch, but as such it should not be detached from the rituals of court life. Speeches in praise of the king in the masques were not the slavish expressions of a culture of sycophancy; they were the conventional modes of address to a sovereign, normal in courtly discourse. Because the masque spoke to the court in the language of the court and expressed the conventions of the court, it should not be read as propaganda or flattery. It should perhaps rather be regarded as a court ceremony at which, as in all ceremonies, those present both perceive and perform, and participate in, an experience in which the everyday and the mystical become one, indistinguishable. The court masque then is a political event; it is kingship in action. When we discuss 'the masque' as a subject, we must not forget that, for contemporaries, it was above all an occasion, differing with each circumstance and changing considerably, like so much of court life, with each monarch.

[2] E. K. Chambers, *The Elizabethan Stage* (Oxford, 1923), I, pp. 234–5. The proscenium arch was used for some court plays that ended in revels, *The Shepherd's Paradise*, for example.
[3] Orgel, *Illusion of Power*, pp. 20–4.
[4] *Ibid.*, p. 39.

It has become conventional criticism to discuss the court masque as a form as well as a genre, as, that is, a mode not only characterized by distinctive features, but one defined by rules of structure.[5] There are problems with such an approach. We know almost nothing of the Tudor masque because texts have not survived for any period before Elizabeth's reign. By 1640 the royal masques had come to an end. We are discussing therefore a short period and, depending upon how rigidly one defines masque,[6] three or four dozen entertainments. Secondly, because one man, Ben Jonson, became the undisputed poet of the masques for twenty-five years, it is difficult to distinguish the idea of a form of the masque from the individual genius of one author. Literary criticism has perhaps tended too much to detach the masque from the artist, instilling it with an independent life and evolutionary cycle so as to observe its step from tottering infancy to the perfection of manhood – to study, that is, 'the development of an art form'.[7] Such an approach may have illuminated the masque as a distinct genre. But emphasis upon the idea of a perfect form by which the successes and failures of such entertainments may be evaluated, has, I believe, dulled our sense of the masque as an occasion, an event in the life of the court; and it has blinded us to the changes, the possibilities of diversity, the conscious alterations that took place within the few decades of the court masque's life. In a recent study, David Lindley has outlined what we tend to think of as the complete or perfected form of the masque – a sequence of poetic induction, antimasque(s), masque, revels and epilogue.[8] But such a form was not common to all masques of the Jacobean and Caroline period, and even in those entertainments that follow this basic structure, the balance of parts, of antimasque to masque for example, could vary greatly. We should not regard such differences necessarily as a failure to achieve perfect form, but as independent statements, ironic treatment, conscious departure from previous practice – as, that is, the expressions of different circumstances and changing tastes which we may not accommodate if we conceive of the masque as a rigidly structured form.

In his brilliant essay on *The Jonsonian Masque*, Stephen Orgel demonstrated how the masque changed considerably during the sixteenth and early seventeenth centuries. In what was essentially a courtly and royal entertainment, the principal changes reflected the different monarchs and their own preferences. Henry VIII evidently danced and led the revels; Elizabeth I did so

[5] See Lefkowitz, *Trois Masques*, p. 12; Lindley, *Court Masque*, p. 1.
[6] Whether, for example, one includes *The Triumphs of the Prince D'Amour* presented by the Inns of Court. Stephen Orgel has reminded me that two masques were performed during Cromwell's Protectorate. This suggests the importance of the masques as representations of authority, a subject to which I shall return in a study of the English court, 1558–1660.
[7] Orgel, *Jonsonian Masque*, preface. Cf. the remarks of Martin Butler on what he describes as a Darwinian approach to literary criticism, *Theatre and Crisis*, pp. 7–8.
[8] Lindley, *Court Masque*, introduction.

only rarely and not at all during her last years. The Tudor masques were not printed; they were performances effected most by occasion and circumstance. The succession of James VI and I brought radical changes. For James, though present at and through his presence the centre of the masque, never took part in the performance. This posed the author of the Jacobean masque a problem. For the transition from the world of sense and disorder to that of divine harmony and order expressed in the revels was no longer centred upon the king: Jonson had to find a way of revolving the action around a monarch who remained off stage. Perhaps as a consequence of this, as well as of Jonson's own inclination, poetry took on an enhanced rôle. James I's tastes – and those of his queen – affected another important alteration. The king took most pleasure in the debates, the humour and the burlesque of court entertainment. In response to royal preferences, Jonson introduced and developed a comic 'foyle or false Masque' into the entertainment, which, as antimasque, became an established part of Jonson's Jacobean productions. The antimasques grew longer and more theatrical; Jonson, drawing upon his dramatic skills and characters, injected it with independent life.[9] In some of Jonson's productions the antimasque becomes the more powerful element and in the conclusion of the masque the antimasque is integrated rather than transcended. The antimasques appear even more dominant of course in the texts of the masques which cannot convey the power of spectacle and illusion. During the later part of Elizabeth's reign the texts of court masques began to be preserved and, as a consequence, the masque became a literary mode as well as an entertainment for the occasion. As a poet and playwright, Jonson attributed considerable importance to the masque as literature as well as performance. In the texts as well as the performances the changes of the early seventeenth century were a reflection of the king. Jonson, Jonathan Goldberg points out, incorporated into printed editions the interjections from the throne as an integral part of the performance.[10] He strove not to find one ideal form of the masque, as criticism might lead us to believe, but to satisfy the monarch.

The tastes of the new king could hardly have been more different. The change of monarch from James I to Charles I saw a radical shift of personal and political style. And Jonson's entertainments for the new king were very different productions. Unfortunately no texts of masques have survived for the first six years of Charles I's reign, so that the first that we have are also the first for which Jonson was commissioned:[11] *Love's Triumph Through Callipolis* performed by the king on Twelfth Night 1631, and *Chloridia*

[9] Orgel, *Jonsonian Masque.*
[10] Goldberg, *James I and the Politics of Literature*, p. 64.
[11] We know, however, that there were two court masques in 1626, two in 1627 and two commissioned for 1628. *Jonsonian Masque*, p. 79.

presented by the queen at Shrovetide the same year.[12] As texts the differences strike the reader immediately. They are much shorter than Jacobean texts and *Love's Triumph* has no antimasque of humorous dialogue. The 'depraved lovers', boasting, whining, froward, corrupt, melancholic, appear, we are told, with 'antic gesticulation' and then exit,[13] leaving the rest of the action to the masque proper – to the triumph of love represented by the queen and the celebration of the royal marriage as the highest expression of love. The emphasis is upon spectacle rather than poetry. The masque, as we have argued, was an expression of kingship. And there could be few better documents of the impact of Charles I's succession than Jonson's first masque for the new reign. The fundamental change for Jonson was the king's enthusiastic participation. Charles I danced in *Love's Triumph* as the heroical lover, one of fifteen lovers who triumphed over the corruptions of Cupid. Jonson's stage directions make it clear that the king was 'the middle person ... placed in the centre'.[14] Participating, the king must now be what James could not be: the centre of the action of the masque. The masque proper and revels may assume a larger rôle now that the king performs in the action of transcendence. We do not know whether Jonson followed a pattern set by the earlier Caroline entertainments, or whether his production, as we may suspect, was tailored to suit royal preferences. But we may be certain that the king's participation was completely to refashion the masque.

Love's Triumph announces a second force for change – in the court and in the masque: the king's marriage to Henrietta Maria, the youngest daughter of Henry IV of France. For the performance of *Love's Triumph* is the first example we have of the king's Twelfth Night masques presented to his wife, and hence the first of what were to be a series of entertainments performed in turn by the king and the queen (at Shrovetide) principally for each other. Anne of Denmark had been an enthusiastic masquer and James I had liked to watch his wife dance. After her death in 1619, however, no royal actor had regularly graced the stage. The Caroline masques, by contrast, not only all revolved around a king *and* his queen, they articulated a dialogue between them and they celebrated a union of virtues greater than either possessed in themselves. The royal marriage determined too the third important change announced by *Love's Triumph*: the emergence as the theme of the masques of the triumph of love over illicit passion, over what Jonson describes here as the 'confused affections' of 'certain sectaries, or depraved lovers, who neither knew the name or nature of Love rightly ...'[15] Jonson informs us that the subject was resolved on 'we the inventors, being commanded from the king to

---

[12] I have used the texts in Orgel and Strong, *Inigo Jones*, I, pp. 405–7; II, pp. 420–2.
[13] *Ibid.*, I, p. 406, lines 16–34.
[14] *Ibid.*, p. 406, lines 103–4.
[15] *Ibid.*, I, p. 406, lines 23–4.

think on something worthy of his majesty's putting in act'.[16] We may be almost certain that Jonson and Jones made their decision after careful consideration of the king's, or queen's, favoured subjects, as other authors who succeeded them were to do. Love's triumph as the subject of the masque, no less than the royal participation, was a hallmark of the new reign.

In some ways the succession of Charles I presented Jonson with a solution to the problem he had faced for years: how to make the monarch the centre of the masque and the effective force of the transformation which was the masque's purpose. When Charles I as chief masquer led the revels he would have taken by the hand his queen and so led her in a dance which enacted in motion their union and the triumph of ordered love over depraved passion which had formed the subject of the poetry. Subject and form were in harmony when what the king was presented as doing, he did. But if the involvement of Charles I resolved some of the tensions of the Jacobean masque, it is evident that it posed Jonson new difficulties. In his masques for James I, Jonson had increasingly employed the debate and dramatic dialogue of the antimasque as an explanatory device by which to facilitate the comprehension of the action, much as a prologue served to introduce a play. Such antimasques are absent from *Love's Triumph* and *Chloridia*.[17] And in the absence of explanatory dialogue, Jonson found it necessary to write a prologue to the text for the benefit of those who had not seen how the antimasque of depraved lovers in *Love's Triumph* expressed 'their confused affections in the scenical persons and habits of the four prime European nations', and who had not beheld the whining lover or fantastical lover whose costumes represented their qualities.[18] Jonson tells his reader how he and Inigo Jones 'after some debate of cogitation with ourselves resolved on the following argument':

First that a person *boni ominis*, of a good character, as Euphemus, sent down from heaven to Callipolis, which is understood the city of beauty or goodness, should come in; and finding her majesty there enthroned, declare unto her that love, who was wont to be respected as a special deity in court, and tutelar god of the place, had of late received an advertisement that in the suburbs or skirts of Callipolis were crept in certain sectaries, or depraved lovers . . .[19]

The prologue was necessary 'To Make the Spectators Understanders' and to make the masque intelligible to those who had not seen it. For as action and spectacle dominated, the masque as literature was threatened. *Love's Triumph*, at just over two hundred lines, was only half the length of Jonson's Jacobean texts. If the king's participation resolved some of the problems of

[16] *Ibid.*, I, p. 405. 'To Make the Spectators Understanders', lines 6–8.
[17] Orgel, *Jonsonian Masque*, pp. 79–80.
[18] Orgel and Strong, *Inigo Jones*, I, p. 406, lines 31–3. Sketches of the costumes may be seen in *ibid.*, pp. 409–14, nos. 149–59.
[19] *Ibid.*, I, p. 406, lines 16–23.

the masque in performance, *Love's Triumph* suggests that it presented new difficulties to the survival of the masque as literature.

The problem and Jonson's response to it are important for our understanding of the Caroline masque. Jonson in 1631 adapted to the tastes of the new king and to the circumstances of the royal marriage, as he had twenty years earlier fashioned his entertainment to please James I and Anne of Denmark. But for all the changes, it is evident that Jonson was concerned to preserve the masque as a literary form as well as an occasional performance, and more importantly that for him the didactic purpose of the masque remained central. The masque, he asserted in his prologue, should seek to inculcate the values which it celebrated:

Where all representations, especially those of this nature in court, public spectacles, either have been or ought to be the mirrors of man's life, whose ends, for the excellence of their exhibitors . . . ought always to carry a mixture of profit with them no less than delight . . .[20]

Jonson's assertion expresses his fear: that as spectacle came to predominate, 'profit' would be banished for pure delight, that the spectators would not become understanders. For twenty years, Jonson had collaborated uneasily in the production of the masques with Inigo Jones, who, Jonson suspected, wished always to make excessive claims for the place of architecture and design to the detriment of the power of poetry, for, as Jonson saw it, the masque as delight rather than profit. Over *Love's Triumph*, the tensions in their relationship flared up into an open quarrel. Though the prologue spoke of the two men as joint inventors, rather than (as earlier) listing Jonson as 'Author' and Jones as 'Designer', Jones was furious to find his name printed second on the title page.[21] His anger suggests that Jones at least believed himself to have been the principal author of the entertainment. If his greater influence seems likely in *Love's Triumph*, it becomes more evident still in the queen's Shrovetide masque that followed it a few weeks later. In *Chloridia*, we discern a greater emphasis than before on the description of scene and the mechanics of spectacle. And despite the long speech of the Postilion from hell, the antimasques of eight entries depend upon costume and scene rather than dialogue. *Chloridia* does not read well as a text: the poetry itself depends upon the performance. Jonson and Jones invented this time, as the prologue declares, 'a new argument, with the whole change of the scene',[22] and the argument was enacted through the mechanics more than the power of poetry. Describing the subject of the masque action, the stellification on earth of the goddess Chloris, the prologue concludes:

[20] *Ibid.*, I, p. 405, lines 1–6.
[21] See D. J. Gordon, 'Poet and architect: the intellectual setting of the quarrel between Ben Jonson and Inigo Jones', *Journ. Warburg & Courtauld Inst.*, 12 (1949), pp. 152–78.
[22] Lines 2–3, *Inigo Jones*, II, p. 420.

Upon this hinge the whole invention moved.[23]

The words resound with irony and ambiguity. For to Jonson the invention or subject of the masque has been reduced to 'ye Machine', and the mystical and didactic purpose of the masque surrendered to the emptiness of mechanical spectacle.[24] Despite their collaboration, it is Jones who has emerged as the dominant partner. *Chloridia* was Jonson's last masque for the court.

It is Jones's triumph over his rival that has engaged the attention of historians and students of the masques. Jones's prominence, however, cannot be isolated from, and is in some ways less important than, the influence of the king and queen. The prologue to *Chloridia* hints that there had been more than two inventors of the masque; and that the king and queen had been closely involved in the production. It may well be that throughout the 1630s the decisive voices in the direction of the court entertainments were those of Charles I and Henrietta Maria themselves. In the case of the queen, who presented over half of the entertainments, there is little direct evidence. We know that Jones was careful to consult with Henrietta Maria about the design and colours of her costumes,[25] and the detailed nature of his sketches for them suggest that this was of great importance to her. Her own comment on *Coelum Britannicum*, that 'Pour les habits, elle n'avoit jamais rien vue de si brave' reinforces the impression.[26] But it is probably wrong to assume that the queen's influence went no further than the costumes. Henrietta Maria, we recall, not only danced in masques, she (notoriously as far as the puritans were concerned) took speaking parts in plays.[27] The queen was a regular attender at plays in which there was relatively little emphasis upon the visual, and, if the text may be our guide, her own production of *The Shepherd's Paradise* can hardly be said to have elevated spectacle over dialogue.[28] Though there is no evidence that the queen helped to write any entertainments, there is a unity of theme and treatment to the masques which she presented, and a style distinct from the king's production, which, given the different authors over a decade, can be explained only by the queen's own

---

[23] *Ibid.*, line 11.

[24] 'And I have mett with those / That doe cry up ye Machine, & ye Showes.' 'An Expostulacon wth Inigo Jones', lines 31–2, *Ben Jonson*, ed. C. H. Herford and P. and E. Simpson (11 vols., Oxford, 1925–53), VIII, p. 403.

[25] Jones wrote a note at the bottom of his sketch for the queen's costume as Chloris, 'This designe I conceave to bee fitt for the invention and if it please hir Matie: to add or alter anything I desier to receave her Mats comand and the deseigne againe by this bearer. The collors allso are in hir Mats choise', *Inigo Jones*, II, p. 445, sketch no. 181.

[26] Adams, *Dramatic Records of Herbert*, p. 55.

[27] *Artenice and The Shepherd's Paradise*, to which it was believed Prynne had referred in *Histrio-Mastix*.

[28] See above, pp. 39–44. We might recall here that *The Shepherd's Paradise* lasted eight hours. This is not to deny that the scenery was also elaborate.

1 Inigo Jones's final design of the queen's costume as Chloris for the masque *Chloridia* performed at Shrovetide 1631

tastes.[29] When on the title page of *The Temple of Love* Davenant described himself as 'her Majesties Servant', it would appear that he not only acknowledged a patroness, but also the mistress of his muse.[30]

The influence of Charles I is more obvious. We know that in the midst of pressing business Charles took the masques very seriously. Newswriters

[29] See below, p. 257.
[30] Orgel and Strong, *Inigo Jones*, II, p. 600.

frequently commented on the time the king devoted to them; in 1637 he
practised for *Britannia Triumphans* daily.[31] His involvement evidently went
beyond participation. Since the masque was an expression of the monarch, it
should not surprise us that a king as concerned with his image as Charles I
collaborated with, or at least oversaw, the production. Charles, we know, not
only read the manuscripts of plays and intervened personally in matters of
censorship, he even suggested a plot to Shirley, perhaps to other
playwrights.[32] Such reflections, together with the echoes of royal speeches
and political allusions in the masques, make at least the circumstantial
evidence for Charles's involvement, as Professor Smuts concluded, 'fairly
compelling'.[33] Inigo Jones himself provides a more explicit testimony. In a
letter to Salvetti, the Venetian envoy, requesting assistance in procuring from
the Duke of Tuscany a book of designs of Italian intermezzi, Jones added: 'I
would like not only the designs and scenes of the interlude, but also the book
which describes the form because I am certain the King wants to see it.'[34] As
Smuts points out, the 'form' of the masque was its meaning. Jones's certainty
that the king wished to see it can have stemmed only from the experience of
working with a monarch who had taken a close interest in the subject and
symbolism of the masque, as he did in the paintings of himself and his family.
This comment suggests strongly that Jones's chief collaborator after 1631
was Charles I himself and that the masques of the 1630s reflect the ideas of
both men.

Indeed the changes in the masque that we have noted – the absence of the
long explanatory antimasque, the greater emphasis upon spectacle – may be
attributable more to the influence of the new monarchs than to the triumph of
Jones over Jonson. Charles I brought to the English court a very different
personal, cultural and political style. James I had come to the English throne
after years as King of Scotland. The organization and nature of the Scottish
court were quite unlike those of England. The royal household was smaller
and the court less formal; relationships between the king and his nobility
were far more direct and familiar than the elaborate rituals of etiquette at the
court of Gloriana. James's own informality and familiarity, his taste for crude
and bawdy humour, his disregard for decorum, were very much the product
of that environment. A belief in debate, in discussion and argument, characterized his kingship.[35] An education under the tutelage of the most learned
humanist of his day, George Buchanan, had not only equipped him for

---

[31] Berks. Record office, Trumbull MS 543/2 (Weckherlin's diary); despatch of Salvetti, 15 Jan.
     1637, B.L., Add.MS 27,962. I owe this reference to Smuts, 'Culture of absolutism', p. 154.
[32] Harbage, *Cavalier Drama*, pp. 101–3.
[33] Smuts, 'Culture of absolutism', p. 190.
[34] *Ibid.*, p. 189.
[35] See J. Wormald, 'James VI and I', and the chapter by Neil Cuddy in Starkey, *The English
     Court*.

political oratory. James VI and I was a scholar, a writer who engaged in ecclesiastical controversy and penned political treatises; moreover he was a poet who besides his own verse composed a tract on the rules of Scottish poetry.[36] Jacobean culture no less than early seventeenth-century politics bears the marks of the king's personality: the Jacobean style is literary and discursive, resonant with debate and tension, argument and counter case. And Jacobean dramatists and poets could in their writings, as the courtiers in personal exchange, engage the king in a debate which aired disagreement whilst it flattered the learning of the scholar-king.[37] In so many ways the opposite to his father, Charles I was formal and grave, stiff and reserved, with no taste for irreverent humour or innuendo. And though he sought a wide range of advice, Charles did not enter into debate with his courtiers or counsellors. The role of kingship he perceived as the resolution of debate and uncertainty; the monarch, he believed, was above politics, not part of the political process. Charles I was no controversialist; to him the royal word was not an argument to be weighed, but an order to be executed. Obsessed with order and uniformity, he was drawn most to those courts, such as Spain, which were most regulated and to those cultural modes that most expressed the order he sought – in art and in life. Van Dyck was Charles I's painter because he presented the king with the idealized order which he sought. And Jones rose to prominence as author of the Caroline masques because he effected on the stage what Van Dyck represented on canvas: the ordering of the world through the majesty of the king's person.

With the accession of Charles I, the masque in some ways achieved a more perfect form. The transcendence from the material and sensual world to that of the intellect and soul now became the centre of the action. Jones's devices became more elaborate; descriptions of scene loom larger because it is the masque proper (rather than antimasque) that dominates the production. The tensions between antimasque and masque and between poetry and spectacle were never, as we shall argue, resolved. But in the 1630s, as the masque more clearly expressed transcendence, the claims of the architect whose art made possible the transformation could be asserted more forcefully than before. The greater prominence of Jones was a direct consequence of the aesthetic preferences and the political values of Charles I and his queen.[38]

Both the succession of Charles I and the ascendancy of Jones were responsible for important shifts of emphasis. But we should be wary, I

---

[36] See, for example, J. Craigie, ed., *The Poems of James VI* (2 vols., Scottish Text Society, 3rd series, 22, 26, 1955, 1958); James VI, *The Essays of a prentise in the divine art of poesie* (Edinburgh, 1585), ed. E. Arber (English reprints, London, 1869); W. W. Skeat, ed., *The King's Quair* (Scottish Text Society, 1911). For a discussion see Goldberg, *James I and the Politics of Literature*, esp. pp. 17–28.

[37] Goldberg, *James I, passim*, and especially the brilliant ch. 3.

[38] See below, ch. 6.

suggest, of concluding that the masque was fundamentally or radically changed in purpose or in treatment. Jonson, as we saw, believed that it was, and complained that the ethical force and mysteries of the poetry were abandoned for 'Painting & Carpentry'.[39] In answer to his accusation, D. J. Gordon and Stephen Orgel have demonstrated beyond doubt that Jones's purpose was no less serious than Jonson's; that he believed in the didactic powers of architecture as expressions of harmony and order, no less than Jonson asserted the claims of poetry as *magister vitae*.[40] But no critic has made a claim for the continued vitality of the Caroline masque as literature – for the poetry or dramatic dialogue – alongside the mechanical brilliance of Jones. In part the poets are themselves to blame. In the first of the court masques after Jonson's retirement, Aurelian Townshend's *Albion's Triumph*, Mercury, though God of eloquence and at times the symbol of poetry, announces: 'we speak in acts and scorn words trifling scenes'.[41] But that of course Mercury does not do, and it would be wrong to take him at face value here. For all that Jonson's successors have been branded as mere adjuncts to Jones,[42] *Albion's Triumph* is a distinctly literary masque that works as a text, as well as performance. At four hundred and fifty lines, it is twice the length of Jonson's last two masques and an equal to many of his Jacobean productions. Like them, too, it consists of a long dramatic antimasque, in which the very purpose and philosophy of the masque is articulated. It is a purpose which is shown to depend upon poetry and prose rather than spectacle. Platonicus's debate with Publius about the nature of perception (of the masque) reads like a philosophical dialogue. Platonicus explains that vision is not necessary to him because he has understanding, and that that understanding has been nurtured by his study – by the word. He accompanies Publius to the triumph at the amphitheatre to educate him in understanding – 'to teach thee to read in thy own book', to discuss the difference between knowledge and observation.[43] Townshend's second masque, for the queen, has been described as little other than spectacle and again the poet would appear to concur.[44] At the critical moment of *Tempe Restored*, the Highest Sphere proclaims:

---

[39]   Oh, to make Boardes to speake! There is a taske
         Painting & Carpentry are ye Soule of Masque.
         Pack wth your pedling Poetry to the Stage,
         This is ye money-gett, Mechanick Age!
         ('An Expostulačõn wth Inigo Jones', lines 49–52, Herford and Simpson, *Ben Jonson*, VIII, p. 404).

[40] Gordon, 'Poet and architect'; Orgel, *Illusion of Power*; Orgel and Strong, *Inigo Jones*, I, ch. 1.

[41] *Albion's Triumph*, line 99, Orgel and Strong, *Inigo Jones*, II, p. 454. Though there may be an irony in 'words *trifling scenes*'.

[42] Parry, *Golden Age Restor'd*, p. 185.

[43] *Albion's Triumph*, line 230, *Inigo Jones*, II, p. 456.

[44] Chambers, *Aurelian Townshend's Poems and Masks*, pp. xvii, 119.

I cannot blame ye if ye gaze,
And give small ear to what I say,
For such a presence will amaze,
And send the senses all one way.[45]

But for all the disclaimer the verse *does* report the action. The Highest Sphere describes what the Whitehall audience is watching. Though the senses are seduced by the sight, the word, as Platonicus explained to Publius, is also necessary to the understanding and for the perception of what is seen. It is 'more th'object than the sight' that is the subject of masque, and the perception of the object depends upon the poet's instruction as well as the designer's arts of illusion.[46] Mere observation without understanding is the subject of antimasque; the masque proper, the perception of 'insides', requires the observer, like Publius, to read in his book.[47] Townshend does not desert Jonson's stand for poetry; though he lacks his predecessor's poetic gifts, he makes a bold claim for the poet's tutelary rôle. Thomas Carew's masque is an even bolder assertion of the rôle of poetry and drama. *Coelum Britannicum* may be read as a literary text more satisfyingly perhaps than any other Stuart masque. Not only is it one of the longest, it speaks with many of the varied voices of literature – the dramatic as well as the poetic, the voice of question as well as statement, a tone of irony as well as celebration. And for all the brilliance of Jones's engineering, *Coelum Britannicum* does not depend upon the mechanics of production. Action in the masque never overrides the poetry.[48]

Ironically, the most spectacular Caroline masque was not a court masque in the strict sense: it was James Shirley's *The Triumph of Peace*, presented by the Inns of Court for the king and queen. The entertainment commenced with the procession from Holborn to Whitehall of the masquers and antimasquers in rich costume and decorated chariots. The intended audience of such a procession was clearly not the court. It was 'the multitude of spectators in the streets besides the windows' who 'all seemed loathe to part with so glorious a spectacle'.[49] Once at Whitehall, the entertainment commenced with a dramatic dialogue befitting the authorship of an experienced playwright and in no way dependent upon the mechanics of scenery. The Caroline masque undoubtedly saw greater refinements of the arts of illusion, and greater visual extravagance. But this did not have to be, and in many cases was not, to the detriment of prose and poetry. Jones in *Tempe Restored* boasted of the

---

[45] *Tempe Restored*, lines 226–9, *Inigo Jones*, II, p. 482. [46] Line 254, *ibid.*, p. 482.
[47] I quote from the speech of Platonicus, 'Outsides have insides, shells have kernels in them, and under every fable, nay almost under everything lies a moral', *Albion's Triumph*, lines 230–2, *Inigo Jones*, II, p. 456. [48] See below, pp. 232–42.
[49] James Shirley, *The Triumph of Peace* (1634). Account of Bulstrode Whitelocke, from *Memorials of the English Affairs* (London, 1682), quoted in *Inigo Jones*, II, p. 543. See below, pp. 215–16.

technical achievements that had brought fifty persons together on the stage.[50]
Triumphant at last over his long-standing rival Jonson, he could not resist the
taunt: that 'these shows are nothing else but pictures with light and
motion'.[51] But even if he meant it seriously, his remark was neither true nor
unchallenged. The poets who followed Jonson may not have been as noisy in
their claims or expostulations, but as worthy members of the tribe of Ben,
they continued in their masques to sustain the place and power of poetry.

The printed editions of the masques are evidence of their literary success.
Texts of the entertainments were carefully produced and purchased both by
those at court who had seen the productions and by interested readers in the
country who had not.[52] The consciousness of a readership at court and
beyond pervades the texts and can never have been absent from the production. *Tempe Restored* is not only prefaced by a summary of the argument of
the masque, but concludes with an explanation of the Allegory which reads
like a key to the action.[53] The text of *Salmacida Spolia* elucidates the
complicated symbolism of the proscenium arch which had probably been
intelligible only to a few who had been present at the performance. *Britannia
Triumphans* sets out 'The Subject of the Masque'. Critics might discern more
subtle manifestations of literary self-consciousness in the internal debates
about the purpose of masque in *Britannia Triumphans* and *Albion's Triumph*
or in Carew's placing himself upon the stage in the character of Momus in
Coelum Britannicum. We need to think more carefully about the relationship
of the performance to the text and of the author's sense of that relationship.[54]
For our purpose, however, it is sufficient to stress that the masque continued
as a literary mode, and that as such spectacle, for all its brilliance, could not
subject poetry. Despite Jonson's fears, the poet was not packed off to the
public stage. In the persons of Carew, Townshend and Davenant, he
remained a commanding presence in the masquing hall at Whitehall.

It is as literary texts and theatre that the Caroline masques await a study.
For concentration on the achievements of Jones's spectacle has diverted our
attention from how the authors who succeeded Jonson responded to the
commissions to write and to the circumstances of the 1630s entertainments.
The dramatic vitality and importance of the antimasques have largely gone
unremarked. In *Love's Triumph* and *Chloridia*, as we have observed, Jonson

[50] 'This sight altogether was for the difficulty of the engining and number of the persons the
greatest that have been seen here in our time', *Tempe Restored*, lines 204–6, *Inigo Jones*, II,
p. 481.
[51] 'The Description of the Scene', *ibid.*, lines 49–50, *Inigo Jones*, II, p. 480.
[52] Humphrey Mildmay bought a copy of *Coelum Britannicum*, having seen it, Bentley, *Jacobean
and Caroline Stage*, II, p. 676, III, p. 108; VII, p. 92. See below, p. 259.
[53] Below, pp. 227–8.
[54] See T. Berger, 'Textual problems in English Renaissance masques, pageants and entertainments', *Research Opportunities in Renaissance Drama*, 17 (1974), pp. 13–16.

dispensed with the long antimasque of dialogue and burlesque which had characterized his Jacobean productions. But this was by no means to be a feature of the Caroline masque. Especially in the case of the king's masques, it is the antimasque that dominates when we experience the entertainment as text, and perhaps too when it was seen in performance. Moreover the antimasque serves, as with Jonson's *Neptune's Triumph*, as an introduction to set out the argument of the masque and to explain how it should be understood.[55] In Townshend's *Albion's Triumph*, as we have seen, Platonicus and Publius debate the meaning of understanding and perception – and the very philosophy behind the masque that follows. Action and Imposture similarly discuss the nature of appetite and virtue by way of prologue to *Britannia Triumphans*, which is concerned with the governance of the senses.[56] The complexity, drama and dialogue of these scenes are central to the authors' intentions. And though they are antimasques in the sense that their debates are ultimately transcended by the harmonious action of the revels, they manage the entertainment rather than provide burlesque comedy. Indeed they often stage antimasques proper of caricatured vices as devices of their discussions. So, for example, Merlin in *Britannia Triumphans* presents a mock romance of a giant, a knight and a damsel as evidence of his powers and claims; Mercury and Momus in *Coelum Britannicum* call down from the heavens the stellified vices to earth; Publius and Platonicus go off together to the spectacles of the amphitheatre which have been the subject of their exchange.[57] Such burlesque antimasques within the discussions tend to raise the debate over the world of sense and appetite to which in form they belong, and elevate the speakers and disputants beyond the antimasque itself. So, for instance, Mercury and Momus not only discuss the reforms of Jupiter, they stay on stage to judge those who would claim by their virtue a place in the stars. They control the stage until the appearance of the masquers; at times they virtually act as Masters of Ceremonies for their entrance. The compelling force of these dialogues is by no means eroded by their final transcendence in apotheosis, spectacle or dance. Platonicus, Momus and Action have told us what to see, and their words remain with us throughout the performance. Such dialogues make some of the 1630s masques didactic drama and philosophical treatise as well as triumphs of the arts of illusion.

A recognition of the drama and dialogue must lead us to question a common charge: that the Caroline masque had as its purpose the creation of an ideal or fantasy, as a retreat from the world of reality. Charles I and his court, it has been said, excluded the world outside Whitehall for the comforts of an illusory kingdom which could be governed, as the realm could not, by

[55] Orgel, *Jonsonian Masque*, p. 94.
[56] Below, pp. 248–9.
[57] Below, pp. 224–5 and note 195.

ideas and by machinery.[58] The masque, by definition, represents an ideal. Its conclusion is the attainment of that knowledge of truths or ideas, the divine harmonies of which are expressed in the final dance. But masque as such does not escape reality. The antimasque features the most grotesque manifestations of the physical world of sense and appetite. Antimasque is, of course, transcended. But, as we have argued, the antimasque is such a forceful feature of some of the Caroline texts that the debates, the doubts and difficulties of the antimasques are never completely dispelled. The masque is made to acknowledge and in some cases integrate the world of problems and imperfections. Publius in *Albion's Triumph* never acquires the understanding that Platonicus attempted to teach him; and yet he cannot be ignored, for, as his name suggests, he stands for the people – a people who will also fail to comprehend the masque. He expresses the limits to Platonicus's own arguments. The ideal remains in *Albion's Triumph* an ideal: the vision of a philosopher and of a philosopher-king who will attempt to rule in accordance with truths that the people will not understand. In *Coelum Britannicum*, Momus's speech in praise of Jove is a catalogue not of achievements but of ideal intentions many of which, as it is acknowledged, will never succeed in reality.[59] Momus knows that edicts will be disobeyed and that 'however the letter of the law runs', human nature will follow its own course.[60]

Even when virtue does triumph, its vulnerability is never disguised. The claims of wealth to a place in the stars are so persuasively delivered (one recalls the seductive eloquence of Comus) that 'feeble virtue' can hardly resist them, and even some gods are shown to have fallen prey.[61] Authority itself is depicted in the masques as falling to temptation. In Davenant's *Luminalia*, watchmen who ought to be apprehending criminals share with thieves the booty of the night.[62] There are many other examples. Ideal and reality exist in tension in several Caroline masques. One scholar has pointed to a recognition of such tensions by Inigo Jones himself. In *Albion's Triumph*, L. F. Barkham points out, the two columns of the proscenium arch, Theorica and Practica, stand for the ideal and the real, and the claim for architecture lies in its resolution of the tension between them.[63] We must note, however, that the resolution of the tension is a result not of the rejection of practice, but the integration of practice and theory, the real with the ideal – or Publius with Platonicus. Whilst 'all the masque's technology is in the service of making the

---

[58] C. V. Wedgwood, *Poetry and Politics Under the Stuarts*, pp. 43–4; Parry, *Golden Age Restor'd, passim*; Ashton, *English Civil War*, pp. 31–4.
[59] See below, pp. 236–8.
[60] *Coelum Britannicum*, lines 325–6, *Inigo Jones*, II, p. 573.
[61] Line 548, *ibid.*, p. 575. The phrase is delivered by Mercury, who speaks for the world of masque, not antimasque.
[62] *Luminalia*, lines 156–60, *Inigo Jones*, II, p. 707.
[63] L. F. Barkham, 'The imperialist arts of Inigo Jones', *Renaissance Drama*, 7 (1976), pp. 257–85.

ideal real', it by no means always succeeds.[64] In *Coelum Britannicum*, as Barkham acknowledges, the tensions between the abstract and the concrete, the ideal and the real, are never resolved. The world of Idea and Intellect never totally supplants that of sense and appetite. The most explicit recognition of the obstacles to fulfilling ideals comes in the last masque of the reign. With the Scots in armed rebellion and murmurs of discontent in the provinces, it was, as Orgel and Strong put it, 'no longer possible for the inventor of Platonic visions simply to reveal the Good and expect men to follow it'.[65] In *Salmacida Spolia*, though the king is still presented as the intellectual light which might lead men to virtue, there is an admission that many may not be led. The blessings of the realm were seen to be vulnerable: 'we grieve they are too great to last'.[66] Circumstances obviously have dictated a more fatalistic tone. But it is wrong to regard this as the first glimmer of realism in the masque. Davenant had revealed his scepticism about the ideal of Platonic love in his earlier masque, *The Temple of Love*.[67] In the *Triumph of Peace*, the world of masque is punctured as a common carpenter and painter rush upon the stage, claiming a place at the entertainment.[68] Though the masque represents the ideals for which Charles I strove, the obstacles and realities were to be found not only in the suburbs and the country; they are to be found in the masquing rooms at Whitehall.

To argue that the masques retained a sense of reality, that they incorporate question and debate, is to challenge the verdict that they were sycophantic. Flattery after all is delusion; it is the protection of its recipient from any unpalatable truths; it glosses over difficulties. And this, we have suggested, the masque does not do. This is not to deny that the masque writers praise or celebrate the monarch: the discourse of masque is the language of praise. But because the masque is concerned with idealizations, it is ideals that are celebrated. The king addressed in the masque is a god, an embodiment of virtue, an idealization of kingship. The masquers, that is the courtiers in disguise, are also gods. Gods, of course, demand no flattery or compliments, as Mercury declares in his commission announcing the triumph in Albipolis:

> This from a god unto a goddess sent
> A god relates, that could use compliment;
> But when such states negotiate by such means,
> We speak in acts, and scorn words' trifling scenes.[69]

Momus in *Coelum Britannicum* makes it clear that he has delivered his praise

[64] *Ibid.*, p. 261; Orgel and Strong, *Inigo Jones*, I, p. 9.
[65] Orgel and Strong, *Inigo Jones*, I, p. 74.
[66] *Salmacida Spolia*, line 309, *Inigo Jones*, II, p. 732.
[67] See below, pp. 244–7.
[68] Below, p. 218.
[69] *Albion's Triumph*, lines 96–9, *Inigo Jones*, II, p. 454.

of Jove 'in a blunt round tale'. Gods need not 'rhetorical elegancies'.[70] The nearer then that the king and courtiers by their virtuous actions approached the deities which they represented, the less they required any praise beyond the renown of their own actions. The masquers represented ideals; but they also in confronting such ideals might perceive what they were and what they should become.[71] The masque was a mirror in which images of the ideal and of the real were juxtaposed and reflected – not only to the audience, but to the performers themselves. Interestingly, the metaphor was one the authors were fond of: Aurelian Townshend concluded his first masque with the admission that 'I was as loathe to be brought upon the stage, as an unhandsome man is to see himself in a great glass.'[72] The comparison came easily to him, for he knew that the stage – of the masque no less than the drama – was a platform of self-realization, of truth rather than delusion; that the masque could reveal imperfections in reflecting the ideals from which they fell short. Similarly in Carew's *Coelum Britannicum* Mercury announces to the king and queen that Jupiter

> When in the crystal mirror of your reign
> He viewed himself, he found his loathsome stains.[73]

In the crystal mirror of the masque, the king may learn his own faults as he plays the god whose 'exemplar life' even Jove would imitate. Praise in the masque is not empty flattery: it is didactic. Like the masque itself, it is a celebration of the highest ideals presented in the belief that what men (performers and audience) see and enact they may become. It is the theatrical form of the poetry of praise which Jonson described in his epistle to Selden, in defending himself against the charge of flattery:

> Though I confesse (as every Muse hath err'd,
> And mine not least) I have too oft preferr'd
> Men past their termes, and prais'd some names too much,
> But 'twas with purpose to have made them such.[74]

To suggest that praise was not necessarily flattery[75] is not our only ground for defending masque against the charge of sycophancy. For in the Caroline masques there is an ironic tone which our ears may have failed to discern because our hearing has been impaired by our assumptions about what we

[70] *Coelum Britannicum*, lines 281–3, *Inigo Jones*, II, p. 572.
[71] On praise and criticism see Goldberg, *James I, passim*, and below, ch. 6.
[72] Albion's Triumph, lines 452–3, *Inigo Jones*, II, p. 458.
[73] *Coelum Britannicum*, lines 82–3, *Inigo Jones*, II, p. 571.
[74] 'An Epistle to Master JOHN SELDEN', lines 19–22, Herford and Simpson, *Ben Jonson*, VIII, p. 159. The idea comes from Aristotle's *Rhetoric*. See Javitch, *Poetry and Courtliness*, p. 117 and Peterson, *Imitation and Praise in the Poems of Ben Jonson*. I am grateful to Richard Peterson for a valuable discussion of this matter.
[75] Jonson made a careful distinction between them, *Timber or Discoveries* (1641), Herford and Simpson, *Ben Jonson*, VIII, p. 566.

should listen for. It has not passed completely undetected. D. J. Gordon pointed to the speech in Jonson's *Love's Welcome at Bolsover* in which Philalethes mocks a court 'where all the true lessons of love are thoroughly read, and taught; the Reasons, the Proportions and Harmonie, drawne forth in analytick Tables, and made demonstrable to the *Senses*'.[76] The mathematical organization of love was not only another jibe at Jones; it suggests a court preoccupied with sterile abstractions which meant little to those beyond its confines. Gordon's example, of course, is Jonson and an entertainment which, though presented to the king, was devised by the poet for presentation in the country. Irony in the court masques is a difficult subject. It is hard when reading a text to tune our ears to the significance of a phrase for a Caroline court audience, or to imagine the style or mode of delivery by the professional actors.[77] Visual irony is a more elusive subject still: though Confidence in the antimasque of *The Triumph of Peace* appears from the description to be dressed like a cavalier, we have no surviving sketch, nor any knowledge of Jones's intentions.[78] But some obvious cases present themselves and indicate that irony awaits further investigation. Let us consider, for example, the rôle of Momus in Thomas Carew's *Coelum Britannicum*. Momus rehearses the reforms of Jupiter as a list which virtually recites the changes announced in orders and proclamations of Charles I: strict regulations for the court, restrictions on tobacco and alehouses, orders forbidding country gentry to come to London, and so on.[79] Not only, however, is Momus's tone ironic and sardonic, it is, as we shall see, a pastiche of the rather lofty style in which royal proclamations were couched. Momus describes serious intentions with scepticism and ribaldry. He is, of course, mythically the god of satire, the very personification of mockery and censure. He is visible as such by his costume. And he imparts to Carew's *Coelum Britannicum* that second, often undermining voice that we have detected in the poetry. A tone of realism and cynicism pervades this masque. Momus is a warning that we should not reduce the masques, before we have carefully studied them, to monotone or monochrome. They may resonate with more tones and reflect more complex images than we have realized.

SUBJECTS AND THEMES: NATURE, LOVE AND GOVERNMENT

The masques of the 1630s then should not be dismissed as a decadent form of the genre, abandoning poetry for spectacle, realism for fantasy or serious purpose for slight flattery. The masque changed with the succession of

[76] Gordon, 'Poet and architect', pp. 171–5.
[77] It is important always to remember that all the speaking parts were taken by actors familiar with the professional stage.
[78] *The Triumph of Peace*, lines 44–8, *Inigo Jones*, II, p. 546.
[79] See below for a full discussion of this masque.

Charles I, but it did not become simply a visual entertainment. Rather in some cases it would seem that as Jones's genius in effecting the transcendence from antimasque to masque by elaborate machinery reached its apogee, the antimasques grew longer and more complex, and the masques as a whole became more dramatic and literary. If the Caroline masque achieved its perfection as a production, it also retained its force and importance as literature – and perhaps allowed the expression of many of the modes of literary discourse.

Such a reappraisal of nature and form is necessary if we are to understand the Caroline masque as a statement of values or to comprehend the themes and treatment of subjects in the 1630s productions. For the subjects of the court masques throughout their history reflected, no less than the changes of form, not only the very different monarchs – a woman, a Scot and a young married English king – but also the circumstances of each performance: the creation of a Prince of Wales, the return from an embassy abroad, or the launching of a ship money fleet.[80] But the handling of subjects, as of the genre itself, remained to a large extent the prerogative of the authors and inventors. A general commission in the visual and literary arts does not, as we know, determine or dictate the end product; nor need a work produced for an occasion be limited by that moment. As we turn to investigate the subjects of masques in general and the treatment of subjects in particular, it may be helpful to bear this in mind and to think in terms first of commissions, and later of executions.

Discussion of the Jonsonian masque has, in accordance with the literary critic's interests, concentrated more on form than on content. As a reflection of James I's kingship and values, and as political statements at particular moments, the Jacobean masque awaits its historian who might study the texts in the context of court intrigue and political debate and so evaluate precisely how they did 'sound to present occasions'.[81] Study of *The Gypsies Metamorphos'd* has confirmed a general impression that the Jacobean entertainments reflected immediate circumstances and political alignments and so changed with the swirls of the vortex of factional intrigue that characterized Jacobean politics.[82] There was a greater unity to the Caroline masques, as there was perhaps a greater degree of consistency and royal direction in the government of the realm. The inspiration behind the Caroline entertainments was the philosophy of Neo-Platonism, and in the light of that philosophy the masques

[80] As were the occasions, respectively, of *Prince Henry's Barriers*, *Neptune's Triumph* and *Britannia Triumphans*.

[81] For an example of the sort of study that might be developed, see S. Pearl, 'Sounding to present occasions: Jonson's masques of 1620–5', in Lindley, *The Court Masque*, pp. 60–77.

[82] Dale Randall, *Jonson's Gypsies Unmasked* (Durham, N. Carolina, 1975). Cf. K. Sharpe, 'The Earl of Arundel, his circle and the opposition to the Duke of Buckingham, 1621–8', in *Faction and Parliament*, pp. 209–44.

2 *Luminalia*: Scene I, Night

take as their subjects the themes of nature, beauty and love, presented as allegories of modes of kingship and rule.

Neo-Platonic philosophy postulates an ascent of cognition from the plane of senses and material objects to a loftier stratum of knowledge of forms and ideas, of which objects were but an imperfect material expression.[83] The Caroline masque enacted that philosophy in the transition from antimasque to masque. The world of sense and appetite was represented in the masque by images of nature as an ungoverned wilderness, threatening, violent, ignorant and anarchic; the sphere of soul was depicted as nature ordered and governed by the patterns of the forms. So in the Caroline masque the transcendence is most often a transformation of nature – from chaos to order and from disjuncture to harmony – through the understanding of the philosopher-kings. The transformation is visually represented as a change from a scene of darkness or storm to one of light or calm. *Luminalia*, for example, opens to a scene of darkness, the City of Sleep. But 'these antimasques being past, the heaven began to be enlightened as before the sun rising and the scene was changed into a delicious prospect wherein were rows of trees, fountains,

[83] Above, ch. 1.

3 *Luminalia*: back shutter for Scene I

statues, arbours, grottos, walks and all such things of delight . . .'[84] More
graphically still, at the start of *Salmacida Spolia*:

A curtain flying up, a horrid scene appeared of a storm and tempest. No glimpse of the
sun was seen, as if darkness, confusion, and deformity had possessed the world . . . the
trees bending, as forced by a gust of wind, their branches rent from their trunks . . .[85]

With the antimasque past, however, 'the scene changed into a calm . . . in the
landscape were cornfields and pleasant trees sustaining vines fraught with
grapes, and in some of the farthest part villages, with all such things as might
express a country in peace, rich and fruitful'.[86] The motif of the masque was
this translation from wild to ordered nature. Antimasques present wild
beasts, and bestial attributes of lust and greed; the masque portrays an
idealized nature, the perfect form of nature.

What accomplishes the transcending from scenes of nature as wilderness to
scenes of nature as harmony and order in the production of the masque is the
stage machinery. What effects it in the allegory is love. Love is the expression
of innocent, pure nature in the masque; and the corrupt forms of nature are
represented by the illicit forms of desire, by passion and by lust. Love is the

---

[84] *Luminalia*, lines 239–42, *Inigo Jones*, II, p. 708. No sketch has survived of the scene of 'trees,
  fountains, statues . . . and all such things of delight'.
[85] *Salmacida Spolia*, lines 111–14, *ibid.*, II, p. 731. Cf. below, p. 253.
[86] Lines 156–60, *ibid.*, II, p. 731. Sketch no. 402, II, pp. 744–5.

4 *Salmacida Spolia*: Scene I, 'a horrid scene . . . of a storm and tempest'

higher understanding, the soul in man, that governs the passions and so orders nature. Lust, the antithesis of love, is anarchy. These associations and representations may be seen clearly in Townshend's masque for the queen, *Tempe Restored*. Circe 'by her allurements enamoured a young gentleman on her person, who a while liv'd with her in all sensual delights'.[87] A creature of sense, she turned him into a beast as she had done before to others under her sway. Her lover, however, escaped, refusing to be slave to her lust or his own baser nature:

> Yet there was in me a Promethean fire
> That made me covet to be man again,
> Governed by reason, and not ruled by sense.[88]

'It is consent,' he knows, that makes man 'a perfect slave' to his passions, and he has the will to flee to a place of virtue.[89] Circe pursues him with all her bestial army and powers. What defies her and saves him is pure love, the union of divine beauty and heroic virtue. Circe resigns her authority to such majesties and Cupid vows to order his own government by their example.[90]

[87] *Tempe Restored*, lines 1–2, *Inigo Jones*, II, p. 480.
[88] Lines 76–8, *ibid.*, II, p. 480.
[89] *Ibid.*, line 91.
[90] On the Circe theme see M. M. McGowan, *L'Art du Ballet de Cour en France, 1581–1643* (Paris, 1963), pp. 72ff.; F. Yates, *The French Academies of the Sixteenth Century* (London, 1947), pp. 240–60.

5 *Salmacida Spolia*: Scene II, 'the sky serene, afar off zephyrus appeared breathing a
     gentle gale; in the landscape were cornfields and pleasant trees . . . there came
   breaking out of the heavens a silver chariot, in which sat two persons, the one . . .
   representing Concord; somewhat below her sat the Good Genius of Great Britain'

'The allegory' clarifies for the reader what the spectator has seen represented:
reason has overruled appetite and enabled man to control his desire; divine
beauty has inspired the reason to order 'the body and affections as instruments' and so has restored the purity of nature which had been kept at least
dimly alight in that Promethean fire which led the lover to flee. Love has
dispelled lust and inaugurated the rule of perfect nature.[91]
     The love that elevates men to the 'rational and highest part of the soul' in
the masque is itself pure and uncorrupted;[92] it has transcended the world of
sense and appetite. The power of such love is the central agent of the subject
and action of the Caroline masques. The Temple of Love, for instance, in the
masque of that name, is re-established in the island and triumphs over the
enemies of chastity who attempted to lead astray the young men who came in
search of purity. In *Britannia Triumphans*, Action and Imposture discuss the
nature of love in the context of a debate about reason and appetite. Imposture
speaks for sensual love; but Action is a 'strict corrector of delights' who
announces that he has come 'To make new lovers here on earth'.[93] In

[91] 'The Allegory', *Tempe Restored*, lines 309–64, *Inigo Jones*, II, pp. 482–3.
[92] *Ibid.*, lines 351–2.
[93] *Britannia Triumphans*, lines 318, 324, *Inigo Jones*, II, p. 664.

Salmacida Spolia, chastity and love stand for all virtues and for that higher reason or understanding that 'gives to men the power of sight'.[94]

The love that we read of in the masques is Platonic love. In the masque, as in Neo-Platonic theory, beauty, that quality which expresses the virtues, perforce attracts men to itself, and so draws those attracted to the love of the good which raises them above the plane of sense and appetite (the anti-masque) to the sphere of reason, of the soul. It enables them to govern their own nature and appetite. Aurelian Townshend explains in *Tempe Restored* that by divine beauty 'is meant . . . a divine beam coming from above, with a good inclination, and a perfect habit of virtue made by the harmony of the irascible and concupiscible parts obedient to the rational and highest part of the soul, making man only a mind . . .'.[95] Similarly in *Albion's Triumph* the text points out that the queen derives her name, Alba, from her nature: her 'native beauties have a great affinity with all purity and whiteness'.[96] Platonic love represents the victory of reason over appetite; it is the ordering of nature. Platonic love then is an ideal form of government. For if beauty and love may kindle the Promethean fire that leads men to shun their baser nature and seek the good, then beauty and love have the best claim to rule – because they teach men self-regulation and lead them to a higher understanding, a discovery of their soul. In the masque the king and queen in disguise represent that love which has the best claim to rule. In reality, of course, they are the rulers who also set an example of love to the court. What they perform is what they are. Just as Platonic love is the masque's mode of government so corrupt forms of love, passion and lust, stand for disaffection and disobedience. The errors of Cupid Jonson describes in *Chloridia* as 'Love's rebellious war'.[97] Love, by contrast, is harmony and order. 'Where love is mutuall, still / All things in order move'.[98] In *Tempe Restored*, Cupid comes to understand that illicit love is corrupt government, and when beauty breaks Circe's spells, he too vows to reform his commonwealth:

> my gentle reign,
> So wronged with acting of a tyrant's part,
> I must restrain,
> My pow'r abused, and right my injured train.[99]

[94] *Salmacida Spolia*, line 415, *ibid.*, II, p. 733.
[95] *Tempe Restored*, lines 348–52, *ibid.*, II, p. 483.
[96] *Albion's Triumph*, lines 10–11, *ibid.*, II, p. 454. The relationship of names to ideas in masques requires further study. See Brian Vickers, 'Analogy versus identity: the rejection of occult symbolism, 1580–1680', in B. Vickers, ed., *Occult and Scientific Studies in the Renaissance* (Cambridge, 1984), pp. 95–164. I owe this reference to Conrad Russell.
[97] *Chloridia*, line 187, *Inigo Jones*, II, p. 421; cf. Mercury's speech, line 57, *Coelum Britannicum*, II, p. 571.
[98] B. Jonson, *Love's Triumph Through Callipolis*, lines 130–1, *Inigo Jones*, I, p. 407.
[99] *Tempe Restored*, lines 269–72, *ibid.*, II, p. 482.

Love teaches virtue. And in the masque the government of Charles and Henrietta Maria engenders virtue because it is founded in love. In *Coelum Britannicum* it is the mutual fire of love burning in the king and queen that releases the masquers on to the stage as 'shapes formed fit for heaven'.[100] The king's example has moulded courtiers who are fit to be stellified as shining examples of virtue. Love rules by example. Sunesis at the end of *The Temple of Love* sings the valedictory to love:

> To Charles the mightiest and the best,
> And to the darling of his breast,
> Who rule b'example as by power.[101]

The royal government is love. Love orders nature: love expresses the purity of nature and the harmony of its forms, and led by the king or queen the revels which celebrate the triumph of the masque over antimasque enact all these ideas: order, harmony, love and government.

It is perhaps within this philosophical rather than a political context that we should understand the place and praise of peace in the masques. For peace in the masques is not presented as a policy, in contrast to war, but as a state, a condition. And that condition is associated with love, concord, harmony and ordered nature.[102] Peace is the state of the sphere of the soul which, inhabiting the world of forms or ideas, is raised above the strife of objects, time and events. We have seen that Thomas Carew, in his answer to Townshend's poem in praise of Gustavus Adolphus, distinguished the subjects of poetry from the turmoils of history, from battles and events.[103] Interestingly, in his masque *Coelum Britannicum*, the sixth antimasque dance is 'the representation of a battle' staged by Fortune as her claim to power.[104] Battles, in other words, like Fortune herself, belong to the world of sense and contingency. 'To the piercing eye of Providence', 'thou dost disappear / Losest thy being, and art not at all', Mercury tells Fortune.[105] The sphere of the soul, or of knowledge, is raised above accidents and events; and above wordly strife. It is the peace of this world that is the subject of masque, as Peace herself sings in *Albion's Triumph*:

---

[100] *Coelum Britannicum*, line 972, *ibid.*, II, p. 576.
[101] *The Temple of Love*, lines 511–13, *ibid.*, II, p. 604.
[102] See R. S. Anselment, 'Clarendon and the Caroline myth of peace', *Journal of British Studies*, 23 (1984), pp. 37–54; Parker, 'Carew's Politic Pastoral'.
[103] Cf. Ben Jonson's comment which might be seen in the same light:
> what is't to me whether the French designe
> Be, or be not, to get the Val-telline?
(quoted by Peterson, *Imitation and Praise*, p. 144).
[104] *Coelum Britannicum*, line 723, *Inigo Jones*, II, p. 576.
[105] *Ibid.*, lines 739–42. Mercury goes on to celebrate the power of wisdom over Fortune in language that evokes Machiavelli as well as the Platonic conceits of masque. See below, p. 240.

> Frighted by day, and in the night diseased,
> I fled to heaven and left the world displeased.
> Fond men, that strive more for a province there,
> Than looking upward to possess a sphere![106]

The masque's purpose was to look upward and to raise men's eyes to the higher understanding of mysteries. No less the purpose of government was to elevate men to that knowledge by which they might order the turmoil of their own nature. Peace therefore was the aim of a government which saw its rôle as educating men to higher understanding. And it was the fitting subject of masques which not only represented that polity but as art effected the transcendence to the higher cognition of the soul. Peace, poetry and government in the masques inhabit the sphere of the soul and seek to attract men to it. It is the complexity of those interrelationships that Townshend put so simply:

> Those princes see the happiest days
> Whose olive branches stand for bays.[107]

The olive branch befits the king and the poet. It is an emblem of nature whose peace and purity both monarchs and poets seek to restore.

The purpose of government is the civilization of nature. In many of the masques, as we have observed, the scene changes from wilderness to ordered and harmonious nature. The transformation is effected in the spectacle by machinery and in the allegory by love and by government. In *Albion's Triumph* the final scene 'is varied into a landscript in which was a prospect of the King's palace of Whitehall and part of the city of London'.[108] Innocency, Justice, Religion, Concord and Peace descend from heaven to grace their union of nature and government. *Britannia Triumphans* opens on a scene of 'English houses of the old and newer forms intermixed with trees and afar off a prospect of the city of London'.[109] London, the seat of government, stands for ordered nature and a commonweal governed in accordance with nature.[110] The antimasques of magic, nature's enemy, emerge from 'a horrid hell ... the nearer part expressing the suburbs', that is an area outside authority – in the wilderness.[111] The contrast is made again visually in *Salmacida Spolia* where the order of the city and the disorder of the suburbs are separated by a bridge which (as it was a favourite metaphor of the time)

---

[106] *Albion's Triumph*, lines 390–3, *Inigo Jones*, II, p. 457.
[107] *Ibid.*, lines 404–5.
[108] *Ibid.*, lines 338–40.
[109] *Britannia Triumphans*, lines 58–61, *Inigo Jones*, II, p. 662.
[110] London too appears to have represented for Charles I a model for the reformation of government; see Sharpe, 'The personal rule of Charles I', pp. 61–2.
[111] *Britannia Triumphans*, lines 231–3, *Inigo Jones*, II, p. 664. Charles planned to incorporate the suburbs as a means to their government. See R. Ashton, *The City and the Court, 1603–1643* (Cambridge, 1979), pp. 163–7.

6 and 7 *Britannia Triumphans*: Scene I, 'English houses of the old and newer forms intermixed with trees and afar off a prospect of the city of London and the river Thames'. Illustration 6 is by John Webb, 7 by Inigo Jones. Orgel and Strong argue that Webb's version more closely fits the text

8 *Salmacida Spolia*: Scene IV, 'Magnificent buildings [and] in prospect . . . the suburbs of great city'

itself represents the arch of government.[112] As Thomas Wentworth put it in 1628:

> the authority of a king is the keystone which closeth up the arch of order and government, which contains each part in due relation to the whole, and which once shaken, infirmed, all the frame falls together into a confused heap of foundation and battlement.[113]

Whitehall and London stand for a government which has, like perfect nature, contained each part in due relation to the whole. But London, as Wentworth's metaphor reminds us, represents not only government but the triumphs of art and architecture. Inigo Jones had for long attempted to make claims for the moral and didactic power of his art. Architecture, he believed, might elevate men to the knowledge of forms and harmonies distilled by its science and realized in its perfect proportions; the arch, in other words, might harmonize all the parts of nature in an ordered frame. In the first scene of *Britannia Triumphans*, as Orgel and Strong observed, 'The back shutter view focuses attention on Jones's work on St. Pauls's' and so asserts the place of

---

[112] *Salmacida Spolia*, lines 451–7, *Inigo Jones*, II, p. 734.
[113] Sir Thomas Wentworth's speech when he first sat as Lord President of the North, December 1628, in J. P. Kenyon, ed., *The Stuart Constitution* (Cambridge, 1966), p. 18.

9 *Albion's Triumph*: proscenium arch

architecture in the highest ideals of government.[114] For Jones the meaning of the masque is that architecture and engineering might order nature and so were inseparable from government. The proscenium arch elaborates this claim. That to *Albion's Triumph*, for example, Jones's first production after Jonson's displacement, showed an imperial crown supported by two columns, Theorica and Practica, which are described as the twin pillars of architecture.[115] For *Coelum Britannicum*, the two sides of the ornament which held up the royal *impresa* displayed, as Jones boasted, the various compositions and inventions of architecture and sculpture.[116] The border of the proscenium arch for the production of *Salmacida Spolia* was the most elaborate of all. Fame is held aloft flanked by the figures of Safety and Riches. The rest of the frieze is composed of figures representing the 'followers of peace and concord'. Supporting them all are columns in which, on the right, stand Reason and Intellectual Appetite, and on the left Counsel and Resolution. Architecture has resolved all the tensions of government and united them in ordered harmony. Here we may understand Jones's claim for

[114] Notes to sketch no. 334, Scene I, *Inigo Jones*, II, pp. 668, 670.
[115] *Albion's Triumph*, lines 23–46.
[116] *Coelum Britannicum*, lines 1–31, *Inigo Jones*, II, p. 581.

10 *Coelum Britannicum*: proscenium arch and 'a new scene . . . of mountains'

architecture to be the soul of the masque and the centre of government. For the proscenium to *Salmacida Spolia* was, as he claimed, 'moral philosophy'.[117] Through the contemplation of the order and forms given concrete expression in stone, the spectator, Jones believed, might come to see by that intellectual light which was government and which it was the purpose of masque to reflect.

The architect, however, was not alone in his claim that art might raise the consciousness to the sublime. Jonson had asserted in his masques as in his verse that poetry necessarily performed a didactic function and so was the indispensable counsellor to kings.[118] In his last production, *Chloridia*, the

---

[117] *Salmacida Spolia*, lines 22–70, *ibid.*, II, p. 730. Orgel and Strong suggest that such an elaborate proscenium 'could have been meaningful only to its inventors' and required the elucidation of the printed text, *Inigo Jones*, I, p. 73.
[118] See below, ch. 6.

poets tell the king and queen they are 'we that sustain thee'.[119] The authors of the masques who succeeded Jonson were not, as we have seen from an examination of their poetry, disposed to compromise the claim. Indeed the power of poetry is affirmed in the Caroline entertainments not only in practice, in the quality of the best verse, but in the action of the masque itself. In *Coelum Britannicum*, Mercury, the god of eloquence and often of the muses, acts as Master of Ceremonies, speaking on behalf of the king and queen and directing the celebration of their virtues. He is indispensable to the masque as is poetry itself to kingship and the presentation of kingship. In *The Temple of Love*, Divine Poesy commands the stage. She protects the temple from the magicians, and through Orpheus' harp leads the young men who have come in search of it to the shrine of virtue. She is the servant of love, of Indamora, and of Queen Henrietta Maria, who performs the part. Davenant, the author of the masque, a poet and playwright, describes himself as 'her majesty's servant'. What the masque presents, Davenant is claiming: the importance of poetry for love and for government, its capacity to make 'sacred catches for the gods'.[120] In several of the productions poetry is the discourse of the masque, prose or blank verse that of the antimasque. Unlike prose dialogue, poetry, like the masque, is concerned with truths, with ideas, outside time, beyond uncertainties and events. As Davenant put it, the poets 'first gave words an harmony' and poets 'shall after death reside above'.[121]

Nature ordered by love and government; architecture and poetry as the arts that civilize man, regulate nature and serve government. The interrelationships of these themes and subjects are common to the Caroline masques and express the king's and queen's values. Nature – and man's nature – are portrayed as potentially wild and anarchic. What may order them is love, a love which transcends sense and appetite. Love then is the ideal government, because through love men are led to self-regulation; coercion becomes unnecessary. The best government by corollary is the presentation of an example of love which might kindle the Promethean fire of virtue in corrupt natures. Love may raise men to their higher nature. Nature too is governed by art, by the knowledge and representation of those forms and ideas which express the harmonies of pure nature. Through architecture and poetry men are lifted by visions of the sublime from the material world of sense to that of the soul. Like love then, architecture, art and poetry are central to government. They are not metaphors for rule, nor even mere allegories of kingship; they perform the very functions of government: the education of men that may lead them to higher cognition. The masque represents love, architecture

[119] *Chloridia*, line 249, *Inigo Jones*, II, p. 422.
[120] *Temple of Love*, line 182; cf. 'The Argument', *ibid.*, II, pp. 600, 601.
[121] *Temple of Love*, lines 96, 149.

and poetry as triumphing over disorder. And through the experience of the masque the spectators and the performers are transformed by love and by art.

When he performed in the masque, Charles executed, as he saw it, the rôle of a king, of a philosopher-king whose function it was to educate and elevate, to be the intellectual light by which his subjects might also come to see. Historians have scorned the masque as a distraction from the reality of governing. To Charles I it was rather a duty, a ritual no less than his participation in the services of the Anglican church. It would be interesting to know the relationship in the king's mind between his intense religious devotions and the Neo-Platonic ideas informing the masque. It is tempting to speculate on the connections between the ideas of the masque and Charles's emphasis upon ceremony and order in church services, upon the 'beauty of holiness', or his apparent discomfort with Calvinist predestinarian theology.[122] But it is most important to realize that the masques were statements of a faith, and that the themes and subjects of the masques of Charles I were the doctrines of his kingship, the creed of God's lieutenant on earth.

DIFFERENCES AND POSSIBILITIES

Hitherto we have discussed the Caroline masques as an entity, as a genre. We have glanced at the constituents of the form of masque and at the subjects and philosophy which provided its common themes. It is useful to have considered the masques in this way; to have identified common characteristics which certainly would not have escaped contemporary observers. But to think of the masques of Charles I's reign as a whole is to risk losing a sense of the primacy of the masque as an occasion, and to risk remaining insensitive to the variations possible within the genre and to the differences between the masques both as spectacles and as texts. We must now turn from generalizations to particular studies, examine some of the masques closely, and even question some of the generalizations that hitherto we have been happy to employ. Just as we have seen that the poetry and drama of the age of Charles I are better understood if we read it for itself rather than as 'cavalier' plays and verse, so the masques can be appreciated only when we investigate them individually and study how general themes are treated on particular occasions.

There are several reasons why we must change our style from the broad sweep of landscape to the individual detail of miniature. First, as an occasion in the life of the court, as a political statement, the masque reflected changed circumstances, attitudes and events — changes which are central to the concerns of political history and the history of ideas. Though the powerful

[122] See below, pp. 280–1.

direction of Charles I himself and the absence of parliaments have led us to characterize the decade of the 1630s as the period of 'personal rule', the eleven years from 1629 to 1640 saw changing issues, questions and attitudes in foreign and domestic affairs which naturally were reflected in the masques. Though performances at Twelfth Night and Shrovetide were common, the occasion and location of a masque could closely echo immediate events. *Salmacida Spolia*, for example, performed on 21 January 1640, was presented to the Queen Mother of France, recently arrived in England.[123] *The Triumph of Peace* was offered by the Inns of Court as a celebration of the birth of Prince James and as an atonement for Prynne's *Histrio-Mastix*.[124] Other entertainments for the king and queen away from the court but taking on some of the characteristics of a masque, Jonson's *King's Entertainment at Welbeck* for example, were occasioned entirely by a royal visit – in this case to Nottinghamshire on the king's progress to Scotland.[125] Such entertainments remind us of the blurred line between masques presented at court and those performed for the court.[126] Most of all they recall us to the masque as an *event* in the life of the court and the history of the reign.

Secondly, though the masque was a court entertainment, it did not speak continuously or uniformly with one voice. Within the court of Charles I we find a broad spectrum of attitudes on all matters of religion and government. Though the king and queen may have made up their own minds, they listened to and acted upon advice – advice that changed and was taken from different men at different times. Between the king and the queen themselves there were, at times, considerable differences of opinion and taste – in matters perhaps of aesthetic judgement as well as politics. We may think of the masques that they presented to each other in turn as a dialogue between them in which, for all the common ground, important differences were aired. And we must come to recognize the king's and queen's masques as quite different productions and texts.[127]

Thirdly, it is important to recall that after the demise of Jonson, Jones, though he rose to greater ascendancy, worked in partnership with several different authors – with Thomas Carew, William Davenant, Aurelian Townshend and James Shirley. The nature of the relationship of each of these writers with Jones evidently differed considerably and consequently the extent to which Jones devised the subject of the masque varied greatly from

---

[123] *Salmacida Spolia*, lines 306–23, *Inigo Jones*, II, pp. 732–3. Marie de Medicis arrived in England on 19 October 1638, Gardiner, *History of England*, VIII, p. 380.
[124] See below, p. 215.
[125] See Herford and Simpson, *Ben Jonson*, VII, pp. 791–803.
[126] As does *The Triumphs of the Prince D'Amour*, written by Davenant and presented to the Prince elector at the Middle Temple in February 1636. For the text see *Dramatic Works of Sir William D'Avenant*, I, pp. 317–40; Lefkowitz, *Trois Masques*, pp. 111–69.
[127] See below, p. 257.

one occasion to another. D. J. Gordon suggested that these different relationships may clearly be seen from the title pages of the masques and in particular from the attribution of the 'invention'.[128] So, for *Albion's Triumph*, Aurelian Townshend himself tells us 'Master Inigo Jones and I were employed in the Invention',[129] but for his *Tempe Restored* the same year he was responsible for the 'verses' but not 'The subject and allegory' which were left to Jones alone.[130] *The Triumph of Peace* – not a masque of course prepared at court – was 'Invented and written' by James Shirley; Jones designed the scenes.[131] *Coelum Britannicum* appears to have been a partnership, both Carew and Jones being billed as 'Inventors'.[132] Davenant's productions all seem to have been worked out together with Jones; in *Salmacida Spolia* the text is explicit: 'The subject was set down by them both'.[133] Different masques, presented by the king and the queen, devised by different authors, the responsibility for the subject sometimes the poet's, sometimes the architect's, sometimes the work of both. Only Davenant wrote more than one masque for the queen and no author was commissioned for more than one of the king's; *Salmacida Spolia* was the only entertainment that they presented jointly.[134] Such a catalogue of permutations should warn us that for all the common influences, the masques of the 1630s were in no way the expression of one mind.[135]

Most important of all, the Caroline authors, as we have seen, were very different men. Thomas Carew was a courtier whose duties involved close attendance upon the king; his poetry, though perhaps the most popular of all the Caroline poets, was his pastime rather than his living. William Davenant was first and foremost a professional playwright. He became attached to the queen's circle but seems never to have been close to the king. As far as we know, he held no court office and probably fulfilled his life ambition when, in the England of the Restoration, he managed his own theatre and company. Townshend, about whom we know the least, was probably never other than on the fringes of the court and of the literary world. Any historian believing that art cannot be separated from the man would like to know more about each of them. But we know enough to suggest that the experiences that they could draw on differed greatly. Townshend, for a start, was over twenty years

---

[128] Gordon, 'Poet and architect', appendix I, 'Notes on the terms used by other writers of masques and pageants', p. 176.
[129] *Albion's Triumph*, lines 2–3, *Inigo Jones*, II, p. 454.
[130] *Tempe Restored*, lines 365–8, *ibid.*, II, p. 483.
[131] *The Triumph of Peace*, title page; Adams, *Dramatic Records of Herbert*, p. 54.
[132] *Coelum Britannicum. A Masque at Whitehall in the Banquetting house, on Shrove Tuesday-night, the 18 of February, 1633.* The Inventors. *Tho. Carew   Inigo Jones* (1640).
[133] *Salmacida Spolia*, line 493, *Inigo Jones*, II, p. 734.
[134] For a suggestion concerning the importance of this, see below, p. 255.
[135] Moreover the large numbers involved in scene, music and choreography made it all but impossible for one person to control the production. Cf. Smuts, 'The failure of Stuart cultural patronage', p. 170.

older than Davenant and a dozen years Carew's senior; born in 1583, he
passed his childhood and adolescence while Elizabeth I was still on the
throne, and was an elderly man in his fifties during the decade of personal
rule. Davenant's father's inn at Oxford was as far removed in lifestyle and
geography from the Townshend family's Norfolk estates and pedigree as it
was from Carew's legal and London background. Later life continued to lead
them along different paths – to the war in France, to the banks of the Tweed,
to miserable poverty in the Barbican. Such diverse experiences formed
different personalities and different styles. One senses a jocular, rumbustious
Davenant playing tricks on his friends,[136] at home in a simple inn and at
court; a somewhat whimsical Carew with a keen sense of irony, often in
turbulent debate with himself; a modest and quiet simplicity in Townshend,
perhaps a discomfort with courtly pomp and a more intense spirituality.
Their literature addressed at times common questions, but they wrote in
different modes and from different angles and perspectives. We have seen too
how the three authors were connected to different political circles. On the
question of England's participation in war, they disagreed publicly and in
verse. In collaborating with our poets and playwrights, Inigo Jones must have
had a greater sense of the differences of each occasion than a conception of
the masque as one form. For all the apparent uniformity imposed by the form
of the masque, each occasion dictated and each author inspired not only
different emphases, but distinct entertainments unlike each other in form and
treatment. Perhaps it is the measure of a great artist to find freedom within
constraint. Though our authors may not claim greatness, their individuality
cannot be denied. We do not know how closely the masques were directed.
Given the numbers involved and changes that occurred, there is no reason to
believe that poetic freedom was circumscribed other than by the need to work
with Jones. A general structure for masques was given; general themes were
known to be to the taste of the king and queen. But within these broad
frameworks, it was quite possible to articulate very varied views and create
quite different productions.

The most obvious example of the flexibility and freedom allowed within
the masque is provided by *The Triumph of Peace*. To some *The Triumph of
Peace* might appear to exemplify the Stuart masque: magnificent in display,
irresponsibly and staggeringly expensive, fawning and sycophantic.[137] It
would be hard to deny the first two charges. The Venetian ambassador's
wonder at the 'numerous, stately and glittering cavalcade' and the admiration
of numerous observers for 'so glorious a spectacle' made good Bulstróde
Whitelocke's boast that this was the 'most glorious and splendid shew that

---

[136] See Aubrey's account of a jest played by Davenant on one Jack Young on a visit with Suckling
to Bath, *Brief Lives*, II, p. 243.
[137] Parry, *Golden Age Restor'd*, pp. 192–4.

ever was beheld in England'.[138] The cost, a staggering £21,000, was more than ten times that of the other Caroline productions.[139] *The Triumph of Peace* too had its origins in a desire to please the king. It was offered by the Inns of Court to atone for the sins of one of their number – that is, to dissociate the legal profession from the recent scandal caused by the publication of William Prynne's *Histrio-Mastix*, with its attacks on theatrical productions and supposedly scandalous remarks against the queen. Anxious to 'testify their affections', the Inns resolved upon 'an expression of their love, and duty to their Majesties'. Whitelocke of the Middle Temple, who helped devise the entertainments, tells us that the idea for it came from within the court itself:

This was hinted at in the Court and by them Intimated to the chief of those Societies, that it would be well taken from them, and some held it the more seasonable, because this action would manifest the difference of their opinion, from Mr *Prynne*'s new learning, and serve to confute his *Histrio Mastix* against enterludes.[140]

Spectacular and extravagant, planned to please the court, its very title the celebration of a royal policy of neutrality, *The Triumph of Peace* seems to represent a court culture which has been described as exclusive and sycophantic. It is important therefore for us to appreciate that this entertainment subjected the form of masque to a radically different treatment, and in so doing articulated clear criticisms of the court within a conventional genre and rhetoric of commendation.

Though the idea for *The Triumph of Peace* originated within the court, the entertainment, quite unusually, began far from the royal palace of Whitehall and indeed was addressed to an audience beyond the confines of the court. For the spectacle commenced at Ely House in Holborn, where gathered a triumphal procession of nearly three hundred masquers, antimasquers, musicians and attendants, in ornately decorated chariots and on foot, richly attired. 'When the Evening was come, all things being in full readiness, they began to set forth . . . down Chancery Lane to Whitehall', on a slow march through Holborn and the West End.[141] Not surprisingly, given the unusual public display of such finery, the cavalcade attracted, as the Venetian ambassador reported, a 'great crowd'.[142] The whole occasion was more evocative of an Elizabethan progress than a Caroline masque. The mob pressed and jostled to see – and it is clear that they were intended to do so.

---

[138] Gussoni to Doge and Senate, 17 Feb. 1634, *Cal. Stat. Pap. Venet., 1632–36*, p. 195; account of Bulstrode Whitelocke, quoted in *Inigo Jones*, II, pp. 541, 543. The masque text is edited in Lefkowitz, *Trois Masques*, pp. 27–109.

[139] Whitelocke's estimate, *Inigo Jones*, II, p. 544; Smuts, 'Political failure of Stuart cultural patronage', p. 174.

[140] *Inigo Jones*, II, p. 539.

[141] *Ibid.*, II, p. 540.

[142] *Cal. Stat. Pap. Venet., 1632–6*, p. 195.

Consisting of beggars, cripples, birds and Northern pipers, part of the procession comprised a Brechtian visual antimasque which appears to have been staged consciously for an audience outside as well as within the court. The rider who begged a patent for sole manufacture of 'a Great Bit' and 'another fellow with a bunch of carrots upon his Head and a Capon upon his fist, describing a *Projector* who begg'd a Patent of *Monopoly* as the first Inventor of the Art to feed Capons fat with Carrots' belong more to the tradition and visual satire of popular carnival than they do to the conventions of masque.[143] Evidently the point was well taken, for Whitelocke, who helped prepare the procession, tells us that 'it pleased the Spectators the more because by it an Information was covertly given to the King, of the unfitness and ridiculousness of these Projects against the Law'.[144] What pleased the people, however, also satisfied the king and queen. When the procession finally reached Whitehall, doubtless some hours after the initial assembly at Ely House, the king, 'delighted with the noble Bravery' of the display, requested that 'the whole Show might fetch a turn about the *Tilt-yard*, that their Majesties might have a double view of them'.[145]

There is no shortage of witnesses to testify to what was a quite extraordinary display.[146] But *The Triumph of Peace* was by no means mere spectacle. At over 830 lines it is one of the longer Stuart masques. From the beginning, it would seem, the text was carefully prepared, and no fewer than a remarkable three thousand copies were printed for sale.[147] The learned gentlemen of the Inns of Court evidently had something to say – and to communicate, both through the streets and the printing press, to an audience far larger than the privileged courtiers seated in the Banqueting House, still awaiting the show. And in order to make their point they employed not the court's own masque author, but the dramatic talents of James Shirley. By 1634, when he was commissioned by the Inns, Shirley had been established as a professional playwright and poet for more than a decade. Though his replies to Prynne's attacks upon the stage made him especially suitable for the occasion, Shirley was no dependent of the court and boasted (in the prologue to *The Maid's Revenge*) that he 'never affected the wayes of flattery; some say I have lost my preferment by not practising that Court sinne'.[148] In writing and preparing the Inns' masque, he remained independent of the court. Though Inigo Jones was acknowledged as designer of 'the scene and ornament' of the masque,

---

[143] See P. Burke, *Popular Culture in Early Modern Europe* (London, 1978), ch. 7.
[144] *Inigo Jones*, II, p. 542.
[145] *Ibid.*, II, p. 543.
[146] See Garrard to Wentworth, 27 Feb. 1634, *Strafford Letters*, I, p. 207; Bentley, *Jacobean and Caroline Stage*, V, pp. 1154–63.
[147] *Ibid.*, VII, p. 1162.
[148] *Ibid.*, V, p. 1161; James Shirley, *The Maide's Revenge* (1639), 'To the Worthily Honoured, Henry Osborne, Esquire', sig. A2.

Shirley claimed that *The Triumph of Peace* was 'invented and written' by himself.[149] His control of the production and independence of Jones were probably greater than that of any other poet.

The masque commenced at Whitehall with a long dramatic exchange. The scene opening on the forum or piazza of peace, Opinion and Confidence enter upon the stage. Their dialogue with Novelty and Fancy presents a satire of the court as the home of such frivolous attributes and a critique of the court's failure to comprehend the serious purpose of the masque and of its trivialization of such entertainments. Fancy, we are told, is welcomed to court for alleged wit which is in reality nothing but emptiness: 'He's a great prince of th'air.'[150] He announces that he has come to assist the masque, but dismisses the 'dull phlegmatic inventions', preferring the spectacles of antimasque without which for him (and the court that welcomes him) there will be no entertainment. 'The soul of wit' he sees as farce, and believes that other courtiers agree with him:

> No anti-masque!
> Bid'em down with the scene, and sell the timber
>
> No antimasque! Let 'em look to 't.[151]

Ironically, Fancy's own denunciations constitute the very antimasque he thinks is lacking. And his dialogue with his companions is an antimasque of the attributes (Fancy, Opinion, Novelty, Laughter and Confidence) which are wrongly valued at court. Such qualities are also, as Fancy acknowledges, the attributes of 'a time of peace', as indeed the characters themselves have assembled in the forum of peace.[152] As 'a representation of the effects' of peace, Fancy changes the scene to a tavern, a forum of 'good fellowship'. Peace, the characters make clear, has fostered drunkenness and moral decay, gambling, whoring and poverty. Opinion can see that 'such base and sordid persons' 'become not here', that they are unsuitable inhabitants for the court and the realm.[153] But they are companions of the peace he liked 'well', as are the projectors who Fancy leads upon the stage children of the king's halcyon days. Opinion fails to see the point, and, like the court he represents, which has similarly failed to see it, he craves more and more fantastic antimasques – of ignorant birds, thieves and satyrs. Fancy obliges him with 'Inventions' which are moral allegories in themselves. But he fails again to understand them and lauds them, as he does the masque itself, only as pleasing visions rather than images of vices to be shunned and virtues to be emulated. Though

---

[149] *The Triumph of Peace. A Masque . . . Invented and written by James Shirley . . .* (1633). All references here are from Orgel and Strong, *Inigo Jones*, II, pp. 546–66.
[150] *Triumph of Peace*, line 224.
[151] *Ibid.*, lines 261–2, 268–78.
[152] *Ibid.*, line 327.
[153] *Ibid.*, lines 368–9.

welcomed at court, Fancy and his friends ought not to belong there, nor ought they to be in the world of masque they misunderstand. They exit from the stage and, the antimasque over, the scene switches to a cloud, bearing the chariot of peace.

Where in the antimasque the companions of peace are presented as debauched and drunken, Irene (Peace), now stepping from her chariot, calls upon her sisters, Eunomia (Law) and Dice (Justice). In the world of forms and truths which is the world of masque, Irene knows that she depends upon her sisters: 'I am but wild without thee,' she tells Eunomia; 'I'm lost with them / That know not how to order me.'[154] Law reciprocates the acknowledgement of their mutual dependence, as with Irene she sings:

> The world shall give prerogative to neither.
> We cannot flourish but together.[155]

Peace, Law and Justice are united. Together the three sisters move 'in a comely figure toward the King and Queen' in order to pay their homage. Charles and Henrietta are addressed as Jove and Themis, divine power and law.[156] The masquers, sons of Peace, Law and Justice, appear and dance their entry, followed by their main dance. In accordance with the form of masque, the world of ignorance and sense has been transcended.

At this very moment of transcendence, however, at the conclusion of the song of homage to the king and queen, the world of antimasque re-intrudes – quite uncharacteristically. 'There is heard a great noise and confusion of voices within.' Peace is broken. 'Then a crack is heard in the works, as if there were some danger by some piece of the machines falling.'[157] The world of masque is shattered. A group of artisans, a carpenter, a painter, a tailor's wife and 'a property man's wife' now 'rush in', their haste and coarse speech in contrast to the measured steps and verse of the masque poetry and dance. They wish to see the masque, and though they know they should not be there, the artisans claim a place by virtue of the skills and labour which they have contributed to the production: 'let us challenge a privilege. Those stairs were of my painting.'[158] Though they know that the masque usually excludes them, they are after all, as they claim, 'the kings subjects, God bless us'.[159] But as they come to learn, 'the masquers will do no feats as long as we are here'.[160] They are reduced to masquerading as an antimasque, to be laughed at and then rejected, in order to resolve their dilemma. Only when they depart are

---

[154] *Ibid.*, lines 531–2, 554.
[155] *Ibid.*, lines 560–1.
[156] Orgel and Strong, *Inigo Jones*, I, p. 66.
[157] *Triumph of Peace*, lines 690–3. Cf. *The Alchemist.*
[158] *Triumph of Peace*, lines 714–15.
[159] *Ibid.*, line 721.
[160] *Ibid.*, line 726.

the masquers 'encouraged' to the revels. The dances do not conclude the masque. For the revels being past, the scene changes to a cloud bearing Amphiluche, 'the forerunner of the morning', that 'glimpse of light which is seen when night is past, and the day not yet appearing'.[161] She calls the masquers away, and so concludes the entertainment.

From the initial procession in Holborn to the startling last interruptions, Shirley subjects what we think of as the form of masque to a quite unusual treatment. This is because he has things to say about not only the court and its policies, but about the masque too as the cultural expression of its values. Peace is the policy, as Shirley knows, advocated by the king, supported by the court and celebrated in the masque. But peace may nurture corruption and vices as well as bring benefits. The masque eulogizes the fruits of peace as an ideal. But in doing so it may blind the court to the dangers that peace may bring in her train in the world. That is, the visions of masque may be miscomprehended – as they are by Opinion, Fancy and Confidence, who mistake 'the soul' of wit for the spectacle.[162] Though the purpose of masque is 'To Make the Spectators Understanders', Fancy, Opinion and the others are not led to see with the eye of understanding. When the masque proper commences, they 'go off fearfully', remaining in ignorance of the 'phlegmatic inventions' that are to follow.[163] In the masque itself the point is made. Peace announces the need for Law and Justice to be her companions. Without them there is no real peace nor masque. 'I am but wild without thee,' Peace tells Eunomia and Dice – and wilderness and disorder do not belong in the world of masque. Together with Law and Justice, however, Peace may present a true masque to the monarch and so inform the king of what should be by celebrating their union in the masque. For Peace, Law and Justice united will produce courtiers, as they here do masquers, who 'love good for itself' (rather than the projectors who seek gain) and who will be worthy subjects of the king.[164]

Shirley employs the vehicle of masque, as Jonson believed it should be employed, to offer counsel as well as praise: peace triumphs only when law and justice preserve it. But the playwright is at pains too to demonstrate that the abstract and idealized world of the masque is not the real world, and that in practice as well as allegory, the law must ensure that a time of peace is not a period of corruption. The long procession of ridiculous antimasquers makes the same point to the spectators in the streets as Opinion and Confidence present to the court. The artisans who rush in towards the conclusion of the

[161] *Ibid.*, lines 668–9. It is not the fact of Amphiluche's final song that is unusual, but its language.
[162] As Jonson believed Jones did, of course.
[163] *Triumph of Peace*, lines 262, 504.
[164] These are the 'children of your reign' whom Genius presents to the king and queen, *ibid.*, 651–68.

entertainment remind the courtly audience and the king of the world outside. They are representatives of a people who, whilst they do not comprehend the neo-Platonic philosophy of the masque, alone make it possible.[165] It is they also who make Charles a king in reality as well as in image: they *are* what they say 'the king's subjects'; they must too enjoy the benefits of peace, justice and law; to deny them is for the monarch to deny his own kingship. If the masque cannot, as it cannot here, incorporate them, then it fails as an expression of kingship. 'Somebody', the artisans believe as they dance off, 'will think this was meant for an anti-masque.'[166] They are right; the courtiers will. But in seeing the king's subjects as an antimasque to be transcended and forgotten, the courtly spectators will invert the truth; they will be guilty of the same misunderstandings about the purposes of masque displayed by Fancy and Opinion. The unusual conclusion of the entertainment may be meant to underline the point. The revels, the realization of the idealizations in harmonious paces, take place in darkness. But reality, the outside world, must dawn. To the court, Amphiluche, who announces the arrival of day and the suspension of the revels, is *'unwelcome* light'. She *'invades'* the sphere of night and masque, 'proclaiming wars' on its mythological emblems.[167] In the final speech to the king and queen, Shirley has the Genius inform the royal pair that the masquers, gentlemen of the Inns, attend on them, 'Acknowledging no triumph but in you'.[168] Whatever took place on the stage at Whitehall, only the king could bring in peace with order, law and justice – throughout the realm and for all his subjects.

The Triumph of Peace subverts the form of masque – from the initial procession to the intrusion of the carpenter and painter. It was a combination of public carnival and royal entertainment, more common in the sixteenth century, but quite unfamiliar by 1634. It may be of significance that the Venetian ambassador did not describe it as a masque at all, but as 'representations, music and dancing for the entertainment of the king and queen'.[169] English observers, however, knowledgeable courtiers, such as Sir Henry Herbert and the Reverend George Garrard, as well as Bulstrode Whitelocke and James Shirley himself, were happy to employ the term, as was Henrietta Maria, who declared by way of thanks 'that she never saw any Masque more noble'.[170] Orgel and Strong have observed that *The Triumph of Peace* illustrates 'how exceedingly clumsy as a mode of political statement the form'

---

[165] Shirley may well have had in mind the Publius of *Albion's Triumph* who never understood what Platonicus told him.

[166] *Triumph of Peace*, line 736.

[167] *Ibid.*, lines 770–9 (my italics). Amphiluche's speech seems to invert the association of masque with light.

[168] *Triumph of Peace*, line 823.

[169] *Cal. Stat. Pap. Venet, 1632–6*, p. 195.

[170] *Inigo Jones*, II, p. 544.

of masque appeared to be.[171] But it is perhaps as important to appreciate that Shirley's entertainment is evidence of what *could* be done within the alleged constraints of the masque form and an example of how the structure of the masque could be manipulated to reinforce the point. *The Triumph of Peace* suggests that in itself the masque as a form imposed few constraints upon the dramatic or poetic invention.

Perhaps more important to the historian is what *The Triumph of Peace* demonstrates about the treatment of theme and subject and the possibilities for criticism within the context of praise. For all the celebration, this was critical both of royal policy and of masque as an expression of royal values. Peace, it is implied, has led to corrupt and illegal practices, and the illusions of masque have blinded the court to the realities of the commonwealth. The masque, Shirley suggests, anticipating later critics, creates a world in which the court views only itself and forgets the 'king's subjects', who find no place in the entertainment but as antimasques to be laughed at. Shirley's own counsel seems clear: like peace and the law, prerogative and the law, the king and the people 'cannot flourish but together'. Court culture must acknowledge and express those realities and truths. And so to the world of idealizations at the court Shirley brings the light of reality and the people.[172]

To suggest that Shirley's masque was intended as criticism is to raise a difficult problem: the reaction of the king and the queen. Did they understand the criticism? If so, how did they respond to it? It is impossible to know what Charles and Henrietta Maria thought of any part of the performance. We do know that in general they greatly approved of it. When the procession arrived at Whitehall, the king and queen, standing at the window, 'sent to the Marshall to desire that the whole Show might fetch a turn about the *Tilt-yard*, that their Majesties might have a double view of them'.[173] A second performance of the whole entertainment was commanded the following week at Merchant Taylors' Hall.[174] The king and queen not only expressed their thanks to the Inns warmly in words and promises; they returned the hospitality by inviting members of the Inns to Thomas Carew's court masque performed a few days later.[175] Evidently the show 'took so well' and the masquers, who dined with the king, were 'well used at Court'.[176] Graham Parry may be right then in stating that the criticism implied passed completely over the king's head.[177] Charles I may have gloried in the praise and remained

[171] *Ibid.*, I, p. 64; cf. Parry, *Golden Age Restor'd*, p. 193.
[172] We may recall the criticisms of Perwiggana (England) voiced at the tavern in Shirley's *The Gamester*, above, ch. 1.
[173] *Inigo Jones*, II, p. 543.
[174] *Strafford Letters*, I, p. 207.
[175] *Ibid.*
[176] *Ibid.*
[177] Parry, *Golden Age Restor'd*, p. 193.

blind to the counsel. But we should not *assume* that this was the case.
Bulstrode Whitelocke himself recorded the people's approval that by the
antimasque of the patentees 'an Information was covertly given to the king, of
the unfitness and ridiculousness of these Projects against the Law'.[178] What
the spectators appreciated clearly should not have been, and evidently was
not thought to have been, too covert for the king. The criticism was
powerfully visible and intended by the devisers of the masque to be so. One of
the members of the planning committee (Whitelocke tells us), who had 'a
great hand in this Antimasque of the Projectors', also had 'most knowledge of
them'.[179] And he was no other than William Noy, of Lincoln's Inn, the king's
own Attorney General; with Prince Charles, Noy had claimed credit for the
Monopolies Act of 1624 and may have endeavoured a decade later to remind
the now king of its purpose. Other members of the committee enjoyed, or
were to enjoy, close relations with the court. Sir Edward Herbert of the Inner
Temple was to become, the next year, Attorney General to the queen and, in
1640, the king's Solicitor General; Edward Hyde, future Earl of Clarendon,
became a Privy Councillor and Chancellor of the Exchequer. Clearly such
men, if Whitelocke is to be believed, found criticism of particular royal
policies reconcilable with loyalty to the crown and with their political
ambitions.[180] Moreover they saw a place in a masque intended as a gesture of
loyalty for drawing the king's attention to abuses. It may well be that Charles I
understood the criticism well whilst seeming to miss the point. But whether
the king recognized the complaints or not, *The Triumph of Peace* not only
illustrates the flexibility of the masque as a form, but also demonstrates that
the masque could be, what Dr Parry has denied, 'a successful vehicle for
critical opinion'.[181]

   The Triumph of Peace, of course, was not a court masque. It was presented
to the court, but it was not performed by courtiers, nor prepared under the
direction of the king or queen. But contemporary observers did not single it
out for this reason – not even the Master of the Revels – and I should like to
suggest that the freedom of form and treatment illustrated by Shirley's
masque was available to and employed by the three authors who devised the
entertainments at court; that the court masques of the 1630s could be no less
ironic and critical. Before we turn to these productions and texts, however, it
may be valuable to remind ourselves of the attitudes to masques expressed by
Carew, Townshend and Davenant in their drama and their poetry. For in
each case, our authors were commissioned to devise a court entertainment,
having already established their reputations in verse and on the stage. We

[178] *Inigo Jones*, II, p. 542.
[179] *Ibid.*
[180] *Ibid.*, II, p. 539.
[181] Parry, *Golden Age Restor'd*, p. 193.

cannot be sure that they had seen a masque. If they had read the texts of masques, they would certainly have read Jonson's, whom they admired as playwright and poet. Before 1630, then, their idea of the masque as a form could hardly have diverged from Jonson's. Whatever the enhanced rôle of Jones, or the tastes of the king and queen, their own reading and experience must have remained the most powerful influence on their careers as the authors of masques.

The poetry and drama of our three authors should be signal sufficient to us that these were men unlikely to subordinate poetry to spectacle, or the serious purpose of art to tinselled entertainment. More particular comments, however, suggest a dissatisfaction with the masques themselves. In 'Hide not thy love' Townshend had dismissed those 'masquers now-a-dayes' who lived through disguise rather than by nature's patterns.[182] Carew, we recall, had in 'To G.N. from Wrest' scorned decorative images which covered a 'naked face' and praised throughout his poems those – courtiers, patrons or lovers – who preferred 'Rather to be in Act then seeme in sight'.[183] Carew had doubted the artist's capacity 'to paint a virtue', but revealed no doubts about the power of poetry.[184] Davenant, for his part, had persistently warned his audiences: 'If glist'ring shows or jingling sounds you pass / For current plays, we justly pay you brass.'[185] In his clearest statement of his attitudes, the preface to *Gondibert*, he had proclaimed the drama and stage to be the best medium for didactic art.[186] Poets and playwrights to such men were not mere acolytes of kings; they provided counsel as well as celebration, criticism as well as compliment. We have seen that all of our authors, though loyal to the king and connected with the court, criticized implicitly or explicitly the policies of the king and the values of the court: peace, Platonic love, absolutist tendencies in monarchy and government. We have argued that they debate the political issues of their age from the perspective of their individual experience and in the context of their own moral values. Did then Carew, Davenant and Townshend compromise their independence or morality when commissioned by the court to write the masques? Or did they, like Shirley in *The Triumph of Peace*, find freedom within the form for expressing at court itself the values that inspired their drama and their poetry? If we recognize that there is a question to be asked, if we acknowledge the possibility within the genre for discussion and even criticism, we must appreciate that the Caroline masque awaits a critical re-examination.

[182] 'Hide not thy love', version 2, lines 47–8 in Brown, *The Poems and Masques of Aurelian Townshend*, p. 39.
[183] Above, p. 173.
[184] Above, pp. 129, 148–51.
[185] Above, p. 85.
[186] Above, p. 108.

'The last Sunday night the king's masque was acted in the banquetting house ... The Inventor or Poet of this masque was Mr Aurelian Townshend, sometimes towards the Lord Treasurer Salisbury.'[187] So one of the best informed newsmongers of the reign of Charles I reported the end of Jonson's quarter century as author of the court entertainments and the beginning, as some would see it, of a new era in the history of the masque.[188] John Pory, the newswriter, however, could not foresee any major change. Ben Jonson, he announced, was '*for this time* discarded by reason of the predominant power of his antagonist, Inigo Jones'.[189] About the masque prepared by Townshend he had evidently heard nothing worthy of special comment. As for the 'predominant power' of Jones, Townshend evidently did not feel overawed by it. *Albion's Triumph*, he tells us, was a co-operative venture: 'Master Inigo Jones and I were employed in the invention.'[190] And if the rival claims of poetry and spectacle are to be a criterion, the masque as a text supports his statement.

Certainly *Albion's Triumph* differed noticeably from Jonson's last entertainment. The text is almost twice the length of *Chloridia* and more than twice as long as *Love's Triumph Through Callipolis*, Jonson's last two productions. Moreover, unlike those two performances, *Albion's Triumph* opens with a long antimasque dialogue which is no less than a dramatic debate concerning the meaning and purpose of the masque – as if Townshend were anxious as a new author to announce the philosophy that inspired his art. Mercury, the messenger of the Gods and god of eloquence, introduces the masque with instruction concerning the purpose of what is to follow:

> Observe! But See ye be not nice,
> Prepare to give and take advice,
> As wise men ought to do.[191]

Mercury exhorts the company to 'observe' and 'admire' the triumph that is to be presented in the masque, and also the triumph that is to be effected through the masque. And, following Jonson, he commands that what the masquers teach, they must also learn. As Mercury re-ascends to heaven, the scene changes to an amphitheatre where Platonicus and Publius debate the spectacle of triumph that is taking place, and the nature of spectacle itself. Publius has seen the triumph and pomp. Platonicus, who remained all this time in his

---

[187] John Pory to Sir Thomas Puckering, 12 Jan 1632, B.L., Harleian MS 7000, f. 318v.
[188] See W. S. Powell, *John Pory 1572–1636: The Life and Letters of a Man of Many Parts* (Chapel Hill, 1977).
[189] B. L. Harleian MS 7000, f. 318v (my italics).
[190] *Albion's Triumph*, lines 2–3. The Bodleian copy (Bodl. Malone 187(8)) contains manuscript notes by Townshend. All references are from Orgel and Strong, *Inigo Jones*, II, pp. 453–78.
[191] *Ibid.*, lines 58–60.

study, claims to have seen it too: 'I did, and a true one; thine was but a show.'[192] Their exchange becomes a philosophical dialogue, in style not unlike those of Plato from whom Platonicus takes his name. Publius retorts, in language directly evocative of Plato's *Republic*, that Platonicus, absent from the amphitheatre, had not seen anything 'but a shadow'.[193] But Platonicus rebukes him; Publius, he maintains, has fed only his bodily senses; he has digested a visual experience as he might meat, and he expels it as he would wind. By contrast Platonicus's 'spirit' has walked though he has remained in his study; though his eyes have not witnessed it, his intellect has perceived the triumph:

> know I have seen this brave Albanactus Caesar, seen him with the eyes of understanding, viewed all his actions, looked into his mind, which I find armed with so many moral virtues that he daily conquers a world of vices, which are wild beasts indeed.[194]

The triumph which they discuss *is* the masque and the nature of masque itself. Townshend tells his audience how the spectacle should be perceived. There is more to the triumph and to the masque than Publius 'can find in the street' or the court will see on the stage. Platonicus tries to educate his plebeian friend to see beyond the scene to the idea, to comprehend the forms that lie behind the objects:

> Outsides have insides, shells have kernels in them, and under every fable, nay almost under everything, lies a moral.[195]

Publius cannot grasp what he is taught; he is confined to a world of the senses. He takes as a literal statement what Platonicus had intended as an allegory, lifting a stone to see what lies beneath it. In the eyes of Platonicus he is a 'fool'.[196]

Mere spectacle, the triumph that Publius has gone to observe without comprehending, or perhaps what many courtiers have come only to see, is an antimasque. The true triumph that Platonicus has perceived 'with the eye of understanding' is the subject of the masque: the union of Cupid and Diana, the conquest by love of a king who has conquered vice. The king and the masquers dance their main dance in celebration of that union of love and victory over vice and the king takes his place beside the queen, enacting the marriage that the masque has represented. The scene changes to the royal

---

[192] *Ibid.*, line 164.
[193] *Ibid.*, lines 165–6.
[194] *Ibid.*, lines 202–7.
[195] *Ibid.*, lines 230–2. Cedric Brown has recently suggested to me that the humour may be double-edged and as critical of Platonicus as Publius. Ideas too have to be made visible if they are to communicate, so Platonicus and Publius go off to see the show together, idea and spectacle joined. Cf. my point below, p. 263.
[196] *Albion's Triumph*, lines 215, 230–2.

palace of Whitehall and the city of London, expressions of the order of government and regulation of nature that are the fruits of love's triumph over vice. Innocency, Justice, Religion, Affection to the Country and Concord, the companions of love, offer the king and the queen 'rich favours as we can afford'.[197] Peace their mistress descends from heaven to join in the valedictory praise.

Albion's Triumph, England's triumph, is the victory of Albanactus, of Charles I, over vice and passion, the triumph of the union of love (Cupid) with chastity, but also with fecundity. Diana was the patroness of virginity, but also the goddess who presided over childbirth. The love celebrated is pure _and_ fertile: it procreates virtues which attract the blessings of concord, peace and justice to the king, the queen and the realm. This seems to be an outright encomium of the royal pair as perfect lovers and model rulers. But the tone is hortatory as well as commendatory. Both the king and the queen are off the stage when the deities come forward to address them:

> _So_ hand in hand live many a day,
> And may your virtuous minds beget
> Issue that shall never decay,
> _And so be_ fruitful every way.[198]

The king and queen too are here urged to perceive as well as to see; to look beyond the representation of their love and marriage in the masque and to comprehend the idea, the ethical and political philosophy which is, in Platonicus's word, the 'inside' of the masque. The end of such perception is action – not only in the masque, but in engendering through government the virtues which may lead others to conquer vice. Gods, kings, Mercury had announced, 'speak in acts and scorn words' trifling scenes'.[199]

Albion's Triumph does not end with the revels, but with a song to the king and queen. Innocence, Concord, Religion, Justice and Affection to the Country address the monarch after he has left the stage, after the main masque dance. They present a triumph to the king and the queen, just as the king has, as Albanactus, performed one. The king is, we might say, now a part of the audience. As such he may, in Mercury's opening words, take advice as well as give it. Concord, Justice, Religion, etc. 'come freely to impart' their favours. It is for the king to accept them.

Though he acknowledged the 'invention and the writing' as his own, Townshend evidently felt uneasy about his debut as author of masques. 'I was as loathe to be brought upon the stage', he tells us, 'as an unhandsome man is to see himself in a great glass.'[200] Townshend is indeed on the stage in his

---

[197] _Ibid._, line 378.
[198] _Ibid._, lines 371–4 (my italics).
[199] _Ibid._, line 99.
[200] _Ibid._, lines 452–4.

masque, first of all explaining the purpose of his production through the dramatic dialogue of Platonicus and Publius, then holding up a great glass in which images may be perceived by the spectators, and even the king. Art, he knew, reflected truths and ought to do so.

It is likely that Townshend received at the same time a second commission – a request to write the queen's Shrovetide masque a few weeks after *Albion's Triumph* for the king's at Twelfth Night. The accounts lend support to the suggestion that the two were conceived together; less than five weeks would have been short notice for the preparation of the production.[201] Two letters further strengthen the case. Sir Thomas Edmondes wrote to Henry Vane on 20 December 1631 that 'The Duke de Vendosme, having obtained permission to return into France, will not stay to see either the king's or the queen's masques, which are to be acted on Twelfth Day and at Shrovetide.'[202] John Pory reported on 12 January: 'The last Sunday at night the kinges masque was acted in the banquetting house, the queen's being suspended till another time by reason of a soreness which fell into one of her delicate eyes.'[203] But if the two were fairly definitely planned at the same time, the productions and texts differed greatly. *Tempe Restored*, written for the queen, has been described as 'perhaps the chef-d'oeuvre of Inigo Jones in its command of scenic effect'.[204] The arrangements between Townshend and Jones were this time clearly altered. The 'subject and allegory' of the masque were now accredited to Jones, and where before the 'invention' here only the verses were attributed to Townshend.[205] The lengthy descriptions of the scenic changes seem obviously to have been written by Jones, along with the famous taunt: 'these shows are nothing else but pictures with light and motion'.[206] Drama and dialogue are absent, the antimasque is visually presented, and the transformation to masque, the triumph of Divine Beauty over Circe, is effected not by poetry, but by a feat of engineering which Jones could not restrain himself from advertising:

This sight altogether was for the difficulty of the engining and number of the persons the greatest that hath been seen here in our time. For the apparitions of such as came down in the air, and the choruses standing beneath, arrived to the number of fifty persons all richly attired.[207]

---

[201] See Orgel and Strong, *Inigo Jones*, II, p. 453.

[202] Sir Thomas Edmondes to Sir Henry Vane, 20 Dec. 1631, *Cal. Stat. Pap. Dom. 1631–3*, p. 207; cf. Edmondes to Vane, 15 Feb. 1632, *ibid.*; p. 270.

[203] B. L., Harleian MS 7000, f. 318v; cf. Chambers, *Poems and Masques of Townshend*, pp. 116–17.

[204] Chambers, *Poems and Masques of Townshend*, p. 119.

[205] *Tempe Restored*, lines 365–8. All references are from Orgel and Strong, *Inigo Jones*, II, pp. 480–3.

[206] *Ibid.*, lines 49–50.

[207] *Ibid.*, lines 204–8.

So powerful was the spectacle and so dependent was this masque upon it that in *Tempe Restored* the text and the poetry are overshadowed. Much of the text of the masque is taken up, as it has to be, by the description of the scene. In addition to the usual explanatory prologue, 'The Argument', the masque text concludes with a lengthy exposition of 'The Allegory' to elucidate for the reader what costume, iconology and machinery would have made apparent to the spectator.

Poetry is not quite relegated. Cedric Brown rightly points out that 'there are some nice touches of comedy in the treatment of Circe'.[208] The speech of the fugitive lover, too, neatly encapsulates the moral message of the masque – the triumph of virtue over illicit love and base desire.[209] As a poem it could stand on its own; here it effectively introduces the action. The fugitive had been transformed into a beast – the symbol of desire's dominance over reason – by the power of Circe's magic. Refusing to be so subject, he covets to be a man again, 'Governed by reason, and not ruled by sense'.[210] Accordingly, he flies to the vale of Tempe, to the shrine of virtue whose powers, he knows, may dispel the charms of desire. The will to virtue is what secures freedom from base appetites or, as the fugitive puts it, 'It is consent that makes a perfect slave.'[211] Where lust and passion blind and subject man, love 'should enfranchise us',[212] for love is virtue. The rest of the masque, for all the spectacle, acts out this verse. The rest of the verse becomes dully formal, as if poetry has acknowledged its own redundancy:

> The music that ye hear is dull,
> But that ye see is sweet indeed.[213]

Divine Beauty and Heroic Virtue dissolve Circe's enchantments and she surrenders her kingdom and powers. Virtue and love reign over desire and lust.[214] Love that enfranchises men for self-government prescribes the model for the government of the realm.

The Venetian ambassador who attended reported to the Doge and Senate 'a sumptuous masque performed with wonderfully rich decorations' and commented particularly on the king's dancing the revels, confirming our impression as readers that the masque made an impact more by display than through poetry.[215] But we should not forget that on this occasion we have a more informed reaction to the performance: that of the poet Thomas Carew,

---

[208] Brown, *Poems and Masques of Aurelian Townshend*, p. 13.
[209] *Tempe Restored*, lines 70–96.
[210] *Ibid.*, line 78.
[211] *Ibid.*, line 91.
[212] *Ibid.*, line 94.
[213] *Ibid.*, lines 230–1.
[214] For a discussion of the Circe myth as a theme of the *ballet de cour* see McGowan, *L'Art des Ballet de Court*, pp. 72–8; Yates, *The French Academies of the Sixteenth Century*, pp. 240ff.
[215] Gussoni to Doge and Senate, 17 Feb. 1632, *Cal. Stat. Pap. Venet.*, 1629–32, pp. 592–3.

upon whom *Tempe Restored* clearly had an impact that penetrated more deeply than the dazzle of visual splendour. Carew had clearly been taken by the 'rich fancie' and 'cleare Action', 'Th'Angelike formes, gestures, and motion' of the 'misterious fable', all of which (despite the clear delineations of responsibility proclaimed in the text) he seems to attribute to Townshend. As poetry the masque impressed him too, by 'the stories curious web, the Masculine stile', by the 'harmonious notes' and 'ravishing sounds'

> ravishing sounds that did dispence
> Knowledge and pleasure, to the soule, and sense.[216]

His comments remind us that most of the verse was sung – this masque being the first occasion when women singers had performed on an English stage.[217] More significantly they inform us that a distinguished contemporary poet and 'son of Ben' did not share Jonson's fear that the masque was becoming no more than poetry and carpentry. To Carew the performance of *Tempe Restored* was still evidence of the powerful transforming force ('ravishing', 'masculine') of poetry.

We know nothing of Townshend's own attitude – unless we may deduce something from Carew's attempt to persuade his friend to return to such works and abandon the heroic vein of his elegy on Gustavus Adolphus.[218] The differences, however, between Townshend's two masques are striking and, I believe, significant. Certainly the two texts cannot be grouped together, as Chambers grouped them in describing their purpose as 'little more than to furnish a *libretto* for the elaborate stage architecture and ingenious machinery of Inigo Jones'.[219] The style of *Albion's Triumph* is quite different from that of *Tempe Restored*: it is more literary, more discursive, more dramatic and more poetic. We may speculate on the reasons for the differences. Did *Albion's Triumph* not meet with royal approval? Did *Tempe Restored*, as seems likely, reflect the different tastes of the queen? And if Jones now devised and directed the performance, was this the queen's decision? Similarly it is tempting to reflect on the reasons for Townshend's not receiving the commission to write the masques of the next year. Had the poet found it difficult to co-operate with Inigo Jones and resented, as had Jonson, the dominance of machinery and architecture? Did he, as Carew implies, turn his muse to 'a loftier pitch', to elegy and verse epitaphs? Or did Townshend's elegy upon the death of the King of Sweden cause the offence that Carew feared? We cannot say. But the poet who took delight 'most in unusual ways'

---

[216] T. Carew, 'In Answer of an Elegiacall Letter upon the death of the King of Sweden from Aurelian Townshend', Dunlap, *Poems of Carew*, pp. 74–7, quotation lines 75–6. See above, ch. 3.
[217] Lindley, *The Court Masque*, p. 117.
[218] Above, p. 146.
[219] Chambers, *Poems and Masques of Townshend*, p. xvii.

may well have found it unacceptable to take second place to Jones, providing only the verse to his invention.[220]

Townshend's ideas about masque may well have been different from Jones's. Townshend did contribute one more entertainment at the court of Charles I: evidently, as has recently been discovered, he penned a short masque to follow the performance of the French pastoral *Florimene* on 21 December 1635.[221] Given the uncertainty about the completeness of the verse or exact form of the masque, it would be dangerous to attempt firm conclusions. But the masque appears to reflect attitudes and positions which echo Townshend's poems but which are implicitly at odds with the court masques, their recurrent themes and their form. In the masque after *Florimene*, the antimasquers are welcomed and embraced by a song that introduces the masque dance:

> Draw neere! And let not your Condition,
> Meane though it be, dismey your Harts:
> Vales have sometimes as full fruition
> Of the bright Sunne, as higher Parts
> And should as oft, if some proud Hill
> Cast not his shadow on them still.[222]

The words recall the lowly huts to which Townshend beckoned his mistress, and the sentiments of 'Come not to me'.[223] But they seem out of place in the world of masque in which those of mean condition, as the artisans discover in *The Triumph of Peace*, belong only to antimasque. There is a radical imperative in the mood of Townshend's verb – 'And *should*'. Those of mean condition (perhaps even poor and pocky poets) *should* have enjoyment in the masque and in the commonweal of the sun of royal protection. Proud courtiers and magnates confine them to darkness.

The subject of the masque may press the points. Its theme is the inspiration of love which has fired the English shepherds for the French shepherdesses, as it has the king for the queen. But the love described is, though chaste, not Platonic, if by that we are to understand the denial or complete transcendence of the sensual and the physical. The masque ends in marriage, which allows for the expression of a love

---

[220] Brown, *Poems and Masques of Townshend*, p. 53.
[221] The verses to an entertainment following *Florimene* were originally discovered in the Huntington Library by Stephen Orgel, who identified them as antimasques to a masque now lost (Orgel, '*Florimene* and *The Ante-Masques*', *Renaissance Drama*, 4 (1971), pp. 135–53). Recently Cedric Brown has argued that the verses represent 'a short masque to follow the play, not, as Orgel suggests, merely antimasques'. See for Brown's suggested reconstruction of the masque *Poems and Masques of Townshend*, pp. 109–14.
[222] Brown, p. 111.
[223] Above, p. 162.

> Whose Operation, in a noble brest,
> Is violent, and gives the limbes small rest.[224]

This is physical as well as spiritual union. It is part of the world of sense as well as soul; it integrates the two. And that is why the antimasques are embraced in the world of masque, as the representation of that integration. Those who inhabit the world of appetite and sense (like Circe's fugitive lover) may be brought to reason through light and incorporated in the world of intellect and understanding. There is clearly a political implication. The king as the sun may offer light to vales as well as hills – to the humble as well as the great. And if marriage unites sensual and physical with spiritual love, the ideal government which marriage and love represent should unite the people with the king. As those of mean condition are embraced in Townshend's masque, so they should be incorporated within the government the masque celebrates – the government of love and virtue personified by the royal marriage. The antimasque is not dismissed, because Townshend is arguing that even those of mean condition have the potential for higher understanding. Beauty and love may raise the lowliest above base nature, as we recall from 'Come not to me':

> And love, they say, as often rests
> In sunnburnt, as in snowy breasts.[225]

It is the court and its culture ('snowy breasts'), most of all the masque, that denies it.

A sense of Townshend's disenchantment with masque, a sense of a criticism of the values and culture of the court, must remain a suggestion. But it is corroborated by Townshend's own sense that he may have spoken too outrightly. The valediction speech of the Pigmy in the masque (perhaps a court dwarf in masque disguise?) is replete with innuendo far removed from the rarefied purity of Platonic abstractions. Ladies at court will give him kisses, 'sometimes claps';[226] they will give their lovers little rest. Courtiers may 'speake out like clerks' but the reality of courtly love is less monastic.[227] Townshend acknowledges this reality and sensuality and incorporates it within the masque. Apologetically he makes 'my own excuse' to the king and queen:

> So many are the faults I make
> In this loose Paper that I feare

---

[224] Brown, *Poems and Masques of Townshend*, p. 112.
[225] 'Come not to me', lines 26–7, *ibid.*, p. 26.
[226] Sometimes they lay me in their lappes
      And give me kisses, sometimes Clappes. (Brown, *Poems and Masques of Townshend*, p. 112)
   'Lay' may have sexual connotations here, as often; 'clap' was an impolite term for gonorrhoea in the seventeenth century, as today (*O.E.D.*).
[227] Brown, *Poems and Masques of Townshend*, p. 113.

> Onely for this poore Pöems sake
> I may hereafter loose your eare:
> I would by your Two bounties live,
> But now, if yee forgive, yee give.[228]

The puns are deliberate and ironic. Had Townshend hoped to 'loose' the king's ear, to open it, through the medium of his 'loose paper', his formless masque and erotic lines, to attitudes to love which were less spiritual and Platonic, and to a mode of government less authoritarian? If so, by forgiving the king might indeed 'give' – the light of reason to all. But Townshend seems to have suspected that rather than his counsel being taken, he would 'lose' the king's ear and the patronage he sought. His fear was well placed. The bright sun of royal favour, at least in commissions for court entertainments, shone no more on the 'poor and pocky poet' of the Barbican.

There may be more than a strange twist of fate in the appointment of Townshend's successor. Thomas Carew, who had so much appreciated *Tempe Restored*, but who had warned Townshend not to risk royal disfavour by dabbling in sensitive subjects, was recruited to write the next masque for Charles I. This is not to suggest, however, that Carew pandered to court tastes and sentiments, where Townshend did not. For not only may *Coelum Britannicum*, Carew's masque, make claim to be the triumph of masque as a genre, both in performance and as literature; it is one of the best examples we have of an ironic and sardonic treatment of the values of the court and of the masques which represented them.[229]

Such an interpretation is not the consensus of criticism. Peter Thomas described the masque as 'sycophantic';[230] G. E. Bentley thought 'Carew's efforts [were] not particularly distinguished'.[231] Stephen Orgel, however, has defended the masque as literature, and Kathleen McLuskie has identified a disruptive irony and an interplay of statement and form.[232] The most recent

---

[228] *Ibid.*

[229] *Coelum Britannicum* is printed in Orgel and Strong, *Inigo Jones*, II, pp. 567–98. I take this as my text. The edition, however, by Rhodes Dunlap (*Poems of Thomas Carew*, pp. 151–85, 273–83) contains valuable annotation, especially for an appreciation of Carew's debt to Giordano Bruno's *Spaccio de la Bestia Trionfante* (1584), trans. and ed. A. D. Imerti, *The Expulsion of the Triumphant Beast* (New Brunswick, 1964). The masque is discussed by Parker in '"Comely Gestures"', and by J. Chibnall, 'The Significance of the Caroline Court Masque in the History of the Court Revels', Cambridge University unpublished Ph.D. thesis, 1982. In what follows my own interpretation departs from all earlier accounts in arguing for a full recognition of the ironic and critical in Carew's masque. I am grateful to Dr Cedric Brown for his comments on a paper at Reading which constituted an earlier draft of this section.

[230] Thomas, 'Two Cultures', p. 181.

[231] Bentley, *Jacobean and Caroline Stage*, III, p. 109.

[232] Orgel and Strong, *Inigo Jones*, I, pp. 66–9; *The Revels History of English Drama*, IV, 1613–1660, pp. 144–5.

commentator of all has denied the ambivalence of treatment and form. The function of Carew's antimasque, Jennifer Chibnall maintains, 'is to purge any critical disbelief by turning it to laughter; to present, and dismiss, those aspects of social reality which could be brought against the harmonious vision'.[233] *Coelum Britannicum* has been the subject of unusual critical controversy. Contemporary opinion was favourable: the queen had never seen such admirable costumes; the more discerning Sir Thomas Herbert singled it out as 'the noblest masque of my time to this day, the best poetry, best scenes and best habits'.[234] This was praise indeed. For Carew had the difficult task of following two weeks after the lavish and extravagant masque of the Inns, *The Triumph of Peace*. Herbert's comment may help to explain Carew's success: *Coelum Britannicum* made an impression both as poetry and as spectacle. The beauty and force of the poetry make this for the modern reader the most powerful of the early Stuart masques. Not only is Carew's by far the longest Caroline masque text,[235] the long speeches of Momus and Mercury assert and display the power of rhetoric. Poetry here is not dominated by spectacle. *Coelum Britannicum* was invented jointly by Carew and Jones and there can never have been a more powerful, or more equal, assertion of the capacities of poetry and architecture. But it is the tone, as well as the force, that makes this masque distinctive. Permeating the text is a tone of irony, of scepticism and cynicism, the existence or possibility of which some commentators would deny, *a priori*, in masque. It is a tone to which Carew's editor, Rhodes Dunlap, was apparently deaf. But it is a tone that will not be unfamiliar to us if we recall, as we examine his masque, the voices of Carew's poetry.

Coelum Britannicum opens with a scene of decayed walls and buildings, 'resembling the ruins of some great city of the ancient Romans or civilized Britons'.[236] Mercury, ambassador from heaven, enters and addresses the state – where both the king (for the moment) and queen are seated – praising the royal pair for their example of love and government. Even the gods, Mercury tells them, have become envious of the royal pattern of purity, and Jove himself has felt shame at the contemplation, in the light of that example, of his past sins – his former base loves, now vices stellified in the heavens. Jupiter

> When in the crystal mirror of your reign
> He viewed himself, he found his loathsome stains;[237]

[233] J. Chibnall, '"To that Secure fix'd state": The function of the Caroline masque form', in Lindley, *The Court Masque*, p. 86; and Chibnall, 'The Significance of the Caroline Court Masque in the History of the Court Revels'.

[234] Adams, *Dramatic Records of Herbert*, p. 55.

[235] The text is 1,143 lines, longer than any other court masque.

[236] *Coelum Britannicum*, lines 36–7; *Inigo Jones*, II, p. 571.

[237] *Ibid.*, lines 82–3.

11 *Coelum Britannicum: Scene I*

and resolved to banish the vices from heaven, in order to immortalize as stars
in their places the British virtues exemplified and engendered by the king and
the queen. The purpose of masque as the apotheosis of the king is here, then,
to find its ultimate expression, and the rôle of poetry in the deification is
enacted in Mercury's discourse.

But the world of praise, and the action of the masque as such, is
immediately disrupted as Momus enters on the stage: 'Good den, cousin
Hermes.'[238] Momus is the god of ridicule, banished from the heavens for
finding fault with the deities.[239] He wears a porcupine in his hat as a symbol
of his prickly disposition and of the darts he is to deliver; his robe is decorated
with 'serpents' tongues', emblems of his venom and malice.[240] In the world of
the masque introduced by Mercury he has no place – and he knows it. He is
conscious of his intrusion upon the stage and before the audience – 'By your
leave, mortals' – but impertinently defiant. Mercury reminds him of the

[238] *Ibid.*, line 106.
[239] *The Oxford Classical Dictionary* (Oxford, 1970).
[240] *Inigo Jones*, II, p. 590.

12 *Coelum Britannicum*: Momus, 'attired in a long, darkish robe all wrought over with poniards, serpents' tongues . . . and upon his head a wreath stuck with feathers and a porcupine in the forepart'

inappropriate familiarity of his intrusion and language in the presence of the king: 'let this presence teach you modesty'. Momus, however, is not to be silenced: 'Let it if it can.'[241] He reminds his audience that for all that the poets call down the gods for the court festivities from Twelfth Night to Shrove Tuesday, he has never been invited. Satire has not been welcomed to the masquing hall at Whitehall. Nor, until now, as the audience well knows, has Carew. But though he has hithertho been excluded, Momus asserts his entitlement to be present — not as a eulogizer of the court, but as a 'Hypercritic of Manners'. He alone, he boasts, has the powers to root out the truth, to investigate 'all the privy lodgings, behind hangings, doors, curtains, through keyholes, chinks, windows, about all venereal [*sic*] lobbies'.[242] Carew is having fun with a presentation of himself (or at least an aspect of himself): as gentleman of the privy chamber he had indeed knowledge of life in the privy lodgings and behind doors and curtains; his personal acquaintance with

[241] *Coelum Britannicum*, line 124.
[242] *Ibid.*, lines, 141–3.

'venereal lobbies' was probably notorious. For those who had not already identified him as the poet, Momus offers another clue: Peter Aretine and Rabelais are, he tells us, birds of his feather, that is ribalds like himself whose writings were compared to Carew's own erotic ode, 'A Rapture', which specifically refers to Aretine.[243] A figure known for his scurrilous language and over-familiarity may well seem, as he does to Mercury, out of place in the masque's 'solemn message'. But Momus defends his style as the discourse of truth (rather than illusion) delivered by one who can boast more independence of the gods than Mercury, who of course is traditionally employed in masque to utter speeches of praise. 'As a freeborn god', Momus asserts, 'I have the liberty to travel at mine own charges.'[244] Like Momus, Carew, new to the masque stage, is telling his audience that he will not flatter. His prerogative as a poet is to speak truths 'whether it be to the behoof or prejudice of Jupiter his crown and dignity', whether it pleases the king or not.[245] Momus's remarkable defiance of the conventions of masque does not stop there. While the scene changes from the ruins of a city to the sphere of the world supported by Atlas, he scarcely interrupts his soliloquy.[246] Even the heavenly splendours presented by masque engineering will not divert Momus, nor will he allow it to distract the 'mortals' from *his* analysis of the state of heaven.

Mercury has proclaimed the virtues of the king and queen familiar to the masque: beauty, love, purity, virtue. Momus now as a 'sedulous acute observer' insists upon his more independent account. The renunciation of vice, he implies, owes more to decayed capacity than to virtue; the new chastity has been taken to such ridiculous lengths that all erotic literature (including Carew's own?) is to be censored in order to protect the fragile new morality. Morality, of course, cannot be imposed by force. And Momus mocks Jupiter's reforms as not only absurd but ineffectual.[247] The catalogue of measures he cites reads almost exactly as a list of the reforming proclamations and orders issued by Charles I since the commencement of his rule without parliament. Heaven has become a cloister; the king, as Lucy Hutchinson observed, ordered moral reformation and enforced strict sobriety at court.[248] New orders have been read by Jupiter in the Presence Chamber: Charles I issued new decrees for the regulation of his court and

---

[243] Cf. 'A Rapture', line 116, Dunlap, *Carew*, p. 52.
[244] *Coelum Britannicum*, lines 181–3.
[245] *Ibid.*, lines 149–50.
[246] This is a rare instance in which a speech continues while the scene changes. I am grateful to John Peacock for drawing this to my attention.
[247] Carew points up the real libertinism that the language of masque normally conceals: Momus has seen Jupiter 'religiously kissing the two-leaved book'; 'I left him practising in the milky way . . .' Parker points out that the two-leaved book is the vagina (' "Comely Gestures" ', p. 84) and for the 'milky way' cf. 'A Rapture', line 70 (Dunlap, *Carew*, p. 51).
[248] Above, p. 13.

household in 1630.[249] Some monopolies were curtailed; the adulteration of standards in manufactures was controlled; new rates were imposed on goods.[250] Charles I had issued (several) proclamations for, as Momus describes it in almost the king's own words, 'the restoring of decayed housekeeping, prohibiting the repair of families to the metropolis'.[251] There were orders and schemes for the stricter regulation of alehouses.[252] The sway wielded by favourites such as Buckingham had been ended: Ganymede, former cupbearer to Zeus, (like Carr and Villiers to James I) was forbidden the bedchamber. The parallels are close to the point of exactitude. No masque had represented immediate politics so precisely. Daringly then, Momus, true to his claim to be hypercritic, makes it clear that reform has been carried to extremes: 'Pan may not pipe . . . but by especial permission.' The penalties of the law have been invoked inappropriately for trivial, non-existent or archaic offences: 'Vulcan was brought to an *ore tenus* and fined for driving in a plate of iron into one of the sun's chariot wheels and frost / nailing his horses upon the fifth of November last.'[253] Few courtiers would have missed the allusion to recent fines on those who, in breach of medieval statutes, had failed to come forward to be knighted, or had encroached upon ancient royal forest. Nothing, Momus implies, has escaped attention but not all has been for the good: 'In brief', Momus concludes, 'the whole state of the hierarchy *suffers* a total reformation.'[254]

But in practice, and by implication fortunately, the realm suffers, that is allows, no such thing. For what Jupiter has decreed is, like the speech of Mercury and the discourse of masque, an ideal. This is not the same as the reality Momus perceives. The rules for the ordering of the court, he believes, are 'too strict to be observed long' (and Carew ought to have known).[255] Whilst decrees forbidding the gentry to come to the metropolis restrain the men, they do not inhibit their wives, who flock to London. For all the talk of chastity, women are arriving in the capital 'soliciting businesses in their own persons, and leaving their husbands at home for stallions of hospitality'.[256] We recall Davenant's courtly lady who would have 'my stallion if I please'

---

[249] P.R.O., Lord Chamberlain's Dept., L.C.5/180; Sharpe, 'Court and Household of Charles I'.
[250] See, for example, 'A Proclamation against the false dyeing of Silke', 9 Aug. 1630; 'A Proclamation against frauds and deceits used in Draperie . . .', 16 Apr. 1633, in *Stuart Royal Proclamations*, II, pp. 289–92, 359–61; F. C. Dietz, *English Public Finance 1558–1641* (London, 1932), p. 269; Gardiner, *History of England*, IX, p. 6.
[251] *Coelum Britannicum*, lines 244–5. Cf. 'A Proclamation commanding the Gentry to keepe their Residence at their Mansions in the Countrey, and forbidding them to make their habitations in London . . .', 20 June 1632, *Stuart Royal Proclamations*, II, pp. 350–3.
[252] P.R.O., P.C. 2/42/263, 9 Nov. 1632; 2/43/157, 198; Garrard to Wentworth, 9 Jan. 1634, *Strafford Letters*, I, p. 176; Bodl., Bankes MS 66/12.
[253] *Coelum Britannicum*, lines 257–60.
[254] *Ibid.*, lines 263–4 (my italics).
[255] *Ibid.*, line 237.
[256] *Ibid.*, lines 247–9.

according to the fashion.[257] Clearly the country's gentlewomen have not, like Jupiter, become converts to marital fidelity, nor followed the example of marriage presented by the king and queen. Momus has exposed the reality behind the masque. Speaking in his 'blunt round' way he has told us enough to know that, in accordance with his name and habit, he means the opposite of what he says when he concludes:

there is no doubt of an universal obedience where the lawgiver himself in his own person observes his decrees so punctually.[258]

We have seen every reason to doubt. Carew and his courtier audience know it too. Mercury's masque, whatever he says or whatever takes place upon the stage, cannot in reality transcend the problems. And even Mercury admits, breaking all masque conventions, 'Momus, thou shalt prevail . . . I must obey necessity.'[259]

The masque proceeds to enact Mercury's speech: the stellified vices are called down from heaven by Jove's decree. What for a thousand years have been praised and worshipped – the stars, the Hydra, the Dragon – are brought down to earth. Carew enjoys the reflection that with such beauties poets have compared their mistresses! The constellation of the crab, fallen to earth, dances an antimasque 'in retrograde paces, expressing obliquity in motion'.[260] Once again Momus interrupts the action by observations from a world, as it were, outside the masque. In a dramatic aside he observes that the crab's backward motion, its disorder and deviation, represents the decay of the arts and sciences and exhorts Mercury to employ his power to reverse the decline – a 'benefit to mankind worthy the power of a god'.[261] That, Momus acknowledges, is not 'the work of this night'. But such, we cannot but hear him (and Carew) reflecting, should more appropriately be the preoccupation of a philosopher-king. Art which might effect improvement in reality was superior to the illusions of such transforming power presented in the form of the masque. But Mercury ignores the aside and proceeds to empty the heavens, summoning the vices of flattery, cowardice and ambition, drunkenness and ostentation 'to this place', that is to the court. One by one they are snuffed out by the power of virtue, whose pure air they cannot breathe. Mercury has performed what he decreed.

The totality and finality of their eclipse disturb Momus: 'In my opinion there were some innocent and some generous constellations that might have been reserved for noble uses.'[262] He challenges the absolute transformations

----

257 Above, p. 64.
258 *Coelum Britannicum*, lines 273–5, 281.
259 *Ibid*., lines 292–4.
260 *Ibid*., lines 349–50.
261 *Ibid*., lines 357–8.
262 *Ibid*., lines 411–12.

of masque, the rejection of antimasque. Momus would have had the Scales and Sword remain in heaven to adorn justice, 'since she resides here on earth only in picture and effigy'.[263] Carew implies that the world of abstract ideas and Platonic forms in masque has replaced the real qualities and virtues of justice for a mere conceit, as in 'To Saxham' and 'Wrest' hospitality had been abandoned for its mere emblems. His criticism strikes at the heart of masque which, to Carew, confuses reality with Idea. And, he suggests, in so far as the masque expresses the king's mind, it expresses a vision and a language in which (as in masque as a form) reality does not intrude. The masque makes the monarch believe that the power of poetry is omnicompetent; that language may determine reality. And so the king, in emulation, believes that his own language may be active – through the power of the word.

We recall Momus' catalogue of Jupiter's decrees, the proclamations of Charles I. Momus now parodies a royal declaration for the evaluation of virtue in language that demonstrates the harmful effects of masque on royal perceptions of power and the power of discourse. It has, Momus mocks;

after mature deliberation and long debate held first in our own inscrutable bosom, and *afterwards* communicated with our Privy Council, seemed meet to our omnipotency, for causes to ourself best known, to unfurnish and disarray our foresaid Star Chamber of all those ancient constellations which have for many ages been sufficiently notorious, and to admit into their vacant places such persons only as shall be qualified with exemplar virtue and eminent desert ... It is therefore our divine will and pleasure, voluntarily and out of our own free and proper motion ...[264]

Momus parodies of course the lofty style of royal decrees and satirizes a style of monarchy in which decisions are made autocratically and *afterwards* presented to the Privy Council. But he is ridiculing too the belief that will expressed in language is action, the illusion that language or representations on the stage may effect a change in reality. The decree endows Momus and Mercury with 'an absolute power to conclude and determine' who may make claim to virtue.[265] But virtue and merit cannot be created by such decrees, nor do they depend upon masque to establish their value.[266] They are absolute qualities which the world of masque may even overturn. A decree that will admit virtue into the Star Chamber, – that is not only the heavens, but the king's prerogative court for the trial of rebels – ironically underlines the criticism. Language can be at odds with value; and masque, as well as representation, can be misrepresentation, the opposite rather than the reflection of truths – truths which must accommodate reality as well as visions of the ideal.

Mercury and Momus, who now proceed to appraise the claims of can-

[263] *Ibid.*, lines 413–14. Cf. 'Upon my Lord Chiefe Justice', lines 4–7, Dunlap, *Poems of Carew*, p. 83.
[264] *Coelum Britannicum*, lines 444–55 (my italics).
[265] *Ibid.*, lines 464–5.
[266] Hence the process of evaluation by Momus takes place elsewhere as the masque continues.

didates with pretentions to virtue, may be seen to stand for both – for the ideal and the real. Momus, who had intruded into the masque, has now been endowed with authority, and a rôle in the action. In accommodating him the masque has introduced a reality and a tone of speech usually absent, or confined to antimasque. It is no longer possible to describe Momus simply as a figure of antimasque: with Mercury he presents and observes the antimasques and so appears to manage the action and performance. Before Momus and Mercury, Wealth, Poverty, Fortune and Pleasure now appear to present their case for a place in the stars. They speak with an unusually persuasive eloquence for figures of antimasque – much as Milton's Comus – and even the gods acknowledge the force of their rhetoric. Once again the world of reality is brought on stage: for in the real world, Wealth, Poverty, Fortune and Pleasure are mighty forces, less easily cast aside than figures in an antimasque. In *Coelum* their claims are finally denied, but they are not dismissed; they are counselled to amend their ways – wealth advised to choose the company of worth, poverty of contentment. They may then be integrated within the world of masque as they are in that of reality; the ideal and the real may be more closely associated. As judges Mercury and Momus, for all their initial mutual hostility, come to complete agreement: virtue lies not in extremes or opposites (not in the attributes of masque or antimasque) but in the mean between them.[267] Virtue rests in nature and both wealth and poverty corrupt nature. The virtuous are too wise to ascribe all to Fortune and too enlightened to succumb to the Circean temptations of Pleasure. But the virtue that can resist the powerful voices of Pleasure and Wealth or Fortune and Poverty must be a mighty force indeed – strong in action as well as in discourse. Accordingly Mercury and Momus

> advance
> Such virtues only as admit excess,
> Brave bounteous acts, regal magnificence,
> All-seeing prudence, magnanimity
> That knows no bound, and that heroic virtue
> For which antiquity hath left no name.[268]

Such virtues, the form of masque demands, are to be found in the king. The false claims exposed, Mercury, the voice of the masque, turns to praise the royal pair whose 'actions plead' their case. The king and queen claim virtue in silence; the debate is transcended as the antimasque gives way to the masque. Significantly, at this point, Momus, who arrived as an intruder, departs abruptly 'without taking leave'.[269] Perhaps an aspect of Carew, who has

---

[267] See below, ch. 6.
[268] *Coelum Britannicum*, lines 666–71.
[269] *Ibid.*, line 46. Cf. his opening speech, 'By your leave, mortals'. Momus forcefully announces his arrival, but mutters his valediction almost as a stage aside.

presented a critique through his masque, who has brought the world of external reality into the theatre of illusion, must also step off stage.

Mercury now describes, as he had in his opening speech, the action that is to follow. He resumes the masque as it might have been had Momus never interrupted him. The scene now shifts to Britain, as Jones's engineering performs the transformation that Mercury has proclaimed. Song replaces blank verse as the celebration of the virtuous king succeeds to the debate between Mercury and Momus.[270] The active virtues of the king and queen, the consummation and the revival of all the ancient virtues of the realm, are expressed in the purity of their love, and represented through the harmony of the masquers' dance. Their beauty and virtue are now, as the masquers lead out the ladies in the revels, depicted as the light that leads others from darkness. Love is the royal mode of government that will direct subjects to virtue:

> And as their own pure souls entwined,
> So are their subjects' hearts combined.[271]

When the revels are over, the masque concludes with a final, magnificent change of scene:

> Out of the farthest part of the heaven begins to break forth two other clouds, differing in colour and shape; and being fully discovered, there appeared sitting in one of them Religion, Truth and Wisdom . . . In the other cloud sat Concord, Government, and Reputation . . . These being come down in an equal distance to the middle part of the air, the great cloud began to break open, out of which struck beams of light; in the midst, suspended in the air, sat Eternity on a globe; . . . In the firmament above him was a troop of fifteen stars, expressing the stellifying of our British heroes; but one more great and eminent than the rest, which was over his head, figured his majesty.[272]

As Orgel and Strong concluded, 'apotheosis can go no further'.[273] The mechanics of Platonism have placed the king in the seat of the gods. It is the function of poetry now to describe what is effected by spectacle.

And yet Momus cannot be forgotten despite his stealthy exit. For all the wonder at the spectacle which 'gave great cause of admiration', Momus's voice still echoes. He is not repudiated; he departs, he tells us, in order to continue to hear the petitions of those who would sue for a place in the stars. He has no place in the transformations made possible by the power of Jones's engineering, but he leaves an uneasy feeling of tension not resolved by it. The tension may well be in Carew. We know that the poet himself had been impressed by the 'dazzling beauties' of Townshend's masque, by the power of

---

[270] We recall Selig's distinction between Carew's singing and speaking voice.
[271] *Coelum Britannicum*, lines 1100–1.
[272] *Ibid.*, lines 1054–78.
[273] *Inigo Jones*, I, p. 70.

illusion. But he had introduced too into the Banqueting House a realism and a scepticism which the masque had, for much of the performance, accommodated. The voices of praise and criticism, of ideal vision and reality, which we have discerned in Carew's poetry, are, in the persons of Mercury and Momus, brought together in the masque.

Indeed the relationship between Carew's poetry and his court masque may be closer and more particular than we have realized. In a recent persuasive essay Michael Parker has drawn attention to the affinities between *Coelum Britannicum* and Carew's 'To my friend G.N. from Wrest'.[274] The poem, Carew's 'secular masque' as Parker describes it, appears to comment on masque in general and reflect *Coelum* in particular. Parker demonstrates that the structure of the poem follows that of the masque, but that the relationship of subject to structure is reversed. Architecture and image, the agents of masque transcendence, as Dorique and 'Corinthian Pillars', function in 'To my friend G.N. from Wrest' as antimasques to the poem. The masque triumph is the victory of reality, not of idea.

In a movement that parallels the climactic dramatic incident of the court masque, the unmasking that reveals the revelers' true identities, the poet calls forth the realities – fire, lord and lady, men – that in other houses remain frozen in architectural disguises. The poet banishes the perverted emblems of hospitality to evoke the spirit of hospitality itself.[275]

Accordingly, as we recall, Ceres and Bacchus are not represented in 'emblemes to the eyes' but 'for service' and 'real use'. Masque is the representation of ideas. Momus has warned us not to confuse it with, or forget, reality. As 'equal judges' together, Momus and Mercury evaluate virtue; the real and the ideal are reconciled. 'To G.N. from Wrest' also advocates their integration; it is an example of the mean that is the best course. So, though Wrest is anchored in the world of nature, 'we decline not all the worke of Art'.[276] Wrest achieves the perfect combination. It is 'with a double crystal heaven embrac'd', by the sky above and below by the lake that man's ingenuity has formed around the house.[277] Having reconciled art and nature, Wrest is envied by the gods themselves. For where Wrest's lake has signs of the zodiac in its life – fishes, swans and boatmen – the heavens enjoy only their symbols. At Wrest 'our refreshing lake' quenches men's thirst. The heavenly constellations 'stick fast nayl'd to the *barren* Spheare / Whilst our encrease in fertile waters here'.[278] The constellations in heaven and on earth recall *Coelum Britannicum*. The king and the British heroes stellified by the

---

[274] M. P. Parker, '"To my friend G.N. from Wrest": Carew's secular masque' in Summers and Pebworth, *Classic and Cavalier: Essays on Jonson and the Sons of Ben*, pp. 171–92.

[275] Parker, '"To my friend G.N. from Wrest"'.

[276] 'To G.N. from Wrest,' line 69, Dunlap, *Poems of Carew*, p. 88.

[277] *Ibid.*, line 80.

[278] *Ibid.*, lines 85–6.

masque, then, inhabit only a 'barren Spheare', just as they do at Wrest. Carew's poem contrasts the sterility of mere image with the richness of reality – and he does so both in the form and the content of his poem. One cannot but sense from the structure and tone of his masque that when Momus departs, a part of the poet leaves too.

Carew's poetry, as we have argued, presents an ideal of the state of nature as a reconciliation, an integration of the worlds of sense and soul. It is a different ideal from that of masque. One purpose of Carew's poetry appears to be to bring men to the peace and order of nature through, and through ordering, the sense, not by an abstract intellectual philosophy, or through representations of the victory of a sterile order over the world of sense. Such a transformation was integral to the form of masque. Momus, the disciple of Rabelais and Aretine, had questioned the philosophy and disturbed the form. Five years later, in 'To G.N. from Wrest', Carew perhaps reiterates in his poem what he had implied in Whitehall: a criticism of masque as a genre and of the values and ideas which masque expressed. If there is something in this suggestion, it may help to answer a difficult question and an unexplained problem: why Thomas Carew never wrote another masque.[279] *Coelum Britannicum* received the critical acclaim of contemporaries. For all the satire and mockery of royal proclamations, Carew remained close to Charles I. For all he disclaimed, on the title page of his own text, any wish to write a masque, we know, from his advice to Townshend, that Carew was not averse to the genre. But it is clear that he had his own ideas of the form that it might take: there is a dramatic force, a poetic power, an ambivalence and irony in *Coelum* that recalls Jonson at his best. It may be that for Inigo Jones, the voice of poetry and ambiguity was raised too loudly, that spectacle was too little esteemed. We cannot know. But we do know that the next masque at court, the queen's Shrovetide masque for 1635, launched the career of a new writer who, unlike his predecessors, became established, in collaboration with Jones, as author of the remainder of the Caroline masques.

Those who would wish to discuss the Caroline masque as mere spectacle must face the fact that the longest serving author of the masques was one of the most renowned playwrights of his age. William Davenant wrote four masques for the king and queen between 1635 and 1640, as well as one for the Inns of Court: the Christmas revels staged for the entertainment of the Prince Elector Charles Louis and his brother Rupert on their visit to England in 1636.[280] The same few years were those of Davenant's greatest activity as a playwright (for the Blackfriars and the Globe) and as a poet. It may be his

---

[279] A problem raised by Sadler, *Thomas Carew*, p. 127.
[280] *The Temple of Love, Britannia Triumphans, Luminalia, Salmacida Spolia, The Triumphs of the Prince D'Amour.*

diversity, his flexibility and adaptability that secured Davenant his position as
successor to Jonson. Certainly his entertainments differed notably from each
other, whether according to patron (king, queen or the Inns) or circumstance.
Evidently he pleased both Charles and Henrietta Maria and was able to
work with Jones. If Davenant received the royal commission for the rest of
Charles I's reign, we might well conclude that he had satisfied where his
predecessors (Townshend and Carew) had not.

But if Davenant pleased his patrons it was not because he sycophantically
flattered them. We have seen from his drama and verse that Davenant
exposed the moral failings of the court to mordant satire and criticism. We
have suggested that even in his poetry of compliment there is ambivalence,
counsel and criticism as well as praise. In his first masque for the queen we
undoubtedly see Davenant the aspirant courtier writing at the behest of a
patron. But we often sense too the playwright sceptical of the commission he
has been given and able, within the form of masque, to convey his strong
misgivings. Davenant's commission was important. On 3 June 1634, James
Howell, a court gossip, wrote to his friend Philip Warwick in Paris:

The Court affords little News at present, but that there is a Love call'd Platonick Love,
which much sways there of late; it is a Love abstracted from all corporeal gross
Impressions and sensual Appetite, but consists in Contemplations and Ideas of the
Mind, not in any carnal Fruition. This love sets the Wits of the Town on work; and
they say there will be a Mask shortly of it, whereof Her Majesty and her Maids of
Honour will be part.[281]

The Temple of Love, the masque here anticipated, was performed four times
in February 1635.[282] Its subject was the triumph of purity and chastity over
the forces of temptation and sensuality through the example of love and
beauty set by the queen. The marriage of higher understanding and will
necessary for the victory over appetite is represented in the union of Henrietta
Maria and Charles. 'The Argument' that prefaces the text describes the action
and proclaims the rôle of 'divine poesy' as the force leading men to the
Temple of Love. Davenant reminds the queen of the service of her own poet,
describing himself on the title page as 'William Davenant, her majesty's
servant'.[283]

Divine Poesy introduces the action, upbraiding the poets whose loose
verses 'made false love in numbers flow'.[284] It is for poets now to celebrate the
reign of Queen Indamora 'In which love's blessings shall be given'.[285] But a

[281] J. Jacobs, ed., *Epistolae Ho-Elianae. The Familiar Letters of James Howell* (London, 1890),
pp. 317–18.
[282] Bentley, *Jacobean and Caroline Stage*, III, p. 218.
[283] *The Temple of Love ... By Inigo Jones ... and William Davenant, her majesty's servant*
(1635). All references are from Orgel and Strong, *Inigo Jones*, II, pp. 599–630.
[284] *Temple of Love*, line 97.
[285] *Ibid.*, line 123.

sense of unease and scepticism intrudes from the beginning. Chastity (as the pox-ridden Davenant knew well!) 'seems somewhat hard doctrine to most young men'.[286] The magicians who control the world of sensual allurements disdain Indamora's reformation and authority. She and her train, they claim, may radiate beauty, but they cannot appeal to the appetite or taste of men. The queen and her ladies, they believe:

> Still carry frozen winter in their blood.
> They raise strange doctrines and new sects of love,
> Which must not woo or court the person, but
> The mind, and practice generation not
> Of bodies, but of souls.[287]

The unnaturalness and sterility of Platonic love is here boldly drawn and the criticism of a cult is expressed in the derogatory terms employed by the king and court in denouncing the puritans – a heterodox 'sect' with its own 'strange doctrines'.[288] Platonic love may have become the court orthodoxy, but we sense the magician is right: 'there will be / Little pastime upon earth without bodies'.[289] Physical union, love expressed physically as well as spiritually, will triumph over the 'dull imaginary pleasures of / Their souls'.[290] Platonic love is no more than a fad and a disease: 'This humour cannot last.'[291] Only in 'a dull northern isle they call Britain', and then only at court, has the doctrine found disciples.[292] Even there the young lords found the new faith 'uncomfortable, sad and new'.[293] The magicians set out to reconvert the Persian youths to the old ways of love, natural ways. If they fail, they claim, 'Nature, our weakness must be thought thy crime.'[294] Though an antimasque, the magicians appeal to nature against the posturings of unnatural, ill-understood ideas. They present the elements of nature – earth, air, water and fire – in the corrupted forms of drunkards, witches, devils and amorous revellers. Their antimasque over, the audience prepares for the masque entry. But the transformation is not clear.

After these was an entry of three Indians of quality of Indamora's train, in several *strange* habits, and their dance as *strange*.[295]

---

[286] *Ibid.*, line 22.
[287] *Ibid.*, lines 189–93.
[288] See above, p. 71.
[289] *Temple of Love*, lines 197–8.
[290] *Ibid.*, lines 203–4.
[291] *Ibid.*, line 204. The word 'humour', of course, conveys multiple meanings and ironies: a fluid of an animal or plant; one of four such 'by the relative proportions of which a person's physical and mental qualities and disposition were held to be determined'; a 'fancy' or whim (*O.E.D.*).
[292] The miracle is more increased, in that
It first takes *birth* and *nourishment* in court. (*Temple of Love*, lines 218–19 (my italics)).
[293] *Ibid.*, line 224.
[294] *Ibid.*, line 272.
[295] *Ibid.*, lines 304–5 (my italics).

The reservation about the masque that is to ensue is confirmed by the page who introduces the Persian masquers. For though he reports the triumph of beauty and love over base appetite, of a love 'what's Platonical', he acknowledges that many are sceptical:

> My master is the chief, that doth protect
> Or, as some say, *mislead* this precise sect.[296]

The tone of his speech is sardonic, only half-serious and suggestive. The Platonists are ridiculed: they are coy, 'quav'ring'; they retreat at a kiss; they are pusillanimous and impotent. Their philosophy, it is implied, may be no more than the expression of their physical incapacities: 'Ladies, I must needs laugh!'[297] Doubtless the less Platonically inclined of the courtly audience laughed too, as they were to, more openly, at Davenant's satirical play, *The Platonic Lovers*, performed a year later. But masque was not the forum for prolonged comic satire and the page, having completed his irreverent discourse, flees the stage 'lest killed with pins and bodkins for my news'[298] – though whether by ladies frustrated at the news of Platonic love, or by Indamora for his having ridiculed it, we cannot be sure.

The dance of the Persian youths ended, the scene changes to prepare the way for Indamora, who calms the winds and waves of wild nature, as she quells the tempestuous appetites of passion. The mists which hung over the temple of love clear. Indamora is crowned by Chaste love, perfect will and strengthened reason, and praised by the poets who serve them. The valedictory address to the king and queen (now seated under the state) praises the uniting of these virtues in the love of the royal couple. This is conventional masque transcendence and celebration. But the ambivalence of the poet may still be heard. As Kathleen Mcluskie observed, even Platonic love is expressed in sensuous poetry that undermines it.[299] Chaste love addresses the king and queen in metaphors of fertility, promising 'fruitful showers' that may 'fructify' – in contrast to the 'barren earth' and 'barren' hearts.[300] It is the language of nature as a physical as well as spiritual force, pregnant and procreative. And this may be Davenant's point. In reality, the king and queen are not of the precise sect that 'retreat at kissing', represented in the masque.[301] Their own marriage is physical as well as spiritual love; it is fecund and has borne fruit and it is as such that the royal marriage may stand as a pattern of virtue:

[296] *Ibid.*, lines 323–4. The acknowledgement throughout of scepticism, a reflection of Davenant's own, imparts an unusual tone to the masque.
[297] *Ibid.*, line 339; cf. this speech with Momus's imputations concerning Jupiter's incapacities; *Coelum Britannicum*, line 198.
[298] *Temple of Love*, line 348.
[299] *Revels History of English Drama IV*, p. 146.
[300] *Temple of Love*, lines 499–510.
[301] *Ibid.*, line 337.

> To Charles the mightiest and the best,
> And to the darling of his breast,
> Who rule b' example as by power,
> May youthful blessings still increase,
> And in their offspring never cease.[302]

Davenant's masque pleased the queen, who performed it three more times within the week. G. E. Bentley suggests that 'his dutiful handling of the queen's favourite subject of Platonic love' may have assisted Davenant's rise in her favour.[303] But the sceptical tone cannot be denied, and is not confined to the antimasque. Davenant argues that the forces of nature cannot be discounted and physical love is natural.[304] It may, however, like the magicians' presentations, be disordered. The solution lay not in the rejection of natural human passions, but in their regulation – in 'a lawful though a loving heart'.[305] In Davenant's drama, as we have seen, that order is often to be found in marriage, marriages which stand for virtue and for order in the commonweal. And it is marriage that Davenant celebrates in the masque, a royal marriage that is physical and pure, which does not deny but orders nature. It is this marriage, *not* Platonic love, that qualifies the king to 'rule b' example', and it is his own beliefs and values that Davenant prefers in his masque.

Davenant's first masque for Charles I is concerned to make the same point. *Britannia Triumphans* was the king's Twelfth Night masque for 1638, and the first performance after an intermission of three years, during which a special masquing hall had been erected, so that the smoke and tapers did not damage the Rubens paintings recently installed in the ceiling at Whitehall.[306] Much had happened in the intervening years: England's relations with Spain had been strained almost to breaking point; ship money had been levied and a substantial fleet was at sea. Some critics have argued that Davenant's masque reflects exactly the immediate political circumstances. For Graham Parry, *Britannia Triumphans* had 'a clear political motivation, to vindicate Charles's dubious demand for ship money'.[307] There may be some truth in this: allusions to naval strength occur throughout the masque. But ship money and the royal fleet are not the central subjects or purpose of Davenant's masque;

---

[302] *Ibid.*, lines 511–15.

[303] Bentley, *Jacobean and Caroline Stage*, III, p. 218.

[304] Unusually the masque is performed by aristocratic men *and* women, which Davenant may have arranged to make his point.

[305] *Temple of Love*, line 454.

[306] I take as my text of *Britannia Triumphans* Orgel and Strong, *Inigo Jones*, II, pp. 661–704. For another edition with music, see M. Lefkowitz, *Trois Masques à la Cour de Charles Ier*, pp. 171–243. On the building of the new masquing room, see Garrard to Wentworth, 9 Nov. 1637, *Strafford Letters*, II, pp. 130, 140.

[307] Parry, *Golden Age Restor'd*, p. 196; 1638 was the year of Hampden's case, the constitutional test case of ship money.

they are metaphors for less particular, more universal concerns which the king, perhaps, no less than the courtiers, is urged to heed. *Britannia Triumphans*, like Davenant's drama, is concerned with the anarchy of nature and its regulation, and with the function of government as the ordering of the potentially destructive but natural passions of men. Within the context of these concerns, it self-consciously debates too the rôle of the arts, of poetry and of masque itself, in the process of educating subjects to self-discipline and virtue. 'Debates' is the most appropriate term. For Davenant's treatment of the ethical and political questions he addresses is discursive and his style is dramatic. Like *Albion's Triumph* and *Coelum Britannicum*, *Britannia Triumphans* opens on two characters, Action and Imposture, engaged in dialogue – about the nature and meaning of the performance that is to ensue.

Illusion, Imposture claims, is what governs all experience: 'everything but seems'.[308] Men, he maintains, live by their senses rather than their reason and so fail to understand the ideas that may be presented to them. The only art, therefore, which has any point is that which panders to men's senses, 'not what pretends at profit'.[309] He represents, in other words, the very attitudes that Davenant attacks in his prologues to his plays. Action replies forcefully. The arts, he asserts, have an ethical and didactic function. He dismisses (in words that echo Davenant's own) the idea that 'we were only born to aim at trifles here . . . to run at sight / Of bubbles, and to leap at noise of bells'.[310] Though he cannot claim that all may come to understanding, 'there are some few 'mongst men', he points out, who rise above the level of sense and the noise of bells and perceive beyond visual images to the philosophy and ideas they should express.[311] To such, his entertainment is addressed. But such men who 'look up / To face the stars' are not puritans, nor perhaps even those of the Platonical inclination. Puritans of both persuasions, in renouncing all sensual pleasures, are as guilty of denying their human nature as are those who chase mere bubbles and never realize their higher reason. There is a middle course between those slaves to sense and appetite and the 'melancholy monks' and 'sullen clerks' who would separate themselves from humanity.[312] Action argues for the motto written in silver letters on his belt: *Medio Tutissima*, the mean is the safest way.[313] Entertainments, recreations, even sensual delights are not, he opines, to be disdained, 'but every act be squared by virtue's rule'.[314] Pleasure may be reconciled to virtue, as appetite and sense

---

[308] *Britannia Triumphans*, line 101.
[309]   That universally shall take which most
        Doth please, not what pretends at profit. (*ibid* lines 117–18).
[310] *Ibid.*, lines 131–4; cf. above, ch. 2, p. 85.
[311] *Britannia Triumphans*, lines 143–8.
[312] *Ibid.*, lines 171, 178. See Action's speech, lines 154ff, for language which contrasts the riches of nature with these 'sullen clerks'.
[313] *Ibid.*, lines 63–7. See below, ch. 6.
[314] *Britannia Triumphans*, line 183.

may be to reason. Natural appetites were to be governed rather than excised. Imposture responds that the virtue which integrates sense and reason is a rare quality indeed:

> admit there's one
> Or two allow in nature such a thing,
> And that it is no dream. These mighty lords
> Of reason have but a few followers,
> And those go ragged too.[315]

But he acknowledges in so saying that the virtue to which Action refers is 'in nature'. Action speaks for the potential of man's nature.

Significantly in order to strengthen his cause against Action, Imposture summons Merlin and the magic which 'soars above the reach of Nature's might', an admission that it is nature's might that lends Action his greatest support.[316] Merlin conjures an antimasque of all that Action has spoken against. A world of noise, knackers and bells (Action's 'noise of bells'); tradesmen from the suburbs – the representatives of ungoverned nature, men slaves to their desire; rebels, Cade and Kett, who have overturned authority; posers and impostors (such as 'a mountebank in the habit of a grave doctor'), who appear other than they are; and 'parasitical courtiers', who mouth words without substance – all 'great seducers' to lead men from virtue. As the 'airy mimic apparitions' fade, Bellerophon, the mythical victor over temptation, arrives to dispel them, mounted on Pegasus.[317] Bellerophon is sure that the good will resist the baits of sense and illusion. But Imposture doubts they will do so 'without help/Of arguments'.[318] And he gloats that those who should lead by virtuous example and counsel have opted out of their responsibility to argue their case:

> the virtuous, sir, of late
> Have got a fine feminine trick to rail
> At all they will dislike, refer what is
> Not easily understood unto a kind
> Obedient faith, and then call reason but
> A new and fancy heretic.[319]

Davenant may be alluding to the courtly cult of Platonic love, worshipped by the virtuous as their faith, but scarce understood by themselves and totally incomprehensible to others who, deprived of more reasoned counsel to virtue, are left subjects to Imposture's false rule.[320] The masques which have celebrated Platonic love have themselves required a faith in apotheosis rather

---

[315] *Ibid.*, lines 186–90.
[316] *Ibid.*, line 221.
[317] *Oxford Classical Dictionary*; H. J. Rose, *A Handbook of Greek Mythology* (London, 1933).
[318] *Britannia Triumphans*, lines 292–3.
[319] *Ibid.*, lines 294–9.
[320] See ch. 2, p. 68.

than proffered moral arguments in intelligible language. Unlike the drama, masque has not addressed itself to those in need of instruction. 'Giving seeming pleasures real attributes', Bellerophon rebukes Merlin, is to disguise sense in reason.[321] Empty 'noise and shows' subvert the didactic function of art.

The dialogue is about the nature of poetry, drama and masque and how they should be understood. In viewing the masques (as with his plays), Davenant is saying that men should not run after bubbles but come to perceive moral truths and it is for the masque itself to assist them – not by celebrating a faith but by the power of arguments. Action and Imposture present these arguments. Merlin who stands for pleasure and appetite now stages a dramatic presentation which, for all its apparently traditional moral content, appeals only to the sense. It is a 'mock romansa', a tale of heroes and chivalry. The subject is trivial; the verse unspeakably banal and trite. Davenant parodies the literature that reneges on the responsibility of drama and poetry to educate. Bellerophon dismisses it: 'How trivial and lost thy visions are!'[322] Action scorns it as a 'shadow'. They banish Merlin and Imposture. The action of the masque may now be understood as it should be – not as an empty show but as an argument, a truth. Virtue will triumph over sense and illusion, now that the misleading clouds of error have passed. Britanocles offers the pattern of virtue that will lead men to see aright. Science, poetry and music (in their right forms) assist and celebrate his triumph. Charles I emerges from the palace of fame as Britanocles, who has 'reduced the land by his example to a real knowledge of all *good* arts and sciences'.[323] His example is that of love. The poets address the queen as well as the king, for together they have reduced 'what was wild before' and show others how to resist Imposture's temptations.[324] The masque may teach men too – provided that it presents 'real attributes' rather than 'shows', arguments rather than an incomprehensible 'feminine trick'. The triumph of *Britannia Triumphans* is the triumph of virtue over vice. The 'argument' of the masque is that it is a triumph enacted through love and marriage. And the rôle of the poet is to represent that reality in verse and on the stage.

It is not the triumph of Platonic love, nor is Platonic love presented as the pattern of virtue to be emulated. The masque concludes in 'A Valediction' that is sensual and erotic in tone: 'Each lady slowly yield, yet yield at last.'[325] Davenant is unusually explicit in his reference to the royal love 'renewed, and bettered every night!'[326] Graham Parry has drawn attention to the valedic-

[321] *Britannia Triumphans*, line 309.
[322] *Ibid.*, line 464.
[323] *Ibid.*, lines 21–3 (my italics).
[324] *Ibid.*, line 606.
[325] *Ibid.*, line 631.
[326] *Ibid.*, line 638.

tion as 'a gauche epilogue praising the king's prowess in the royal bed, an extraordinary failure of tone, as if Davenant had quite forgotten the Temple of Chaste Love of his previous masque or the whole tradition of platonic love.'[327] But the only failure of tone is Parry's own. Davenant had not forgotten Platonic love; his masque (like *The Temple of Love*) is a rejection of it. The royal marriage, a physical as well as spiritual union, is his subject. For the royal marriage represents that virtue which 'one or two allow in nature', that reconciliation of pleasures and virtue which Action had held up as the pattern of virtue and subject for poetry. Passions and pleasures may be governed through marriage, as Britanocles, Nature's Admiral, has through love suppressed the raging seas of appetite. Marriage is that best middle course that Action had advocated between slavery to one's appetites and the sterile faith and self-denial of 'sullen clerks'. Since the purpose of poetry was to inculcate virtue and educate men to self-government, marriage was its appropriate subject. And it was a 'real attribute', or argument more fitting for representation in masque than the visions and faiths of Platonic love that the spectators failed to understand. Davenant's valediction encapsulates his argument: love and marriage that order nature but do not deny it are the pattern for virtue and hence the subject for poets.

Davenant's last masque, and the last royal masque of Charles I's reign, from its first conception was a representation of the royal marriage. For this was the first and only Caroline masque presented and performed by the king *and* the queen, as opposed to being presented by one for the other. By January 1640, when it was first presented, the political circumstances had changed dramatically. The halcyon peace of personal rule, praised in the masques, had been ruptured by the revolt of the Scots. Order had collapsed into chaos; government was challenged by rebellion. And the personal rule of Charles I was at an end; writs had been issued in December for a parliament to meet in April. Davenant's masque, *Salmacida Spolia*, could not but reflect these changes. G. E. Bentley has described it as 'the swan song of the Caroline court'.[328] Professors Orgel and Strong have argued that it presents the monarch in a 'new rôle of the patient and suffering king'.[329] But for all the differences of circumstance, the masque may be understood not as radically different in purpose, rather as a more explicit statement of the ethical and political values implicit in Davenant's drama and poetry, and in his earlier masques of the decade.

The complicated proscenium arch represented the philosophy of the masque.[330] Two figures of women stood in a square niche on the right. 'One

[327] Parry, *Golden Age Restor'd*, p. 199.
[328] Bentley, *Jacobean and Caroline Stage*, III, p. 214.
[329] Orgel and Strong, *Inigo Jones*, I, p. 72.
[330] *Salmacida Spolia*, lines 22–70. All references to *Salmacida Spolia* are from Orgel and Strong, *Inigo Jones*, II, pp. 729–85. No sketch has survived.

of them expressing much majesty in her aspect' was Reason; the other stood for Intellectual Appetite, 'who while she embraceth Reason, all the actions of men are rightly governed'. This is the union celebrated in *The Temple of Love* and represented through the royal marriage. The association with government is clarified by the figures on the left: Resolution and Counsel whose own marriage (like that of Reason and Appetite), the description informs, is 'necessary to the good means of arriving to a virtuous end'. Above both flew Prudence and Fame. In the frieze were represented the benefits that accompanied the virtues of ordered nature and a naturally ordered polity: Riches, Commerce, Safety, Success, Felicity, Innocence and Affection to the Country;

all these expressing the several goods, followers of peace and concord, and forerunners of human felicity; so as the work of this front, consisting of picture qualified with moral philosophy, tempered delight with profit.

The marriage of potential opposites (counsel and resolution, for example) is represented as virtue, the mean. In presenting this masque *together* the king and queen actually presented their own union, as the active virtue to be emulated.

The subject, like the proscenium, of *Salmacida Spolia* was unusually complex and it is hard to imagine the performance. The text, which was obviously intended for a wider audience, has to explain the two proverbs from which the masque takes its theme – that of the fountain of Salmacis whose waters calmed 'fierce and cruel natures' and the story of the Thebans' counter attack on their enemies the Argives which ended in bloody victory.[331] Their application to the circumstances of 1640 is clear. Davenant presented in the masquing hall the two responses to the Scottish rebellion which were debated within the Privy Council: conciliation and force.[332] More broadly he discusses two modes of kingship and government: the military and the didactic, the imposition of order by force, or the inculcation of order by instruction and example. The text makes the poet's own position apparent: 'The allusion is that his majesty, out of his mercy and clemency approving the first proverb, (that of the fountain of Salmacis) *seeks* by all means to reduce tempestuous and turbulent natures into a sweet calm of civil discord.'[333] The present indicative of the verb 'seeks' is important. Here, as so often in the masques, what is presented as a statement of fact is offered as a counsel to persuade. Davenant was not describing a firm royal decision – the treaty of Berwick was a truce and the king had not abandoned the military option[334] – he was offering advice. And we shall not understand this masque, nor perhaps

---

[331] *Inigo Jones*, I, p. 73.
[332] Gardiner, *History of England*, IX, pp. 72–80.
[333] *Salmacida Spolia*, lines 107–10.
[334] Gardiner, *History of England*, IX, ch. 89.

any masque, if we do not read it as advice as well as praise. Here, what the king and queen perform on the masque stage they are exhorted to enact: the governing of nature and ordering of chaos not by force, but by virtue, moderate courses, and love.

The scene opens on a storm and tempest, darkness.[335] The sea is now wild and untamed – not the calm waters ruled by Britanocles's trident. The ordered nature of the masques has been rent. The fury who enters threatens with 'wild disorders', storms, 'humours', 'nature's funeral', an England that has been for too long at peace. This antimasque being past, 'the scene changed into a calm', an idealized landscape rich in nature's fruits. The genius of Great Britain (that is of *Scotland* as well as England) tells Concord that the people have ceased to appreciate the blessings of peace; but that Philogenes, literally the lover of his people, still bids Concord stay, for he knows her worth. Concord agrees. But the world of reality is acknowledged; the king is alone in desiring peace

> 'tis his fate to rule in adverse times,
> When wisdom must a while give place to crimes[336]

and the task of persuading others to his view will be more difficult than subjecting them by force:

> When it is harder far to cure
> The people's folly than resist their rage?[337]

Heroism lies in patience rather than in military victory. Davenant knows that the king will receive advice from all quarters, much of it absurd and dangerous. The antimasque entries represent the Politic Would-Bes with their absurd proposals for the resolution of the problems of the realm. Wolfgangus Vandergoose, a magician of the order of the Rosicross, 'undertakes in short time to cure the defects of nature and diseases of the mind'.[338] He is, however, himself a defect and a disease; his cures are false and ridiculous. They include potions 'to make one dance well', as if (as some courtiers who misunderstood masque were inclined to believe) revels could effect change – in reality as well as in representation. Other spurious counsellors see the answer in money, bravura, history, scholarship, magic, pastoral, chivalric posturing. Because none understand the right courses, however, their advice must be discounted, whether proferred by Englishman or Scot, courtier or peasant, young or old. Only the king himself knows the virtuous and honourable course of action,

---

[335] *Salmacida Spolia*, lines 111–16; see illustration on p. 201. Cf. the description in Carew's 'To G.N. from Wrest'.
[336] *Salmacida Spolia*, lines 190–1.
[337] *Ibid.*, lines 198–9.
[338] *Ibid.*, lines 203–4. The antimasques would repay further study; Vandergoose is taken from Jonson's *Masque of Augurs*.

and should not be misled by uninformed suggestions, nor by the illusions of masque. He must resist the temptation to arms, and triumph instead through patience and peace.

Davenant's masque then enacts on the stage what it advocates: the triumph of peace. The king appears with his nobles in the Throne of Honour, 'adorned with palm trees between which stood statues of the ancient heroes', victorious over his enemies and over war.[339] Whilst seated he is addressed by a song in a scene quite unusual in masque, where normally speeches are delivered to the king only when he is off the stage, and seated under the state (a throne with a canopy). Here Charles I is assured:

> If it be kingly patience to outlast
> Those storms the people's giddy fury raise
> Till like fantastic winds themselves they waste,
> The wisdom of that patience is thy praise.[340]

The king is told what he has often performed: that he is the Reason that may order the giddy furies of appetite. Honour will come to him, as it has in earlier masques, for fulfilling the rôle of a king as an instructor of his people, not through subduing them by force. The king is a philosopher:

> He's fit to govern there and rule alone
> Whom inward helps, not outward force, doth raise.[341]

Caroline masques had represented the queen as the example of pure love which civilized the chaos of passion. Davenant had held up the royal marriage as a model for self-regulation and the government of the realm. Now, in *Salmacida Spolia*, with the king raised by patient virtue to the seat of honour, the queen descends on a cloud. She, the song announces, 'gives to men the power of sight', and may help the king restore order.[342] The king and queen dance together before the court representing the unification of patience and virtue, reason and will, love and government which, Davenant argues, must prevail over the resort to arms. When Charles and Henrietta Maria are seated under the state, the deities instruct them in the meaning of their own performance – of the dance and the masque which they have just presented. Their love, they are told, stands for harmony, and where there is harmony, there is no ruler and subject; obedience and will are reconciled:

> All that are harsh, all that are rude,
> Are by your harmony subdued;
> Yet so into obedience wrought,
> As if not forced to it, but taught.[343]

---

[339] *Ibid.*, lines 346–7. That the chief masquer was the Scottish Duke of Lennox added peculiar force to the argument for reconciliation.

[340] *Ibid.*, lines 360–3.

[341] *Ibid.*, lines 378–9.

[342] *Ibid.*, line 145. Davenant appears to allude to *Luminalia*, the queen's Shrovetide masque of 1638.   [343] *Salmacida Spolia*, lines 471–4. Cf. Carew's 'To my Lord Chief Justice', ch. 3.

Such is the end of government: to instil order through examples of harmony, here the royal marriage. The final scene, with 'magnificent buildings composed of several selected pieces of architecture' separated from the suburbs by a bridge, reasserts the claims of art to aid kings in the task of government.[344] The poet's function, like the architect's, is that of the king himself: to teach patterns of virtue. Many at court urged the king to war. Davenant reaffirms a view of government and the power of example – even in the circumstances of the winter of January 1640. There was no denying the circumstances and harsh times: wisdom had for a while given way to crimes. But Davenant adhered to the belief, which in the midst of civil war he did not abandon, that virtuous examples would in the long run persuade; that it was the responsibility of the king to present them and of the poet to represent them. Accordingly he exhorts the king:

> Live *still*, the pleasure of our sight,
> Both our examples and delight.[345]

Salmacida Spolia has been seen as the final gesture of masque flattery: the justification of the king's political isolation and weakness and praise of a Christ-like patience, fortitude in adversity, all at odds with the realities of the political situation.[346] The masque, however, should not be interpreted simply as an endorsement of royal policy. The king was inclined to war. He doubted whether love and enlightened leadership were the best response to rebellion. Davenant does not tell the king what the king was thinking. We recall that in 1640 or 1641 Davenant appealed to the queen to act as an intermediary, to moderate the 'high singleness' – the rigidity of the king.[347] In *Salmacida Spolia* Davenant brings the king and queen together on the stage at Whitehall, to present a powerful example (to them as well as the court) of mutual love and union. The queen's pregnancy added powerfully to the argument for the fruits of love.[348] 'Court sophisters' were telling the king that to compromise, not to fight, was to renounce his kingship. Davenant instead attempts to win him to moderation and reconciliation and presents patience and love, the royal marriage, as the model for Charles's government of his people, as it is for Philogenes in the masque. 'The lastingnesse of government', Davenant was to reflect in the preface to *Gondibert*, 'is the principal work of art.'[349] At

---

[344] *Salmacida Spolia*, lines 451–5; see illustration on p. 207.
[345] *Salmacida Spolia*, lines 475–6 (my italics). The 'both' refers to example *and* delight, and the king *and* the queen, so encapsulating Davenant's point.
[346] Parry, *Golden Age Restor'd*, pp. 199–203; Inigo Jones, I, pp. 72–5; Harbage, *Cavalier Drama*, pp. 175–6.
[347] Above, ch. 2.
[348] Harbage, *Cavalier Drama*, p. 18.
[349] Above, p. 106.

a time in 1640 when government was collapsing, it was a work that certainly needed to be done. Davenant rose to the responsibility: he counselled a policy which might avert conflict and so hoped to demonstrate what he believed, that art might bring men to peace and order. *Salmacida Spolia* was not sycophantic flattery. It was Davenant's most important statement of his own values, offered as advice to the king.

THE CAROLINE COURT MASQUE: SOME RECONSIDERATIONS

If we think of the masque as a form, rigidly defined, in which antimasque is completely transcended by masque, and the entertainment concludes in the revels, we may naturally be inclined to interpret them as statements that rise above any uncertainty and as praise that ascends to apotheosis. The structure and meaning of masques are interrelated. Recently and radically, Professor Leah Marcus has argued that far from being constrained within a strait-jacket of form, the Jacobean masques reveal how the conventional structure, the moment of transformations or unmasking, could be manoeuvred in order to point up doubts and ambiguities. Liberties taken with the structure, she has reminded us, must affect the message of masque. And with this reflection as a starting point, she urged further critical exploration:

Until we have studied the question further, we cannot assert that all masques made use of the form's potential for complexity of statement. But once we recognize that the potential was there, masques can no longer appear to us as fixed and predictable entities . . . Instead they begin to sparkle with tension and nuance and to take on a life of their own, anchored in their occasion and in certain principles of decorum, but free to expand beyond these givens into a new and independent statement about the relation of history to symbol.[350]

As far as the Caroline masques are concerned, these extremely rich suggestions appear to have fallen on deaf ears. At the time of writing, in an essay on the Caroline masque form, Dr Jennifer Chibnall has rehearsed many of the familiar charges against masques, dismissing them as literature and discussing them as evidence of Charles I's withdrawal into a world of fantasy, alone within his control. Significantly, Dr Chibnall has interpreted the Caroline form as characterized by the *complete* eclipse of antimasque by masque, or, more appropriately perhaps, by the transformation from darkness to light.

In the antimasque, the threatening elements are embodied in such a way that they can be defeated, or, more precisely, *obliterated* by the masque vision. Where Jonson

---

[350] L. S. Marcus, 'Masquing occasions and masque structure', *Research Opportunities in Renaissance Drama*, 24 (1981), pp. 12–13. I am grateful to Leah Marcus for several stimulating discussion of this subject.

sought to reconcile the elements, to reorder the disorder and vitality of the anti-masque, the Caroline masque attempts only to contain it.[351]

In the same volume, *The Court Masque*, John Creaser concurs. The threat of the antimasque, he argues, 'is dismissed abruptly and imperiously by the main masque'.[352] It is such assumptions that we have seen are open to question and re-examination. The Caroline masques varied considerably both in form or structure and in their treatment of subject. We must reconsider some of these differences.

The most obvious difference between the masques is that between those presented by the king and those performed by the queen. The masques written for Henrietta Maria, albeit by three different authors, are recognizably distinct from the king's. They lack the long antimasque dialogues that characterize *Albion's Triumph*, *Coelum Britannicum* or *Britannia Triumphans*. As texts they are much shorter – less than half the length. In general they are less successful as texts, more dependent upon visual effects, less literary and less dramatic. The suggestion must be that in the queen's masques, the emphasis was placed on the performance – on dance, music and stage mechanics. It may be that they owed more than the king's entertainments to the influence of the *ballet de cour* of the French court in which Henrietta Maria had spent her childhood. It is unfortunate that we know so little about the development of music and dances of the Caroline masques, for the French ballets provide abundant evidence of the potential for flexibility, for satire as well as eulogy, within the allegories of dance.[353] Without such knowledge the queen's masques appear to modern readers as monochrome and one-dimensional and, in consequence, as simpler statements of unquestioned truths. In the case of the king's masques, by contrast, the structure clearly allowed for considerable freedom and adaptability, evident in text as well as performance. The antimasques are long and complex, often self-conscious discussions of the form of masque itself. They stage a drama which may be transcended by masque, but which introduces, explains and often controls the masque action. In the king's masques, action follows on debate rather than crushing vice and error.

Secondly, as we have detected, in the king's masques in particular, antimasque is not 'obliterated'. It intrudes into the world of masque and may even, like Jonson's, be accommodated within it. We may think most obviously of Momus, who receives the royal commission to judge virtue, or (though not in a court masque strictly defined) of the artisans who invade the stage at the end of *The Triumph of Peace*. Tensions within the Caroline

---

[351] Chibnall, 'The function of the Caroline masque form'; Lindley, *Court Masque*, p. 81.
[352] J. Creaser, '"The present aid of this occasion": The setting of *Comus*', in Lindley, *Court Masque*, pp. 123–4.
[353] See McGowan, *L'Art du Ballet de Cour, passim*.

masques, debates – between Platonicus and Publius for example – are never completely resolved. Nor is the relationship between poetry and spectacle harmonized. In some instances, *Tempe Restored* for example, verse seems to serve the arts of illusion. But in other masques dialogue and poetry resonate with uncertainties that subvert the absolute statements of architecture. Such tensions could profitably be further examined.

Thirdly, we must consider the masque as drama, the direction, the staging, the movement of actors and masquers, the subject of timing, position, entrance, space and so on – subjects normal in the discussion of plays but unexplored for the masque. One obvious example presents itself: the position of the king and queen during the performance of a masque. Critics have drawn attention to this in general. Stephen Orgel has demonstrated the significance of the king's seat as a spectator, placed for the most perfect view of the perspective stage and the most perfect comprehension of the illusion.[354] More important still, in the reign of Charles I, unlike that of his father, the king's place was *on* the stage – as a performer. Dr David Lindley has argued that the change had important repercussions. When the masque was presented *to* the king, it may have a hortatory dimension. When it is presented by him it was difficult to avoid 'the risk of the masque becoming mere self-confirming narcissism'.[355] Whilst the suggestion is fruitful in general, it needs to be worked out in particular. For Charles I performed (apart from joining in the revels) in only half the masques: the others were presented *to* him and *for* him, albeit by his wife. The author of the queen's masques, like Jonson in writing the Jacobean entertainments, could address the king, seated under the state, as does Harmony in *Tempe Restored* or Divine Poesy in *The Temple of Love*. The king and the queen were in the audience for half the Caroline masques and so, in the words of *Albion's Triumph*, took as well as gave advice. Then, of course, even when he presented a masque, the king was not always on the stage. After the main masque dance of *Albion's Triumph*, the king takes 'his seat by the queen' for the rest of the performance. In all masques the valedictory songs are addressed to the king and queen now retired from the stage. Such songs, as we have argued, could proffer counsel to the royal couple, as well as celebration of them. In the case of *Coelum Britannicum*, the position of the king at various moments may well be of significance. We must assume that when Momus delivers his railing parody of royal reform, the king is neither in the audience, nor on the stage, but under it concealed in the rock whence he emerged as the British Hercules.[356] In *Salmacida Spolia*, we have suggested,

---

[354] S. Orgel, 'The royal theatre and the role of king', in G. F. Lytle and S. Orgel, eds., *Patronage In the Renaissance* (Princeton, 1981), pp. 261–73.
[355] Lindley, *Court Masque*, p. 3.
[356] I am grateful to John Peacock for discussions of this question.

the joint performance of king and queen may have underlined Davenant's point. There is more work to be done here. But once we recognize the dramatic significance, of the king's and queen's position for example, we may appreciate the possibilities for dramatic interplay and dialogue between spectators and performers.[357]

Once we begin to think about the masque as drama and performance other questions pose themselves. What was the significance of the location of the Caroline entertainments? Clearly *The Triumph of Peace* which began at Ely House in Holborn was very different for that reason from the court masques staged in the Banqueting House at Whitehall – as were the entertainments presented to the king and queen on progress, at Richmond, at Welbeck and at Bolsover.[358] The Banqueting House was the scene of diplomatic receptions, public dining, audiences, the normal rituals of court life. Clearly the masques held after 1635 in the wooden masquing room built especially for that purpose 'only weather boarded and slightly covered', took place in a very different atmosphere and environment.[359] We can only guess at the scenic, logistic, perhaps most important of all, the psychological differences necessitated or evoked by the different rooms and facilities within Whitehall and the royal palaces. During the 1630s, royal entertainments were held at Somerset House, in the Merchant Taylor's hall, the Great Hall at Whitehall and, if we count *The Triumphs of the Prince D'Amour* (presented to the Elector Palatine and Henrietta Maria in disguise), the Inns of Court, as well as the Banqueting House and masquing room. There was not one, but many stages for the Caroline court.

The modern reader of masques, left with only the text, will ask several other questions.[360] Some will concern the status, preparation and supervision of the text itself and its relationship to the performance. Others, more difficult still, relate to interpretation: the tone of a speech, the conjunction of images, the congruity (or incongruity) of gesture and language (let us not forget the antimasquers were professional actors), the harmony or dissonance of song, the ordered measures or burlesque antics of dance. Were second and third performances revised in the light of their reception?[361] And if so how? Such questions may remain unanswerable. The texts of masques may present more problems than they can yield answers. But such questions should remind us that the form of the masque allowed such diversity of

[357] *Salmacida Spolia* and *Luminalia* name the actors of the antimasque.
[358] See W. Bang and R. Brotanek, eds., *The King and Queenes Entertainment at Richmond* (Louvain, 1903).
[359] Garrard to Wentworth, 9 Nov. 1637, *Strafford Letters*, II, pp. 129–30.
[360] See S. Orgel, 'What is a text?' *Research Opportunities in Renaissance Drama*, 24 (1981), pp. 3–6; T. Berger, 'Textual problems in English Renaissance masques, pageants and entertainments', *ibid.*, 12 (1974), pp. 13–16.
[361] The text of *The Triumph of Peace*, for example, appears to have been prepared before the performance, Bentley, *Jacobean and Caroline Stage*, V, p. 1162.

interpretation. Performance, as we know, can overturn our interpretation of a work read as text. The balance of parts, slightly adjusted, may tilt the meaning the opposite way. The basic structure of the masque may have remained fixed. But within the basic design there was room for contrast, innovation and independent expression. Now, once we suggest that the form of the Caroline masques was fluid, we open ourselves, in Professor Marcus's words, to the nuances and tensions of the entertainment, to its ambiguities and ironies. Once we distinguish, that is, form and treatment of form, we may differentiate general themes and subjects from the interpretation of those subjects by individual authors (and designers, actors, masquers) on particular occasions.

It is customary to regard the masques as political propaganda in general and, in some cases, as the endorsement of particular royal actions and policies. The relationship of masques to historical moments cannot be denied and could be fruitfully studied. *Albion's Triumph* undoubtedly lauds the peace of England and the king's affection for his country at a time when Gustavus Adolphus was the active champion of Protestantism in Germany and Sir John Eliot, imprisoned in the Tower for his activities in the stormy session of 1629, symbolized the king's rule without parliament. *Coelum Britannicum* boasts the moral reformation at court and the proclamations for the better government of the country which were the pride of Charles I after five years of personal rule. In *Britannia Triumphans*, the achievements of the ship money fleet which had, if little else, at least forced the Dutch to purchase licences to fish in English waters, are alluded to both in the references to Britanocles' naval victories and in the representation in scenes of the pride of the royal navy, the *Sovereign of The Seas*, built in 1637.[362] *Salmacida Spolia* obviously condemns the rebellious fury of the Scots and the puritans, and even echoes the king's own language: the Book of Sports licensing Sunday games and the royal proclamations condemning the rebels for using religion as the cloak for rebellion.[363] There are numerous allusions both in scene and in verse to current circumstances or issues – to puritans (in *The Temple of Love*),[364] to the ceremonies of the church (Religion appears in a surplice in *Albion's Triumph*)[365] to St Paul's as the visible symbol of the king's aesthetic and religious values (in *Britannia Triumphans*).[366] But the presence of topical references should not be confused with the uncritical

[362] *Inigo Jones*, II, p. 680.
[363] *Salmacida Spolia*, lines 41–6, 193–4.
    And make religion to become their vice,
    Named to disguise ambitious avarice. (*ibid.*, lines 152–3)
    Cf. 'A Proclamation declaring those of Scotland ... to be Rebels and Traitours to His Majestie', *Stuart Royal Proclamations*, II, pp. 726–8.
[364] *Temple of Love*, lines 273ff.
[365] *Albion's Triumph*, line 352, *Inigo Jones*, II, p. 457.
[366] See illustration on p. 206.

13 *Britannia Triumphans*: Scene VI, A heaven with a citadel, and a large ship that may
be the *Sovereign of the Seas*

endorsement of current policies. Momus, we have seen, refers very specifically to the proclamations of Charles I only to mock them. In *Britannia
Triumphans* the naval achievements are used only as a metaphor for the right
government which, it may be implied critically, was of much greater importance than victories at sea. We know little of the specificity of visual images,
but religion represented with a surplice *and* a book, justice with a sword *and* a
crown, may have been intended to exhort the king to moderation and
reconciliation,[367] as costume might have pointed all too close a connection
between the courtier gallants and the world of antimasque buffoons.[368]

What is more striking, however, than the topical pointers in the masques is
their failure or reluctance, for the most part, to 'sound to present occasions'.
As a historian of the 1630s, I have found fewer close allusions to contemporary events in the texts than one might have expected. Even *Salmacida Spolia*
eschews close engagement with the immediate issues and circumstances of the
Scots war. This may be, as doubtless some commentators would have it,
evidence of the court's deliberate isolation from the political realities of the
reign. But I would suggest rather that the authors of the masques shunned
close or narrow preoccupation with contemporary events, not in order to
escape but rather to engage the larger ethical and political questions of the
age.

The theme of disorder and order in the realm of human passions, society

---

[367] *Albion's Triumph*, lines 348–55, *Inigo Jones*, II, p. 457.
[368] Above, p. 197.

and politics was central to the drama and poetry of the English Renaissance. The uncertainties of an age of social change, economic dislocation, religious flux and intellectual turmoil were exacerbated in England by the dislocation of foreign threats, war and the memory and threat of disputed succession and political instability. If some of these problems had been resolved by the reign of Charles I, there were many and some fresh causes for concern. Between 1625 and 1629 England failed ignominiously to fight wars against France and Spain. Men feared for the future of Protestantism. The king's favourite and minister, the Duke of Buckingham, was impeached and then assassinated. Sessions of parliament proved abortive and (to the king) uncooperative. Charles I was not alone in his sense that the commonweal faced collapse into disorder and that authority faced the challenge of anarchy – of distempered spirits who ate at the very marrow of monarchy and society. To George Wither, who analysed the ills of the realm in his poem *Britain's Remembrancer*, the explanation for England's crisis lay in God's desertion of his chosen nation – a diagnosis shared by many of the king's puritan subjects.[369] To Charles I himself the events of 1625–8, even more the fracas of 1629, appeared like a world of antimasque in which those who knew not how to rule themselves and lacked any understanding of the nature of government subverted the natural order – royal authority, harmony, the union of the king and his people, peace. The king's decision to rule without parliaments and to enact reforms through proclamations was an attempt to impose order on chaos, as the higher perceptions and order of masque transcend the disorder and ignorance of antimasque. In his efforts to reform in church and state, Charles saw himself as re-establishing the stability that was natural in the English polity. Believing, if his proclamations are anything to go by, in the good inclinations of his people when not misled,[370] he hoped through his personal example to lead the realm back to order and virtue, like Britanocles in the masque. If, as a proclamation of 1629 declared, the people came to understand the king, it was not possible that they would not co-operate with him.[371] Charles I hoped to assist them, by his actions, to that understanding.

Such a hope may seem to us naive, the quest for an unrealizable ideal. But we must understand it if we are to comprehend the king – and the masque. And we must also acknowledge that it was a hope shared by intelligent ministers of the king, hard-headed men of practical affairs. Sir Thomas Wentworth, future Earl of Strafford, the 'black Tom Tyrant' of parliament's fears, shared the king's ideal vision of a world of perfect order created by

---

[369] George Wither, *Britain's Remembrancer* (1628).

[370] Charles I early on articulated a belief in a conspiracy by a few seditious hotheads to upset the natural order, e.g. 'A declaration of His Majesties cleare intention, in requiring the Ayde of His loving Subjects . . .', 7 Oct. 1626, *Stuart Royal Proclamations*, II, pp. 110–12.

[371] 'A Proclamation for suppressing of false Rumours touching Parliament', 27 Mar. 1629, *Stuart Royal Proclamations*, II, pp. 226–8.

royal authority and example. He could never understand why what was decreed by royal command was not enacted in fact,[372] could never, that is, understand the gap between discourse and action, or between representations of power and power itself. Momus had mocked a king who confused masque with reality. But when we read the speeches and letters of Wentworth we realize that the vision – or blindness – did not stop with the king. On 15 July 1634, Wentworth addressed the Irish parliament as Lord Deputy on the subject of the late difficulties with those assemblies in England:

This was the spirit of the air that walked in darkness, abusing both, whereon if once one beam of light and truth had happily reflected it, it had passed over as clouds without rain, and left the king far better contented with his people and them much more happy.[373]

Here is the language and vision of masque applied to the realities of politics. Again, in a letter to Laud:

I am confident that the king . . . is able by his wisdom and ministers to carry any just and honourable action through all imaginary opposition for real there can be none.[374]

As the historian S. R. Gardiner said of him, Wentworth was a man prepared to defy 'the sluggishness of men and the very forces of human nature' in order to pursue a goal.[375] His friend William Laud, Archbishop of Canterbury, accused Wentworth of living in 'Plato his commonwealth'.[376] Like Wentworth's own words, the comments of contemporaries and historians evoke the world of masque.

It may then seem that we have come full circle to the old familiar charge: that masque fostered the illusion that because disagreements, doubts and disorder could be transcended by the king on the stage, they could be as easily dispelled from the commonweal. But this is not the conclusion of our investigation. The authors of the Caroline masques we have examined did not share Wentworth's vision. Rather they seem to have been aware of the dangers of the distortions of illusion and to have exposed them. If, as John Creaser has argued, the form of the masque involves transcendence rather than integration, the substitution of ideal visions for reality,[377] then the Caroline masques often subverted that form. They force the ideal to acknowledge and accommodate the real, certainty to face the doubts of debate, Platonicus to deal with and accommodate Publius, the courtiers to remember the artisans who burst upon the stage. The model of government presented in

---

[372] For a perceptive insight into Wentworth's character, see Gardiner, *History of England*, VII, pp. 27–8, 135–8; VIII, p. 36; also C. V. Wedgwood, *Thomas Wentworth* (London, 1961).

[373] Gardiner, *History of England*, VIII, p. 49.

[374] *Ibid.*, VIII, pp. 30–1.

[375] Gardiner, *History of England*, VIII, p. 63.

[376] Laud to Wentworth, 14 Oct. 1633, *Strafford Letters*, II, p. 132.

[377] Creaser, '"The present aid of this occasion"'.

the masque is not that of an abstract authority that obliterates all who do not see its light. The masque represented, through the royal marriage, a politics of reconciliation: the reconciliation of pleasure with virtue, of the king with his people, of freedom with authority. *Salmacida Spolia*, written at the time of the Scots invasion, did not mark a break in the masques. It was the final statement of what the entertainments of a decade had been advocating – a plea to the king not to rule *over* his people by authority, but to rule in conjunction with them, to lead them to virtue and understanding through example and love.[378] Within weeks of the last masque of his reign, Charles prepared *not* for civil war, but for a parliament which, he hoped, might unite him in love with his subjects.

[378] See below, ch. 6.

6

Criticism and compliment: the politics of love

The study of Caroline literature, we have argued, has been obstructed or distorted by preconceptions: by assumptions about the political polarization of the court and the country, about the nature of the court, and about the rôle and position of the poet or playwright who wrote for the court. Such preconceptions and assumptions have led historians and critics to denigrate the literature of the reign of Charles I as limited by narrow concerns and marred by particular, indeed partisan, loyalties. It has been the intention of this study to question the preconceptions concerning the intellectual and political contexts in which the drama and verse were written. It has been our purpose, in other words, not to study the literature from the perspective of political values that we assume or believe to have characterized the court of Charles I, but to examine the poems, plays and masques as vital *primary* evidence for an understanding of political attitudes and ideas in the England of the 1620s and 1630s.

For it is one contention of this study that the literature of Caroline England is a rich source of primary evidence for the political and intellectual history of the period, a source that historians have for long neglected and cannot afford to ignore. The claim for a more serious study of literature as historical evidence could be made, and is now being made, for other periods. But in the England of Charles I, the study of culture takes us to the centre of politics in an age when the boundary between theatre and life, between representation and reality, never as clearly marked or delineated as we sometimes pretend, was all but eroded. Masques were, as we have seen, political occasions. And in Charles I's own character, we may suspect, the distinctions that we make between theatre and life were never firm or clear. If the king's trial and execution reads like a gripping tragedy, it was not least because the rôle was played, for this last time as so many times before, by an experienced actor with a magnificent sense of the dramatic gesture and moment. It did not go

265

unappreciated. For to the courtiers, gentlemen, merchants and even common people of Caroline London, the theatre had become an intrinsic part of urban life. A frequent and sophisticated acquaintance with the playhouse enabled men not only to identify allusions on the stage to contemporary figures, or topical issues;[1] it led them at times to a language, and a perception, of politics and life that also owed something to the theatre.[2] Courtly figures fashioned rôles for themselves to perform on the stage of Westminster and Whitehall; the queen and her ladies garbed themselves as humble folk.[3] Courtier playwrights, such as the Earl of Newcastle, court poets, be they aristocrats such as Lord Percy, or gentlemen of the king's chamber like Carew or Suckling, exemplify a society in which literature and politics inhabited one world and shared a common discourse.[4] To fail to study the politics of the courtly literature of Caroline England, then, is to neglect a powerful voice of the literature of politics – one through which contemporaries at the centre of power articulated important observations on and anxieties about the nature of government.

As we have examined the poems, plays and masques of the three figures who succeeded Ben Jonson as authors of court entertainments, two terms have persistently forced themselves on the centre of our stage: 'nature' and 'love'. Far from the particular concerns of the 1630s or the trivial diversions of the courtly precieux with which the cavalier poets and playwrights were allegedly preoccupied, these words themselves point to an engagement with universal questions in the literature of Caroline England. For through reflection on nature and love man confronts the two fundamental issues of his existence: his interaction with the created world, and his relationship with his fellow man. And through reflection upon these, man is forced to speculate beyond – on the very nature of his own created being as body and spirit; upon his social being as father, husband or lover; and upon his political being as subject, ruler, overlord or client. In the preceding chapters, we have seen how, in different ways, William Davenant, Thomas Carew and Aurelian Townshend examined the problems, and often criticized the values, of their society through their examination of love and passion, of nature and human nature. It is important now for us to return to these common themes.

Since the Romantic movement, the very idea of nature has been associated with an ideal and an escape; and pastoral poetry has evoked idealization, fantasy or dream rather than reality. If we are to understand the significance of the idea of nature in Caroline literature, we must exorcize such conno-

---

[1] See Butler, *Theatre and Crisis*, ch. 6.
[2] See below, p. 296.
[3] See S. Greenblatt, *Renaissance Self-Fashioning from More to Shakespeare* (Chicago, 1980); Bentley, *Jacobean and Caroline Stage*, III, p. 219.
[4] There is a volume of plays and poetry by William Percy in The Huntington Library, MS HM4, 'Wm Percy Comedies and Pastorals'.

tations from our thinking. There is, as we have seen, an ambiguity and contradiction in seventeenth-century usage. Nature, in one sense, described the material world and its phenomena, the natural world, fallen, often wild, disordered and menacing. But in the early seventeenth century, the term was also employed to represent a force, 'the creative and regulative physical power which is conceived of as operating in the material world and as the immediate cause of its phenomena'.[5] To the Christian, that is to almost all early Stuart Englishmen, that force came from God and expressed the original condition of the created universe. As Dante put it in *De Monarchia*, 'Nature is in God as its prime mover'; 'God wills what nature intends.'[6] In this sense, nature prescribed laws to all men, indeed had instilled in man its laws for his moral good. Man had fallen from his perfect created state. But nature, the creative force of the universe, the first lawgiver to man and society, was looked to as the guidance for man and society, as the hope for living well in a degenerate world. In his essay on *The Advancement of Learning* in 1605, Francis Bacon affirmed as one of his principles that 'there are in nature certain fountains of justice, whence all civil laws are derived but as streams'.[7] During the 1630s, in his sermons at Gresham College, the preacher Richard Holdsworth concurred: all moral laws, he pronounced, were founded in nature.[8] Nature for early seventeenth-century England was not only the creative force that regulated and ordered the material world; it enshrined the codes and mores by which man might live rightly and happily in it.

That man did not always live rightly and happily in the material world escaped no one. Nature was conceived as and represented what was ordered, moral, peaceful, harmonious, and good; the material natural world was stained by vice, and torn by chaos and war. But the disjuncture was not regarded as a difference between ideal and reality. Nature, as harmony, peace and good, was not conceived as an idealization, but as a reality. If it was not that reality in which men lived, that was only because men had fallen from perfect nature and had corrupted nature, not because perfect nature was an unrealizable ideal. For nature had endowed men with the potential to inhabit a moral, ordered universe. This belief in an attainable real natural world of 'social harmony, natural fecundity, political peace, economic security and personal happiness' was recurrent in classical literature.[9] Christianity adapted the concept and located it in the garden of Eden, a real (rather than symbolic or metaphorical) location of man's virtue and nature's perfection.

[5] *O.E.D.*
[6] Dante Alighieri, *On World Government. De Monarchia*, ed. H. W. Schneider (Indianapolis, 1949), pp. 25, 53.
[7] Quoted in *O.E.D.*
[8] Kearney, *Scholars and Gentlemen*, p. 86. Cf. Donne, 'All sinne is very truely said to be against nature' (*O.E.D.*). See too A. P. D'Entrèves, *Natural Law* (London, 1960).
[9] Giametti, *Earthly Paradise*, p. 29. Cf. Levin, *The Myth of the Golden Age in the Renaissance*.

For both the pagan classical and Christian traditions, the quest of man in this world was the quest for a return to that state.[10] Man, Dante put it, is ordained for the bliss of eternal life, but ordained too 'for the bliss of this life, which consists in the functioning of his own powers, and which is typified by the earthly Paradise ...'.[11] The quest for nature was not aspiration to an unrealizable ideal, still less the pursuit of a dream; it was striving for the restoration of a reality, of a condition that was literally natural and right for man, or, we might say, both normal and normative. The poetry of nature, pastoral, was not then a poetic of fantasy or escape. It was, as Paul Alpers put it in his study of Virgil's *Eclogues*, a way of engaging reality, and of effecting reality.[12]

Virgil and Horace presented in their verse images of perfect nature as the condition of man's original state from which he had deviated.[13] And the Renaissance disciples of the classical poets followed them in this. Christianity taught that nature had fallen along with man, that the fecundity of paradise had given way to wilderness. But the original state of nature was still an image of perfection. And the poet was of all men the most able to represent that golden age. In what was to become the handbook of English Renaissance poetics, Sidney claimed that the poets 'goeth hand in hand with nature' because poetry represented a perfected nature.[14] And nature, so perceived, was for Sidney the source of moral good and hence the principal subject of the poet's art.

A few decades later, in the axiomatic jottings that encapsulate his own aesthetic philosophy, Ben Jonson came close to saying the same thing. Knowledge of nature was the goal of man and teaching that knowledge was the responsibility of the poet. Nature, Jonson believed, inclined men to understanding its courses, if they would take the pains; virtue was not irrecoverable. Men may have been corrupted, but 'I cannot think *Nature* is so spent, and decay'd, that she can bring forth nothing worth her former yeares. She is always the same, like her selfe ...'[15] For Jonson, as for Sidney, nature was synonymous with what was ordered and good; it was by images of perfect nature that poetry performed its didactic function as the force that might restore man to knowledge and virtue. Vices, in Jonson's drama, are expressions of artifice, of the unnatural. In *Mercury Vindicated from the Alchemists at Court*, Jonson employed alchemy 'to express that deplorable

---

[10] Giametti, *Earthly Paradise, passim*.

[11] Dante, *De Monarchia*, p. 78.

[12] P. Alpers, *The Singer of The Eclogues: A Study of Virgilian Pastoral* (Berkeley, 1979), p. 143.

[13] *Ibid*., p. 241; Giametti, *Earthly Paradise*, p. 42.

[14] Philip Sidney, *An Apology for Poetry*, ed. G. Shepherd (Manchester, 1973), p. 100. For a fuller discussion, see below, pp. 274–5.

[15] B. Jonson, *Timber or Discoveries*, Herford and Simpson *Ben Jonson*, VIII, p. 567; see below, p. 275.

flight from Nature which . . . he saw in the literature and society of his time'.[16] Towards the end of his career when, one feels, his sense of the need for the moral regeneration of society pressed even more urgently, Jonson abandoned the metropolis of his earlier city drama to locate a play, *The New Inn*, in the country. Significantly he refers in the play to an academy in which the nobility might be educated to 'the harmony of nature'.[17] In a life lived according to nature, Jonson believed, man might recover his virtue and the society of man the innocence of its first condition.

It is against this classical, humanist and recent English background that we must understand the preoccupation with nature in the poetry of Carew and Townshend, in the drama of Davenant, and in the masque. To Davenant, as to Jonson, the corruption of society was synonymous with its departure from nature, its concern with artifice and fashion: 'Now nothing is good that is naturall . . . Nothing is fashionable, till it bee deform'd . . .'[18] In Davenant's plays, as we have seen, fashion overturns natural hierarchy and order, subverts language and truth, and perverts normal (natural) human relationships. Men who fall from virtue are shown as having abandoned their very humanity and surrendered their manhood.[19] Only those, like Francis Manners, Earl of Rutland, who live virtuously are seen to have fulfilled themselves and so become 'Nature's selfe'.[20] In *Gondibert*, Davenant made explicit the identification between the good and nature, 'which is the only visible power, and operation of God'.[21] And he attributed so much power to poetry because it embraced the 'general History of Nature' and contained 'the utmost strength and activity of Nature'.[22] Only by a return to nature, the preface to *Gondibert* argues, may man recover himself and society restore its order and peace. In the poetry of Thomas Carew, too, we have seen an identification of nature and reformation. In Townshend's verse an accord with nature is closely associated with man's recovery of himself. From nature, he implies, man may learn how to rule himself and society how to govern itself in peace and harmony.

The preoccupation with nature in cavalier poetry, then, was not the escapist fantasy of a court coterie devoted to frivolous games. Like Milton's insistence on a harmony with nature, the cavaliers' preoccupation exhibits a concern, even an optimism, for the reformation of man and society which is central to an understanding of humanism. And, like Milton's, their concern

---

[16] Barton, *Ben Jonson, Dramatist*, p. 136.
[17] *Ibid.*, ch. 12. I am grateful to Anne Barton for an earlier discussion of this play.
[18] *Timber or Discoveries*, Herford and Simpson, *Ben Jonson*, VIII, p. 581.
[19] See above, ch. 2.
[20] Above, ch. 2, p. 91.
[21] W. Davenant, *Gondibert*, ed. D. F. Gladish (Oxford, 1971), p. 7.
[22] *Ibid.*, pp. 5, 40. Cf. the comment (p. 3) that the heroic poem 'in a perfect glasse of Nature gives us a familiar and easy view of ourselves'.

evidences the responsibility of the poet to effect that reformation – through both representations of the virtue of nature which men might emulate and through criticisms of the artificial values and priorities of society by which men had lost their innocence. Caroline pastoral in drama, poetry and masque was engaged with the loftiest aspirations of Renaissance humanist literature: with didactic counsel and moral prescription.

The principal medium through which that counsel was proferred was the literature of love. Davenant, Carew and Townshend explored through love the nature of man, of society and of government. To argue for the centrality of love in the drama and poetry of our three authors is not to distinguish them as preoccupied with an unusual concern: it is to locate them, or relocate them, in the world of Renaissance humanism. The humanists, as A. J. Smith has recently observed, 'took love for a pattern of our struggle to live well in the world'.[23] Love expressed the perfection of nature and of man's nature. To many sixteenth-century cosmologists, moreover, love was the force that held the entire universe in cohesion and order. Spenser identified political virtue, order in the commonweal, with love; Sidney in the *Arcadia*, like Castiglione in *The Courtier*, described an aristocratic society in which love was a main preoccupation.[24] Like reflection about nature, the discussion of love involved speculation concerning the metaphysical, the ethical and the political condition of man in the universe.

Love more than any other force exposed, indeed exposes, the fundamental ambiguities and poses the existential questions of man's mortal state. Love, like man himself, is particular, temporal, mortal: the poet/lover sings of his Stella or his Celia. But love too is universal and infinite. Through love of a particular woman, man may be raised to experience the sublime force of love in the created world. In Christian belief, he may be brought closer to God: God is love. Secondly, love, like man, may be base, violent, animally sexual, the ultimate expression of the appetite of man unordered by reason or regulation. But love too, like man, could be noble, spiritual. Love, we might say, identified the tensions within, and within reflection about, man and the universe; and love revealed clearly the metaphysical and ethical problems concerning the material corporeal world and the world of spirit. The nature of that relationship was the central concern of ancient and Renaissance philosophy. Though they disagreed about the nature of the symbiosis, Plato and Aristotle both posited a world in which all created entities consisted of particular material substances and universal forms. In the language of Christian metaphysics, the relation between them throughout the created world, as well as in man, was that of the body and the soul.[25] In the natural

[23] A. J. Smith, *The Metaphysics of Love* (Cambridge, 1985), p. 12.
[24] D. Norbrook, *Poetry and Politics in the English Renaissance* (London, 1984), pp. 85–7, 92.
[25] See below, p. 282.

world, the soul was that which framed and ordered matter; in man it was the soul (the reason) that regulated the appetites of the body and instilled a moral sense; in the body politic the prince was, as Jonson put it, summarizing a whole literature of political theory, 'the soule of the Commonwealth'.[26] The soul expressed the order and good of nature. When, then, Jonson and Jones quarrelled about whether poetry or architecture ('painting and carpentry') were the 'soule of masque', they were quarrelling about the capacity of art to express nature and so effect its order and morality.[27] In *Gondibert*, we recall, Davenant described poetry as the 'soul's powder'.[28] The realm of the aesthetic, like the physical and political spheres, consisted of body and soul. Love might express both. Love was a motif through which Renaissance thinkers reflected upon all experience, indeed upon the very nature of being. Discussions about the right mode of love were not merely debates about personal and social morality; they reflected differences in thinking about the nature of the cosmos, of man and of society.[29] Love poetry, far from the literature of a court game, engaged all these questions and problems.

Later we must return to the specific discussions of love in the work of Carew, Davenant and Townshend. For the moment it is important for us to appreciate that the *subjects* that engaged their attention, nature and love, place our authors in the mainstream of Renaissance humanism rather than, as criticism of Caroline literature has tended to suggest, outside the serious concerns of humanist poetics. Whatever the literary merits of their poetry and drama (which now awaits revaluation), the questions and problems they posed and their attempts to answer and resolve them could hardly have been more ambitious. Carew, Davenant and Townshend cannot be comprehended unless we appreciate that they wrote from the fundamental convictions of Renaissance humanism: that, as Dante put it, 'man's basic capacity is . . . a potentiality of power for being intellectual';[30] and that poetry had the power and responsibility to address that potentiality with a view to man's reformation. In Caroline England, poetry was concerned with the rediscovery of the good life: it was a literature of moral philosophy. And because the state existed to make the good life possible, the poet was inextricably involved with politics.

The language of love expressed political as well as moral values. Kings spoke of being wedded to their subjects as suitors addressed their 'sovereign mistress' as vassals. Because right love, self-regulation and good government were all interrelated, it was natural for Ben Jonson to speak of '*Passions*' as

---

[26] *Timber or Discoveries*, Herford and Simpson, *Ben Jonson*, VIII, p. 602.
[27] 'An Expostulačõn wᵗʰ Inigo Iones', *ibid.*, VIII, pp. 402–6.
[28] Davenant, *Gondibert*, p. 18.
[29] See Smith, *The Metaphysics of Love*.
[30] Dante, *De Monarchia*, p. 6.

'spirituall Rebels [that] raise sedition against the understanding'.[31] In a society organized around personal connections, in a commonweal founded upon patronage and clientage, personal relationships were often intrinsically and obviously political, as indeed political relationships were personal. Love poetry had a public and political dimension and must be studied as part of the discourse of politics.[32] And, thus appreciated, it must be studied too as another aspect of the humanist literature of counsel, offered to all men but directed primarily at those of influence and authority in the commonweal.

If the theme of counsel recurs persistently in humanist rhetoric, it was in part because the age of humanism was also the period of the consolidation of the princes' authority. But there were idealistic as well as pragmatic reasons for the address to kings, princes and noblemen. Men still believed that nobility reflected virtue, that the nobles were gifted by nature with a knowledge and understanding denied to others. And princes were regarded as the soul of the commonwealth because, as Cratander (who had compiled a discourse on the soul) in *The Royal Slave* reminds us, in their own persons their soul governed their body and their reason restrained their appetite. True princes ordered their own nature and hence constituted that power which might order others by example.[33] As Jonson put it in *The King's Entertainment at Welbeck*:

> A Prince, that's Law
> Unto himselfe! Is good, for goodnesse-sake;
> And so becomes the Rule unto his Subjects![34]

Kingship, the rule of the soul over the body politic, might lead man back to his earthly paradise. Significantly the term 'paradise' comes from a Persian word meaning a royal park.[35] Experience, of course, showed that not all princes were possessed of the right qualities. And even virtuous rulers could be misled at times by their own appetites, or by the influence of natures less noble than their own. Good counsel then was central to good kingship. Counsel might ensure that the good king was redirected when he was so misled and encouraged when he acted according to the dictates of his own higher nature: counsel, as we shall argue, implied criticism as well as compliment. But whence was good counsel to be taken? Poetry, it was often argued, might

[31] *Timber or Discoveries*, Herford and Simpson, *Ben Jonson*, VIII, p. 564.
[32] The failure to perceive the political in love poetry is one of the consequences of the demarcation as separate spheres of the metaphysical, ethical and political that took place in the later seventeenth century. See Sharpe and Zwicker, *Politics of Discourse*, introduction, and below, p. 274.
[33] This of course is inherent in the symbolism of the equestrian portrait. The emperor on horseback displays not only martial prowess but nature (and his own nature) tamed and regulated.
[34] *The King's Entertainment at Welbeck 1633*, Herford and Simpson, *Ben Jonson*, VII, p. 802.
[35] Giametti, *Earthly Paradise*, p. 11.

offer monarchs the best counsel because poetry distilled the essence of perfect nature. The poet and the prince were, then, in the most literal sense, natural companions. They were both concerned with the regulation of the potential chaos of the material world and of the appetites of man. They were both intent on effecting a reformation of man and the commonweal through images of nature's perfection, of which the good king was the example. The poetry of nature and love did not renege on the public responsibility of the poet: it gave powerful expression to the humanist concept of counsel.

The humanists were concerned not only with man's relationship with nature but with what Douglas Bush termed the harder problem of man's control over himself.[36] For all the different responses to this problem (which cannot be our subject here), its centrality to all *literae humaniores* should not pass without comment. For what perhaps unites all the humanist poets and playwrights is a belief in the *possibility* of a solution, in man's potential for self-regulation and in the restoration of a more perfect commonweal. And it is important to remember that in this sense, for all his puritanism inclined him to stress the sin and depravity of man, Milton belongs among the humanist poets, and should not be separated from them. Milton wrote from the conviction that 'our degeneration from the created state will be made good not when we renounce or transcend our human capacities but when we recover and realize them fully'.[37] And, as his Commonplace Book shows, in the 1630s Milton believed strongly that drama and poetry might, by presenting images of virtue, lead men to that realization and reformation.[38] In *Paradise Regained*, it is the human powers of Christ on which the poet lays his emphasis.[39] To make this point is not to deny the differences that separated Milton from our authors, Davenant, Carew and Townshend. But it is to reinhabit both Milton and them within that common world of Renaissance humanism which is all too often fragmented by those who erect too rigid boundaries of 'court' and 'country', or 'Anglican' and 'puritan'.[40] Like the cavaliers, Milton advocated an ideal based upon a life according to nature; the necessity for human struggle to establish reason's mastery over appetite; the responsibility of princes for the moral reformation of their subjects and kingdoms; and the power of poetry as a force in that regeneration.

In early seventeenth-century England, politics could not be separated from

[36] D. Bush, *Classical Influences in Renaissance Literature* (Cambridge, Mass., 1952), p. 11.
[37] Smith, *Metaphysics of Love*, p. 251.
[38] Cedric Brown, *John Milton's Aristocratic Entertainments* (Cambridge, 1986), p. 130. I am extremely grateful to Cedric Brown for allowing me to see a copy of his text in advance of publication.
[39] Smith, *Metaphysics of Love*, p. 325.
[40] Norbrook has recently drawn the contrast sharply, *Poetry and Politics*, pp. 239ff. I am not convinced, however, that Milton 'undermines the confidence in human self-sufficiency ...' (p. 256), and believe that Norbrook's analysis is affected by such historical assumptions.

metaphysics, religion or morality, nor humanist poetry from politics. Indeed the English civil war, as Steven Zwicker and I have argued elsewhere, was, at least partly, a consequence of an inability to distinguish them. After the civil war, it appears that there was a conscious attempt to do so: metaphysics, ethics and politics begin to be more clearly demarcated. The languages of Scripture and moral absolutism become anathema for politics.[41] Interestingly, as A. J. Smith has recently demonstrated, 'love no longer offered a proving ground for the issues which really confronted people'.[42] The language of love was no longer a recurrent voice of the discourse of politics, as the world of politics began to be marked off as a realm independent from religion and ethics. Already by the time of Pope, a critical appreciation of the cavaliers had become obstructed by such developments. It is important for us to understand that Carew, Davenant and Townshend did not, any more than Milton, look forward to that world. Nor were they merely the last faint tinkle of a voice that had sounded earlier with sonorous authority. Rather they articulated insistently and powerfully the ethical and political authority and responsibility of the aesthetic and of the artist which had been given fullest theoretical exposition in the treatises of Sidney and Jonson.

Sidney maintained that God had made man in his highest capacity capable of understanding nature. But men had not lived according to the light of reason. Man had fallen from the life of nature's happiness and perfection and his fall had corrupted nature. Yet Sidney's sense of man's sin did not entirely negate his humanist belief in man's potential. Man's degeneration did not preclude all possibility of knowledge nor the recovery of a good life. Indeed it was the function of education to lead men back to virtue. Sidney defined the purpose of knowledge in the language of redemption: 'to lift up the mind from the dungeon of the body to the enjoying his own divine essence'.[43] Knowledge of perfect nature was the source of man's moral sense, 'seeing in nature we know it is well to do well'.[44] And the source of that knowledge, Sidney claimed, was to be found in poetry.[45]

The most forceful, his contemporaries might have said the most hectoring, exponent of Sidney's claim was the figure who perhaps best represents the intellectual bequest of Renaissance humanism to England: Ben Jonson. In all Jonson's work, comedy, masque or verse compliment, we may discern the humanist creed that literature should teach men self-knowledge and self-realization, as a means of self-improvement and reformation. At times we might be led to doubt it – to wonder whether a drama in which men cozen each other and fool themselves does not exhibit more cynicism than any belief

---

[41] Sharpe and Zwicker, *Politics of Discourse*, introduction.
[42] Smith, *Metaphysics of Love*, p. 234. I am grateful to Jim Smith for discussions of this subject.
[43] *Ibid.*, p. 104.
[44] *Ibid.*, p. 113.
[45] *Ibid.*, p. 103.

in the possibility of human reformation. But Jonson's scepticism, I would suggest, was not the product of a fundamental doubt about the capacity of man to be taught. Jonson's life's work makes little sense if we ascribe to him such a negative pessimism. Rather Jonson's cynicism emerged from a sharp perception of a reality which he saw as the business of art to engage. Like Machiavelli (many of whose maxims he would have deplored), Jonson took as his starting point men as they were rather than as they could or ought to be. It is precisely man's own acceptance of this reality, his own reality, which is for Jonson the first step to improvement. Self-deception, or language which disguised the reality of men or truths, was what confined humanity to debasement. Language that announced truth could lead to regeneration. But language, as Jonson realized, was often a social artefact, not an expression of the nature of things. And Jonson's pessimism, I would suggest, was a pessimism about *society* rather than about the nature of man. For beneath the social being, deeply corrupted by the vanities of the world, Jonson still discerned an inner virtue which men might cultivate by searching within themselves.[46] Society and fashion were what distanced men from nature and truth: for Jonson, as for Davenant, it was 'pould'ring, perfuming, and every day smelling of the taylor . . .' that deprived man of the nobility of his humanity.[47] And 'wheresoever manners and fashions are corrupted', as he put it, 'language is'.[48] Jonsonian characters, it has been observed, are often satirical portraits of Renaissance aspirations, of social values and vanities which the poet spurned; they become human only when stripped of the accoutrements and 'authorities' which define their place in society – when they come closer to their nature.[49] Compliance with nature is, throughout Jonson's career, the formula for the good life. It is only articulated with more urgency in the later plays – through rural settings, idealistic visions of country life and neo-Elizabethan pastorals – perhaps because Jonson turned from a preoccupation with social vices to be shunned (the city comedy) to presenting a model of life to be emulated.

The fullest and most succinct statement of these beliefs is to be found in Jonson's still little-studied *Timber or Discoveries*. Though it doubtless subsumed the reflections of a working lifetime, it is important to note that *Timber* is a Caroline document, evidently written after Jonson's library burned in 1623, and published only after the author's death in 1641. In *Timber*, Jonson makes explicit his belief in a natural good and the evil of a social existence that has corrupted it. 'There is no doctrine will do good', he

[46] Peterson, *Imitation and Praise in the Poems of Ben Jonson*, p. 71.
[47] *Cynthia's Revells*, 'To the Speciall Fountaine of Manners and The Court', Herford and Simpson, *Ben Jonson*, IV, p. 33.
[48] *Timber or Discoveries, ibid.*, VIII, p. 593.
[49] A. Kernan, *The Cankered Muse: Satire of the English Renaissance* (New Haven, 1959), p. 180.

asserts, 'where nature is wanting . . .'[50] Sophistry and social posing, however,
had inverted truth and nature: 'Now nothing is good that is naturall . . .';
'Nothing is fashionable, till it bee deform'd.'[51] Those who ordered their lives
in accordance with nature could not want for contentment. But society's false
values diverted men from it and condemned them to baseness and misery.
Almost all men had the strength and human resources to secure their own
fulfilment: 'It is a false quarrell against nature, that shee helpes understanding, but in a few; when the most part of mankind are inclin'd by her thither, if
they would take the paines.'[52] But the temptations of the world's vanities
were strong and men were often weak. Like children, men could be distracted
from the true pleasures and riches of the upright life by sensual delights and
attractions: 'They are pleas'd with Cockleshels, Whistles, Hobby-horses, and
such like: wee with Statues, marble Pillars, Pictures, guilded Roofes.'[53] Men
came to knowledge therefore only through personal effort and by means of
instruction that taught them to look beyond the tinselled attractions to the
appetite: 'if we will looke with our understanding, and not our senses, we
may behold vertue and beauty, (though cover'd with rags) in their bright-
nesse'.[54] The senses were not negated or denied in Jonson's thinking. Man, he
knew, was a creature of sense as well as reason, of body *and* soul. But it was
necessary for man to learn to govern his appetite, not be ruled by it.
Knowledge led to the rule of reason, but men could and did come to
knowledge through an appeal made to the sense; pleasure and virtue were not
at odds:

> *Knowledge* is the action of the *Soule*; and is perfect without the *Senses*, as having the
> seeds of all *Science*, and *vertue* in it selfe; but not without the service of the *senses*; by
> those Organs the *Soule workes*.[55]

The responsibility in society for leading men back to nature, to knowledge
lay with the prince. The prince was the 'soul' of the commonwealth who
might lead men to regulate the polity of their own nature. Men owed
obedience to the prince for their own good, not for his. Disobedience to the
ruler was an act of self-abnegation, a denial of one's own creation and
fulfilment: '*After God*, nothing is to be lov'd of man like the Prince: He
violates nature, that doth it not with his whole heart.'[56] But Jonson was
realist enough to accept that men who had not come to knowledge could not
appreciate that their own good lay in obedience to the prince. '*The vulgar*', he
put it, employing now the phrase in its literal sense, 'are commonly *ill-*

[50] *Timber or Discoveries*, Herford and Simpson, *Ben Jonson*, VIII, p. 584.
[51] *Ibid.*, p. 581.
[52] *Ibid.*, p. 619.
[53] *Ibid.*, p. 607.
[54] *Ibid.*, p. 607.
[55] *Ibid.*, p. 588.
[56] *Ibid.*, p. 594.

natur'd; and always grudging against their *Governours*.'[57] As a result, 'the Prince has more busines, and trouble with them, then ever *Hercules* had with the Bull, or any other beast'.[58] Princes required assistance and advice in the difficult task of governing. But their aids and counsellors had themselves to be men of rare and special qualities:[59] 'In being able to counsell others, a Man must be furnish'd with a universall store in himselfe, to the knowledge of all *Nature*.'[60] Such men were those who most closely imitated nature herself, that is painters and poets: 'For they both invent, faine and devise many things, and accommodate all they invent to the use, and service of nature.'[61] Both the literary and visual arts had the service of nature as their end and dedicated themselves to the representation of nature in images for man's emulation. 'Yet of the two, the Pen is more noble than the Pencill. For that can speak to the Understanding; the other, but to the Sense.'[62] It was the poet then who might best aid the prince in the task of government. The poet, Jonson vaunted, could 'faine a *Common-wealth*, ... governe it with *Counsels*, strengthen it with *lawes*, correct it with *Iudgements*, informe it with *Religion*, and *Morals*'.[63]

Poets and princes, in other words, were engaged upon the same work and depended upon each other for their success. It was the prince's duty to heed the poet, for 'A *Prince* without letters, is a Pilot without Eyes.'[64] But without the authority of the prince the poet lacked the position in society from which to impart his counsel. Poet and prince lived then, as had Jonson and James I, in a relationship sometimes tense, sometimes harmonious, but always, as he idealized it, mutually dependent because based upon a responsibility which they shared. The poet had therefore to behave towards the prince with respect and modesty – 'Yet free from *flattery*'.[65] Rather than chide or lecture he was to speak at times 'as the *Prince* were already furnished with the parts he should have'.[66] This was not sycophancy. Compliment, like oblique criticism (and often they were not distinct), was a mode of counsel, directed at persuading the prince to 'take care of the *Common-wealth* of Learning', and to heed its dictates for the reformation of man and society.[67]

Like Sidney's *An Apology for Poetry*, Jonson's treatise on poetics owed most to the predominant influence of Aristotle. The sixteenth century in

[57] *Ibid.*, p. 593.
[58] *Ibid.*, p. 593.
[59] 'The good counsellors to Princes are the best instruments of a good Age', *ibid.*, p. 601.
[60] *Ibid.*, p. 565.
[61] *Ibid.*, pp. 609–10.
[62] *Ibid.*, p. 610.
[63] *Ibid.*, p. 595.
[64] *Ibid.*, p. 601.
[65] *Ibid.*, p. 566.
[66] *Ibid.*, p. 566.
[67] *Ibid.*, p. 592.

Europe witnessed a revival of interest in Aristotelian philosophy after the
fashion for Neo-Platonic ideas had all but monopolized the academies of the
fifteenth century.[68] The Neo-Platonists, especially Ficino, had gone much
further than Plato himself in their emphasis upon the separation of the worlds
of material and form, of sense and spirit. They had little place in their system
for the arts that appealed to the senses or represented, as they regarded it, only
the semblances of things rather than the true reality of the ideas or forms that
lay behind them; Plato, they observed, had banished poets from his Republic.
In Aristotelian philosophy, the relationship of matter and form was one of
integration, not separation: 'it is', he put it in *De Anima*, 'in the sensible forms
that the intelligible forms exist'.[69] Aristotle, and the Aristotelians, laid greater
emphasis upon the unity of nature and of man's human nature, and upon the
interdependence of the body and the soul in the created being: 'in most cases
soul neither acts nor is acted upon apart from body'; 'the attributes of the soul
appear to be all conjoined with body'.[70] Accordingly, Aristotle believed that
the arts which addressed themselves to the sensibility might *thereby* come to
have influence in the soul. Music and dance, he argued in the *Poetics*,
conveyed the rhythms of nature.[71] But the art that most imitated nature was
poetry: 'an expression of the universal element in human life'.[72] Poetry alone
presented in images a purified form of nature through which man might come
to understand it. Poetic images were not mere visions or faint reflections of
reality, as the Neo-Platonists maintained, but a more powerful expression of
reality. Art, and especially poetry, in Aristotelian philosophy, revealed the
perfection of nature to the sense and soul of man and so was efficacious in
fulfilling man's nature in his attainment of virtue and happiness. Aristotle did
not in the *Poetics* develop his ideas about the didactic function of the arts: he
was attempting to separate a theory of aesthetics from morality.[73] But
throughout the treatise he assumes the existence of a man capable of moral
insight; and he takes it as a premise that art may be an influence that 'trains
the moral sympathies, and acts as a curative and quieting influence on the
passions'.[74] Horace went on to state categorically what in Aristotle's *Poetics*
was implied. The purpose of poetry, he declared in the *Ars Poetica*, was 'the
giving of pleasure with some useful precepts for life', or, as he put it more

[68] Smith, *The Metaphysics of Love*, p. 200 and *passim*.
[69] Aristotle, *De Anima*, ed. R. D. Hicks (Amsterdam, 1965), Bk. III, ch. 8, p. 145.
[70] *Ibid.*, Bk. I, ch. 1, Hicks, p. 7. Cf. 'The soul . . . can not be separated from the body,' Bk. II,
ch. 22, Hicks, p. 57.
[71] S. H. Butcher, *Aristotle's Theory of Poetry and Fine Art* (London, 1895), p. 140; Aristotle, *On
the Art of Poetry*, ch. 9, in T. S. Dorsch, ed., *Classical Literary Criticism* (Harmondsworth,
1967), pp. 43–4.
[72] Butcher, *Aristotle's Theory of Poetry and Fine Art*, pp. 140–2.
[73] *Ibid.*, p. 221.
[74] *Ibid.*, pp. 129–30. Aristotle, *Poetics*, *passim*.

tersely, 'profit with delight'.[75] The Neo-Platonists would have doubted the possibility of the combination. They distrusted pleasure as the titillation of the senses and could see no profit to be derived from poets who offered only imitations of shadows of reality. Neo-Platonic ideas were not without influence on English poetry of the sixteenth and seventeenth centuries.[76] But it is clearly the influence of Aristotle and Horace that is more discernible in the handbooks of poetics in the late sixteenth and early seventeenth centuries. And it was the metaphysical, the ethical and the political philosophy that was integral to Aristotle's *Poetics* that most influenced English humanism.

It is impossible to understand the relationship of literature to morality and politics in the English Renaissance without a sense of the relationship within the Aristotelian system of philosophy of the *Poetics*, the *Ethics*, the *Politics*, and the metaphysical treatises *On Nature* and *On the Soul*. As we have seen, Aristotle depicts man as a creature of both body and soul. Part of man's soul springs from the appetite and sense, but part participates in reason.[77] The end of all created beings is their progress towards a greater good, the realization of their nature.[78] The end of man, therefore, is the development of the highest part of his being by which he fulfils his humanity: 'The function of man is the exercise of his non corporeal faculties of "soul" in accordance with . . . a rational principle.'[79] Man had the innate capacity to achieve the perfection of his moral virtue, but he did not always exercise it: 'Nature prepares in us the ground for their reception, but their complete formation is the product of habit.'[80] Men could be misled by the siren pleasure.[81] It was therefore the task of the political philosopher to establish 'the standard by reference to which we are enabled to say whether anything is absolutely good or bad'.[82] In the *Ethics*, Aristotle announced that goodness lay in the middle course between extremes: 'goodness is that quality that hits the mean',[83] manifesting itself in liberality rather than meanness or prodigality. Once the standards of good were established, it was the responsibility of the statesman to make good behaviour habitual: 'What the statesman is most anxious to produce is a certain moral character in his fellow citizens, namely a disposition to virtue and the performance of virtuous actions.'[84]

The prince taught his citizens the good by his example: he exemplified in

[75] Horace, *On the Art of Poetry*, Dorsch, *Classical Literary Criticism*, pp. 90–1.
[76] See Norbrook, *Poetry and Politics in the English Renaissance*.
[77] Aristotle, *De Anima*, Bk. III, ch. 3.
[78] Aristotle, *Ethics*, Bk. I, ch. 1, p. 25.
[79] *Ibid.*, Bk. I, ch. 7, p. 38.
[80] *Ibid.*, Bk. II, ch. 1, p. 55, Bk. III, ch. 4, p. 88, and cf. 'we must be born with an eye for a moral issue which will enable us to form a correct judgement . . .', *ibid.*, Bk. III, ch. 5, p. 92.
[81] *Ibid.*, Bk. III, chs. 4, 5, pp. 88–9.
[82] *Ibid.*, Bk. VII, ch. 2, p. 217.
[83] *Ibid.*, Bk. II, ch. 6, p. 65.
[84] *Ibid.*, Bk. I, ch. 9, p. 44.

himself the mean between too little authority and too much rigour. Because he ruled over men who had the capacity to become moral beings, his government was like that of a father over his children, as indeed the family was the origin of political society.[85] The difference between the ruler and the ruled was that between a rational man and those who had the capacity for reason as yet undeveloped.[86] Such a rule was not that of absolute dictate or cruel repression, but of loving persuasion: 'the rule of mind over body is absolute, the rule of intelligence over desire is constitutional and royal'.[87] The end of the state was the common good of the citizens.[88] So the only good rule was that directed by kindness to the good of the subjects: 'it is clear then that those constitutions which aim at the common good are right . . . while those which aim only at the good of the rulers are wrong'.[89] A right mode of government is monarchy; for doing good defines the business of kingship: 'The tyrant thinks of nothing but his own advantage, the king studies the good of his subjects.'[90] The king guides the intelligence of his citizens with whom he lives in a relationship of 'friendship', and for whom, like a father, he feels 'benevolence'.[91] Because Aristotle's citizens are not mere beasts of appetite (such creatures are nature's slaves),[92] because the government of his state is 'rule over free and equal persons', the ruler's power is not absolute, but limited, not harsh but loving.[93] Its end is not the suppression of men but the realization of humanity. It is less a rule *over* men, than, like the process of education which it is, a government *for* and in conjunction *with* them. Aristotle's prescribed mode of government arises from his metaphysics and his ethics. The *Politics*, like the *Ethics* and the *Poetics*, derives from a belief in the innate good of man and in the potential for its realization. The Christian preoccupation with the Fall did not negate that belief for all that at times, in this as other matters, Christianity and Aristotelianism were reconciled only in uneasy tension. The humanists forcefully reasserted it.

In early modern England, however, the conviction of man's potential for virtue faced two fundamental challenges. One came from puritanism – that is from strict predestinarian Calvinism. Strictly held puritan theology was intrinsically at odds with the humanist belief in man's innate good and potential for reformation. The puritans rigorously maintained that the Fall had stained man for ever and irrevocably with sin. Sinful man stood helpless

---

[85] Aristotle, *Politics*, Bk. I, ch. 12, p. 50.
[86] *Ibid.*, Bk. I, ch. 13, pp. 51–2.
[87] *Ibid.*, Bk. I, ch. 5, p. 33.
[88] 'The good life is indeed the chief end of the state both corporately and individually,' *ibid.*, Bk. III, ch. 6, p. 114.
[89] *Ibid.*, Bk. III, ch. 7, p. 115.
[90] Aristotle, *Ethics*, Bk. VIII, ch. 10, p. 246.
[91] *Ibid.*, pp. 248–9.
[92] Aristotle, *Politics*, Bk. I, ch. 5, p. 34.
[93] 'The government of a state is rule over free and equal persons,' *ibid.*, Bk. I, ch. 7, p. 37.

before the omnipotence and judgement of God. From the beginning of time, the puritans believed, God, who foresaw and forewilled all things, had ordained that certain men should be elected to eternal life while the rest of mankind was damned by sin to reprobation. In strictly held Calvinist theology, there was no possibility for men by their own human effort to hear the gospel and come to grace. Salvation was the exclusive gift of a munificent God to his elect. Even assiduous reading of Scripture and godly recreation and life could not be efficacious in winning eternal life; such activities were the signs, but they could not be the causes or means of election. It was then in their premises about the nature of man, rather than over issues of morality, that the puritans and humanist poets were divided. This is not to argue that all those we call puritans were antagonistic to the arts.[94] But it is to recognize that the logic of puritan theology precluded the didactic function of the arts in the regeneration of man claimed by the apologists for poetry. Jonson's attitude to humanity and to poetry, more than his Catholicism, distanced him from the puritans. If Milton appears to stand as an exception to such an argument, it is, as we have seen, because his humanist convictions never surrendered to the logic of his religious beliefs, but cohabited with them at times, one senses, in uneasy tension.[95]

The authors we have examined appear unsympathetic to the puritans: Davenant's irritation with the hypocrisy of the 'Geneva band' is obvious in *The Wits*.[96] But the quarrel is more fundamental than an irritation with hypocrisy. For a central premise of Davenant's drama, like Jonson's, is the possibility of man's improvement. During the 1620s and 1630s, Davenant adhered to a belief that man was a creature of reason. In the preface to *Gondibert*, he writes: 'we must side with reason, according to our duty, by the law of Nature; and Nature's law . . . hath taken deep impression in the heart of man'.[97] Thomas Carew's poetry exhibits too an optimism in man's capacity for reformation. The most direct rejection of puritan theology, however, comes from Aurelian Townshend. Townshend appears to have specifically denied the doctrine of original sin and to have refuted the belief that when men 'Maie doe amisse . . . they doe'. The world, he argues as if in debate with the puritans 'is not so full of sin'.[98] Those who strive to live morally need not fear that they will fall. The Caroline poets and playwrights replied to the puritans by a powerful reassertion of the humanists' creed.

In Caroline England that creed faced another challenge: the philosophy

[94] See above, ch. 1, pp. 11–13.
[95] Cf. these remarks with Smith, *Metaphysics of Love*, pp. 141ff, and Brown, *John Milton's Aristocratic Entertainments*, p. 82.
[96] Above, ch. 2.
[97] Davenant, *Gondibert*, pp. 36–7.
[98] 'Hide not thy love', Brown, *Poems and Masques of Aurelian Townshend*', pp. 34–7. See above, ch. 4, pp. 165–6.

and politics of Neo-Platonism. Neo-Platonic metaphysics, like Aristotelian metaphysics, implied an ethical and political system.[99] Platonic love, the expression of Neo-Platonism fashionable at court, was founded upon attitudes to human nature, and prescribed a mode of government. The doctrine of Platonic love did not deny man's capacity for improvement: the attainment of Platonic love represented man's realization of his highest capacities, his elevation to knowledge and an understanding of the reality of forms. But Platonic love involved *not* the reconciliation of the sensual, corporeal nature of man with his rational soul, but the abnegation of the senses, the suppression of the appetite. Platonic love was the love of minds, not of minds *and* bodies. In the body politic, the constitution of Platonic love was that of the absolute rule of the king, as the soul of the commonwealth, over creatures inhabiting a world of sense and illusion.[100] In the polity of Platonic love the problem of the regulation of the baser expression of human nature, of passion and appetite, was resolved by either the suppression or the transcendence of those facets of human nature.

It is, I would suggest, the metaphysics and politics, rather than merely the fashion of Platonic love to which Carew, Davenant and Townshend took exception. Each of them, like Aristotle, perceived human nature as an entity consisting of body *and* soul, physical *and* spiritual attributes, both of which must be integrated not denied. As Jonson put it, by the senses 'the *Soule workes*'.[101] A different attitude to love exemplified this metaphysics. Sexual love, our authors concur, could express either the base or loftier attributes of man's nature. But man was fulfilled as a human being only when both were reconciled. To deny, abnegate or suppress the physical appetites of man was to limit his nature. To Carew only 'fooles' adored the 'mystique' charms of a mistress to the neglect of her body's delights.[102] Carew's poetry sees both the sensuality and spirituality of man, the need to integrate not separate them, and right love as that which gave expression to both in perfect harmony. Carew understood that appetite must be ordered, but he knew too that it must not be suppressed:

> For the sense not fed, denies
> Nourishment unto the minde.[103]

No less the language of Townshend's poetry, like Carew's, is rich in images of

---

[99] See Orgel and Strong, *Inigo Jones*, I, ch. 4.

[100] We recall Aristotle's comment, 'The rule of mind over body is absolute,' above, p. 280.

[101] *Timber or Discoveries*, Herford and Simpson, *Ben Jonson*, VIII, p. 588, cf. the explicitly political analogy made by Bishop Joseph Hall: 'Every Man hath a Kingdom within himself. Reason as the princess dwells in the highest and inwardest room: the senses are the Guards and attendants on the court, without whose aid nothing is admitted to the Presence ... violent Passions are as rebels...', *The Works of Joseph Hall* (3 vols., London, 1628), I, p. 14.

[102] Above, ch. 3, pp. 116, 139.

[103] 'Separation of lovers', lines 21–2, *Poems of Carew*, p. 62.

sensuality, fertility and reproduction, underlining the physicality of man and of sexual love, and the nobility and naturalness of such sensuality that was denied by the Platonists. To Davenant, Platonic love was an empty abstraction, a sterile denial of humanity. Most men, he knew, like himself, could understand only 'warme contaction' and 'reall sight'.[104] In *The Temple of Love*, he did not, or could not, mask his antagonism to the cult. Queen Indamora and her Platonic band carry 'frozen winter in their blood'.[105] They lack human warmth and life. Practising generation not of bodies but only of souls, they appear an unnatural 'sect' who, defying nature, will soon be extinct.[106] In devoting an entire play to the subject of Platonic love, however, Davenant exhibited a concern far greater than that merited by a fashionable cult soon to expire. The concern of all our authors went beyond that. For Platonic love, as Davenant put it, had become a 'faith' at court – a faith that dimmed the light of reason, and challenged a premise of humane learning.[107] It was a faith too that the court had substituted for the responsibility of all art (and especially courtly literature and entertainment) to instruct. Platonic love to Davenant symbolized the court's failure to fulfil the function of government prescribed in Aristotle's *Ethics*: to lead men to understanding through the force of example and argument which appealed to their reason.

Platonic love represented a mode of government which our authors appear to have found objectionable. In the *Ethics*, Aristotle had outlined clearly the logical connections in Platonic philosophy between metaphysics and politics, and the style of government consequent upon a view of human nature which rigidly separated the body and soul. Such a polity was to Aristotle a perverted form of constitution, a tyranny:

in the perverted constitutions friendship ... goes but a little way ..., for under a tyranny there can be little or no kindness between ruler and ruled. They have nothing in common, so there can be no friendliness between them, just as there can be no justice. The relations between them are those *of the skilled workmen to his tool, or of the soul to the body.*[108]

The passage, I would suggest, evokes some of the anxieties about government that we have seen expressed by our authors. Does not Davenant suggest that the king and his people are not sufficiently united in love and friendship? Did not Carew in his poem upon the romance of the Lord Chief Justice imply, what Aristotle argues in the *Ethics* and *Politics*, that justice was a relationship between free men who were ruled by love not rods?[109] Have we not

---

[104] Prologue to *The Platonic Lovers, Works of Davenant*, II, p. 6; 'To I.W. Upon the death of his Mistresse', lines 47–8, Gibbs, *Shorter Poems*, p. 49.
[105] *The Temple of Love*, line 189, *Inigo Jones*, II, p. 601; above ch. 5, pp. 244–6.
[106] *The Temple of Love*, lines 191–3.
[107] Above, ch. 2, pp. 71–2, ch. 5, p. 245.
[108] Aristotle, *Ethics*, Bk. VIII, ch. 2, p. 249 (my italics).
[109] *Ibid.*, Bk. V, ch. 6, p. 156, *The Politics*, Bk. III, ch. 9, pp. 118–19.

heard Aurelian Townshend assert that sunburnt breasts contained as noble
hearts and natures as the snowy breasts of courtly ladies?[110] Did not *The
Triumph of Peace* criticize a court which subordinated the people as
creatures to be ordered rather than citizens for whose good government
existed, and a court culture, the masque, which here literally ranked the
artisans who made it possible as mere tools wielded by a higher intellect?[111]
We have seen that in the queen's masque that most enshrined the court's
philosophy, Davenant aired his reservations about Platonic love. In a later
masque for the king he subjected it again to critical examination. Let us recall
the debate between Imposture and Action that opens *Britannia Triumphans*,
performed in January 1638. Imposture presents a view of men as creatures
who are slaves to their senses. The masque does not address them because
they are incapable of comprehending the forms which it realizes. Such men,
he argues, have no place at court; they are subjects to be ruled over by a higher
authority and understanding. Action, the personification of Aristotelian
virtue, questions this cynical view of human nature. He grants that many are
creatures of appetite, but rejects the assumption that men 'were born only to
aim at trifles . . .'[112] Men have the capacity for reason, and some will exercise
it, all may. It is therefore for rulers to assist in educating them, and for court
culture to accept this responsibility, not to neglect them. Pleasures of the
sense, Action goes on to explain, should not themselves be disdained. For
images of nature made attractive to the sense might lead men to understanding and reason. Poetry, in other words, as Horace, Sidney and Jonson had put
it, reconciled pleasure with profit. It was the king's responsibility, like
Bellerophon in the masque, to present and represent such an image, rather
than the empty noise of knackers and bells that comprise antimasque or, at
the other extreme, the little comprehended faith of 'sullen clerks'. Platonic
love, no less than untutored sensuality, is an Imposture which, like the figure
of that name, denies reason and virtue. The masque urges a more optimistic
perception of human nature and that Action which might truly lead men to
reason by whose government 'every act be squared by virtue's rule'.[113] The
action that concludes the masque is love, physical coupling, sexual union
'renewed and bettered every night'.[114] The final song is a celebration of
integrations of body and soul, pleasure and virtue, the king and his people,
not the abstract intercourse of minds of Platonic love.

Davenant, like Carew and Townshend, rejects the metaphysics, ethics and
politics of Neo-Platonism in his critique of Platonic love. But if, as our

---

[110] Above, ch. 4.
[111] Above, ch. 5, p. 218.
[112] *Britannia Triumphans*, lines 131–2, *Inigo Jones*, II, p. 663.
[113] *Ibid*., line 183; cf. ch. 5, note 248.
[114] *Ibid*., lines 627–44, *Inigo Jones*, II, p. 667.

authors appear to have believed, Platonic love suppressed man's senses, denied his body and part of his nature, it was just as clear to them that human appetites and passions could not be given free rein. Licence and lust meant the dissolution of all morality, the debasement of man himself to the condition of a slave, the subversion of all political order, in sum the rejection of the laws of nature. Wherein then lay a course in love between unbridled appetite and passion and an inhuman denial of man's physical nature, or in politics between anarchy and tyranny? Wherein might be found that integration of all parts of human nature, that reconciliation of body and soul in harmonious order so that 'every act be squared by virtue's rule'? In the *Ethics*, we recall, Aristotle had postulated that virtue was 'the quality that hits the mean'. In the *De Monarchia*, Dante had argued that human nature stood at the centre of a spectrum which ran from the corruptible corporeal world to the incorruptible realm of spirit. Man, he maintained, is 'a kind of mean between the corruptible and the incorruptible, like every mean, he partakes of the nature of extremes'.[115] The mean, the virtue of human nature, as all else, was that course 'opposed to both extremes'.[116] I should like to suggest that it was the course for man's ethical and political condition advocated by our authors.

The tenet that the right course lay in the mean would have been the common heritage of any who had received a university education founded on Aristotle. In more popular discourse the idea may well have been expressed in the familiar wisdom of proverb.[117] But it is perhaps of interest that each of our authors alludes specifically to the doctrine. For example, in his epilogue to a play presented to the king and queen at their entertainment by the Lord Chamberlain at Whitehall, most probably in 1633, Carew argued that

> The pleasure lyes, not in the end, but streames
> That flowe betwixt two opposite Extreames.[118]

In the masque *Coelum Britannicum*, as has been observed, 'the Aristotelian conception of virtue as a mean lying between the extremes of vice determines Carew's selection of antimasque figures'.[119] Wealth and Poverty are both denied their place in the stars. Davenant appears to make specific visual allusion to the axiom. In the course of his drama, he suggested that

---

[115] Dante, *De Monarchia*, p. 78.
[116] Aristotle, *Ethics*, Bk. II, ch. 8, p. 72.
[117] See Filippo Picinelli, *Mundus Symbolicus* (Cologne, 1694), ed. A. Erath (2 vols., New York, 1976), I, pp. 153–4, 167.
[118] *Poems of Carew*, p. 127. Carew had read Aristotle's *Ethics, ibid.*, p. 247.
[119] Parker, '"Comely Gestures"', p. 88. See above, ch. 5, pp. 239–40.

philosophy had scarcely advanced since its greatest teacher, Aristotle.[120] And we have suggested that in the masque *Britannia Triumphans*, Action appears to defend views of human nature and the power of the aesthetic that echo Aristotle's *Ethics* and *Poetics*. It is significant, then, that Action is described as wearing a belt on which is emblazoned in silver letters the motto *Medio Tuttissima*, the middle course, the mean, is the safest way.[121] Action's emblem may also be the summation of his counter argument to Imposture: there is a mean to be found between total cynicism and naive optimism about human nature, and a middle polity between anarchy and repression. In that middle course lay the good of man and of the commonweal. It was in a specifically political context that Aurelian Townshend had occasion to echo the doctrine that the mean was the best course. For the occasion was the advice he gave to his daughter at the time of her affair with Charles Louis, the Elector Palatine, in 1640, at a time too when the best mode of government was a contentious question. It is appropriate here to remind ourselves of the verse in which the poet counselled his daughter how to conduct herself as a monarch of love's commonwealth:

> A State in evry princely brow
> As decent is required,
> Much more in thyne to whom they bow
> By Beauty's lightning fired.

> And yet a state so sweetly mixd
> With an attractive mildness,
> It may like Vertue sit betwixt
> Th' extremes of pryde and vildness.[122]

Townshend's language prescribed the middle course between two little and too much authority for *both* love and government.[123] For government, like love, was, as Aristotle put it, rule over 'free and equal persons'.

But wherein lay the mean? In the polity of love, as we have seen, our authors advocated a middle course between unregulated passion and the suppression of man's natural appetite. At times they looked to marriage as the

---

[120] *Fredeline:*
> Since your great Master Aristotle died,
> Who fool'd the drunken Macedon out of
> A thousand talents to buy books, what have
> The multitude of 's learned successors done?
> Wrote comments on his works . . .
> . . . Have you so many ages toil'd
> T' interpret what he writ in a few years?
> (*Platonic Lovers*, Act III, Scene I, *Dramatic Works*, II, p. 56).

[121] *Britannia Triumphans*, lines 63–70, *Inigo Jones*, II, p. 662.

[122] 'Let not thy beauty', Brown, *Poems and Masques of Townshend*, p. 67; above, ch. 4, p. 169.

[123] We may note here that in *The Alchemist* the whore Doll Common refers to herself as a republic, the political extreme that expresses the anarchy of her sexual morality.

course by which body and soul, passion and love are reconciled in society. The physical and spiritual union with another in matrimony is presented by Davenant and Carew as the resolution of a moral dilemma and as the means by which man may recover innocence. Marriage in the words of the *Book of Common Prayer* was 'instituted of God in paradise in the time of man's innocency'; it was 'ordained for a remedy against sin'.[124] In the *Ethics*, Aristotle describes marriage as an expression of nature and hence of the good: 'The love between husband and wife is evidently a natural feeling, for Nature has made man . . . a pairing animal'.[125] Since the state emerges from the family, being too a natural creation, love and marriage may be said to imply too a political as well as a personal relationship.[126] Marriage, then, might describe or represent the virtuous middle course in politics as in ethics.

Marriage was not only a common concern of our authors, it appears to have become a topical subject of the literature of the 1620s and 1630s. Anne Barton has recently drawn attention to Jonson's new concern with marriage in his late plays – *The New Inn*, for example, or *The Magnetic Lady*, which concludes with three marriages – and suggests that in the late 1620s and 1630s Jonson had become nostalgic for the romance of Elizabethan drama.[127] Professor Barton is sceptical about attempts to read *The New Inn* as a parody of Neo-Platonism, a cult which, as she argues, was perhaps still an uncontaminated ideal in 1629. Lovel's definition of love in the play, she reminds us, draws upon Plato's *Symposium* and advocates a union of 'two soules' celebrated in masque, and indeed in Jonson's last two entertainments for the court.[128] And yet, as Professor Barton acknowledges, Lovel has his critics in the court of love, one of whom, Beaufort, spurns 'these philosophicall feasts; / Give me a banquet o' sense.'[129] In the end the resolution of this disagreement lies in the middle course between them. Lovell himself comes to marriage, as indeed the host and Irish nurse of the inn are reunited in their marriage. Love and marriage are the forces of order and of hope in the society of the inn, and characters outside them seem subhuman, and appear unnatural. Multiple marriages provide the conclusion to the discussions and games of the 'court of love' set up at the inn; and it is, undoubtedly, a happy ending.[130] In his later plays, Jonson shows a concern with the idea of community as well as with marriage. In the *Tale of a Tub* he depicts a rural community at Tottenhall, as a model, in Anne Barton's words, of the capacity of people to 'communicate with each other as individuals, and their aware-

---

[124] *The Book of Common Prayer 1559*, ed. J. E. Booty (Washington, D.C., 1976), pp. 290–1.
[125] Aristotle, *Ethics*, Bk. VIII, ch. 12, p. 251.
[126] Aristotle, *Politics*, Bk. I, chs. 1, 2.
[127] Barton, *Ben Jonson, Dramatist*, pp. 259, 281, 290.
[128] *Ibid.*, pp. 264–5.
[129] *Ibid.*, p. 265.
[130] *The New Inn*, Herford and Simpson, *Ben Jonson*, VI.

ness of mutual dependence and solidarity as a community'.[131] Marriage and community carried political implications. A quarter of a century earlier, in his wedding masque for the Earl of Essex, Jonson had taken the occasion of the marriage to present the removed mystery of political union (and to allude too to that union of Britain so dear to James VI and I in 1606).[132] Marriage stood for him as a constitution as well as a personal relationship. And we may begin to see clearly that it did so for others. Fulke Greville's objection to Platonic love conveyed political criticism. To Greville, love meant 'a relationship of equals . . . based on a clear idea of mutual obligation'.[133] In his essay *Of Reformation*, Milton listed the marriage bed as one of those institutions or customs in which 'well knows every wise Nation that their *liberty* consists . . .'.[134] As that which reconciled the appetites and reason of man, integrated the body and soul, regulated but did not suppress human passions, marriage offered a virtuous mean between licence and a too sterile ordering of human nature. And as the relationship of 'free and equal persons' who had regulated their own appetites, it prescribed a model polity.

In previous chapters we have seen how marriage represented a political relationship. In *The Fair Favourite*, a searching study of kingship, Davenant depicts a monarch dethroned and unmanned by passion, who recovers both his humanity and regal authority only through right love in marriage.[135] Good government, in Davenant's drama, is not oppressive or harsh; it is founded upon mutual love. In 1640, in his poem to Henrietta Maria, it was Charles I's 'high obnoxious singleness' that Davenant identified as the obstacle to a settlement between king and parliament. And it was to the queen – the king's wife – that Davenant appealed for a solution to the problem.[136] Marriage was the ultimate relationship of equals in love. Accordingly the queen might counsel her husband to change his policies without arousing any suspicion that she wished to compromise his authority. And their relationship too might form the basis of that change of policy: towards a polity of community and mutual love. Love, as Thomas Carew described it in his poem on the romance of Chief Justice Finch, might soften authority and substitute for the dreadful rods of harsh rule the mild courses of love's prescription. Such a government, founded upon love rather than coercion, would win 'loyal hearts', which lovers enjoyed.[137] The people, Townshend reminded his

[131] Barton, *Ben Jonson, Dramatist*, p. 336.
[132] *Hymenaei, Inigo Jones*, I, pp. 105–14; cf. *Ben Jonson Poems*, ed. Ian Donaldson (Oxford, 1975), p. 9 and n.
[133] Norbrook, *Poetry and Politics in the English Renaissance*, p. 165.
[134] 'Of Reformation', *Complete Prose Works of John Milton* (5 vols., New Haven, 1953–71), I, p. 588.
[135] Above, ch. 2.
[136] 'To the Queen', line 11 (my italics); Gibbs, *Shorter Poems*, p. 139; see above, ch. 2, pp. 98–9.
[137] Above, ch. 3, p. 142.

king, were not 'beasts' or servile creatures from whom a ruler should look for love 'custome free'.[138] Government, as Aristotle and Dante had argued, was a reciprocal relationship for the common good; its constitution framed for the mutual good promulgated the laws of love. Love's kingdom, we recall Townshend told his daughter, was a mixed polity, 'sweetly mixd', 'with an attractive mildness'.[139] Such a mode of government too, Townshend suggests in 1640, might restore love between the king and his people. Like Jonson and others, Carew, Davenant and Townshend counselled by means of the drama and poetry of love a politics of integration and reconciliation, a reconciliation founded on mutual dependence and reciprocal love.

The preface to *Gondibert* offers the clearest statement of this argument. In *Gondibert* ethics and politics, the private and public realms, love and government are integrated and inseparable realms, partaking of a common discourse. The commonwealth about which Davenant writes exists like Aristotle's for the good of its citizens. It derives its coherence from 'an universall communion of bosoms', from love.[140] The men who are its citizens are creatures of both body and soul, appetite and reason. Their nature inclines them to reason, but that nature is often corrupted. Government, then, is necessary in order to regulate men's passions. Power belongs to those of Nature's chosen, who are endowed with virtue; their duty is to persuade others to realize their potential for goodness. Their rule is for the good of the citizens, but not all men will appreciate it. Those most subject to their baser appetites are likely to resent an authority that, as they see it, restrains them: 'and so the State and the People are divided, as we may say a man is divided within himselfe, when reason and passion ... dispute about consequent actions.'[141] Lust, the corruption of love, Davenant takes as the expression of these baser natures and of their anarchic resistance to government.[142] Lust required regulation and firm rule. But despite the experience of civil war, Davenant did not abandon the belief, more strongly held during the 1620s and 1630s, that men were not necessarily slaves to appetite, nor beyond hope of reformation. As a consequence he retained his commitment to moderate government based upon the mutual dependence of ruler and ruled. Reason and love, he believed, were united: love showed men the way to reason. Kingship was a government of gentle, loving persuasion directed at appealing to man's rational faculty, in the hope that men may be led by example to virtuous habits and self-government. Such a rule Davenant described as akin to the condition of marriage:

---

[138] 'When we were parted', line 8, Brown, *Poems and Masques of Townshend*, p. 61.
[139] Above, p. 286.
[140] Preface, *Gondibert*, p. 10.
[141] *Ibid.*, p. 36.
[142] *Ibid.*, p. 13.

and then when the minde is conquer'd, like a willing Bride, Force should so behave it selfe, as Noble Husbands use their noble power; that is by letting their wives see the Dignity and prerogative of our Sex . . . continually maintain'd to hinder Disobedience rather than rigorously impose Duty . . .[143]

After the upheavals of the 1640s, Davenant could not be blind to the difficulty of that task. But his awareness of the difficulty served to sharpen his sense of the power and responsibility of poetry to assist in the business of government:

to such an easy government, neither the People (which are subject to Kings and States) nor wives (which are subject to Husbands) can peacefully yield unless they are first conquer'd by Vertue; and the Conquests of Vertue be never easy, but where her forces are commanded by Poets.[144]

The force of poetry could be mightier than troops used by rulers in conquering men's minds. Love poetry might restore the peace and harmony of government. Davenant practised what he advocated. In the preface to *The Siege of Rhodes*, performed in 1656, he described his story as 'intelligibly convey'd to advance the characters of Virtue in the shapes of Valour and *conjugal love*'.[145] Those characters of virtue in shapes of conjugal love had graced Davenant's stage throughout the 1630s, because the poet had always offered assistance to the prince. And it was the duty of kings worthy of the title, bent on ruling for the common good, to heed the poet's counsel – albeit it was counsel proferred at times through criticism as well as praise.

THE POLITICS OF CRITICISM

In the drama and poetry of Davenant, Carew and Townshend we have detected a tone of criticism as well as the voice of praise. Our authors pilloried the court for obsession with ridiculous and unnatural fashion, for disimulation, for ambition and intrigue and for advancing corrupt men and factions dedicated to their own ends rather than virtuous men dedicated to the common good. The culture of the court, they suggest, confused action and illusion and so failed to fufil its purpose: the representation of images of virtue. Most importantly, in the court literature of the 1630s there are hints and implications that the king himself is unduly cynical about human nature, about his subjects, and that he is thereby inclined to a too authoritarian mode of government, and that his own masques and entertainments had failed to be what Jonson had declared they should be: 'mirrors of man's life, whose ends . . . ought always to carry a mixture of profit with them no less than

---

[143] *Ibid.*, p. 39; Bk. I, Canto II, verse 19, 'I that Love and Reason thus unite'.
[144] *Ibid.*, p. 39.
[145] 'To the Reader', *The Siege of Rhodes, Dramatic Works*, III, p. 235.

delight'.[146] Such comments echo other criticisms by contemporaries which have been identified by historians as expression of 'country' opposition to the court. Were not the vanities of the court, the corruption of court politics, the selfish machinations of favourites, the failure to prescribe a model for moral conduct, the charges levelled by those of the country? And have not historians and critics described the entertainments of the court as narrow and exclusive, an escape from the reality of politics into a world of illusion? Did not Sir Simonds D'Ewes criticize Charles I for elevating his will and prerogative above the law?[147] Did not Milton upbraid the court for its failure of civil and spiritual leadership and subject its values and its culture to critical examination in *Comus*?[148] Because our answers to such questions are in the affirmative, we may begin to reflect whether the distance between our authors and these others, between Carew and Milton for example, is as great, or the divide between court and country as wide a gulf, as is usually supposed. The equation of the court with sycophancy cannot stand; criticism, we have now seen, was articulated insistently from *within* the court as well as from outside.

How, some may be prompted to ask, could this be? How could the court poets and playwrights of Caroline England reconcile criticism with their positions as court retainers and with their duty to praise? And how could they voice criticism from within the forms of those very literary genres, verse compliment or masque for example, which had their raison d'être in encomium of the king and the court? Such questions come naturally to us, but they would have appeared artificial problems to Carew, Davenant and Townshend because they reflect assumptions and polarities common to the twentieth-century mind but not to that of the Renaissance. Let us begin with the position of the courtier and the meaning of patronage. We think immediately of a political allegiance (even a party affiliation) and a position of fawning dependency. But in early seventeenth-century England the court was not a party; it was the focus of all politics. And patronage describes not a condition of servility, but all social and political relationships, relationships of *mutual* dependency. To be a courtier or to receive court patronage was not to be a propagandist for a policy.[149] The court in Caroline England, as we have seen, contained a wide spectrum of political attitudes and ideas in matters of religion, domestic and foreign affairs. And those at court, as well as those outside in the country, shared a belief that the court ought to set moral standards and govern for the good of the realm.[150] It was the responsibility of counsellors, they agreed, that the king and his ministers ruled virtuously.

---

[146] B. Jonson, *Love's Triumph through Callipolis*, lines 1–5, *Inigo Jones*, I, p. 405.
[147] Butler, *Theatre and Crisis*, p. 21.
[148] Brown, *Milton's Aristocratic Entertainments*, p. 73 and *passim*.
[149] It is important to recall here the important article by Smuts, 'The failure of Stuart cultural patronage'.
[150] Above, ch. 1.

Membership of the court, still less attachment to the court, did not negate the possibility of criticism. The very idea of free, loyal counsel implied criticism. Criticism and loyalty were not in conflict. They were both a duty of counsel.

Nor were criticism and praise necessarily opposites or irreconcilable polarities. Rather, they were both strategies of counsel, directed to the common end of persuading princes to the best government. In Carew and Davenant as in Jonson we have seen (what Parry and others have denied) that praise is often also exhortation – what the king or a mistress is said to be is what he or she ought to be; the present indicative of the verb is hortatory as well as celebratory. Praise was the discourse of address in making suits, be they amorous or political, but the discourse of praise could be deployed as a vehicle of criticism. Praise should not be confused with flattery. Flattery involves misrepresentations: of the flatterer, of the patron and of the truth. It presents its idealizations as synonymous with the real person or action lauded. But the encomium of humanist poetry praises the ideal as a standard to which the recipient of the address *should* aspire.[151] It presents images of perfect nature as an inducement to the realization of a perfected nature. The poets did not in the verse of celebration, or even masque, confuse, as some would argue, the ideal with the real. They retained a sharp sense of the distance between them. But because they also believed strongly in the capacity of man as he was, to become man as he ought be, they believed in the possibility that ideals might be made real, that reality might approach ideal. The praise of good kings and the criticisms of the shortcomings of princes or courtiers shared this common objective.

If our anachronistic assumptions about patronage and the nature of praise have dulled our sensitivity to the language of criticism, it is probably our rigid categorization of modes and genres that has deafened our ears to its voice.[152] For once we have labelled a work of literature as 'verse compliment', perhaps most obviously as a 'court masque', there is a danger that we have predetermined our expectations – of form, of content and of language, or at least of the meaning of language. The most courtly modes, we tend to assume, *could not* be vehicles of criticism. But in Jonson's hands, the verse compliment or epitaph so often stands not merely as the paean of a patron, but as the occasion for the poet's articulation of his own ethical and political position, and of attitudes critical of courtly society. In the poems celebrating the Earl of Rutland, the Lady S., the Countess of Huntingdon and the Crofts of Wrest, we have seen how Davenant, Carew and Townshend, like Jonson (and Donne), turn praise of an individual into a social and political commentary on an age. The mode of address does not confine the freedom of statement. Indeed it sharpens it and lends it force as what is praised is,

---

[151] Cf. Davenant, 'Praise is devotion fit for mighty minds,' *Gondibert*, p. 28.
[152] On this history of genre, see Sharpe and Zwicker, *Politics of Discourse*, introduction.

explicitly or implicitly, contrasted with what deserves only opprobrium. Perhaps most importantly (and there is more to be done here) we have suggested that the poets were able to articulate their own values, concerns and criticisms about both the politics and the culture of the court through the most courtly of all modes, the masque.[153] Again the recognition of that possibility involves ridding ourselves of assumptions about genre. For if we think of the masque as a genre of rigid form, in which the world of masque supplants all vices, uncertainties and debates, criticism can have no place, except in the burlesque of antimasque, of which the form demands the transcendence. But if we recognize that change and flexibility were possible within the form of masque, then we may come to understand that the manipulation of the balance of the components of masque could itself be the device of criticism.

As the most recent critical schools have begun to appreciate, forms themselves partook of a 'fundamentally political character': to manipulate them was itself a political gesture.[154] *The Triumph of Peace*, we recall, makes its argument concerning the king's obligation to guarantee the benefits of law for all his subjects through carnival and intrusions in the masque of artisans who do not belong there. It questions the political values of masque, that is, primarily by a challenge to its form. Similarly during the 1630s, Townshend, Carew and Davenant debate, within masque, the meaning, nature and ideology of masque; and they play with the form of masque, leaving doubts about the transcendence of masque over the world of antimasque, and so arouse reservations about the reality of the ideas or forms to which, in Neo-Platonic theory, masque gives expression. To perceive or demonstrate this criticism is not to argue that the masques of the 1630s were not gestures of praise: *The Triumph of Peace*, after all, emerged from an intention to please the king. It is to argue rather that within a genre of celebration, criticism remains a powerful possibility and may be expressed through subtle deployment of language and form rather than obstructed by conventions of language and form. This is to recognize that Carew speaks through both Mercury and Momus in the masque. And it is to appreciate that *Coelum Britannicum* must stand as one of the finest examples of the observation that the most extravagant praise could accommodate and incorporate some of the sharpest criticism.

Indeed it may be that by working within courtly modes and by drawing upon the languages of courtly discourse, criticism could be more effectively voiced, without any suspicion of disloyalty. Jonathan Goldberg has recently

---

[153] As was first argued by Leah Marcus in 'Masquing occasions and masque structure'.
[154] Norbrook, *Poetry and Politics in the English Renaissance*, pp. 7–8. The deconstructionists, as Norbrook observes, have identified radicalism in literary texts 'not in their overt political content, but in their subversion of the conventional processes of signification'.

demonstrated how Jonson was able to adopt James I's favourite metaphors and adapt them subtly to point to criticisms within a discourse of praise.[155] Kings themselves, after all, spoke the languages of love and communion: Charles I participated in masque that celebrated the purity of his love and represented his marriage as a model for government. But a common language did not necessarily mean a shared ideology or attitude. The love *represented* by the king and the queen was that of a Platonic union of minds or souls which was raised above the material world of illusion and triumphant over the rebellious passions and creatures of sense. The love celebrated in the poetry and drama of Carew, Davenant and Townshend reflects a different perception of love, of human nature and hence a different attitude to government. Their understanding of love our authors found exemplified in the fertile *reality* of the royal marriage and in the royal progeny. Celebration of the fertility and fecundity of the royal marriage could not, at one level, be construed as anything other than conventional praise of a dynasty. But in the context of the courtly Platonic love cult, it powerfully drew attention to the physical nature of man and of his sexuality, and to the possibilities of ordering appetite, integrating the body and the soul, reconciling order and disorder. This is, one might say, to integrate the worlds of antimasque and masque. And thus it is that we feel at times structural tensions within the thirties masques. For in the hands of our authors, as in Jonson's earlier entertainments, masques played subtly with such tensions in order to make their point.

Perhaps in every age, theatre has permitted freedoms greater than those tolerated in life. Play is always a form of licence. In seventeenth-century England, it was a freedom and licence institutionalized in social customs such as 'putting out' in schools, Christmas revels of social inversion, May queens and lords of mis-rule.[156] This has its most obvious demonstration in popular customs and festivals. But even at court, theatre made possible the articulation of criticism which could shelter, if necessary, under the umbrella of play. And it may be that in the reign of Charles I, when the style of royal government was characterized less by debate and discussion, poetry and theatre offered the best opportunity for the most searching discussions of issues and the best platform for criticism – directed to, as well as at, the king and the court. Several literary scholars have expressed surprise at what playwrights were able to 'get away with' in the 1620s and 1630s.[157] Recently it has been observed that 'certainly Charles I permitted a greater degree of

---

[155] Goldberg, *James I and the Politics of Literature*. I have had stimulating discussions with Jonathan Goldberg on this subject.

[156] See for example, K. V. Thomas, *Rule and Misrule in the Schools of Early Modern England* (Reading, 1976).

[157] E.g. Barton, 'Harking back to Elizabeth', p. 18.

freedom to his poets than his courtiers'.[158] Of course, in the cases we have been examining, his poets were in a real sense also his courtiers. Yet far from being sycophants they deployed the licence of play to offer counsel through compliment and through criticism. Hence they offer the historian of politics some of the best evidence not only of what men at court felt, but also of what they believed that the king and the country should be told.

Drama and poetry, some might say, enjoyed this freedom because they were in practice irrelevant to the actual business of politics and even to the discourse of political ideas. Aristocratic audiences, it has been said, exhibited 'a sophisticated ability to separate life from art'.[159] But we should not draw the wrong conclusions from this observation nor underestimate the contribution of theatre to politics. For the sophistication of the audience could be, and was, exploited as much to underline the contingencies and interactions of theatre and life, of play and of politics, as to demarcate or divide them. Indeed the common device of the play within the play, of games like the court of love in *The New Inn*, or the slave Cratander's reign of 'misrule' in *The Royal Slave* seems consciously to undermine any clear separation between theatre and reality. Evidently kings too found it hard to make such clear distinctions. When Jonson incorporated a satire on projectors in his play *The Devil Is An Ass*, 'the king desired him to conceal it'.[160] Charles I demanded the removal from Massinger's play *The King and The Subject* of a passage that implied an unconstitutional method of raising money.[161] But what is as significant here as the king's recognition of the place of theatre in political criticism is the fairly explicit nature of the references (to immediate and particular events) which were censored. Such direct allusions are only one of the modes by which theatre may contribute to the discourse of politics, and it is not, perhaps, the most important one. For the culture of the court, we have seen,[162] did not represent or attempt to sustain particular courses or policies as much as to promulgate a vision of kingship. Even *Britannia Triumphans* is less about ship money than about the regulation of the human appetite by the rational faculty. And it is less to the particular than to the larger, universal debates that our authors addressed, and were able to address, themselves. If we do not find in Carew, Davenant and Townshend frequent pointers to, or echoes of, current events or controversies, it is not because their literature

---

[158] Parker, ' "Comely Gestures" ', p. 110.
[159] *Ibid.*, p. 110.
[160] Briggs, *This Stage-Play World*, p. 121.
[161] Adams, *Dramatic Records of Herbert*, p. 23:
    Monys? Wee'le rayse supplies what way we please,
    And force you to subscribe to blanks, in which
    Wee'le mulct you as we shall think fit.
    Charles also banned a play 'because it has relation to the passages of the king's journey into the north', *ibid.*, p. 66. See above, ch. 1, p. 37.
[162] Above, ch. 5, pp. 260–2.

eschewed political comment or responsibility. It is because it contributed to a wider political debate, a dispute about attitudes to human nature and government which constituted the fundamental premises of Caroline government.

This very non-specificity, the universal concerns of their poetry and drama, enlarged the artist's freedom without compromising the force of his counsel. The subjects of lust and love, passion and honour, have simultaneously universal *and* particular application. The modern mind is accustomed to thinking of these as opposites. Accordingly criticism has been inclined to underplay the political dimension of great art – Shakespeare is the most obvious example[163] – and to deny to the obviously topical a more universal import. But Jonson, once again the exemplar of his world, provides the best illustration of the topical comment or address that drew force from the timeless, and of the rich reworking of universal themes through a sharp sense of occasion. Working within courtly modes, Jonson enjoyed a freedom for political commentary and counsel proferred through compliment and criticism. We cannot, of course, be certain how such statements were interpreted or read by individuals on particular occasions. But we can affirm with conviction that contemporary theatre audiences were quick to make connections – not only between one play and another, but also between theatre and life, the politics of the stage and the stage of politics. Both Prince Charles's journey to Spain and Prince Rupert's Madagascar venture were described as 'romances' by contemporaries; and Middleton's *Game At Chess*, as we know, took the court as well as the playhouse by storm.[164] Theatre was politics and was seen to be political. The freedom allowed and taken by theatre, it would appear, was itself something of a game in which both princes and playwrights played by certain rules. The freedom of dramatic commentary was virtually unbounded provided it did not obviously reflect topical controversy. The freedom of the theatre depended upon its ambiguity, indeed upon a series of ambiguities between the universal and the particular, the common reference and the topical allusion, between 'simple' entertainment and political allegory. They were ambiguities which could be skilfully manipulated for political comment. Such ambiguities too, as modern criticism would put it, enabled the audience, be it ordinary folk, courtiers or king, to perform a variety of readings, that is to perform or not perform any particular interpretation. For many, doubtless, a play provided no more than a pleasing entertainment and diversion from the cares of business. But we should never forget that in a society where children were educated by plays at school, a

[163] See D. Norbrook, '*Macbeth* and the Politics of Historiography', in Sharpe and Zwicker, *Politics of Discourse*.

[164] Gardiner, *History of England*, V, p. 9; above, p. 95, n. 229; Heinemann, *Puritanism and Theatre*, ch. 10.

court and metropolitan society in which figures fashioned for themselves
rôles to perform as if in a drama, there was no shortage of men capable of
multiple and sophisticated readings and of political interpretations.[165]

Among the most experienced of the Caroline theatre lovers were the king
and queen themselves. What then, we must conclude by asking ourselves,
might Charles I and Henrietta Maria have made of the arguments and the
criticisms that we have been discussing? Could they have comprehended
them? And if they did understand them, why did they not censor them? The
conditional character of our clauses points to our greatest problem, perhaps
the central problem in the history of ideas: the problem of reception. Apart
from a few instances (some of which we have already cited) where the king or
queen quite clearly expressed their approval, disappointment or irritation, we
do not have any evidence of their responses to plays or poems. The simplest
solution, that posited by Graham Parry, is to assume that any criticism passed
over their heads.[166] But we know that the king and queen attached great
importance to theatre both as audience and as performers, and that both as
actors and audience they ought to have developed a sophisticated sensitivity
to the discourse of the literary arts. Charles's intimate knowledge of paintings
suggests a more than receptive interest in the aesthetic, a view reinforced by
the annotated copies of books in the royal library and the evidently close
attention he gave to written documents and literary texts.[167] His appreciation
of the political dimension of the aesthetic can hardly be in doubt. Carew,
Davenant and Townshend, too, spoke, as we have seen, a language familiar
to the king and played with associations (between love and government)
familiar to the early Stuart age. Charles I himself perceived and articulated
those associations when he wrote to Sir Thomas Wentworth, 'I will end with
a rule that may serve for a statesman, a courtier or a lover . . .'[168] I should like
to close this study by a suggestion, for such it must remain, that our authors'
attitudes and criticisms might not only have been comprehended, but have
actually influenced the course of politics and royal counsels.

[165] Briggs, *This Stage-Play World*, p. 112; Greenblatt, *Renaissance Self-Fashioning*; Greenblatt,
Sir Walter Raleigh: The Renaissance Man and his Roles (New Haven, 1973). Cf. the incisive
comments of Annabel Patterson, *Censorship and Interpretation* (Madison, Wis., 1984),
which I read after this book was written. Patterson talks of 'functional ambiguity'.
[166] Parry, *Golden Age Restor'd*, p. 193.
[167] On Charles's intimate knowledge of paintings, see Smuts, 'The culture of absolutism';
Charles I's folio copy of Shakespeare's *Works* is in The Royal Library at Windsor; his
annotated copy of Bacon's *On the Advancement of Learning* is in the British Library. The
best evidence for Charles's personal attention to letters and papers showing a careful scrutiny
of words and phrases is to be found in the papers of Sir John Coke at Melbourne Hall,
Derbyshire. (I am grateful to Lord Lothian and to the archivists of Derbyshire Record Office
for permission to spend some weeks with these papers.) *The Dramatic Records of Sir Henry
Herbert* offer indications that Charles paid an equally close attention to the texts and
language of plays.
[168] Krowler, *Strafford Letters*, II, p. 32.

During the 1630s, the decade of personal rule, Charles governed without parliaments and, in some eyes, ruled not with the love of his people, but only their grudging compliance. The language of necessity and an emphasis upon the prerogative replaced the rhetoric and traditions of communion between the king and his subjects.[169] We have suggested that our authors shared some of the reservations and voiced some of the criticisms of Charles's style of government, advocating a more optimistic view of human nature and a closer union between the king and the people. One expression of that union was the summoning of a parliament in which the king literally came together with hundreds of his leading subjects in the community of the realm. During the 1630s leading figures in the queen's household, Holland and Northumberland for example, had attempted to persuade the king to summon a parliament. In 1640 in *Salmacida Spolia*, and in 1641 in his poem to the queen, Davenant added his voice to the call for conciliation and a parliament.[170] In the spring of 1640 the Short Parliament convened but failed in its three short weeks either to satisfy quickly the king's urgent need for supply or to resolve any of the country's grievances. When, later in the year, another parliament was resummoned we may detect a new tone of conciliation. Charles gave his assent to the bills of the first session that dismantled the taxes and machinery of the personal rule, and even accepted the impeachment of the ministers who had been charged with dividing the king from his people. Charles's hand of course was restrained by circumstances – most of all by the presence of a powerful Scottish army and his dependence on parliament to pay for it. But significantly we may detect during these months a new language informing the king's speeches, and new counsels close to the king. 'I am resolved to put myself freely and clearly on the love and affection of my English subjects,' Charles told the Long Parliament in his first address to both houses.[171] And the Lord Keeper, speaking on his behalf, went on to expound the king's meaning. The monarch, he explained, is, '*Anima – Deliciae Legis* ... of rare endowments and Abilities of Nature'.[172] One expression of nature was love[173] and it was the king's love, his marriage, that the Lord Keeper (Finch) dwelt on as he proclaimed the virtues of the king:

Behold him in another Part of himself, in his dearest Consort, our gracious Queen, the Mirror of virtue; from whom ... never any Subject received other than gracious or benign influence: And I dare avow, as she is nearest and dearest to our Sovereign, so there is none, whose Affections and Endeavours ... have, or do, or can co-operate

---

[169] See Sharpe, 'The personal rule of Charles I', p. 57.
[170] Above, ch. 2, p. 98; ch. 5, p. 255.
[171] *The Parliamentary or Constitutional History of England from the Earliest Times to the Restoration of Charles II* (24 vols., 1751–62), IX, p. 17.
[172] *Ibid.*, IX, p. 19.
[173] We recall Charles I's own note in his copy of *Of the Advancement of Learning* (p. 318): 'Love is the Mother of all noble actions'.

more to the happy Success of this Parliament, and the never-to-be-equall'd Joy and Comfort of a right understanding between the King and his People.[174]

Lord Keeper Finch might have reflected upon Thomas Carew's poem on his own earlier romance. He might have thought of William Davenant's verse as he went on to inform the Houses that it was the queen who had persuaded her husband to resummon parliament. And we have seen too that, though unconsciously, he echoed all our authors in his exhortation to parliament to assist the king 'to make us steer between the Tropicks of Moderation . . .'[175] The language of moderation, union and love continued to pervade the king's speeches as Charles came under the influence of new counsellors who drafted his addresses to parliament. 'Your Majesty well knows', one wrote, 'that your greatest strength is in the hearts and affections of those persons who . . . are in love with your inclinations'.[176] Over a decade earlier, Edward Hyde, who penned these words and most of the king's speeches, had shared chambers and friendship with Davenant and Carew.[177] The language of love and its politics were not new to him in the autumn of 1641.

Love and union, however, were not to be the outcome of the parliament. Hyde almost spoke the language of antimasque as he reflected upon the ills that befell the realm.

The excellent envied constitution of this kingdom hath been of late distempered . . . the king and people have been robbed of the delight and comfort of each other, and the blessed peace of this island been shaken and frightened into tumults and commotion.[178]

Like Charles, he had come to view politics from the vision of masque. Ultimately Hyde, like Charles I himself, blamed a few evil factious persons ruled by their private will and ends for undermining love and harmony. The king's worst suspicions about some men appeared to be confirmed. Counsellor and king became united now in a conviction that the time for conciliation was over.

During the years before his execution, Charles I reflected upon his reign, the traumas of rebellion and war, and the nature of kingship and govern-

---

[174] *The Parliamentary or Constitutional History*, IX, p. 20.
[175] *Ibid.*, IX, p. 21.
[176] B. H. G. Wormald, *Clarendon: Politics, History and Religion, 1640–1660* (Cambridge, 1951), p. 80.
[177] E. Hyde, *Life of Clarendon*, pp. 7, 30; Nethercot, *Sir William Davenant*, pp. 66–7.
[178] R. W. Harris, *Clarendon and the English Revolution*, (London, 1983), p. 67.

ment.[179] 'He deserv's to be a slave', he is said once to have uttered, 'that is content to have the rational Soveraigntie of his soul and libertie of his will . . . captivated.'[180] The statement offers an explanation of some of Charles's most fundamental premises. For in his metaphysical world it was essential that the appetite be firmly governed, for only such government guaranteed true freedom, the liberty of men, as Rousseau was later to put it, to fulfil their higher natures. With rational men, Charles I believed, kings, the embodiment of reason, could live, as our 'authors had urged, in love and communion. Accordingly, parliaments of a 'right constitution' were 'interchangings of Love, Loialtie and Confidence betwen a Prince and His People'.[181] But popular tumults had subverted the good designs of rational men and undermined the counsels of reason.[182] At Holdenby Charles had prayed: 'deliver the Honor of Parliaments from the insolencie of the vulgar'.[183] The threat of populism could not be quelled by love; it demanded firm rule if it were not to overturn all order and reason:

Miscarriages in Government may escape, rather through ill Counsel of *som men* driving on their private ends, or the peevishness of others envying the Publick should be managed without them . . . than anie propensitie a Prince hath of himself to injuriousness, or oppression.[184]

It was right and proper, Charles believed, for a king to compromise to meet 'modest and sober desires', but wrong for a ruler to give too much countenance to unreasonable demands;[185] for reason was 'the divinest power'.[186] And it was the duty and responsibility of a king who derived his power from God to sustain the sway of reason if it did not by itself persuade those men who were slaves to appetite to follow its light. In the 1640s, Charles became certain of what he had long suspected: that he confronted men dominated by appetite and passion, who threatened to subvert all reason. In 1641 he had been prepared to compromise with them. Later he came to know and

---

[179] I refer here to the *Eikon Basiliké*, published as the authentic work or dicta of the king in 1649. Considerable controversy has surrounded the question of Charles's authorship (see F. F. Madan, *A New Bibliography of the Eikon Basiliké*, Oxf. Bibl. Soc. 3, 1950; H. R. Trevor-Roper, 'Eikon Basilike. The Problem of the King's Book', *History Today* (September 1951), pp. 7–12). I have always inclined to the view that the work, though probably written by John Gauden, was a faithful record of the king's words as well as sentiments, and this case is convincingly put by Professor J. P. Kenyon in a hitherto unpublished paper, 'Charles I and the *Eikon Basiliké*'. I am most grateful to John Kenyon for allowing me to see this paper.

[180] *Eikon Basiliké, part II, Apothegmata*, p. 23.

[181] *Eikon Basiliké*, pp. 216–17.

[182] *Ibid.*, pp. 15–18.

[183] *Ibid.*, p. 195.

[184] *Eikon Basiliké, Apothegmata*, p. 36.

[185] *Eikon Basiliké*, p. 1.

[186] *Ibid.*, p. 175; cf. *Apothegmata*, p. 4: 'It is God's will that we should maintain our native, rational and religious freedom.'

prophesy that he would rather wear a crown of thorns than exchange one of gold for one of lead

Whose *embased flexibleness* shall be forced to bend and complie to the various, and oft-contrarie Dictates of anie Factions; when, instead of Reason and Publick concernments, they obtrude nothing but what makes for the interest of Parties, and flow's from the partialities of Private Wills and Passions.[187]

Such men of passion, Charles believed, would subvert the peace and order of the commonweal. He owed it as his duty to 'his loving subjects'[188] – he never ceased to use the phrase – as to his God to stand and fight against them.

Thomas Carew died before that war. William Davenant lived not only to be caught up in it, but, for all his criticism of royal government, to risk his life for his king and queen. For the events of civil war made him too, at least for a time, 'hopeless'[189] of a people, weak in mind. The people he began to see, like his friend Hobbes, as beasts, creatures of sense but not reason, and the government of such creatures as necessarily harsh: 'who can imagine lesse than a necessity of oppressing the people . . .?'[190] When such men rose against government, there was only one side that Davenant could take, whatever his earlier position:

and so the State and the People are divided, as we may say a man is divided within him selfe, when reason and passion . . . dispute about consequent actions; and if wee were called to assist at such intestine warre, we must side with Reason, according to our duty, by the law of Nature.[191]

---

[187] *Eikon Basiliké*, p. 33. Compare the language and metaphor with Carew's in 'To T.H. a Lady resembling my Mistresse', *Poems of Carew*, pp. 26–7; above, ch. 3, p. 141.
[188] See the proclamations issued by the king during the civil war in *Stuart Royal Proclamations*, II.
[189] Davenant, *Gondibert*, p. 13.
[190] *Ibid.*, p. 12. Cf. *Gondibert*, Bk. II, Canto I, p. 121:
    But now the People's passions run too farre;
    Their untaught love, artless extremes does wed.
[191] *Ibid.*, p. 36.

INDEX

303